THIRD EDITION

MARKETING RESEARCH
AN INTEGRATED APPROACH

ALAN WILSON

Department of Marketing, University of Strathclyde

**Financial Times
Prentice Hall**
is an imprint of

PEARSON

Harlow, England • London • New York • Boston • San Francisco • Toronto • Sydney • Singapore • Hong Kong
Tokyo • Seoul • Taipei • New Delhi • Cape Town • Madrid • Mexico City • Amsterdam • Munich • Paris • Milan

Pearson Education Limited
Edinburgh Gate
Harlow
Essex CM20 2JE

and Associated Companies throughout the world.

Visit us on the World Wide Web at:
www.pearson.com/uk

First published 2003
Second edition 2006
Third edition 2012

ISBN 978-0-273-71870-3

British Library Cataloguing-in-Publication Data
A catalogue record for this book is available from the British Library

Library of Congress Cataloging-in-Publication Data
Wilson, Alan M.
  Marketing research : an integrated approach / Alan Wilson. – 3rd ed.
     p. cm.
  ISBN 978-0-273-71870-3 (pbk.)
1. Marketing research.   I. Title.
  HF5415.2.W558 2011
  658.8′3–dc23

                                        2011027689

10 9 8 7 6 5 4 3 2 1
15 14 13 12 11

Typeset in 10/12 pt Minion by 35
Printed and bound by Rotolito Lombarda, Italy

MARKETING RESEARCH

Visit the *Marketing Research*, third edition Companion Website at **www.pearsoned.co.uk/wilson** to find valuable **student** learning material including:

- An online glossary to explain key terms
- Flashcards to test your understanding of key terms
- Links to relevant sites on the web
- Multiple choice questions to test your learning

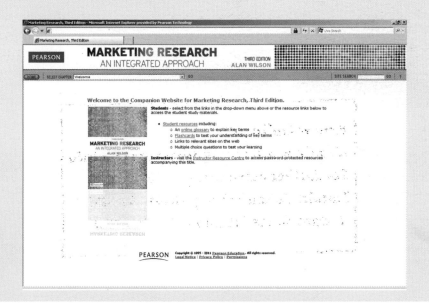

To Sandra, Duncan and Kirsty

Contents

3 Secondary data and customer databases   50

4 Collecting observation data and monitoring online user-generated contents   83

5 Collecting and analysing qualitative data   101

6 Collecting quantitative data   129

7 Designing questionnaires   153

8 Sampling methods   180

9 Analysing quantitative data   204

10 Presenting the research results   232

Marketing research in action: case histories   249

Current issues in marketing research   287

Supporting resources

Visit **www.pearsoned.co.uk/wilson** to find valuable online resources

Companion Website for students
- An online glossary to explain key terms
- Flashcards to test your understanding of key terms
- Links to relevant sites on the web
- Multiple choice questions to test your learning

For instructors
- Complete, downloadable Instructor's Manual
- PowerPoint slides that can be downloaded and used for presentations

Also: The Companion Website provides the following features:
- Search tool to help locate specific items of content
- E-mail results and profile tools to send results of quizzes to instructors
- Online help and support to assist with website usage and troubleshooting

For more information please contact your local Pearson Education sales representative or visit **www.pearsoned.co.uk/wilson**

Foreword

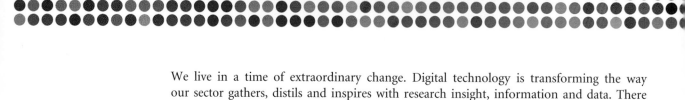

We live in a time of extraordinary change. Digital technology is transforming the way our sector gathers, distils and inspires with research insight, information and data. There has never been a more dynamic time to work in market research, and this makes it both extremely exciting and challenging. More and more people and businesses are entering our sector, bringing new ideas, new technologies and new ways of doing research. This trend is beginning to challenge our own ideas of what constitutes research.

As the chair of the Market Research Society I recognise that we all need to learn and embrace the new thinking and new methodologies, while still insisting on what makes good research. Good research is, after all, the lifeblood of our sector. It is what determines our skill and value to our clients and those we advise. Without good research, our sector cannot stand for a world where people understand that market research not only ensures people get the products and services that they deserve, but also facilitates democracy.

This is why it is critical that the MRS continues to support standards and education in our sector. The training qualifications and publications the society provides help us all recognise and promote good research. This book is a testament to this goal.

Vanella Jackson
Chair of the Market Research Society

Preface

Introduction

Whatever the type of organisation, market and customer information is critical if strategic goals are to be achieved and customer needs are to be met effectively. Successful managers take an orderly and logical approach to gathering information; they seek facts and undertake new marketing approaches on a systematic basis rather than simply through a procedure of trial and error.

Marketing research has always played a valuable role in providing a significant proportion of these facts and information. However, it has now been augmented by developments in:

1 data capture and database management in customer databases;
2 the quality of Internet information resources on market characteristics and trends;
3 the growth in consumers conversing with companies and airing their views about products and services on Facebook-type sites, customer review sites and blogs on the Internet.

This has resulted in a growing number of managers combining information from these resources to develop a more comprehensive view of their marketplace. Integrated information is critical to effective decision making. Marketing information sources can be thought of as separate jigsaw pieces; only when they are connected does the whole picture become clear. Taking decisions by looking at each of the pieces individually is not only inefficient but is likely to result in wrong assumptions and decisions being made.

Therefore the theme of this third edition of this book continues to be about integration, and this is developed over six key dimensions:

1 The integration of marketing research with other information sources such as customer databases, customer loyalty programmes, user-generated content (online social media, customer review sites, blogs) and other Internet-based information sources.
2 The integration of marketing research and marketing decision making. Research should not be perceived as some tedious technical activity separate from the practice of marketing management. In reality, marketing research is rarely tedious, and an understanding of marketing research is critical to effective marketing decision making. It therefore needs to be explained in a manner which is both user-friendly and which demonstrates its application to real-life decisions.
3 The integration of traditional marketing research approaches with newer developments in social media monitoring, Internet-based surveys, computer-assisted interviewing, simulated test markets, ethnography, mystery shopping, etc.

4 The integration of knowledge of marketing research techniques with an understanding about the real world of marketing research, highlighting some of the current issues affecting the use of these techniques (declining response rates, representativeness, multi-mode surveys, data protection issues, etc.).

5 The integration across international borders as more and more research studies involve multi-country data collection.

6 Finally, the integration of the perspectives of practising marketing researchers, users of marketing research and academics, providing academic rigour with real-life practicality.

Audience

This book is intended for students who are taking their first course in marketing research. The content has been carefully chosen to benefit both those who will eventually be directly responsible for undertaking marketing research and also for those marketing or strategy personnel who will be managing, purchasing or overseeing a research project undertaken by others. To cater for this dual audience, the book is written in a non-technical yet authoritative style.

The book is also aimed at supporting:

1 The Chartered Institute of Marketing's Professional Certificate in Marketing Module: Marketing Information and Research

Knowledge and skill requirements of the CIM Marketing Information and Research Module	Relevant chapters
The importance of marketing information	1 The role of marketing research and customer information in decision making 10 Presenting the research results
The role of databases in information management	3 Secondary data and customer databases
The nature of marketing research	1 The role of marketing research and customer information in decision making 2 The marketing research process
Research methodologies	3 Secondary data and customer databases 4 Collecting observation data and monitoring online user-generated content 5 Collecting and analysing qualitative data 6 Collecting quantitative data
Research tools	7 Designing questionnaires 8 Sampling methods

2 The Market Research Society's Diploma Module: Principles of Market and Social Research and Information

Knowledge and skill requirements of the MRS Market and Social Research and Information Module	Relevant chapters
1 Information and research for decision making	1 The role of marketing research and customer information in decision making 2 The marketing research process
2 Ethics, professionalism and legislation	2 The marketing research process
3 Market and social research in context	1 The role of marketing research and customer information in decision making 2 The marketing research process
4 Research methodologies	3 Secondary data and customer databases 4 Collecting observation data and monitoring online user-generated content 5 Collecting and analysing qualitative data 6 Collecting quantitative data 7 Designing questionnaires 8 Sampling methods
5 Presenting and evaluating information to develop business advantage	5 Collecting and analysing qualitative data 9 Analysing quantitative data 10 Presenting the research results

New for the third edition

The feedback from the first two editions praised many elements of the format and the writing style of the first two editions. While retaining these desirable features, the third edition has been enhanced through:

- The inclusion of material relating to user-generated content, in terms of monitoring such online material and the use of social media for researching with customers and potential customers;
- The updating and enlarging of the content, addressing the current and future use of the Internet for marketing research with enhanced sections covering online surveys, online group discussions and online samples;
- The inclusion of 'Integration: an international perspective' sections in each chapter to demonstrate the issues involved in doing marketing research across international borders;
- The inclusion of material on the new MRS Code of Conduct which was published in 2010;
- An expansion and enhancement of the material on customer databases, qualitative research analysis and online qualitative and quantitative research methods;
- The replacement of a number of the cases and chapter introductory vignettes with more recent examples of marketing research in action;
- An increase in the number of articles on current issues in marketing research appearing at the end of the book. In addition, some of the articles appearing in the second edition have been replaced with those that are more critical to the marketing research industry today;
- Throughout the text, material and particularly references to websites and further reading have been comprehensively updated.

Key features of the text

The book is structured in ten chapters relating to the key aspects of marketing research, customer information and the main stages of the research process. Each chapter has the following features:

- **Opening vignettes:** each chapter starts with a mini case history related to how marketing research is used for 'real' in organisations such as MTV, Virgin Atlantic, London Underground and Ford.
- **Learning outcomes:** these set out the objectives for each chapter and provide a template of the outcomes that a student should be seeking from the chapter content.
- **Key words:** at the start of each chapter, the key words that will be used in the chapter are set out. These words also appear in the Glossary at the end of the book. Students find these key word lists particularly useful during their revision for exams.
- **Boxed features:** boxed features are used to show examples.
- **Researcher/client quotes:** quotes from real-life researchers and clients are used to reinforce some of the key messages in the text.
- **International perspectives:** a section in each chapter demonstrates how elements of the content apply in multi-country research studies.
- **Summary and an integrated approach:** each chapter concludes with a summary that summarises the chapter contents and highlights the role of the material in developing an integrated approach to marketing research.
- **Discussion questions:** discussion questions allow students to check on their understanding at the end of each chapter and direct attention to the core concepts of the chapter.
- **Additional reading and web links:** sources for additional reading that amplify the content are also listed at the end of each chapter.

In addition to these learning tools, the book also has:

- **Ten recent case histories:** these explain how marketing research has been used by leading organisations and brands such as Sony Ericsson, Lynx, AIR MILES, the *Metro* Newspaper, Dove and Allied Domecq. Each of these has been previously published in *Research* and are therefore very readable and practitioner oriented.
- **Twelve articles on current issues in marketing research:** these articles relate to topics such as declining response rates, the growth in customer insight departments, using social media for research, multimode research, international research observation using surveillance cameras, etc. These have also appeared recently in *Research* and some take the form of discussions among key industry experts.
- **SNAP software:** a CD providing a 'Demo' version of SNAP, one of the leading fully integrated survey software packages for questionnaire design, data collection and analysis. The CD, combined with the Getting Started Guide printed in the text, will enable you to practise producing short questionnaires that can be printed or formatted for use on the Internet or the telephone. Data, either from the questionnaire or from the data sets provided on the CD, can also be analysed and reported on using various chart and graph options
- **Internet sources of marketing information:** within Chapter 3 there is an extensive listing of Internet sources of information on customers and markets.
- **Glossary:** there is a glossary of all key terms at the end of the text, providing an ideal reference source.

Ancillary material

A lecturer's support package is available on the website **www.pearson.co.uk/wilson** consisting of:

- **A *Lecturer's Manual*:** this sets out suggested approaches and answers to the discussion questions, potential student projects and tasks to support the learning in each chapter, additional Internet sources, and suggestions as to how the case histories and research issues can be used for teaching purposes.
- **PowerPoint slides:** a comprehensive, fully integrated PowerPoint presentation for each chapter. This PowerPoint presentation gives the instructor the ability to completely integrate the classroom lecture with the chapter material.

Guided tour

Each chapter opens with a fascinating **Opening vignette**. This looks at a range of well-known national and international companies and how they apply marketing research theory to strategic business decisions.

Virgin Atlantic – journeys to work

Road-traffic congestion is growing in the vicinity of major airports resulting in increased noise and emissions concern, not to mention time-delays. Employers based at airports have been looking closely at staff travel-to-work policies, mindful of the implications for staff welfare, but also with an eye on the environmental impact.

Virgin Atlantic employs over 8,000 UK staff based mainly in the Gatwick and Heathrow areas. The objective of having satisfied and healthy staff could be adversely affected by the cost and stress of journeys to work. With no existing data on staff behaviour and attitudes towards journeys to work, Virgin Atlantic sought a research agency to get the insight it lacked. The information was needed

TRISTAR PHOTOS/Alamy

both as evidence for an external transport policy document about Virgin's actions to meet environmental obligations and to support internal plans that could improve journeys, staff satisfaction and wellbeing.

The chosen agency used an online survey sent to all UK-based staff, plus follow-up group discussions involving over 70 individuals to gain a more in-depth understanding. The online survey required about ten minutes to complete and consisted of a variety of question types including open-ended questions. Such a question mix was considered to be essential, if employees are to feel valued and empowered to express their

Learning outcomes

Marketing research process
The sequence of activities and events involved in undertaking a marketing research project.

After reading this chapter you should:

- understand the key steps in the **marketing research process**;
- be aware of the importance of the research brief and its contents;
- understand the process involved and the criteria used in selecting marketing research agencies;
- be aware of the importance of the research proposal and its contents;
- appreciate the broad types of research design;
- understand the need for an ethical and professional approach towards marketing research;
- be aware of relevant data protection legislation and professional codes of conduct.

Learning outcomes enable you to focus on what you should have achieved and help structure your learning.

The **Key words** section highlights which words you should be looking out for as you read the chapter.

Key words

'beauty parades'
causal research
conclusive research
cross-sectional studies
data protection legislation
descriptive research
experimental research

marketing research process
observation
primary data
professional codes of conduct
qualitative research
quantitative research
research brief

Each **Researcher quote** pulls out key perspectives from practising marketing researchers.

addresses, reference numbers, etc.) have been removed from the data. This means that respondents can request a copy of the primary data record (e.g. a questionnaire) only as long as it contains information that identifies the respondent.

Researcher quote

The data protection legislation means that every organisation must ensure that one individual in the organisation is made responsible for the area of data protection – it is a critical area!

However, these exemptions apply only if the data are used exclusively for research purposes and if the following conditions are met:

- the data are not processed to support measures or decisions with respect to the particular individuals;

Descriptive research
Research studies that describe what is happening in a market without potentially explaining why it is happening.

Cross-sectional studies
Research studies that involve data collection at a single point in time, providing a 'snapshot' of the specific situation. The *opposite* of longitudinal studies.

Longitudinal studies
Studies involving data collection at several periods in time enabling trends over time to be examined. These may involve asking the same

Descriptive information of this type is gathered through **descriptive research**. It provides the answers to the **who**, **what**, **where**, **how** and **when** of marketing research. The findings describe what is happening; they generally do not explain why it is happening. Descriptive research is appropriate when the research objectives include the description of the characteristics of marketing phenomena, determination of the frequency of occurrence, or the prediction of the occurrence of specific marketing phenomena.

Descriptive research of this type may be required in relation to one point in time. These are called **cross-sectional studies** and involve the research being undertaken once to explore what is happening at that single point in time. Alternatively, the organisation may wish to measure trends in awareness, attitudes or behaviour over time. Such repeat measurement studies are called **longitudinal studies**. These may involve asking the same questions on a number of occasions of either the same respondents or of respondents with similar character-istics. The cross-sectional survey is the most commonly used descriptive research design in marketing research, as many research studies are aimed at obtaining a picture of a market-place at one point in time. However, longitudinal studies do enable researchers to go back to the same respondents again and again to detect ongoing changes in behaviour, awareness and attitudes which may come about as a result of advertising campaigns, pricing policies or even through changes in the economy. The cost and complexity of maintaining a group

These handy **Margin definitions** help to explain key marketing research terms and acronyms.

Each chapter is full of **Boxed examples**. These boxes pick out practical examples used in international business, displaying perfectly the application of marketing research theory for marketers. They also provide essential information on the best available marketing research resources.

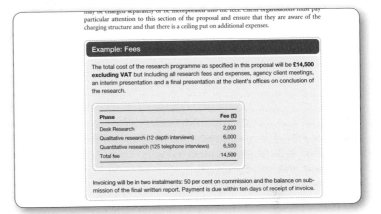

may be charged separately or be incorporated into the fees. Client organisations must pay particular attention to this section of the proposal and ensure that they are aware of the charging structure and that there is a ceiling put on additional expenses.

Example: Fees

The total cost of the research programme as specified in this proposal will be **£14,500 excluding VAT** but including all research fees and expenses, agency client meetings, an interim presentation and a final presentation at the client's offices on conclusion of the research.

Phase	Fee (£)
Desk Research	2,000
Qualitative research (12 depth interviews)	6,000
Quantitative research (125 telephone interviews)	6,500
Total fee	14,500

Invoicing will be in two instalments: 50 per cent on commission and the balance on sub-mission of the final written report. Payment is due within ten days of receipt of invoice.

---

surveys on their own do not provide sufficiently detailed information to allow management to identify and correct weaknesses in the service delivery process.

Client quote

I need to know if staff are saying and doing everything according to our stated stand-ards of quality. Only mystery shopping can tell me if this is happening.

Mystery shopping studies are used for three main purposes:
• to act as a diagnostic tool, identifying failings and weak points in an organisation's service

The **Client quote** boxes give an interesting insight into how businesses can decide on various marketing research options.

Located at the end of every chapter, the **Discussion questions** can be used for self testing, class exercises or debates.

Discussion questions

1 Why should a team rather than an individual be used to develop a research brief?
2 How should one go about selecting a marketing research agency?
3 What role does exploratory research play in the marketing research process?
4 Describe the various ways that a multi-country research project can be managed.
5 Discuss the proposition that the research proposal is the most important part of the whole marketing research project.
6 Explain the difference between cross-sectional studies and longitudinal studies. Give examples of studies for which each may be appropriate.
7 What is the relationship between exploratory, descriptive and causal research?
8 Why is ethics particularly important for the marketing research industry?

Additional reading

Baskin, M. and Coburn, N. (2001) Two tribes divided by a common language? The true nature of the divide between account planners and market researchers. *International Journal of Market Research*, **43**(2), pp. 137–69.
Birn, R.J. (2004) *The Effective use of Market Research: How to Drive and Focus Better Business Decisions*, 4th edn. Kogan Page, London.
Butler, P. (1994) Marketing problems: from analysis to decision. *Marketing Intelligence and Planning*, **12**(2), pp. 4–13.
Callingham, M. (2004) *Market Intelligence: How and Why Organisations use Market Research*. Kogan Page, London.
Chapman, R.G. (1989) Problem definition in marketing research studies. *Journal of Services Marketing*, **3**(3), pp. 51–9.
Moorman, C., Desphande, R. and Zaltman, G. (1993) Factors affecting trust in market

The **Additional reading** section will give you some support for additional study.

Custom publishing

Pearson Education's custom publishing programme began in response to customers' desire to create textbooks and online resources that match the content of their course. Every university course is unique and custom publishing allows a bespoke product created by you for your students and your course.

As a result, content choices include:

- Chapters from one or more of our textbooks in the subject areas of your choice
- Your own authored content
- Case studies from any of our partners including Harvard Business School Publishing, Darden, Ivey and many more
- Third party content from other publishers
- Language glossaries to help students studying in a second language
- Online material tailored to your course needs

The Pearson Education custom text published for your course is professionally produced and bound – just as you would expect from a normal Pearson Education text. You can even choose your own cover design and add your university logo.

To find out more visit **www.pearsoncustom.co.uk** or contact your local representative at: **www.pearsoned.co.uk/replocator**

Acknowledgements

My thanks go to the Market Research Society, and in particular the editorial team at *Research* for their help and support during the writing of this book. My sincere appreciation also goes to the anonymous reviewers and also the students who generously provided suggestions for refining the contents of the second edition. My thanks also go to the publishing team at Pearson Education, in particular Rachel Gear and Mary Lince. Finally, a great hug of gratitude to my wife and family for their continuing love and support.

Publisher's acknowledgements

We are grateful to the following for permission to reproduce copyright material:

Text

Case 1 from The sweet smell of success *Research*, April (Muscroft, Job 2010), Market Research Society; Case 2 from Sony Ericsson, *Research*, March, pp. 46–48 (2005), Market Research Society; Case 3 from Air Miles, *Research*, August, pp. 37–38 (Hayward, Sarah, Mennis, Helen and Cork, Bethan 2000), Market Research Society; Case 4 from The Metro – newspaper media research and understanding the reader, *Research*, April, pp. 20–23 (Saunders, Jenny 2003), Published with the permission of the Market Research Society Media; Case 5 from Birmingham Airport – researching customer satisfaction, *Research*, December, pp. 35–36 (Baker, Tim 2000), Published with the permission of the Market Research Society; Case 6 from The proof is in the pudding *Research*, March (Fowler, C. 2010); Case 7 from English Rugby – researching participation, *Research*, October, pp. 26–28 (Wilson, Vivienne 2003), Published with the permission of the Market Research Society; Case 8 from Sun, sea, sand and surveys *Research*, September, pp. 36–37 (Elphinstone, S. 2010); Case 9 from Allied Domecq – researching lifestyles, *Research*, November, pp. 36–41 (Acreman, S. and Pegram, B. 1999), Market Research Society; Case 10 from Dove – researching beauty for a communications campaign, *Research*, July, pp. 38–41 (Scott, Jennifer, Henderson, Janette, Emmers, Tomas and Iles, Erin 2005), Published with the permission of the Market Research Society; Issue 1 from Marketing research versus customer insight *Research*, May, pp. 20–21 (Gofton, Ken 2001), Published with the permission of the Market Research Society; Issue 2 from Merging marketing research with customer databases, *Research*, September, pp. 28–31 (McElhatton, Noëlle 1999), Published with the permission of the Market Research Society; Issue 3 from Watching you, watching me *Research*, October (2007); Issue 4 from Declining response rates *Research*, March (Bain, R. 2010); Issue 5 from Challenges of business-to-business research, *Research*, May, pp. 30–35 (Shreeve, Peter 2002), Published with the permission of the Market Research Society; Issue 6 from Difficulties in achieving representative samples,

Research, September, pp. 20–25 (Savage, Mike 2000), Published with the permission of the Market Research Society; Issue 7 from People who need people *Research*, August (Phillips, T. 2007); Issue 8 from Multi-mode interviewing *Research in Business*, March, pp. 19–22 (Macer, Tim 2004), Published with the permission of the Market Research Society; Issue 9 from Using technology for data collection, *Research Decisions*, June, pp. 19–22 (Gofton, Ken 2005), Published with the permission of the Market Research Society; Issue 10 from Clients going direct to respondents, *Research*, October, pp. 38–39 (Savage, Mike 2000), Published with the permission of the Market Research Society; Issue 11 from International Research – Think global, act local, *Research*, July, pp. 36–37 (Anderson, Kate and Edmunds, Holly 2005), Published with the permission of the Market Research Society; Issue 12 from In their own words *Research*, March (Eccleston, D. 2010); Appendix on pages 339–388 from Snap Surveys, www.snapsurveys.com; Extract on page 18 adapted from Down to Earth *Research*, February, 44–45 (Smith, A. 2006); Extract on page 40 from Data Protection Act 1998, Crown Copyright material is reproduced with permission under the terms of the Click-Use License; Extract on pages 42–47 adapted from MRS Code of Conduct, The Market Research Society; Article on pages 77–79 from *Research*, April (2005), Published with the permission of the Market Research Society; Extract on pages 83–84 from Public transport: the role of mystery shopping in investment decisions, *Journal of the Market Research Society*, October, pp. 285–94 (Wilson, A. and Gutmann, J. 1998); Article on pages 185–186 from Ipsos Mori broadcasts its solution to the BBC World Service, *Research Business* (2006); Extract on pages 204–205 adapted from Developing a rounder tea, *Market Research Society Conference Proceedings*, pp. 289–308 (Phillips, A., Parfitt, J. and Prutton, I. 1989), Published with the permission of the Market Research Society; Extract on page 232 adapted from MTV dissects the youth of today *Research*, October (Bain, R. 2007).

Photographs

Alamy Images: [apply pictures]/Alamy 289, 327, Blend Images/Alamy 281, Bon Appetit/Alamy 153, Christian Lagerek/Alamy 303, clive thompson rugby/Alamy 270, Craig Holmes/Alamy 331, Creative Element Photos/Alamy 204, CreativeAct – Technology series/Alamy 180, D. Hurst/Alamy 264, D. Hurst/Alamy 300, Datacraft – QxQ images/Alamy 250, DBURKE/Alamy 307, Dmitriy Shironosov/Alamy 292, Hayden Richard Verry/Alamy 254, Iain Masterton/Alamy 323, Image Source/Alamy 50, 296, Image Source/Alamy 50, 296, Jack Sullivan/Alamy 101, 129, John Tomaselli/Alamy 316, Keyfoto/Alamy 267, lifestylepics/Alamy 312, Liz Boyd/Alamy 274, Matthew Richardson/Alamy 1, Mint Photography/Alamy 258, PhotoSpin, Inc/Alamy 277, Radius Images/Alamy 83, Simon Belcher/Alamy 320, Simon Ritter/Alamy 232, TRISTAR PHOTOS/Alamy 18, UpperCut Images/Alamy 261

In some instances we have been unable to trace the owners of copyright material, and we would appreciate any information that would enable us to do so.

1

The role of marketing research and customer information in decision making

Ford – integrated customer information drives product development

Ford Motor Company manufactures or distributes automobiles across six continents. With about 224,000 employees and about 90 plants worldwide, the company's core and affiliated automotive brands include Ford, Lincoln, Mercury, Volvo and Mazda. In the UK, Ford is the largest motor company with seven manufacturing and administrative locations as well as over 550 dealerships. The company sells around 440,000 cars and commercial vehicles each year, with its most popular car being the Ford Focus.

The company has research and development centres throughout the world working on new vehicles, engines and components aimed at addressing one of the five key priorities of the company: *To constantly innovate new products that customers want and value.*

Matthew Richardson/Alamy

Ford conducts market research online and in person, refining and creating new data-gathering processes that influence product development and marketing campaigns. The company engages consumers through group discussions and through one-on-one interviews before vehicles reach market. They also collect feedback from their dealership networks regarding faults, customer concerns and product ideas. Surveys are undertaken with Ford customers online, over the telephone and through the post to examine customer satisfaction with existing vehicles and identify any improvements required.

In addition to these traditional marketing research approaches, Ford searches for information appearing in customer reviews, chat rooms and blogs about Ford vehicles and vehicles built by their competitors. There are thousands of consumer reviews for every Ford model and these reviews have an influence on other consumers' purchase decisions as well as the product development itself.

Ford also has its own Facebook site, where reactions to new ideas can be monitored. This is supported by a variety of Twitter accounts, such as FordTrucks, FordDriveOne, FordDriveGreen, FordCustService, FordRacing, with each account serving a specific purpose as a two-way communication channel with different market segments. In addition, Scott Monty, Head of Social Media at Ford, has his own personal Twitter account with over 44,000 followers to demonstrate Ford's commitment to conversing with customers/potential customers.

By taking a disciplined and integrated approach to gathering consumer feedback from a wide variety of sources, Ford is gaining a better understanding of consumer expectations, and meeting and exceeding them with a strategic mix of design concepts and unique features.[1]

Learning outcomes

After reading this chapter you should:

- understand the need for an integrated approach to the collection, recording, analysing and interpreting of information on customers, competitors and markets;
- be able to define the terms marketing research, customer database and user-generated content;
- understand the need for marketing information and the marketing concept;
- be aware of some of the difficulties and limitations associated with the growing levels of information available;
- be able to describe the structure of the marketing research and database industry.

Key words

blogs	marketing concept
cookies	marketing research
customer database	online communities
data analysis services	product review sites
data elements	profilers
field agencies	social networks
full-service agencies	specialist service agencies
information explosion	triangulation
list compilers and brokers	Web 2.0

Introduction

Marketing research
The collection, analysis and communication of information undertaken to assist decision making in marketing.

This chapter introduces the concept of an integrated approach to **marketing research** and customer information/databases. It also places information and the marketing research industry in the context of marketing decision making.

An integrated approach

Traditionally information on customers, their behaviours, awareness levels and attitudes was only available to organisations through the utilisation of marketing research techniques where customers would be surveyed or observed. Organisations did hold limited information on their customers, but what they held was frequently in the form of paper files, invoices and salespersons' reports. The material was generally difficult to access, patchy in its coverage and rarely up to date. Over the past twenty years significant improvements in computerisation, database management and data capture have meant that many organisations now hold significant amounts of data on their customers. For example, a grocery store operating a loyalty card scheme will have details on each cardholder relating to:

- their home address;
- the frequency with which they visit the store;
- the days and times they visit the store;
- the value of their weekly grocery shopping;
- the range of products purchased;
- the size of packages purchased;
- the frequency with which they use promotional coupons;
- the consistency with which they purchase specific brands;
- the extent to which they trial new products;
- the extent to which purchasing behaviour is influenced by the timing of advertising campaigns.

In addition, the range of products may indicate whether they live alone, have a family, have pets, are vegetarian or tend to eat ready-prepared meals.

At the same time as databases have developed, **Web 2.0** and the advent of user-generated content has resulted in consumers conversing with companies and airing their views about products and services on Facebook-type sites, customer review sites and **blogs**. Companies such as Starbucks run their own customer feedback website (www.mystarbucksidea.force.com) alongside their Facebook and Twitter sites, allowing customers to share their insights, feedback and ideas. Their Facebook site has over 12 million friends and they use it to complete the feedback loop. Not only do they get ideas from customers, but they update the customers on what ideas have been implemented, encouraging more customers to air their views.

The availability of customer databases and user-generated content has changed the role and nature of marketing research in many organisations. Nowadays research may focus more on awareness and attitudes than behaviour, or may focus more on potential than existing customers. **Customer databases** and user-generated content may also be used to assist in identifying potential respondents or topics for research. In addition, customers who are known to the organisation and have a specific relationship with them may be more willing to take part in research on a regular basis. Finally, budgets that were used solely for marketing research may now be split between the managing of a database, administering online social media and marketing research.

These interrelationships between customer databases, user-generated content and marketing research mean that many organisations are starting to adopt an integrated approach to the collection, recording, analysing and interpreting of information on customers, competitors and markets. However, care must be taken to ensure that marketing research is not involved in collecting personal data that will be used in selling or marketing activities directed at the individuals who have participated in a research survey. Marketing research is dependent on respondents providing information voluntarily on their behaviours and attitudes. Respondents may not be willing to provide such information if they think the information that they provide is likely to be misused for purposes other than research. Marketing researchers must therefore understand their professional duty of providing integrated information to marketing decision makers while protecting the rights of their main information resource, the respondent.

Web 2.0
Web applications that facilitate interactive information sharing, interoperability and collaboration on the Internet.

Blogs
An abbreviated title for the term *web logs*, meaning frequent, chronological publications of personal thoughts and ideas. Twitter is a form of microblogging service that allows an individual to publish their blog-type opinions and ideas in short Tweets (text-based messages of up to 140 characters).

Customer database
A manual or computerised source of data relevant to marketing decision making about an organisation's customers.

Marketing research: a definition

In defining marketing research, it is important to consider the key characteristics of the discipline:

- Marketing research provides commercial and non-commercial organisations with **information to aid marketing decision making**. The information will generally be externally focused, concentrating on customers, markets and competitors, although it may also report on issues relating to other stakeholders (e.g. employees and shareholders).

- Marketing research involves the **collection of information** using a wide range of sources and techniques. Information may be acquired from published sources, observing behaviours or through direct communication with the people being researched.
- Marketing research involves the **analysis of information**. Obtaining information is different from achieving understanding. Information needs to be analysed, developed and applied if it is to be actionable and relevant to the marketing decisions that need to be taken.
- Marketing research involves the **communication and dissemination of information**. The effective presentation of information transfers understanding of its content and implications to a wider audience of relevant decision makers and interested parties.

Taking these characteristics together, marketing research can be defined as:

> The collection, analysis and communication of information undertaken to assist decision making in marketing.

The customer database: a definition

The customer database can be defined as:

> A manual or computerised source of data relevant to marketing decision making about an organisation's customers.

Data elements
The individual pieces of information held in a database (e.g. a person's name, gender or date of birth). These elements mean little independently but when combined they provide information on a customer or group of customers.

This definition distinguishes the customer database from a computerised accounting or invoicing system, as the data about customers has to be **relevant to marketing decision making**. The data in the customer database may be collected from many parts of the organisation and may be augmented by data from outside. Data are the basic raw material from which information and, ultimately, understanding are derived. A database consists of a store of **data elements** (see Table 1.1) that mean little independently but, when combined, provide information on a customer or group of customers. In other words, information is derived from the

Table 1.1	Typical data elements held on retail and business consumers
Typical retail consumer data elements	**Typical business data elements**
Customer identification number/loyalty card number	Company number
Name	Industry type
Gender	Parent company
Postal address/post code	Number of employees
Telephone/e-mail	Postal address/postcode
Date of birth	Telephone/Fax/e-mail
Segmentation by lifestyle/demographic code	Credit limit
Relationship to other customers (i.e. same household)	Procurement manager
Date of first transaction	Turnover
Purchase history, including products purchased, date purchased, price paid, method of payment, promotional coupons used	Sales contact
	Purchase history, including products purchased, date purchased, price paid, method of payment
Mailings received	
Response to mailings/last promotion	

relationship between data elements. For example, if an organisation wishes to know how long a particular customer has had a relationship with it, then the data elements associated with the current date and the customer's first transaction date have to be combined to calculate the relationship length.

The transaction record, which often identifies the item purchased, its value, customer name, address and postcode, is the building block for many databases. This may be supplemented with data which customers provide directly, such as data on a warranty card, and by secondary data purchased from third parties. Several companies, such as CACI with their product ACORN(**www.caci.co.uk/acorn**) and Experian with their product MOSAIC (**www.business-strategies.co.uk**), sell geodemographic profiling data that can be related to small geographic areas such as postcodes. Such data show the profile of people within an area and are typically used for location planning and target marketing. Each postcode in the country is allocated a specific geodemographic coding which identifies the typical lifestyle of people living in that postal code area. For example:

ACORN Type 28 – Working families with mortgages

These are family suburbs in relatively prosperous post-industrial areas. Households tend to be larger families often with primary school children. They are typically buying their three- or four-bedroom semi-detached house on a mortgage.

Incomes are above average. These people either work in middle management or clerical jobs, or have a skilled trade. Most will have made adequate pension provision through company or private schemes. Many are likely to save regularly, perhaps into a child savings plan.

Leisure activities include golf, going to the cinema, watching TV and listening to music. Package holidays to Europe and the Mediterranean are popular but many will holiday at home, perhaps in self-catered accommodation.

With larger families the food bill is relatively high, so price is important and stores such as Asda are popular.

Many families will have a home PC which may be used by the children for education and playing computer games. Some shop online and also use the Internet for purchases. Some may be regularly selling goods on eBay.

ACORN Type 5 – Older affluent professionals

These people typically live in villages within commuting distance of major towns or more rural villages where they choose to retire. They live in large detached houses and most have paid off their mortgage.

Households are typically couples over the age of 45. They will often have children who have left home. Those who have yet to leave will typically do well in their exams, achieving much better than average results.

They are a highly qualified type and those that are working tend to be high earners in professional and managerial jobs. Given their affluence, car ownership is high. The majority of households have at least two cars and the main car is usually expensive and bought as new. They also invest significantly in stocks and shares, high-interest accounts and guaranteed income bonds.

In their leisure time these people like golf, hill walking and gardening. Their social life tends to be home-based, where they enjoy a glass of wine rather than going out to restaurants. They like to spend their money on holidays. They travel abroad regularly either to the Mediterranean or long-haul for their main holiday. They also take winter sun and weekend breaks. Most are happy to research and book their holidays online.

The Internet is used by many to make purchases of books and CDs and to research and monitor their financial investments. Some spend significant amounts buying luxury food, wine, clothes and home furnishings mail order.

These are avid *Daily Telegraph* and *Sunday Telegraph* readers, with readership for these papers at twice the national average.[2]

Researcher quote

You can check out the ACORN profile for any postcode in the UK by going to **www.upmystreet.com**, typing in the postcode and looking under 'My Neighbours'.

Cookies
Text files placed on a user's computer by web retailers in order to identify the user when he or she next visits the website.

In addition to physical transactions, databases can be created from virtual transactions. Web-based retailers and suppliers have a two-way electronic link with their customer. This is often done through the use of **cookies**, which are text files placed on a user's computer by the web retailer in order to identify the user when he or she next visits the website. They can record a customer's actions as they move through a website, noting not only the purchases but also the areas that the customer has browsed. This may indicate what the customer may buy on the next visit if the correct promotional offer is made. Also, unlike traditional retailers, an online retailer can alter the website in real time to test particular offers with specific potential customers.

Customer databases are generally developed for four main reasons:

1 **Personalisation of marketing communications:** to allow personalisation of direct marketing activity, with postal, telecommunication or electronic correspondence being addressed specifically to the individual customer. The offers being promoted can also be targeted at the specific needs of the individual. For example, a bank may be able to send out specific information on their student account offerings to the 16–18-year-old market segment.

2 **Improved customer service:** when a customer seeks service from a branch office or a call centre, the organisation is better able to provide that service if details about the past relationship/service history with the customer are known. For example, Amazon's bookselling website makes book suggestions to customers based on their previous purchases.

3 **Improved understanding of customer behaviour:** the organisation can better understand customer profiles for segmentation purposes and the development of new product/service offerings. For example, Sea France was able to categorise its customers into eight segments by analysing customer postcode data with variables such as ticket type, distance from the port, type of vehicle and frequency of travel. This was cross-tabulated with ticket values, allowing Sea France to determine which segments were of most value.

4 **Assessing the effectiveness of the organisation's marketing and service activities:** the organisation can monitor its own performance by observing the behaviour of its customers. For example, a supermarket may be able to check the effectiveness of different promotional offers by tracking the purchases made by specific target segments.

Although customer databases can fulfil these functions, it should be stressed that they tend to hold information only on existing and past customers; information on potential customers is generally incomplete or in some cases non-existent. This may limit their usefulness in providing a comprehensive view of market characteristics.

User-generated content: a definition

User-generated content can be defined as:

> Material such as personal opinions, news, ideas, photos and video published by users of social networks, blogs, online communities and product/service review sites using the applications of Web 2.0.

There is a growing willingness among many people to express themselves in public and to reveal their habits, purchases and opinions. Online social networks allow individuals to communicate with one another and to construct a public or semi-public profile of themselves as well as sharing a variety of content. There are two types of **social networks**: those that focus on the individual, such as Facebook or LinkedIn, and those that focus around objects, such as Flickr (where photographs form the object), YouTube (where videos are the object) and del.icio.us (where hyperlinks form the object). Blogs (a blend of the term 'web logs') is a frequent, chronological publication of personal thoughts and ideas. Twitter is a form of microblogging service that allows an individual to publish their blog type opinions and ideas in short Tweets (text-based messages of up to 140 characters). Organisations interact with customers and potential customers on social networks and blogging sites, but they also interact through **online communities** in order better to understand their customers and target markets. Examples include **www.mumsnet.com** (a British community website set up by mothers to give advice on parenting and family issues) and **www.huggiesclub.co.uk** (a site set up by Huggies Nappies for new parents). Consumers also feedback their views and recommendations through product/service review sites such as **www.tripadvisor.com** or the customer review sections of sites such as **www.amazon.co.uk**. All of these interactive sources of feedback, ideas and opinion can provide an organisation with a wealth of information about consumers and their behaviours, actions and attitudes. Obviously the material may not always be either honest or representative of the views of the wider population but it may provide access to opinion formers, open two-way communication with consumers as well as identifying potential ideas/hypotheses for further testing.

Social networks
Online social networks allow individuals to communicate with one another, construct a public or semi-public profile of themselves as well as share a variety of content.

Online communities
A community of individuals who interact online focusing on a particular interest or simply to communicate.

Product review sites
Online sites that allow individuals to feed back their views on products and services. These sites may be independent or operated by manufacturers, retailers and other forms of intermediaries.

Researcher quote

Product review sites and sites like Facebook give you an idea about the important themes and issues that should be focused on in a survey or group discussion.

The marketing concept and the need for marketing information

Marketing concept
The proposition that the whole of the organisation should be driven by a goal of serving and satisfying customers in a manner which enables the organisation's financial and strategic objectives to be achieved.

The need for marketing information stems from the adoption of the **marketing concept**. Although there are many definitions of marketing, the basic concept of marketing is that the whole of the organisation should be driven by a constant concern for its customers, without whose business the organisation simply would not exist. In other words, the marketing concept requires an organisation to define who the customers or potential customers are, focus on their particular needs, then coordinate all of the activities that will affect customers, in order that the organisation achieves its financial and strategic objectives through the creation of satisfied customers.

The ethos of satisfying customers has to be spread throughout the whole organisation and not limited only to those who are in immediate or direct contact with the customer. The more the marketing concept can be spread through an organisation, the better will be the achievement of the organisation's commercial, charitable, political or social objectives.

This book uses the term *customer* in its widest sense, as some organisations may not sell products or services to consumers or companies but may still have similar types of stakeholder groups that the organisation is seeking to satisfy. For example, charities may view both the recipients of the charitable support and the donors as their customers. Similarly, political parties may view the electorate or their supporters as their customers. Even the prison service has stakeholders that may be classed as 'customers' and these could be seen as being either the prisoners within the walls of the prisons or the general population that lives outside.

Whatever the type of organisation, information is critical if the correct products, services and offerings are to be provided to the customers. In small organisations, such as the village shop, the owner may personally know (a) the customer's buying habits and attitudes, (b) the competitors' activities and (c) the changes occurring in the local market (e.g. new houses being built). However, as an organisation becomes larger, the amount of direct contact the decision maker has with the customer becomes significantly less. As a result, management take decisions as to how best to serve their customers based on information that is gathered from a variety of sources rather than from personal experience.

In particular, effective marketing decisions are reliant on information in three main areas:

1 **Information on customers:** the marketing concept can only be realistically implemented when adequate information about customers is available. To find out what satisfies customers, marketers must identify who customers are, what their characteristics are and what the main influences on what, where, when and how they buy or use a product or service are. By gaining a better understanding of the factors that affect customer behaviour, marketers are in a better position to predict how customers will respond to an organisation's marketing activity.

2 **Information on other organisations:** if a commercial organisation wishes to maintain some form of advantage over competitors, it is essential that information is gathered on the actions of competitors. Comparison of performance relative to competitors helps managers recognise strengths and weaknesses in their own marketing strategies. Even in non-commercial organisations, gathering information on other charities, political parties or government departments can produce new ideas and practices that will allow the organisation better to serve its own customers.

3 **Information on the marketing environment:** the environment consists of a large number of variables, which are outside the control of an organisation, but which have an influence on the marketing activities of the organisation. These variables, such as government policy, the economy, technological developments, changes in legislation and changes in the demographics of the population, have to be monitored continuously if an organisation is to keep pace with changing customer and market requirements.

Examples of changes in demographics within Europe

- *A continuing decline in children of school age*, a threat to producers of teenage magazines, confectionery, soft drinks, etc.
- *An increasing proportion of older people (over 75)*, influencing the demand for retirement homes, hearing aids and special holidays.
- *An increasing proportion of single-adult households*, influencing the demand for smaller accommodation, online dating sites and food packaged in smaller portions.
- *An increasing proportion of working women* and the resultant demand for convenience foods, microwaves and child daycare centres.

All of the above information types have to be collated and their implications for an organisation's marketing activities have to be assessed. Although uncertainty is inherent in decision making, the gathering and interpretation of information can make the process more objective and systematic. Successful managers take an orderly and logical approach to gathering information; they seek facts and undertake new marketing approaches on a systematic basis rather than simply through a procedure of trial and error.

The key roles and application of marketing information

Information for marketing may have descriptive, comparative, diagnostic or predictive roles. Its **descriptive role** answers the '**What**', '**Where**' and '**When**' questions that marketing managers may have, such as:

- **What**, **where** and **when** are customers buying?
- **What** level of donation is made to specific charities?
- **What** knowledge do customers have of a brand or range of products?
- **What** attitudes do customers have towards specific brands or products?
- **What** advertising and marketing communications have customers seen or been exposed to?

Its **comparative role** answers the '**How**' questions used for performance measurement, such as:

- **How** did this service performance differ from previous experiences?
- **How** does our product compare with the competitors?
- **How** does this political party's policies compare with those of another party?

Information's **diagnostic role** answers the '**Why**' questions and provides explanations, such as:

- **Why** do customers believe that advertisement?
- **Why** do customers buy this product rather than one of the alternatives?
- **Why** are prisoners dissatisfied with the conditions?

The **predictive role** answers the '**What would happen?**' type of questions and helps to determine future trends, such as:

- **What would happen** if the competitors reduced their prices?
- **What would happen** if this new product was launched?
- **What would happen** if government expenditure in this area was to reduce?

These descriptive, comparative, diagnostic and predictive roles result in information that addresses the key decision areas of an organisation's strategic and tactical marketing activities. In developing a strategy, the management team need to address marketing decisions such as:

- **The area of the market on which to focus:** specifically, what range of products or services should be produced and delivered? Which market segments should be targeted? What methods of delivery are required to reach these target segments? Information will assist organisations in answering these questions and determining the direction of their core business activities and their core customer segments. For example, an organisation such as Tesco may need to determine which European markets to enter or whether it should move into the selling of other non-grocery products such as cars or furniture.
- **The method of differentiation:** how will the organisation compete with other organisations? What will differentiate its offering from those of other organisations? How can the organisation better serve the needs of the target market? To answer these questions, marketers need to know which product or service benefits create most value for the potential customer. For example, when purchasing a car, is the target segment more interested in speed, comfort, economy or brand name? This may help determine the brand values that an organisation should adopt. These may go well beyond the physical features of the product: for example, the Virgin Airline brand values are associated with fun, innovation

and quality service. Such brand values are developed as a result of researching the views of the target market and are refined or modified based on ongoing information on customer attitudes and competitor activities.

- **The establishment of objectives:** information is critical in determining the objectives for a product, a brand or for an organisation's marketing activities. Objectives may relate to market share, profit, revenue growth, awareness, levels of customer satisfaction or level of donations (for a charity). This is dependent on having information regarding the organisation's performance currently as well as answers to predictive-type questions about what is likely to happen in the market.

- **The development of the marketing programme:** at a tactical level, marketing information can provide detailed information to assist with decisions relating to:
  - product or service features;
  - packaging;
  - distribution channels;
  - ordering and delivery procedures;
  - pricing and discounting policies;
  - marketing communication approaches;
  - communication messages and media;
  - brand image and logo to be associated with the brand;
  - service support and complaint handling procedures;
  - design and location of retail or service outlets.

- **Implementation and the monitoring of performance:** marketing information is needed to determine whether elements of the marketing programme are meeting their objectives. Performance measurement is dependent on specific objectives having been set, with marketing information providing the measures against these objectives. Are market share or sales targets being achieved? If not, why not? Should elements of the marketing programme be changed or continued? A company such as Ford will need to monitor which models of car are selling, as well as the optional extras that customers are buying, to determine how a model's specification will need to change in the future.

The information explosion

Information explosion
The major growth in information available in a wide range of formats from a wide range of sources. This growth has principally resulted from improvements in the capabilities and speeds of computers.

In the past, marketing managers often had difficulties in gathering sufficient information to make sound marketing decisions. Today's problems relate more to the filtering of relevant data from the **information explosion** available in a wide range of formats from a wide range of sources. These sources may be internal to the organisation, coming from customer databases, performance reports and electronic barcode scanning devices, or they may be from the Internet, user-generated content or marketing research sources. More information does not always mean better decision making. It is important that the levels of information presented to the decision maker are kept to a manageable scale. Therefore, marketing managers need to be specific about what information they need as well as the accuracy and reliability of the information they require. Decision makers need to be systematic in their use of information if they are to fully understand its meaning and avoid going through the same information more than once.

Researcher quote

The main task isn't so much the finding of information; it is more to do with ensuring that the information is relevant and of a scale and format that is manageable.

This also means that suppliers of information, whether marketing researchers or database managers, must develop a willingness to accommodate available information from each other. It has to be recognised that data obtained from several sources are likely to provide a more reliable guide for marketing decision making than data drawn from a single source. This is the concept of **triangulation**, where different sources of data are used to counterbalance the weaknesses in some sources with the strengths of others. The term 'triangulation' is borrowed from the disciplines of navigation and surveying, where a minimum of three reference points are taken to check an object's location. As such, it is important that marketing managers are using information in an integrated manner rather than following the piecemeal approach of databases separate from competitor intelligence separate from marketing research. This may mean that information professionals such as marketing researchers need to develop skills in integrating information from marketing research surveys with information from customer databases and Internet resources if they are to prove invaluable to the marketing decision maker. Such integration is more than simply pulling information together; it is also about deciding which information is worth accessing, which should be rejected and which should be stored.

Triangulation
Using a combination of different sources of data where the weaknesses in some sources are counterbalanced with the strengths of others. The term 'triangulation' is borrowed from the disciplines of navigation and surveying, where a minimum of three reference points are taken to check an object's location.

The limitations of information

Information should not be seen as the ultimate panacea for poor marketing decision making. Decisions still have to be taken based on the judgement of the managers concerned. However, better informed judgement should result in better decisions. Wrong decisions may still be made but the incidence of these should reduce with the provision of relevant marketing research and customer information. Sometimes research results may be ignored, particularly where the decision maker has an overriding belief in the product or where a decision maker's reputation will suffer as a result of abandoning a new product development project or by taking a risk and launching. Occasionally the decision makers who ignore the research will be proved correct – the Dyson bagless vacuum cleaner and the Sony Walkman are examples of products that were launched contrary to marketing research recommendations. If the product concept is so unique and different from existing products, consumers and certain research approaches may provide misleading feedback. Therefore, managers need to make judgements not only about the decisions that are to be taken but also with regard to the reliability of the information available.

The marketing research and database industry

Marketing research and customer database information can either be produced by employees internal to an organisation or can be outsourced from an external supplier. The internal supplier for marketing research is the marketing researcher or marketing research department. Such departments tend to be found only in larger organisations where there is a regular and possibly constant need for marketing research. Their incidence also tends to be greater in large organisations involved in consumer products or services rather than business-to-business products. Within some organisations (e.g. Britvic Soft Drinks, Ford, Van den Bergh, Diageo, Walker Snacks), internal marketing researchers have been renamed and are now called customer insight managers. This reflects a change from managers who simply managed the marketing research process to the creation of managers who manage information on an integrated basis from a variety of information sources. These managers may also be responsible for commissioning external suppliers to undertake marketing research or supply information. The external suppliers can be categorised as shown in Figure 1.1.

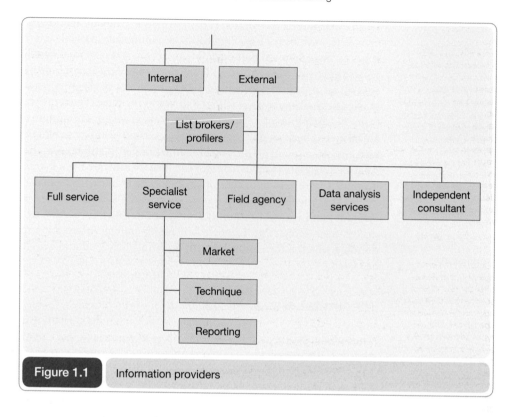

Figure 1.1 Information providers

List brokers/profilers

List compilers and brokers
Organisations that sell off-the-shelf data files listing names, characteristics and contact details of consumers or organisations.

Profilers
Organisations that gather demographic and lifestyle information about consumers and combine it with postal address information. They take this base information and use it to segment an organisation's database of existing customers into different lifestyle and income groups. They may also be used to identify additional prospective customers whose characteristics match those of an organisation's existing customers.

List compilers and brokers capture lists of individuals and organisations and then sell them to companies that wish to augment their own customer databases and mailing lists. They capture names and other details from a wide range of sources, including:

- the names of shareholders and directors of public companies from public records;
- the names of subscribers to magazines;
- the names of people who replied to special promotions, direct mailings or competitions;
- the names of people replying to lifestyle questionnaires;
- warranty records for electrical products;
- the names of voters from the electoral role;
- a country's census records;
- data on bad debt from public records or by sharing data between credit providers.

Profilers are different from list brokers, inasmuch as their work will involve them interacting directly with an organisation's database, whereas a list broker will tend to simply sell an off-the-shelf data file. Profilers such as CACI (**www.caci.co.uk**) gather demographic and lifestyle information from many millions of individual consumers, which enables them to classify every neighbourhood in Great Britain into one of 17 groups and 56 subgroups. They then take this base information and combine it with the postal address information on an organisation's database to segment existing customers by factors such as lifestyle and income. This allows organisations to target their offerings to existing customers more accurately. Profilers will also be able to identify additional prospective customers whose characteristics match those of an organisation's existing customers.

Full-service agencies

Full-service agencies
Marketing research agencies that offer the full range of marketing research services and techniques. They will be able to offer the entire range of qualitative and quantitative research approaches as well as be capable of undertaking every stage of the research, from research design through to analysis and report writing.

External suppliers of marketing research services can be classified as being **full-service agencies** or **specialist service agencies**. Full-service agencies offer the full range of marketing research services and techniques. They will be able to offer the entire range of qualitative and quantitative research approaches as well as being capable of undertaking every stage of the research, from research design through to analysis and report writing. Full-service agencies tend to be the larger research companies such as TNS (**www.tns-global.com**), BMRB (**www.bmrb.co.uk**), Ipsos MORI (**www.ipsosmori.com**) and Research International (**www.research-int.com**).

Specialist service agencies

Specialist service agencies
Marketing research agencies that do not offer the full range of services (see **Full-service agencies**) but tend to specialise in certain types of research. For example, a specialist agency may only do research in a specific market sector such as the automotive sector or children's products, or in a geographic region of the world. Alternatively, the agency may be a specialist in terms of the research techniques it undertakes, focusing on telephone research or qualitative research.

These agencies do not offer a full range of services but tend to specialise in certain types of research. For example, a specialist agency may only do research in a specific market sector such as the automotive sector or children's products, or a geographic region such as the Middle East. Alternatively, the agency may be a specialist in terms of research techniques, and may only do qualitative, telephone or online research. Some agencies may specialise in particular types of reporting approach. For example, certain agencies may only focus on syndicated reporting services, where, rather than carrying out a unique research project for a specific client, they research a market or product area and sell the resulting reports or data to a number of subscribing organisations. In some ways these syndicated research suppliers are like publishers selling books as they sell the same report or data to a number of organisations. Examples of these agencies include Datamonitor (**www.datamonitor.com**), Key Note (**www.keynote.co.uk**) and Mintel (**www.mintel.co.uk**). Syndicated research is a major source of retail sales information and media consumption, such as television viewing and press readership.

Field agencies

Field agencies
Agencies whose primary activity is the field interviewing process, focusing on the collection of data through personal interviewers, telephone interviewers or postal surveys.

As the name suggests, **field agencies**' primary activity is the field interviewing process, focusing on the collection of data through personal interviewers, telephone interviewers or postal surveys. Questionnaire and sample design as well as the analysis will therefore need to be undertaken by the client organisation itself or by another subcontractor.

Data analysis services

Data analysis services
Organisations, sometimes known as *tab shops*, that specialise in providing services such as the coding of completed questionnaires, inputting the data from questionnaires into a computer and the provision of sophisticated data analysis using advanced statistical techniques.

Small companies, sometimes known as 'tab shops' (because they provide tabulations of data), provide coding and **data analysis services**. Their services include the coding of completed questionnaires, inputting the data from questionnaires into a computer, and the provision of sophisticated data analysis using advanced statistical techniques. Within this grouping of organisations there are also individuals or small companies that transcribe tape recordings of qualitative research depth interviews or group discussions.

Independent consultants

There are a large number of independent consultants in the marketing research and customer information sector who undertake small surveys, particularly in business-to-business markets, manage individual parts of the marketing research process or advise on information collection, storage or retrieval.

The professional bodies and associations in the marketing research industry

There are a number of international and national associations and professional bodies representing the interests of marketing researchers and the marketing research industry.

The largest bodies are the Market Research Society (MRS) and ESOMAR. The MRS (**www.mrs.org.uk**) is based in the UK and has over 8,000 members in more than 70 countries. It is the world's largest international membership organisation for professional researchers and others engaged or interested in market, social and opinion research. It has a diverse membership of individual researchers within agencies, independent consultancies, client-side organisations and the academic community, and from all levels of seniority and job functions. All members of the Society agree to comply with the MRS Code of Conduct, which ensures that marketing research is undertaken in a professional and ethical manner. The MRS also offers various training programmes and is the official awarding body in the UK for vocational qualifications in marketing research. ESOMAR (**www.esomar.org**) was founded in 1948 as the European Society for Opinion and Marketing Research. Its membership now reflects a more global positioning as it unites over 4,000 members (users and providers of research in 100 countries). Other associations and professional bodies are listed in Table 1.2.

Maintaining the distinction between marketing research and direct marketing

Marketing research is dependent on the willing cooperation of both the public and organisations to provide information of value to marketing decision makers. Such cooperation is likely to be prejudiced by suspicion about the purpose of research projects and concerns about the validity of the guarantees of confidentiality which are given to respondents. As highlighted in the codes of conduct of both the MRS and ESOMAR, as well as the 1995 European Union Directive on the Protection of Personal Data, information collected for marketing research purposes cannot be used for developing marketing databases that will be used for direct marketing or direct sales approaches. The principle of transparency is the key consideration in all dealings with respondents. It must be made clear to respondents that all personal data collected during a research project will be treated confidentially for genuine marketing research purposes and that no attempt will be made to sell something to the respondent as a result of their having taken part in the research. Also, direct marketing activity should not imply to the customer that it is some form of marketing research – any questionnaires or other data collection methods used for direct marketing should make clear at the time of collection that the information provided may be used for sales or sales promotion purposes. As such, the use of questionnaires as part of a database-building exercise for direct marketing purposes cannot be described as 'marketing research' and should not be combined in the same data collection exercise. Where the results of a marketing research project are to be used to enrich and extend the information held on a marketing database, then personal data is not allowed to be used in a respondent-identifiable basis by the various professional codes of conduct. This means that research data being added to a database should not be in the form of personal data, but should instead be anonymous and partly aggregated data. For example, consumer profiles built up from aggregated research data may be used to categorise all consumers in a database, whereas personal information relating to individual respondents should not be used.

Therefore the integration perspective upon which this book is based refers to the marketing researchers managing the information outputs coming from sources such as customer databases, rather than managing the inputs to such databases or managing the databases for other (non-marketing-research) purposes.

Table 1.2	Professional bodies and associations representing marketing research

Name	Representing	Country	Website
The Market Research Society	Marketing research professionals	International (UK based)	www.mrs.org.uk
Chartered Institute of Marketing	Marketing professionals	International (UK based)	www.cim.co.uk
ESOMAR	Marketing research professionals	International (Netherlands based)	www.esomar.org
AIMRI	European marketing research institutes	Europe (UK based)	www.aimri.net
EFAMRO	European marketing research associations	Europe (UK based)	www.efamro.com
VMÖ	Marketing research professionals	Austria	www.vmoe.at
FEBELMAR	Marketing research bureaux	Belgium	www.febelmar.be
FMD	Marketing research institutes	Denmark	www.fmd.dk
FAMRA	Marketing research institutes	Finland	www.smtl.fi
SYNTEC Etudes Marketing et Opinion	Marketing research professionals	France	www.syntec-etudes.com
ADM	Marketing research agencies	Germany	www.adm-ev.de
BVM	Marketing research professionals	Germany	www.bvm.org
AGMORC	Marketing research agencies and professionals	Greece	www.sedea.gr
PMSZ	Marketing research agencies	Hungary	www.pmsz.org
AIMRO	Marketing research agencies	Ireland	www.aimro.ie
ASSIRM	Marketing research agencies	Italy	www.assirm.it
Markt Onderzoek Associatie	Marketing research professionals	Netherlands	www.moaweb.nl
Norwegian Marketing Research Association	Marketing research professionals	Norway	www.nmf-org.no
APODEMO	Marketing research professionals	Portugal	www.apodemo.pt
AEDEMO	Marketing research professionals	Spain	www.aedemo.es
ANEIMO	Marketing research agencies	Spain	www.aneimo.com
SMUF	Buyers of marketing research	Sweden	www.smuf.com
ASC	Survey computing professionals	UK	www.asc.org.uk
AQR	Qualitative research professionals	UK	www.aqr.co.uk
AURA	Users of marketing research agencies	UK	www.aura.org.uk
ICG	Independent Market Researchers	UK	www.indepconsultants.org

*Details of professional bodies and associations located in other countries are available on the ESOMAR and MRS websites.

Integration — An international perspective

Many of the organisations involved in marketing research are truly international with offices throughout the world. For example, the full service agency TNS employs more than 15,000 staff in 80 countries across Africa, the Americas, Asia Pacific, Europe and the Middle East. Market research projects are frequently undertaken simultaneously in a number of different countries for global brands such as Ford, Nokia and Nestlé. Undertaking cross-border studies brings additional challenges relating to language, national customs, costs and quality of data. There may also be regulatory issues with regards the holding of customer information in different countries which may impact on databases being held by global operators in sectors such as financial services, airlines and hospitality. The implications of an international perspective will be explored further in later chapters.

Summary and an integrated approach

The marketing concept promotes the idea that the whole of the organisation should be driven by the goal of serving and satisfying customers in a manner which enables the organisation's financial and strategic objectives to be achieved. It is obvious that marketing decision makers require the best customer, competitor and market information available when deciding on future courses of action for their products and organisations. Therefore, the source of the information is less important than the quality of information. Marketing researchers need to adapt to these changing circumstances and be willing to integrate information from a range of sources, such as customer databases and user-generated content on the Internet, as well as from marketing research itself, in order to develop better knowledge of market conditions.

The definition of marketing research in this book reinforces this need by stating that marketing research is the collection, analysis and communication of information undertaken to assist decision making in marketing. The type of information is not specified, apart from the fact that it should assist decision making in marketing. Therefore, customer databases and user-generated content should be seen as appropriate sources of information to be included within the remit of marketing researchers. Such information can be used to assist decision making in descriptive, comparative, diagnostic and predictive roles. However, information does not in itself make decisions; it simply enables better-informed decision making to take place. Managers still need to use judgement and intuition when assessing information, and with the growth in information sources as a result of computerisation and the Internet, managers need more guidance and help in selecting the most appropriate information to access and use. Guidance of this type must take account of the manner in which the information was collected and analysed. The marketing research industry, involving many different types of information supplier, should be best qualified to do this.

Discussion questions

1 Marketing research has traditionally been associated with consumer goods. Today an increasing number of non-profit organisations (charities, government departments) are using marketing research. Why do you think this is the case?

2 Explain the importance of marketing research to the implementation of the marketing concept.

3 Using the **upmystreet.com** website, enter a postcode (it may be your own) and look at the detailed ACORN profile for that postcode. Report on the contents of the profile in class.

4 Consider a frequent flyer programme for an airline. What type of information is such a programme likely to hold on each of its members?

5 Why do organisations maintain customer databases?

6 Considering the demographic changes mentioned on page 8, what are the likely implications of these changes for a manufacturer of tinned baked beans?

7 Explain the meaning of each of the following information roles: descriptive, comparative, diagnostic and predictive.

8 What is meant by the term 'information explosion' and what are its implications?

9 When Sony first undertook research into the potential for the Walkman, the results suggested that the product would be a failure. Why do you think that was?

10 Why are marketing research departments in many large organisations changing their names to customer insight departments? To justify this change, what activities should the renamed department be involved in?

Additional reading

Baker, S. and Mouncey, P. (2003) The market researcher's manifesto. *International Journal of Market Research*, **45**(4), pp. 415–33.

Comley, P. (2008) Online research communities: a user guide. *International Journal of Market Research*, **50**(5), pp. 679–94.

Cooke, M. and Buckley, N. (2008) Web 2.0, social networks and the future of market research. *International Journal of Market Research*, **50**(2), pp. 267–90.

Smith, D. and Culkin, N. (2001) Making sense of information: a new role for the marketing researcher? *Marketing Intelligence and Planning*, **19**(4), pp. 263–72.

Smith, D.V.L. and Fletcher, J.H. (2001) *Inside Information: Making Sense of Marketing Data*. John Wiley, Chichester.

Tapscott, D. (2008) *Grown up Digital: How the Net Generation is Changing the World*. McGraw-Hill Professional, New York.

Tapscott, D. and Williams, A. (2008) *Wikinomics*. Atlantic Books, London.

References

[1] Adapted from **http://www.reliableplant.com/Read/3802/market-research-drives-product-development-at-ford**.

[2] Adapted from *ACORN User Guide*, available from **www.caci.co.uk**.

2 The marketing research process

Virgin Atlantic – journeys to work

Road-traffic congestion is growing in the vicinity of major airports resulting in increased noise and emissions concern, not to mention time-delays. Employers based at airports have been looking closely at staff travel-to-work policies, mindful of the implications for staff welfare, but also with an eye on the environmental impact.

Virgin Atlantic employs over 8,000 UK staff based mainly in the Gatwick and Heathrow areas. The objective of having satisfied and healthy staff could be adversely affected by the cost and stress of journeys to work. With no existing data on staff behaviour and attitudes towards journeys to work, Virgin Atlantic sought a research agency to get the insight it lacked. The information was needed

TRISTAR PHOTOS/Alamy

both as evidence for an external transport policy document about Virgin's actions to meet environmental obligations and to support internal plans that could improve journeys, staff satisfaction and wellbeing.

The chosen agency used an online survey sent to all UK-based staff, plus follow-up group discussions involving over 70 individuals to gain a more in-depth understanding. The online survey required about ten minutes to complete and consisted of a variety of question types including open-ended questions. Such a question mix was considered to be essential, if employees are to feel valued and empowered to express their opinions fully. The research found that eight out of ten ground-based staff, and two out of three flight crew, drove to work. However, it also showed that there was significant potential for reducing single occupancy car journeys particularly around Gatwick. The findings enabled Virgin Atlantic to negotiate possible discount schemes with local bus operators as well as the provision of free car parking spaces to those staff willing to car share. The survey also highlighted considerable ignorance, particularly among flight crews regarding public transport options and the fare concessions already available to airport-based staff. As a result, the airline worked on more effective internal communications including travel-to-work information points in office receptions. The research was also used as strong evidence to support the business case for a number of initiatives such as staff shuttle buses from Gatwick to the major Virgin Atlantic office sites in Crawley.

The open-ended questions in a survey combined with group discussions can be extremely useful for highlighting unexpected issues. For example, concerns surfaced amongst female flight crew about gaining unwanted attention from men, as a result of their uniform, when on public transport. While no obvious solutions were identified, it was important for the company to appreciate this issue and understand that public transport is not a suitable solution for all staff.[1]

Learning outcomes

Marketing research process
The sequence of activities and events involved in undertaking a marketing research project.

After reading this chapter you should:

● understand the key steps in the **marketing research process**;

● be aware of the importance of the research brief and its contents;

● understand the process involved and the criteria used in selecting marketing research agencies;

● be aware of the importance of the research proposal and its contents;

● appreciate the broad types of research design;

● understand the need for an ethical and professional approach towards marketing research;

● be aware of relevant data protection legislation and professional codes of conduct.

Key words

'beauty parades'	**marketing research process**
causal research	**observation**
conclusive research	**primary data**
cross-sectional studies	**professional codes of conduct**
data protection legislation	**qualitative research**
descriptive research	**quantitative research**
experimental research	**research brief**
exploratory research	**research proposal**
GANTT chart	**secondary data**
longitudinal studies	

Introduction

This chapter is designed to introduce you to the key steps involved in undertaking a marketing research project. These steps represent the marketing research process, the sequence of activities and events that need to be addressed if a marketing research project is to provide information that is valuable to the marketing decision maker. This process will also provide the basic framework for the structure of the remainder of the book, with individual chapters examining some specific aspect of the process. The marketing research process is shown in Figure 2.1.

Stage 1: identification of problems and opportunities

The marketing environment is constantly changing and therefore marketing managers have to address new issues which may create opportunities or problems for their organisations. For example, the development of a new product may offer potential opportunities to develop business or may simply result in major costs in terms of finance and corporate reputation. A drop in sales may mean that the product range is out of date and needing an expensive

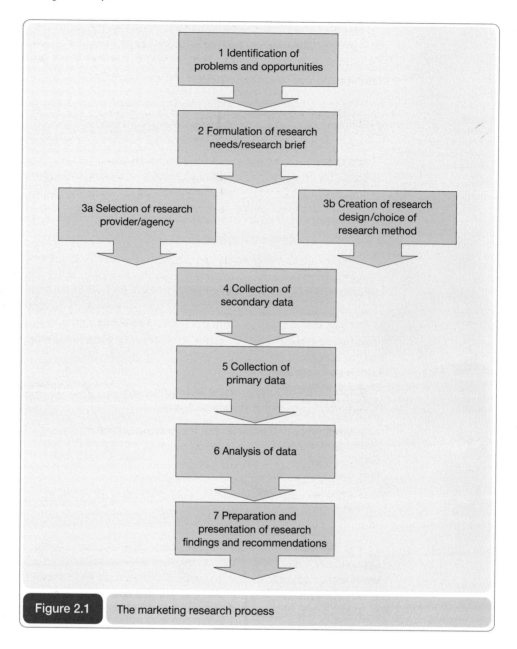

Figure 2.1   The marketing research process

revamp, or it may have come about as a result of short-term price-cutting by the competition. Issues such as these raise questions that need to be answered before decisions can be made. Marketing research may provide the answers to some of these questions.

The precise definition of the problem aids in understanding the information that will be needed and therefore also helps in identifying the research objectives. The organisation should assess the nature or 'symptoms' of the issue that it is currently facing. These may stem from what is known about:

- market conditions;
- competitors' actions;
- the organisation's own objectives, plans and capabilities;
- previous marketing initiatives and their effectiveness;
- the nature of the existing and new products or services;
- the awareness, attitudes and behaviour of customers.

It is critical that this assessment is done in as objective a manner as possible and is based on fact rather than assumption and hearsay. Any gaps in the information may also indicate areas where research is needed. The example of Thomas Cook (see below) illustrates how problems and opportunities are turned into research needs.

Thomas Cook

Thomas Cook is a large and well-known international travel company, operating travel agencies, charter airlines and foreign currency bureaux. Smaller and less well known is its profitable commercial foreign exchange business, which, as the name suggests, provides foreign currency payment services for businesses.

The problem/opportunity

The commercial foreign exchange business (CFX) was charged with significantly increasing the size of its share of the market. A quick look at its existing customer profile soon revealed that a small number of top customers accounted for a disproportionately large amount of its total revenue. As it could not sell more to these customers, it recognised that the most effective way to significantly increase revenue was to get more top customers. But to do this effectively it needed to improve its sales prospecting.

The questions

Before Thomas Cook could develop a more effective sales strategy it needed marketing research to answer questions such as:

- What types of company offer the greatest potential?
- How do we target these companies?
- What approaches should we use?
- What messages should we communicate?
- What pricing offers should we employ to win their business?[2]

It is arguably better to make plans and take decisions based on data gathered from objective marketing research than based on subjective feelings, 'hunches' and assumptions. There are no guarantees that decisions based on marketing research will always be correct and result in success, but there is a higher likelihood of success if research is used to verify or discount these feelings, 'hunches' and assumptions.

Stage 2: formulation of research needs/research brief

In formulating the specific research needs of a project, it is important to consult all of the managers and departments that will be involved in making and implementing the decisions that will flow from the research results. Their input at this early stage will reduce the likelihood of individuals or departments complaining at the end of the project that the wrong questions have been asked or that the research is worthless, as it simply replicates information already held within the organisation.

In particular, the consultation should focus on understanding:

1 The events that led to the decision that marketing research was required. It is necessary to understand the context in which the need for information occurs. If an organisation wishes to look at customer satisfaction as a result of a significant decline in sales then they may require greater urgency and detail than would be the case if customer satisfaction data is simply required as an input into an organisation's performance measurement programme. It is also important to be aware of any internal politics within an organisation which may be influencing the decisions that have to be taken. Any related tensions that may exist may influence the type and quality of both the information and decisions that will be required.

2 The alternative courses of action available to the organisation. Setting boundaries around the problem is critical. If all of the potential courses of action relate to new product features, then that is where the focus should be. There can often be the danger of decision makers taking the opportunity to add peripheral research questions, for example about other topics such as pricing or distribution, that can significantly change the nature of the project. As a result, the research can lose focus and fail to address the information requirements of the core decision area.

3 The individual pieces of information that are required to evaluate the alternative courses of action. Understanding the information that is required behind a decision is important. If a company wishes to consider the suitability of opening a new cinema in a particular city, it isn't appropriate to simply ask city residents if they would like a new cinema, as they are all likely to say 'yes, that would be nice'. Instead the decision needs to be based on information such as the disposable income of city residents, the cinemas residents currently travel to, their propensity to watch movies, their use of other leisure facilities, etc.

4 The time scale within which decisions have to be taken. It may not be appropriate to plan a large marketing research study if a decision is required within the next ten days. Alternatively, where a final decision is not required for several years, it may be more appropriate to establish a phased approach to the gathering of information.

5 The budget available for obtaining the information. The scale of the budget will have a direct influence on the scale and type of information that can be obtained.

6 The appropriateness of marketing research for some or all of the information that is required. Information may be gathered from a variety of sources, some may be available in an organisation's files or customer database. Other information may be readily available in published reports or on the Internet. Alternatively some of the information requirements may not even relate to marketing but may be more technical relating to materials and their suitablity for different applications. It is important to determine the most reliable and economic sources for all of the information that is required for the decisions that have to be taken.

The consultation can be managed by establishing a small project team which represents all of the interested parties within the organisation (for example, it may include representatives from marketing, operations, research and development, distribution, sales, corporate strategy, etc.). Alternatively, where the number of interested parties is large, it is generally more manageable to have a small core team who have discussions and meetings with all of the interested parties, and who then filter the information from these meetings and determine the specific research requirements. It may be necessary to appoint a senior manager as sponsor of the team in order to ensure full cooperation from the various departments.

This team would also be responsible for determining what information already exists within the organisation. It often seems easier and more interesting to develop new information than to delve through old reports and data files. However, if relevant data do exist, they can reduce the cost and time involved in undertaking the research and may also help to formulate the specific information targets and the most appropriate respondents for the research.

Research brief
A written document which sets out an organisation's requirements from a marketing research project. This provides the specification against which the researchers will design the research project.

The research brief

If marketing research is required, the project team should develop a written **research brief** setting out the organisation's requirements. This will provide the specification against which the researchers will design the research project. A written brief in comparison with a verbal briefing of the researchers allows the specifics of the briefing to be circulated and verified by all of those involved in or affected by the specific area of decision making. In particular, it enables all of the interested parties within the organisation to:

1 verify that the need for the research is genuine and is not simply:
   - a way of using up this year's marketing research budget, in order to guarantee the same level of funding on marketing research next year;
   - supporting a decision that has already been made as a way of reassuring the management team that they have made the correct decision;
   - a way of stalling a decision that management do not wish to make;
   - reiterating information that already exists within the organisation.
2 ensure that the information obtained will be relevant and of sufficient scope for the decisions that need to be taken;
3 ensure that the time scales and reporting procedures are compatible with the internal decision-making processes and timings.

Unfortunately, given the natural desire of managers to move things forward and the short time frame that is often set aside for marketing research, the development of the brief is often not given proper attention. The tendency to short-circuit the formulation of the research needs is unfortunate, as it can be very costly. A considerable amount of time, money and effort can be wasted in pursuit of the wrong research questions.

Researcher quote

I regularly experience presentations of research findings at the end of a project where members of the client organisation, who were not involved in the original briefing, ask why certain research questions were or were not asked. Surely this should have been sorted out by the organisation at the start of the project!

The contents of the research brief are therefore very important; the typical structure for such a brief is set out in Table 2.1.

Considering each of the sections of the brief, the following guidelines should be followed:

1 Background: this section should set out a brief explanation of what is happening within the organisation, the nature of its products or services as well as current market trends. This will enable the researchers to understand the context within which the problem or opportunity

Table 2.1	Contents of the research brief

The research brief

1 Background
   - the organisation, its products and its markets
2 Project rationale
   - origin and development of research need
   - decision areas to be addressed by research
3 Objectives
   - Definition of discrete areas of problem and opportunity that have to be explored
4 Outline of possible method
5 Reporting and presentational requirements
6 Timing

and the research need exists. It will also assist in the design of the research method and may actually speed up the research process, as less time is spent researching information that is already known. To augment the information in this section, the organisation may provide the researcher with copies of annual reports, brochures, previous research studies, etc.

2 Project rationale: this section sets out the reasons for the research being required. What areas of decision will be addressed by the research and what are the implications of these decisions to the organisation? This will enable the researchers to identify the priorities and also to develop recommendations at the end of the research project which will directly assist the organisation's decision making.

3 Objectives: the objectives set out the precise information needed to assist marketing management with the problem or opportunity. They should be clear and unambiguous, leaving little doubt as to what is required. Some organisations may also list the specific information targets under each objective to ensure that there is no misunderstanding. For example, the following objective from a study for computer printers considers attitudes towards the operation of a printer and uses information targets such as 'speed of printing' to highlight the specific areas of attitude to be examined.

To examine customer attitudes towards the operation of the new computer printer in terms of:

- speed of printing;
- quality of printing;
- use of the printer control panel;
- procedures for loading paper;
- procedures for installing print cartridges.

In developing the objectives, it is critical that the brief includes only those objectives that relate to what the organisation 'needs' to know rather than to information areas that would be 'nice to know'. In other words, the findings from the research should be 'actionable' and provide decision-making information rather than simply being 'interesting'.

4 Outline of possible method: at this stage in the research process, this section should only give a broad indication of the approach to be undertaken in the research. The researcher, once briefed, should be allowed to use his or her experience to develop the most appropriate research design. Therefore, this section of the brief should simply highlight the parameters within which the design can take place. It should indicate the types of respondents or market segments to be included in the research. It should also indicate whether the study should be large scale and statistically significant with a large amount of quantitative information or whether it should provide more detailed qualitative information on a much smaller scale. Ultimately the organisation will need to consider the trade-offs that are involved – for example, the trade-off between costs or time and the scale of the research. The larger the project, the more expensive and time-consuming it will be.

5 Reporting and presentational requirements (sometimes described as 'Deliverables'): this section of the brief sets out the organisation's requirements in terms of the nature of the written documents required from the researchers, such as the research proposal, any interim reports produced during the research and the final report. It should also highlight what formal stand-up presentations will be required when the proposals are submitted and also for the final results at the end of the project.

6 Timing: the brief should also set out the time scales for the submission of the proposal and the completion of the research.

The budget available for the project is rarely included within the brief. This is to ensure that the research is tailored to the needs of the organisation rather than the size of the budget. However, management should establish a maximum budget and keep this in mind when selecting the research provider or agency.

Stage 3a: selection of research provider/agency

The next stage of the research process is the selection of the researchers who are to do the research. The research could be undertaken by the in-house marketing research department within the organisation or by an external research agency. Larger organisations are more likely to have formal marketing research departments. Moreover, the incidence of such departments has been found to be higher in consumer products and services than in business-to-business products.

In many organisations the marketing research department primarily manages the research activity of external agencies rather than undertaking projects on its own. Many related considerations influence the decision to go outside and use external agencies:

- Internal personnel may not have the necessary skills or experience. Few but the very largest companies can afford to have specialists in the full range of research techniques.
- It may be cheaper to go to an agency that has encountered similar studies with other clients and is therefore more likely to be more efficient at tackling the research.
- Agencies may have special facilities or competencies (a national fieldforce; group discussion facility with one-way mirrors; a telephone research call centre) which would be costly to duplicate for a single study.
- Internal politics within the organisation (e.g. the product under investigation is the pet project of a particular senior manager) may dictate the use of an objective outside agency whose credentials are acceptable to all parties involved in an internal dispute. The internal research department may be well advised to avoid being on one side or the other of a sensitive issue.
- If the research is to be undertaken on an anonymous basis without the name of the sponsoring organisation being divulged then an external agency may need to be used.

With the growth in online surveys, many marketing departments are starting to do their own surveys using survey design and webhosting sites such as **www.surveymonkey.com** or **www.zoomerang.com** (see page 142). These sites allow marketing staff to design their own questionnaires on the web hosting site's server, administer the distribution of the survey and undertake basic data analysis. The sophistication of the questionnaires and the analysis may be limited; however, this may satisfy the research needs of a small research project on areas relating to customer satisfaction or awareness. The research may also be undertaken by an internal marketing research department when time is critical, or if product knowledge is important (for example, on complex financial products or industrial products). Otherwise, an external agency will be selected to undertake all or part (e.g. the fieldwork) of the project.

Selection of external research agencies

It is first necessary to identify a shortlist of three or four agencies which will be briefed on the organisation's research requirements. Without prior experience it is difficult to prejudge the effectiveness and likely research output of an agency. Like any service, there are few tangible cues to assist in the selection of the shortlist.

Therefore, decision makers within organisations tend to rely either on their own personal experience or the experience of others such as colleagues in other departments or other

Integration	An international perspective

Where a multi-country international marketing research project is undertaken (for example, if Nokia wished to examine and compare customer attitudes towards its mobile phone brand across ten countries), then more than one agency may be used to undertake the project. International research is more complex as a result of factors such as differences in language, culture, marketing research practices, privacy and data protection legislation. Therefore, the management of the agencies and the research is also more complex. There are a number of options available to organisations:

1 *They can appoint different agencies in each of the countries that they are researching*. This ensures that the researchers have local knowledge of the country being researched, the marketing research practices of the country and the local language. However, the selection process becomes more complex, with the client organisation having to shortlist, brief and select a separate agency in each country. This may be particularly difficult if the organisation has no experience of agencies in these countries. The management of the relationship with a number of agencies throughout the project may also be very onerous.

2 *They can appoint one agency to do the project in all of the countries*. This reduces the workload placed on the management of the client organisation and provides greater consistency in quality control over all the countries being researched. However, the agency may lack detailed knowledge of the markets and the accepted marketing research practices of the individual countries.

3 *They can appoint one of the large multinational agencies to undertake the research*. These would use their own subsidiaries in each of the countries being researched. There should be consistency in quality control and the individual subsidiaries should have local knowledge. The suitability of this option will depend on the countries being researched, as these agencies are only likely to have subsidiaries in the major markets of the world.

4 *They can use one marketing research agency as the project manager responsible for a consortium of research agencies*. This provides the client organisation with one point of contact. The day-to-day management is the responsibility of the project-managing agency, which briefs, selects agencies and manages their quality. In certain cases the project management agency may use overseas agencies with which it has had a previous relationship. The drawback of this approach is that some marketing research agencies may be good at undertaking research but less good at managing and coordinating the research of other agencies.

Whichever approach is adopted, agencies are almost always selected using the procedures outlined in the following subsections.

companies. Some may also seek recommendations from the trade association for their own industry (pharmaceuticals, toys, cars, etc.), or from bodies such as the Market Research Society, ESOMAR or the Chartered Institute of Marketing. In the UK the Market Research Society also produces an annual *Research Buyer's Guide* which lists agencies and their expertise.

The shortlist is normally drawn up on the basis of the following factors:

- previous experience in appropriate market sector (cars, groceries, advertising, etc.);
- previous experience in appropriate geographical market (for international research);
- appropriate technical capabilities (e.g. able to undertake telephone research);
- appropriate research facilities and fieldforce (e.g. call centre, national fieldforce, group discussion facilities);

- reputation for quality of work and keeping to time scales;
- evidence of professionalism (membership of professional bodies such as the MRS, adoption/compliance with recognised quality standards, etc.)
- communication skills (both written and verbal);
- financially stable/well established.

Once a shortlist of three or four agencies has been established, briefing of each of the agencies should take place using the written brief supported by a meeting between the organisation's project team and the agency. This should enable the agency personnel to fully understand the organisation's requirements, allowing them to develop a research proposal.

The research proposal

Research proposal
The submission prepared by the research agency for a potential client specifying the research to be undertaken. On the basis of the research proposal, the client will select an agency to undertake the research. The proposal becomes the contract between the agency and the client company.

The **research proposal** is the submission prepared by the research agency for a potential client specifying the research to be undertaken. On the basis of the research proposal, the client will select an agency to undertake the research. The proposal then becomes the contract between the agency and the client company. In many respects the proposal is as important as the research brief – if not more important. The typical structure for such a research proposal is set out in Table 2.2.

Table 2.2	Contents of the research proposal

The research proposal

1 Background
2 Objectives
3 Approach and method
4 Reporting and presentation procedures
5 Timing
6 Fees
7 Personal CVs
8 Related experience and references
9 Contract details

Researcher quote

The proposal is the most important part of the whole research project. It provides both the template and the contract for all of the subsequent research.

The content of the various sections is similar to the research brief.

1 Background: the background section puts the research into context by briefly describing the client organisation, its markets and products, and the rationale for doing the research. The following example sets out the background section for an organisation which was seeking research into horticultural equipment.

Example: Background section in a proposal

Smith Brothers are agents for a range of professional grass-cutting machinery and small industrial engines.

In the grass-cutting sector, the company has specialised in the Atlas range of products in terms of both product sales and parts and service support.

In the small-engine market, the company holds agencies for several major manufacturers of petrol engines (from 3 hp. to 20 hp.) for use in a variety of applications including mowers, cultivators, pumps and generators, etc.

The company is particularly strong in the municipal authority and golf course sectors and now wishes to increase sales by market expansion and increasing sales of grass-cutting and horticultural equipment to other market sectors.

Prior to developing a marketing strategy, Smith Brothers would like to obtain a much better understanding of the opportunities and the requirements for horticultural machinery in the following market sectors:

- ☐ Leisure
  - hotels with extensive grounds
  - caravan sites
- ☐ Institutions/government bodies
  - hospitals (public and private)
  - universities
  - private schools
  - government departments
- ☐ Major landowners
  - private estates (stately homes, zoos, etc.)
  - factories, private companies
- ☐ Contractors
  - landscape and building contractors
  - suppliers of contract maintenance

2 Objectives: the objectives are similar to those in the brief, although they may in certain cases be more precisely defined. The following example of an objective relates to the project set out above.

Example: Objectives

To investigate the horticultural machinery needs of the four market sectors under consideration (leisure, institutions/government bodies, major landowners, contractors) in terms of:

- types of machinery currently used;
- makes of machinery currently used;
- age of current machinery;
- source of supply;
- level of expenditure on machinery during last 12 months;
- maintenance provision.

3 Approach and method: this section sets out the methodology of the research approach, highlighting the types of research to be used, the sample, the method of analysis and any limitations of the proposed approach.

Example: Approach and method

In developing an approach for the project, the following elements were considered:

- the need to cover a wide spread of market sectors in sufficient detail to provide actionable findings;
- the geographical spread of the potential respondents;
- the need for a cost-effective research solution.

Based on these, the schedule, method and presentation procedures to be adopted for the research programme can be summarised as follows:

Project planning

A further meeting between representatives of Wilsontec Research and Smith Brothers to clarify any points outstanding on the proposal, finalise the checklist of information areas to be covered and agree timing.

Desk research

This stage of the research exercise will consist of a short programme of desk research to gather information on the market for horticultural equipment over the last ten years. These trend data should give a useful indication about the nature of the market, and should also help to identify the number of establishments in each market sector. A sample list of potential respondents will also be generated from published sources. In order to undertake this research, we would expect access to any internal market reports or industry directories that Smith Brothers hold.

An external search will also be undertaken looking at market reports on the horticultural, hospitality and landscape contracting market. A variety of key directories and websites will be used to assist in the development of a sample list. Brochures covering competing products will also be collected to assist with developing marketing intelligence.

Fieldwork

Qualitative research

In order to fully understand the purchasing procedures and criteria used in the acquisition of horticultural equipment, a small-scale programme of qualitative depth interviews will be undertaken in 12 organisations with the management function principally responsible for decisions relating to the purchase of horticultural equipment. Possible job titles will include:

- facilities manager;
- administration manager;
- company secretary;
- hotel manager/estate manager;
- gardening and grounds superintendent.

The 12 depth interviews will be allocated across the following market sectors:

- hotels with extensive grounds   2
- hospitals (public and private)   2
- universities and Colleges   2
- government Departments   2
- major private landowners   2
- landscape Contractors   2

The interviews will be undertaken by the research executives working on the project and are each expected to be of around 45–60 minutes duration.

Quantitative research

Following the qualitative phase of the research, a programme of 125 telephone interviews will be undertaken amongst a quota sample of companies/organisations located in the target geographic area within the pre-specified end-user sectors. The interviews will be undertaken using a questionnaire with CATI (Computer Assisted Telephone Interviewing). Telephone is the optimum methodology for this study as it enables us to select the correct decision makers accurately and swiftly.

The sample

A quota sample of 125 interviews will ensure that all of the key sectors will be covered in a manner that is likely to give a spread of responses. The proposed quotas are as follows:

	Number of interviews
Leisure • hotels with extensive grounds • caravan sites	25
Institutions/government bodies • hospitals (public and private) • universities • private schools • government departments	35
Major landowners • private estates (stately homes, zoos, etc.) • factories, private companies	25
Contractors • landscape and building contractors • suppliers of contract maintenance	40
TOTAL	**125**

Procedure

The questionnaire will be semi-structured with the majority of questions being pre-coded and it is anticipated that each questionnaire will take no longer than 15 minutes to complete. The interviews will be undertaken by Wilsontec Research interviewers based at our central telephone interviewing unit. All interviewers are fully trained and are supervised through random 'listening in' facilities. All fieldwork meets the industry standards laid down by our professional bodies, the MRS and ESOMAR.

The analysis will produce computer tabulations, in the form of cross tabulations and frequency distributions. Further statistical analysis will be discussed, once the initial data is evaluated.

4 Reporting and presentation procedures: this section highlights the structure of the report and the agency's proposals for interim and final presentations.

Example: Reporting and presentation procedures

Following the qualitative phase of the research, an interim presentation/discussion will be held, at which the questions for the quantitative phase will be agreed. At the end of the project, the findings of the research will be presented in the form of a PowerPoint presentation. This will be followed by a report (three copies) summarising the findings of all phases of the research. The final report will consist of two parts:

1 **Executive report**
   Interpretation of the findings of the research programme in terms of their implications for the future development of Smith Brothers. Among the points covered by Wilsontec Research under recommendations will be the following:
   - market potential available in each sector;
   - segmentation strategy in terms of:
     - prime business activity areas on which to concentrate activity
     - products in addition to grass cutting equipment to be offered.
   - management functions within organisations at which sales activity should be directed;
   - product and service requirements to be met by Smith Brothers taking account of:
     - purchase occasion (breakdown, age, change in requirements)
     - decision-forming factors/market requirements
     - pre- and after-sales services to be offered.
   - communications mix to be developed (website, direct mail, etc.);
   - perceived strengths and weaknesses upon which to build.

2 **Main report**
   Detailed presentation of research findings and relevant working papers

---

5 Timing: this should set out the time the project will take from the time of commissioning and should highlight any proposed break points between different phases of the research. This is frequently laid out in the form of a table as below or in a Gantt chart (see page 36).

Example: Timing

The research programme as summarised in this document will take approximately ten weeks to complete and can be initiated within ten days of written instructions to proceed being received.

Week	Activity
1–2	Desk research and project planning
3–4	Qualitative fieldwork
5	Interim presentation and questionnaire design
6–7	Quantitative fieldwork
8	Data analysis
9	Presentation
10	Final report

6 Fees: this should set out the total fees for the project. Expenses (e.g. travel, room hire, etc.) may be charged separately or be incorporated into the fees. Client organisations must pay particular attention to this section of the proposal and ensure that they are aware of the charging structure and that there is a ceiling put on additional expenses.

Example: Fees

The total cost of the research programme as specified in this proposal will be **£14,500 excluding VAT** but including all research fees and expenses, agency client meetings, an interim presentation and a final presentation at the client's offices on conclusion of the research.

Phase	Fee (£)
Desk Research	2,000
Qualitative research (12 depth interviews)	6,000
Quantitative research (125 telephone interviews)	6,500
Total fee	14,500

Invoicing will be in two instalments: 50 per cent on commission and the balance on submission of the final written report. Payment is due within ten days of receipt of invoice.

7 Personal CVs: this section sets out details about the background and experience of the key researchers who will be involved in this project.

Example: Project management and resources

Project Manager

Day-to-day management of the project will be undertaken by **Alan Wilson**, an Associate Director at Wilsontec Research. An MBA graduate from Edinburgh University, Mr Wilson started his professional career with an industrial market research consultancy before joining Wilsontec Research in 2004.

Mr Wilson has much experience of directing research projects involving the identification of new marketing opportunities. He has undertaken projects of this type for companies such as Shell, Dobbies Garden Centres, Siemens and EDF. Of relevance to this project he has undertaken diversification research into agricultural dealerships for a national company and examined the requirements for preventative maintenance schemes in the off-highway equipment market for Volvo BM.

Project Executive

Mr Wilson will be assisted by **Debbie Black**, a BSc Honours Graduate from Sheffield University. Ms Black has been in research for three years and joined Wilsontec Research in January 2006.

8 Related experience and references: this section sets out the background on the research agency, outlining what experience it has had in projects similar to or relevant to this one. Certain clients may also require the agency to provide references from previous clients.

> ### Example: Related experience
>
> Wilsontec Research is a specialist marketing research-based business, marketing and product/service planning consultancy. The company was formed in 1998. Turnover in 2008 was £3.9 million, and there is a full-time staff of 45.
>
> Clients of Wilsontec Research include government departments, trade associations, manufacturing and service companies. The agency has undertaken a large number of qualitative and CATI telephone surveys with public and private sector respondents. A list of recent clients is attached. For further details about Wilsontec Research, please see our web pages at **www.wilsontecresearch.co.uk**.

9 Contract details: if the proposal is accepted by the client, it will become the contract for the research that is to be carried out. As such, it is common for contractual details to be enclosed at the end of the proposal, these are normally drawn up by the research agency's lawyers.

'Beauty parades'

Beauty parades
The procedure of asking a number of agencies to present their proposals verbally to the client company. The procedure is used to assist clients in selecting the research agency that will undertake a research project.

In addition to the written proposal, agencies will generally be asked to present their proposals verbally in a form of '**beauty parades**'. From the client organisation's perspective this has three major benefits. First, it demonstrates the competence of the individuals in the agency. Second, it provides a check on the quality of their presentational skills and materials. This obviously gives an indication of their communication skills, which will be important in the presentation of the final research results, but in addition it gives an impression of the care and attention that they put into their work. Finally it allows the organisation to use questioning to check on the agency's understanding of the organisation's research need.

> ### Client quote
>
> You learn a great deal about an agency in the presentation, particularly with regard to whether their understanding is superficial or detailed.

Selection criteria to determine the successful agency

Agencies will be judged on a whole range of criteria, but the core criteria that tend to be used are as follows:

1 the agency's ability to comprehend the research brief and translate it into a comprehensive proposal;
2 the compatibility of the agency staff with the members of the project team (as they are going to have to work together on this project);
3 evidence of innovative thinking in the proposal (the research has been designed for this client and is not a standard off-the-shelf solution);
4 evidence of the agency understanding both the market in which the client organisation operates and the specific problem facing the organisation;
5 confidence in the ability of the agency to deliver and communicate actionable results that meet the decision maker's requirements;
6 sound and appropriate methodology for the specific research needs;
7 meeting the organisation's requirements in terms of time scale and budgets;
8 relevant past experience and references.

Once the successful agency has been selected, the agency and client organisation will confirm that the proposal meets the client's needs or make minor adjustments where they are required. The proposal will then become the contract for the completion of the research.

Stage 3b: creation of research design/choice of research method

In developing the research proposal, the agency will have been involved in designing the formal research project and identifying the appropriate sources of data for the study. Where the research is being undertaken by a marketing research department, the process of research design will also have to be undertaken. In determining the design, it is important to be aware of a combination of both the broad types of information required and the resultant decisions to be made. There are three main categories of marketing research that can be undertaken:

1 exploratory research;
2 conclusive – descriptive research;
3 conclusive – causal research.

A classification of marketing research designs is shown in Figure 2.2.

Exploratory research

Exploratory research
Research that is intended to develop initial ideas or insights and to provide direction for any further research needed.

Exploratory research is research intended to develop initial ideas or insights and to provide direction for any further research needed. It is a preliminary investigation of a situation involving a minimum expenditure of cost and time. Typically, there is little prior knowledge on which to build. It may be used to help define detailed objectives for a subsequent marketing research programme, or to examine whether it is valuable to undertake further research at all. The research may be aimed at exploring whether there is any interest in a new product idea or at examining a new market that an organisation wishes to enter. Exploratory research is also useful for establishing priorities among research questions and for learning about the practical problems of carrying out further research. What questions will respondents be willing to answer? What

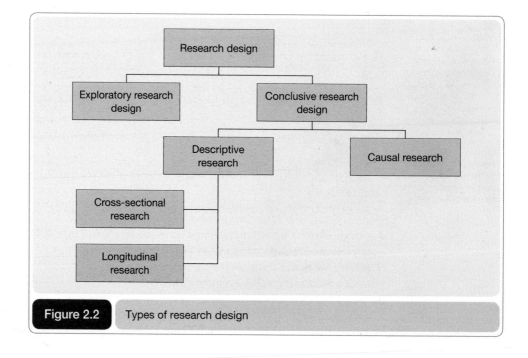

Figure 2.2   Types of research design

respondents should be included in a further study? Such questions may be able to be answered by examining published data (see Chapter 3) or through a small programme of qualitative research (see Chapter 5) or even telephone research. Overall, exploratory research tends to be flexible and unstructured reflecting the tentative nature of the research objectives at this stage.

Conclusive research

All other research that is not exploratory in nature and that is aimed at evaluating alternative courses of action or measuring and monitoring the organisation's performance is described as **conclusive research**. Conclusive research can provide information that is inherently descriptive in nature or causal in nature.

Looking first at descriptive information about a market, examples are:

Conclusive research
Research aimed at evaluating alternative courses of action or measuring and monitoring the organisation's performance.

- the proportion of the population reading a particular section of a daily newspaper;
- the customers' attitudes towards an organisation's products;
- the level of awareness of a particular advertising campaign;
- the extent to which customers are satisfied with the service they receive.

Descriptive information of this type is gathered through **descriptive research**. It provides the answers to the **who**, **what**, **where**, **how** and **when** of marketing research. The findings describe what is happening; they generally do not explain why it is happening. Descriptive research is appropriate when the research objectives include the description of the characteristics of marketing phenomena, determination of the frequency of occurrence, or the prediction of the occurrence of specific marketing phenomena.

Descriptive research
Research studies that describe what is happening in a market without potentially explaining why it is happening.

Descriptive research of this type may be required in relation to one point in time. These are called **cross-sectional studies** and involve the research being undertaken once to explore what is happening at that single point in time. Alternatively, the organisation may wish to measure trends in awareness, attitudes or behaviour over time. Such repeat measurement studies are called **longitudinal studies**. These may involve asking the same questions on a number of occasions of either the same respondents or of respondents with similar character-istics. The cross-sectional survey is the most commonly used descriptive research design in marketing research, as many research studies are aimed at obtaining a picture of a market-place at one point in time. However, longitudinal studies do enable researchers to go back to the same respondents again and again to detect ongoing changes in behaviour, awareness and attitudes which may come about as a result of advertising campaigns, pricing policies or even through changes in the economy. The cost and complexity of maintaining a group of respondents for a longitudinal study tends to be greater than for one-off cross-sectional projects. Panel research, one form of longitudinal study, is discussed in Chapter 6.

Cross-sectional studies
Research studies that involve data collection at a single point in time, providing a 'snapshot' of the specific situation. The *opposite* of longitudinal studies.

Longitudinal studies
Studies involving data collection at several periods in time enabling trends over time to be examined. These may involve asking the same questions on a number of occasions of either the same respondents or of respondents with similar characteristics. Sometimes known as *continuous research*.

Descriptive research can tell us that two variables seem to be somehow associated, such as advertising and sales, but cannot provide reasonable proof that high levels of advertising cause high sales. Research that does examine information on relationships and the impact of one variable on another is called **causal research**. This addresses research questions such as:

Causal research
Research that examines whether one variable causes or determines the value of another variable.

- the relationship between family income and expenditure on groceries;
- the relationship between time spent watching the MTV cable channel and expenditure on music downloads;
- the relationship between advertising awareness and purchasing behaviour.

Causal research provides the type of evidence necessary for making inferences about rela-tionships between variables: for example, whether one variable causes or determines the value of another variable.

Causal research and descriptive research should not be seen as mutually exclusive, as some studies will incorporate elements of both. Conclusive projects should be seen as falling along a research continuum with 'purely descriptive with no specific testing of the relationship between variables' at one extreme and 'purely causal with strict manipulation and testing of

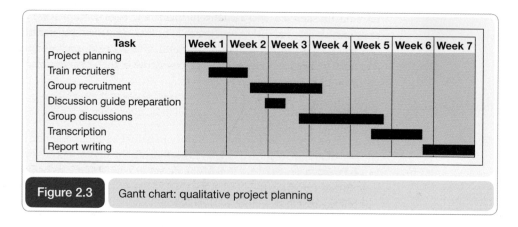

Figure 2.3 | Gantt chart: qualitative project planning

Experimental research
Research which measures causality and involves the researcher changing one variable (e.g. price, packaging, shelf display, etc.), while observing the effects of those changes on another variable (e.g. sales) and controlling the extraneous variables.

GANTT chart
A managerial tool used for scheduling a research project. It is a form of flowchart that provides a schematic representation incorporating the activity, time and personnel requirements for a given research project.

Secondary data
Information that has been previously gathered for some purpose other than the current research project. It may be data available within the organisation (internal data) or information available from published and electronic sources originating outside the organisation (external data).

relationships' at the other. Virtually all marketing research projects fall somewhere along this continuum, although the point where descriptive ends and causal begins is subjective and somewhat arbitrary.

Studies that are nearer to the causal end of the continuum will require an **experimental research** design in comparison to more standard data gathering for a descriptive study. Experimental research allows changes in behaviour or attitudes to be measured while systematically manipulating one marketing variable (e.g. price) and holding all other variables constant.

For example, Lyons Tetley Tea, when launching the round tea bag, experimented by analysing purchasing behaviour while altering the shape of the tea bag, all other variables, such as price, packaging, advertising, etc., being kept constant. This was done by recruiting a panel of tea drinkers who had to make all their tea and beverage purchases from an interviewer who called at their homes once a week (see page 204).

The distinction between descriptive and experimental research designs is more a matter of degree than of kind. While descriptive survey data may merely suggest causation (through, say, a positive correlation between price and sales), data generated through experimental research will increase the degree of confidence one can have in any suggested relationship. Although in pure science a completely controlled experiment can indicate for sure whether something is caused by something else, in marketing practice complete control is rarely possible. Therefore, seldom can causation be conclusively established in practical settings, although most experimental research designs will provide reasonable establishment.

In addition to the determination of the data collection method, the research design phase will also consider the nature and number of respondents (sampling) to be included in the research. Timing, scheduling and project planning are also important at this stage.

Several managerial tools can be used for scheduling a research project. The most frequently used technique is the **Gantt chart**. This is a form of flowchart, named after its creator Henry Laurence Gantt (1910), which provides a schematic representation incorporating the activity, time and personnel requirements for a given research project. When a research project is under way, a Gantt chart is useful for monitoring progress. You can immediately see what should have been achieved by a certain date, and can therefore take remedial action if necessary to bring the project back on course. Most researchers use software packages such as Microsoft Project to build and manage Gantt charts. An example of a Gantt chart is shown in Figure 2.3.

Stage 4: collection of secondary data

Secondary data consist of information that has been previously gathered for some purpose other than the current research project. There are two basic sources of secondary data: data available within the organisation (internal data) and information available from published and electronic sources originating outside the organisation (external data). Internal data may include sales reports, information from customer loyalty cards and information in the internal marketing information system. External data may include government reports, newspapers, the Internet and published research reports. More detailed discussion of secondary data and their use is set out in Chapter 3.

Secondary data are used in many studies because they can be obtained at a fraction of the cost and time involved in primary data collection. They are most commonly obtained prior to the primary research as they:

Primary data
Data collected by a programme of observation, qualitative or quantitative research, either separately or in combination to meet the specific objectives of a marketing research project.

- can help to clarify or redefine the research requirements as part of a programme of exploratory research. Internal data held on customers may provide more information on the detail of customer behaviour and may therefore clarify which customers or which behaviours should be researched further;
- may actually satisfy the research needs without the requirement for further primary research. Someone else, within or external to the organisation, may have already addressed identical or very similar research questions;
- may alert the marketing researcher to potential problems or difficulties. Secondary information about previous research studies may identify difficulties in accessing respondents through, for example, the telephone and therefore may persuade a researcher to switch to some other data collection method.

There are a number of weaknesses relating to the accuracy of the data and their relevance to the research project, which are discussed in more detail in Chapter 3.

Stage 5: collection of primary data

Observation
A data-gathering approach where information is collected on the behaviour of people, objects and organisations without any questions being asked of the participants.

Qualitative research
An unstructured research approach with a small number of carefully selected individuals used to produce non-quantifiable insights into behaviour, motivations and attitudes.

Quantitative research
A structured research approach involving a sample of the population to produce quantifiable insights into behaviour, motivations and attitudes.

Primary data will be collected by a programme of **observation, qualitative research** or **quantitative research**, either separately or in combination. Each of these types of research and their application will be discussed in detail in later chapters. At this stage, it is sufficient to signpost their existence and define them.

Depending on the type of research being carried out, this phase is also likely to involve the development of data collection forms, the determination of the sample of respondents to take part in the research and the actual collection of the data.

Developing data collection forms

Primary data are frequently collected through questionnaires, but in some instances, are also gathered through observation (see Chapter 4) and through qualitative research (see Chapter 5). Regardless of the data collection method used, some instrument or form must be designed to record the information being collected. This is a skilled task requiring careful thought and planning (see Chapter 7). A poorly designed questionnaire can jeopardise response rates and provide incomplete or inaccurate data. With the growth of computer-assisted interviewing where respondents' answers are fed directly into a computer terminal or through the Internet, computing skills may also be critical.

Determination of the sample

Determining the sample involves clearly specifying the types of respondent to be included in the research, the numbers of respondent required and the method by which individual respondents will be selected. There are a large number of sampling approaches (see Chapter 8) and their selection is influenced by factors such as the level of accuracy required, the nature of the project, the characteristics of the potential respondents, and time and cost constraints.

Collection of the data

Once the data collection form and the sample design are prepared, the data can be collected. If the research involves observation, then different types of equipment may be used (see Chapter 4). If it is qualitative, researchers need to use specific skills and techniques to gather detailed information from respondents (see Chapter 5). Quantitative research may require significant logistical management activity to coordinate the dispatch of large postal surveys, the operations of a telephone call centre or the management of geographically dispersed field-force interviewers (see Chapter 6). Quality control is critical at this stage to ensure that the research approach is implemented in a manner which is complete, consistent and adheres to any prespecified instructions.

Stage 6: analysis of data

The types of analysis undertaken in a project depend on the nature of the data and the specific data collection method used, as well as on the use to be made of the findings. In particular, there are significant differences between the analysis approaches adopted for qualitative research (see Chapter 5) and those used for quantitative research (see Chapter 9). The data may need to be prepared for data analysis, which may involve validation, editing and computer data entry. It may then be tabulated or analysed using a wide variety of statistical and non-statistical techniques before being fed into any presentation of the research results.

Stage 7: preparation and presentation of research findings and recommendations

Generally, most projects would be completed by the research team preparing a formal written report and an oral presentation. Often the presentation and communication of the research findings is as important, if not more important, than is the research itself. It is difficult for client organisations to take research findings seriously if they are confusing, inaccurate or lack relevance to the key marketing decision makers. There is a need to understand the requirements of the audience for any research report or presentation, and to develop quality materials to match these needs (see Chapter 10).

Managing the client/agency relationship

Throughout the marketing research process it is important that the project team in the client organisation and the researchers work as a team in order to maintain the quality and relevance of the research. This means that the project team should seek regular meetings during the project in order to maintain their awareness of what is going on and also to suggest alternative courses of action if the research is encountering problems, such as high refusal rates among respondents or the sample lists provided by the client being inaccurate. It may be worthwhile phasing the research into different stages and having interim presentations at various points throughout the research. At these presentations, decisions could be taken as to whether to continue with the proposed research, make amendments to the research design or abort the project. Certainly the project team should be involved throughout the project and not simply at the beginning and end, if they are going to maximise the benefits derived from the marketing research.

Ethics in marketing research

Marketing research ethics refers to the moral guidelines or principles that govern the conduct or behaviour in the marketing research industry. Ethics is particularly important in marketing research, as the industry is dependent on:

- **Goodwill:** the goodwill of the individual respondents for their willingness to volunteer information on their awareness, attitudes and behaviours. Any practice that erodes that goodwill makes future marketing research studies more difficult to undertake.
- **Trust:** marketing decision makers trust researchers to provide accurate information that has been collected in a professional manner. Researchers also trust decision makers to divulge all information that may have an impact on the completion of a marketing research study.
- **Professionalism:** if respondents are to answer questionnaires in a serious and thoughtful manner, they have to feel that the research is going to be used in a professional manner.
- **Confidentiality:** respondents are more willing to express their views and opinions, if they know that the information is going to be used in a confidential manner (in other words, taking part in marketing research will not result in the respondent becoming subject to sales calls, political lobbying or fundraising).

The behaviour of marketing researchers is controlled by the data protection laws enforced by the government of the country in which the research is being carried out, and also by the relevant self-regulatory **professional codes of conduct** drawn up by the professional bodies that represent the marketing research industry.

Professional codes of conduct
Self-regulatory codes covering acceptable practices in marketing research developed by the professional bodies responsible for the research industry (e.g. the Market Research Society or ESOMAR).

Data protection legislation
Legislation created to protect against the misuse of personal data (i.e. data about an individual person).

Data protection legislation

Individual European countries each have their own national **data protection legislation**. These all tend to fit within the framework of the European Union Directive on Data Protection. This Directive was passed in 1995 and required member states to implement the Directive into national legislation during 1998. Although the intention was to have a common data protection law for Europe, each country has added to or changed the detailed meaning of some parts. This means that researchers undertaking research in non-domestic markets should always check the specific laws of the country in which they are researching.

Despite the different nuances of the different laws, the guiding principles are common, and these are:

- **Transparency:** individuals should have a very clear and unambiguous understanding as to why their personal data (i.e. data that identify a living, individual, natural person) are being collected and for what purpose they will be used.
- **Consent:** at the time when their personal data are being collected, individuals must give their consent to it being collected and they should also, at this time, have the opportunity to opt out of any subsequent uses of their personal data.

It is important to note that data protection legislation only covers data (including audio and video records) that identify a living, individual, natural person. Once any identifiers linking data to a specific person have been removed then the data no longer constitute 'personal data' and are therefore not covered by the legislation. Information about companies is also outwith the remit of the legislation unless it identifies information about individuals within the companies.

The UK Data Protection Act (1998)[3] is relatively typical of data protection legislation in most countries and has the following eight data protection principles, which form the fundamental basis of the legislation:

1 Personal data shall be processed fairly and lawfully and, in particular, shall not be processed unless the individual agrees to the processing (some exemptions exist – but none relates to marketing research).
2 Personal data shall be obtained only for one or more specified and lawful purposes, and shall not be further processed in any manner incompatible with that purpose or other purposes.
3 Personal data shall be adequate, relevant and not excessive in relation to the purpose or purposes for which they are processed.
4 Personal data shall be accurate and, where necessary, kept up to date (with every reasonable step being taken to ensure that data that are inaccurate or incomplete, having regard to the purpose(s) for which they were collected or for which they are being further processed, are erased or rectified).
5 Personal data processed for any purpose or purposes shall not be kept for longer than is necessary for that purpose or those purposes.
6 Personal data shall be processed in accordance with the rights of data subjects under this Act.
7 Appropriate technical and organisational measures shall be taken against unauthorised or unlawful processing of personal data and against accidental loss or destruction of, or damage to, personal data.
8 Personal data shall not be transferred to a country or territory outside the European Economic Area unless that country or territory ensures an adequate level of protection for the rights and freedoms of data subjects in relation to the processing of personal data.

Researcher quote

Too often researchers receive demands by sales or marketing personnel for access to results and the names and telephone numbers of respondents. Thankfully, the Data Protection Act now makes it crystal clear that this is not allowed without the prior permission of the respondent!

The Act provides for various exemptions in respect of the processing of data for marketing research purposes:

- Personal data collected for research can be reprocessed, provided that this is not incompatible with what was described to respondents initially.
- Personal data can be kept indefinitely for certain types of projects involving longitudinal research, such as panels (note that in all cases where further interviews with a respondent may be required, consent for the subsequent interviews must be gained during the initial interview and not retrospectively). If personal data are removed then the anonymised elements of the data can be kept indefinitely with no restrictions.
- The rights of respondents to request access to the personal data held about them does not apply once any personal identifiers (e.g. name and address, telephone numbers, e-mail

addresses, reference numbers, etc.) have been removed from the data. This means that respondents can request a copy of the primary data record (e.g. a questionnaire) only as long as it contains information that identifies the respondent.

Researcher quote

The data protection legislation means that every organisation must ensure that one individual in the organisation is made responsible for the area of data protection – it is a critical area!

However, these exemptions apply only if the data are used exclusively for research purposes and if the following conditions are met:

- the data are not processed to support measures or decisions with respect to the particular individuals;
- the data are not processed in such a way that substantial damage or substantial distress is, or is likely to be, caused to any data subject.

In addition to data protection legislation, the human rights legislation being introduced in many countries may have an impact on marketing research. Such legislation does cover wider ground than data protection – for example, in the area of respect for private and family life, but the exact impact at present is unclear.

In the UK there is also the Freedom of Information Act 2000. This gives people a general right of access to information held by or on behalf of public authorities. Information requests may be made to a government body relating to any of their activities including any research they may have undertaken. This may impact on a research agency or researcher that has undertaken a project or produced materials such as tender documents, contacts or research reports for a public body. Accordingly, research organisations preparing documents for public authorities should be aware that the information that they contain could be subject to an information request. The authors of such documents should take this into account, particularly as many public authorities are moving towards a position of greater openness, favouring releasing information in the absence of compelling reasons against doing so.

Codes of marketing and social research practice

In addition to legislation, there are professional codes of marketing and social research practice. These are self-regulatory codes of conduct developed by the professional bodies responsible for the research industry. The first such code was published in 1948 by the European Society for Opinion and Marketing Research. In the UK, the Market Research Society Code of Conduct was first introduced in 1954. Other national marketing research societies and the International Chamber of Commerce (ICC), which represents the international marketing community, produced their own codes. In 1976 ESOMAR and the ICC produced a single international code instead of two differing ones, and the joint ICC/ESOMAR code was established. This has been revised on a number of occasions since. National organisations such as the MRS in the UK have also been revising their own codes during this time, to the extent that most European national codes are now fully compatible with the ICC/ESOMAR International Code of Marketing and Social Research Practice.

Before considering the most recent version of the MRS code revised in 2010, it is important to note that these codes are self-regulatory and are not controlled by law. Breaches of these codes can only result in disciplinary action relating to an individual's membership of the relevant professional body. Such disciplinary action may involve membership being withdrawn, demoted or suspended and the publication of information about such actions.

The MRS Code of Conduct

Designing and setting up a research project

1 Members must not knowingly take advantage, without permission, of the unpublished work of another research practitioner that is the property of that other research practitioner.

Researcher quote

This means, where applicable, that Members must not knowingly carry out or commission work based on proposals prepared by a research practitioner in another organisation unless permission has been obtained.

2 All written or oral assurances made by any Member involved in commissioning or conducting projects must be factually correct and honoured by the Member.
3 Members must take reasonable steps to design research to the specification agreed with the client.
4 Members must take reasonable steps to design research which meets the quality standards agreed with the client.
5 Members must take reasonable steps to ensure that the rights and responsibilities of themselves and clients are governed by a written contract and/or internal commissioning contract.
6 Members must not disclose the identity of clients or any confidential information about clients without the client's permission unless there is a legal obligation to do so.

Use of client databases, lists and personal contact details

7 Where lists of named individuals are used, e.g. client databases, the list source must be revealed at an appropriate point in the interview, if requested. This overrides the right to client anonymity.

Respondents' rights to anonymity

8 The anonymity of respondents must be preserved unless they have given their informed consent for their details to be revealed or for attributable comments to be passed on.

Researcher quote

Members should be particularly careful if sample sizes are very small (such as in business and employee research) that they do not inadvertently identify organisations or departments and therefore individuals.

9 If respondents have given consent for data to be passed on in a form which allows them to be personally identified, Members must: demonstrate that they have taken all reasonable steps to ensure that it will only be used for the purpose for which it was collected and fully inform respondents as to what will be revealed, to whom and for what purpose.

10   If respondents request individual complaints or unresolved issues to be passed back to a client (for example in customer satisfaction research) the Members must comply with that request. The comments/issues to be passed back to a client must be agreed with the respondent and must not be linked back to any other data or used for any other purpose without the explicit consent of the respondent.

Re-interviewing respondents

11   A follow-up interview with a respondent can be carried out only if the respondent's permission has been obtained at the previous interview. The only exception to this is re-contact for quality control purposes.

12   Any re-contact must match the assurances given to the respondent at the time that permission was gained, e.g. when re-contact was to occur, the purpose and by whom.

13   Respondent details must not be passed on to another third party for research or any other purposes without the prior consent of the respondent. The only exception to this is if the client is the Data Controller of the respondent data.

Designing the data collection process

14   Members must take all reasonable steps to ensure all of the following: that the data collection process are fit for purpose and clients have been advised accordingly; that the design and content of the datacollection process or instrument is appropriate for the audience being researched; that respondents are able to provide information in a way that reflects the view they want to express, including don't know/prefer not to say where appropriate; that respondents are not led towards a particular point of view; that responses are capable of being interpreted in an unambiguous way; that personal data collected are relevant and not excessive.

Preparing for fieldwork

Communicating with respondents

15   If there is to be any recording, monitoring or observation during an interview, respondents must be informed about this both at recruitment and at the beginning of the interview.

16   Members must not knowingly make use of personal data collected illegally.

Fieldwork

17   Respondents must not be misled when being asked for cooperation to participate.

18   A respondent's right to withdraw from a project at any stage must be respected.

19   Members must ensure that respondents are able to check without difficulty the identity and bona fides of any individual and/or their employer conducting a project (including any subcontractors).

20   Calls for face-to-face in-home interviews and calls to household landline telephone numbers or mobile telephone numbers (including text messages) must not be made before 9 am Monday to Saturday, 10 am Sunday or after 9 pm any day, unless by appointment.

21   Members must ensure that all of the following are clearly communicated to the respondent: the name of the interviewer (an interviewer's identity card must be shown if face to face); an assurance that the interview will be carried out according to the MRS Code of Conduct; the general subject of the interview; the purpose of the interview; if asked, the likely length of the interview; any costs likely to be incurred by the respondent.

22 Respondents (including employees in employee research) must not be unduly pressurised to participate.

23 Members must delete any responses given by the respondent, if requested, and if this is reasonable and practicable.

24 Recruiters/interviewers must not reveal to any other respondents the detailed answers provided by any respondent or the identity of any other respondent interviewed.

Incentives

25 Where incentives are offered, the Member must clearly inform the respondent who will administer the incentive.

26 Client goods or services or vouchers to purchase client goods or services must not be used as incentives in a research project.

> ### Researcher quote
>
> Incentives need not be of a monetary nature to be acceptable to a respondent as a token of appreciation. With the client's permission, an offer to supply a brief summary report of the project's findings can sometimes prove a better alternative encouragement for a respondent's participation in a research project. Other alternatives are, for example, charity donations, non-monetary gift, prize draws (for prize draws the rules, as detailed in the MRS Prize Draws Guidance Note, must be adhered to).

Children

27 Consent of a parent or responsible adult (acting in loco parentis) must be obtained before interviewing a child under 16.

28 Where the consent of a parent or responsible adult is required Members must ensure that the adult is given sufficient information about the nature of the project to enable them to provide informed consent.

29 Members must ensure that the parent or responsible adult giving consent is recorded (by name, relationship or role).

30 For self-completion postal/paper collection, Members must ensure that when it is known, (or ought reasonably to be known) that all or a majority of the respondents are likely to be under 16, these are addressed to the parent or responsible adult; and when it is known (or ought reasonably to be known), that all or a majority of respondents are likely to be under 16, that all questionnaires carry a note or notice explaining that consent is required for all children to participate.

31 For projects administered using an electronic communications network or service, it is known (or ought reasonably to be known) that some respondents are likely to be under the age of 16. Members must ensure that respondents are asked to give their age before any other personal information is requested. Further, if the age given is under 16, the child must be excluded from giving further personal information until the appropriate consent from a parent or responsible adult has been obtained and verified.

32 In all cases Members must ensure that a child has an opportunity to decline to take part, even though a parent or a responsible adult has given consent on their behalf. This remains the case if the research takes place in school.

33 Personal information relating to other people must not be collected from children unless for the purposes of gaining consent from a parent or a responsible adult.

Qualitative research

34 At the time of recruitment (or before the research takes place if details change after recruitment), Members must ensure that respondents are told all relevant information as per rule 21 and the location of the discussion and if it is to take place in a viewing facility; whether observers are likely to be present; and when and how the discussion is to be recorded; and the likely length of the discussion including the start and finish time; and the Member, moderator and/or research agency that will be conducting the research.

35 Members must ensure that completed recruitment questionnaires, incentive and attendance lists, or any other information or outputs that identify respondents, are not passed to or accessed by clients or other third parties without the explicit permission of the respondents and Members must take reasonable steps to ensure that the information or outputs are used only for the purpose agreed at the time of data collection.

36 If Members have agreed with clients that observers are to be present, Members must inform all observers fully about their legal and ethical responsibilities.

37 Members must make clear to participants the capacity in which observers are present; clients must be presented as such, even if they are also researchers and/or Members of MRS.

38 There are some situations where observers could adversely affect respondents' interests or wellbeing and, in such instances, Members must ensure that respondents are told at an appropriate stage the identity of any observer who might be present during the exercise.

39 Members must ensure that in instances where observers may know respondents (as may occur in business-to-business research), respondents are informed before the start that their interviews are to be observed with a warning that the observer may include clients who already know them.

40 The issue of anonymity and recognition is a particular problem in business and employee research. If guarantees cannot be given then Members must ensure that observers are fully introduced before the group/interview begins and respondents given a chance to withdraw.

41 Members must ensure that respondents on attendance at a venue are informed about the nature of any observation, monitoring or recording and respondents are given the option of withdrawing from the exercise.

42 Members must ensure that any material handed to clients or included in reports, without consent from respondents, is anonymised, e.g. transcripts containing verbatim comments and projective material.

Mystery shopping projects

Researcher quote

In mystery shopping exercises the 'respondent' will be a staff member who is subject to the mystery shop and as such there are different levels of allowable disclosure and data usage.

43 For mystery shopping of a client's own organisation, the Members must take reasonable steps to ensure that: client's employees have been advised by their employer that their service delivery may be checked through mystery shopping; and the objectives and intended uses of the results have been made clear by the employer to staff (including the level of reporting if at branch/store or individual

level); and if mystery shopping is to be used in relation to any employment terms and conditions, this has been made clear by the employer.

44 Since competitors' employees cannot be advised that they may be mystery shopped, members must ensure that their identities are not revealed. Members must ensure that employees are not recorded (e.g. by using audio, photographic or video equipment). This applies in all instances where employees cannot or have not been advised that they could be mystery shopped.

45 Where there is mystery shopping of client's agents or authorised distributors (as well as any organisations which are responsible to a compliance authority) Members must ensure that: the employees to be mystery shopped have been advised by their employer and/or regulator that their service delivery and/or regulatory compliance may be checked by mystery shopping; and the objectives and intended uses of the results have been made clear by the employer and/or regulator (including the level of reporting if at branch/store or individual level); and if mystery shopping is to be used in relation to any employment/contractual/regulatory terms and conditions this has been made clear by the employer and/or regulator.

46 Members must take reasonable steps to ensure that mystery shoppers are fully informed of the implications and protected from any adverse implications of conducting a mystery shopping exercise.

Researcher quote

For example, mystery shoppers must be made aware by the Member that their identity may be revealed to the organisation/individual being mystery shopped if they use personal cards to make a purchase, loan arrangements, etc. and credit ratings may be affected.

Observation

47 Members must ensure that all of the following are undertaken when observation equipment is being used: clear and legible signs must be placed in areas where surveillance is taking place; cameras must be sited so that they monitor only the areas intended for surveillance; signs must state the individual/organisation responsible for the surveillance, including contact information and the purpose of the observation; the need to be sensitive to the possibility that their presence may, at times, be seen as an unwarranted intrusion; here safeguards, and the ability to end the observation quickly, must be built into any ethnographic situation; the need to be sensitive to the possibility that respondents may become over-involved with them at a personal level; the need to be sensitive to the possibility of 'observation fatigue'; again there is value in having the ability to end the observation quickly within an ethnographic situation.

Using research techniques for non-research purposes

48 Members must adhere to the rules in the separate regulations for *Using Research Techniques for Non-research Purposes*, when conducting exercises which are for purposes in addition to or other than research.

Analysis and reporting of research findings

49 Members must ensure that conclusions disseminated by them are clearly and adequately supported by the data.

50 Members must comply with reasonable requests to make available to anyone the technical information necessary to assess the validity of any published findings from a project.

51 Members must ensure that their names or those of their employer, are only used in connection with any research project as an assurance that the latter has been carried out in conformity with the Code if they are satisfied on reasonable grounds that the project has in all respects met the Code's requirements.

52 Members must allow clients to arrange checks on the quality of fieldwork and data preparation provided that the client pays any additional costs involved in this.

53 Members must provide clients with sufficient technical details to enable clients to assess the validity of results of projects carried out on their behalf.

54 Members must ensure that data tables include sufficient technical information to enable reasonable interpretation of the validity of the results.

55 Members must ensure that reports include sufficient information to enable reasonable interpretation of the validity of the results.

56 Members must ensure that reports and presentations clearly distinguish between facts and interpretation.

57 Members must ensure that when interpreting data they make clear which data they are using to support their interpretation.

58 Members must ensure that qualitative reports and presentations accurately reflect the findings of the research in addition to the research practitioner's interpretations and conclusions.

59 Members must take reasonable steps to check and where necessary amend any client-prepared materials prior to publication to ensure that the published research results will not be incorrectly or misleadingly reported.

60 Members must take reasonable steps to ensure that findings from a research project, published by themselves or in their employer's name are not incorrectly or misleadingly presented.

61 If Members are aware, or ought reasonably to be aware that findings from a research project have been incorrectly or misleadingly reported by a client, they must at the earliest opportunity refuse permission for the client to use their name further in connection with the incorrect or misleading published findings; and publish in an appropriate forum the relevant technical details of the project to correct any incorrect or misleading reporting.

Data storage

62 Members must take reasonable steps to ensure that all hard copy and electronic lists containing personal data are held securely in accordance with the relevant data retention policies and/or contractual obligations.

63 Members must take reasonable steps to ensure that all parties involved in the project are aware of their obligations regarding security of data.

64 Members must take reasonable steps to ensure that the destruction of data is adequate for the confidentiality of the data being destroyed. For example, any data containing personal data must be destroyed in a manner which safeguards confidentiality.

In addition to the formal code of conduct, ESOMAR, MRS and other national marketing research societies provide written guidelines to their members on specific areas and issues involving the practice of marketing research such as:

● Internet research;
● research among children and young people;

- qualitative research;
- conducting research in town centres;
- mystery shopping research;
- the use of incentives;
- the use of free prize draws;
- questionnaire design;
- business-to-business research;
- employee research;
- public opinion research;
- using surveys for consultation;
- responsibilities of interviewers;
- marketing research and the Data Protection Act.

These are regularly updated and can be obtained from the MRS (**www.mrs.org.uk**) and ESOMAR (**www.esomar.org**) websites.

Summary and an integrated approach

The research process consists of a series of stages that guide the research project from conception through to final recommendations. Care must be taken in the early stages of a project to formulate what is expected from the research, and a research brief should be written to act as a specification against which researchers will be able to design the research project.

The research proposal is the submission prepared by the researchers for a potential client specifying the research to be undertaken. The proposal is also critical in the agency selection process. In developing the research proposal, the research design is determined by the nature of the research required. This may be exploratory in nature or conclusive research. This chapter has defined these, along with descriptive and causal research.

The later sections of the research process, such as collection of primary research, analysis of data and the presentation of research findings, will be examined in more detail in later chapters. Secondary research is discussed in the next chapter.

Marketing research is dependent on the goodwill of the individual respondents for their willingness to volunteer information on their awareness, attitudes and behaviours. It is therefore important that the whole of the marketing research process is undertaken in an ethical and professional manner. This requires researchers to conform to their professional codes of conduct and relevant data protection legislation.

In terms of integration, the early stages of the marketing research process may highlight decision making areas and information needs that can be better met by analysing internal and external databases than through the use of qualitative or quantitative research techniques. If the customer database can provide information on areas such as buying behaviour, then the research can be more tightly focused on areas such as brand awareness and attitudes. In addition to reducing the cost and time involved in doing the research, it may also be beneficial to the respondents as they end up responding to shorter and more focused research instruments or questionnaires. Overall, a blended approach to information gathering may therefore be advantageous where database information and Internet sources are used at any of the stages of the research process to satisfy the information needs of the project and assist in the design and the execution of the research. In doing so, however, care must always be taken to ensure that the data obtained about and from individuals is protected within the parameters established by the relevant data protection legislation and the self-regulatory codes of conduct established by the research industry.

Discussion questions

1 Why should a team rather than an individual be used to develop a research brief?

2 How should one go about selecting a marketing research agency?

3 What role does exploratory research play in the marketing research process?

4 Describe the various ways that a multi-country research project can be managed.

5 Discuss the proposition that the research proposal is the most important part of the whole marketing research project.

6 Explain the difference between cross-sectional studies and longitudinal studies. Give examples of studies for which each may be appropriate.

7 What is the relationship between exploratory, descriptive and causal research?

8 Why is ethics particularly important for the marketing research industry?

9 Explain the difference between a marketing research code of conduct and data protection legislation.

10 How does the code of conduct attempt to protect the rights of children in relation to marketing research studies?

Additional reading

Baskin, M. and Coburn, N. (2001) Two tribes divided by a common language? The true nature of the divide between account planners and market researchers. *International Journal of Market Research*, **43**(2), pp. 137–69.

Birn, R.J. (2004) *The Effective use of Market Research: How to Drive and Focus Better Business Decisions*, 4th edn. Kogan Page, London.

Butler, P. (1994) Marketing problems: from analysis to decision. *Marketing Intelligence and Planning*, **12**(2), pp. 4–13.

Callingham, M. (2004) *Market Intelligence: How and Why Organisations use Market Research*. Kogan Page, London.

Chapman, R.G. (1989) Problem definition in marketing research studies. *Journal of Services Marketing*, **3**(3), pp. 51–9.

Moorman, C., Desphande, R. and Zaltman, G. (1993) Factors affecting trust in market research relationships. *Journal of Marketing*, **57**(1), pp. 81–102.

References

[1] Adapted from Smith, A. (2006) Down to Earth, *Research*, February, pp. 44–45, and published with the permission of the Market Research Society.

[2] Adapted from Adams, G. and Bunt, K. (2000) B2B travel takes off, *Research*, May, pp. 34–5, and published with the permission of the Market Research Society.

[3] A basic guide to the Data Protection Act 1998 for marketing researchers is available from the MRS website (**www.mrs.org.uk**).

3 Secondary data and customer databases

Wal-Mart's data warehouse

At over 500 terabytes, Wal-Mart's data ware-house is the largest in the world. It contains point-of-sale, inventory, products in transit, market statistics, customer demographics, finance, product returns and supplier performance data from Wal-Mart's 3,600 stores in the US. The data is analysed in three broad areas of decision support: analysing trends, managing inventory and understanding customers. By examining individual items for individual stores, the system can create a seasonal sales profile of each item. In terms of marketing research, the company can analyse relationships and patterns in customer purchases. This can lead to the creation of linked promotions as well as improved floor and shelving layouts.

Image Source/Alamy

The system is also the basis for Wal-Mart's Retail Link decision-support system that Wal-Mart's suppliers use to study item-level inventory and sales information. This type of data warehouse has also been rolled out to its stores in Germany and its Asda stores in the UK.

Learning outcomes

After reading this chapter you should:

- understand the benefits and limitations of secondary data;
- understand how to evaluate secondary data;
- be aware of how to assess the accuracy of secondary data;
- be aware of the various sources of secondary data available inside and outside the organisation;
- be aware of the value of customer databases and the manner in which they can be used for generating marketing information;
- be aware of the components of a marketing decision support system.

Key words

database
data conversion
data fusion
data mining
deduplication
directories
external data
geodemographic profiling

internal data
lifestyle databases
lifetime value
marketing decision support system
newsgroups
search engine
secondary data

Introduction

With the growing capabilities of computers and the Internet, there is a large amount of secondary data within customer databases and external sources available to the marketing researcher. However, these data are only of value if they are relevant to the objectives of a particular research project. Marketing researchers should therefore be aware of the vast array of secondary data available and the factors to consider in evaluating the quality and worth of the data. This chapter will consider these issues within the context of a rapidly changing digital age.

The uses, benefits and limitations of secondary data

Benefits of secondary data

Secondary data
Information that has been previously gathered for some purpose other than the current research project. It may be data available within the organisation (internal data) or information available from published and electronic sources originating outside the organisation (external data).

Secondary data are almost always faster and less expensive to acquire than primary data. This is particularly true when electronic retrieval is used to access digitally stored data. From the Internet alone information can often be found on market size and trends, competitor activity, distributors, ownership patterns, environmental trends, etc. Gathering such information from primary research would be very expensive and time consuming. Here is an example of data available at a touch of a button on the UK fast-food and takeaway market from Key Note, an organisation that provides market reports in electronic and physical format.

Takeaways and fast-food outlets have become part of the lifestyle of the young, and much of the marketing and promotional efforts of the leading chains are aimed at younger age groups, from young children through to teenagers and young families. Penetration rates for visiting a fast-food outlet varied widely around the average of 40 per cent, especially in terms of factors such as age (79 per cent of respondents aged 16 to 19 years visited, compared with 13 per cent of those aged 65 years and over), household size (63 per cent of respondents in four-member households visited, compared with 23 per cent of one-person households), and age of children (69 per cent of households with children aged 5 to 9 years visited, compared with 32 per cent of households with no children). The marital status of respondents was also a fairly influential factor affecting visits to fast-food outlets, with the single and separated groups having the highest penetration rates (51 and 46 per cent, respectively). In the older age groups, the fish and chips takeaway is still popular, but newer takeaway concepts, particularly pizzas and ethnic foods, are largely ignored.[1]

Such information may:

1 help to clarify or redefine the definition of the organisation's research requirements (for example, if research is required into new ethnic takeaway concepts, it would be appropriate to focus the research on the 15–44 age band);
2 answer some or all of the organisation's research needs (for example, if the research is simply aimed at highlighting the trends in the takeaway market);
3 assist in the research design, highlighting aspects such as who to interview, where to interview (outside which types of takeaway restaurants) and the most appropriate questions or multiple response answers;
4 enable researchers to interpret primary data with more insight, letting them see the broader picture of what the data mean in the context of other current or historical developments in the market (for example, a research finding that shows price sensitivity in the pizza market may be explained by the age profile of the customers for takeaway pizzas);
5 provide a source of comparative data to check on the reliability of data gathered from primary research;
6 provide information that cannot be obtained using primary research such as government spending, export figures, etc.

> ### Researcher quote
>
> There is often so much secondary information, you don't know where to start. At least the Internet is making the searching process far quicker.

Limitations of secondary data

Despite the main advantages of secondary data, it has its limitations. These limitations stem from the fact that the information was not designed specifically to meet the researchers' needs, and relate to the availability, applicability, accuracy and comparability of the data.

Availability

For some research questions there will be no available source of data. If SAS airlines wishes to evaluate customer attitudes towards a new seat design, it may find information about aircraft seats but there will be no specific secondary data which will provide information on attitudes towards the new seat design. If IKEA wants to consider the levels of awareness of its brand and product range in Belgium, it may have to undertake primary research. Overall, questions that relate to awareness and attitudes are unlikely to be answered by secondary data, whereas information on market size, market conditions and buying behaviour may be more likely to be available from secondary research sources.

Applicability

It is not uncommon for secondary data to be expressed in units or measurements that cannot be used by the researcher. This is commonly called a 'data-fit' problem. Philips may wish to determine the number of mobile phones sold in Norway per annum but may find that government and other secondary sources only publish the total value of mobile phones sold in Norway rather than the volume. In some countries data about mobile phones may not be distinguished from data for all types of telecommunication equipment.

The manner in which information is classified by size may also cause problems. For example, a researcher may want to know the Irish market for 5–10 mm steel tube but may find that official sources classify and publish information on tubes in the following categories: 0–25 mm, 26–50 mm and over 50 mm. None of these directly matches the information requirements of the researcher.

Data conversion
The reworking of secondary data into a format that allows estimates to be made to meet the researcher's needs.

When secondary data is reported in a format that does not exactly meet the researcher's needs, it may be possible to undertake **data conversion**. This involves reworking the original form of the data to a format that allows estimates to be made to meet the researcher's needs. For example, by considering the value of mobile phones sold in Norway and the average price of a phone, it should be possible to estimate the overall volume of phones sold.

In addition to problems with the units of measurement, the information may also fail to be applicable if it is out of date or does not match the time frame that the researcher is interested in.

Accuracy

As the researcher was not involved in the original collection of data, there is also no control over the accuracy of the secondary data. Research conducted by other persons may be biased to support the vested interest of the source. For example, companies and pressure groups (e.g. the anti-smoking lobby, environmental groups and even shampoo companies) often undertake and publish surveys to raise awareness of their products or their causes. The researcher must assess the reputation of the organisation that gathered the data and critically assess the research objectives and the research design to determine whether the research is unbiased. In order to do this, it is important that the researcher goes back to the original source for information rather than relying on Internet or newspaper reports of the research findings. By going back to the original source, there is a higher likelihood of obtaining details of the research design, and the complete set of the research results. Where the researcher cannot access the original source, the data should be treated with a great deal of caution.

An assessment of accuracy should take account of factors such as:

1 The nature of the organisation undertaking the research. The source of the secondary data is often a key to its accuracy. Government departments and large commercial marketing research agencies are liable to be more reliable than research being undertaken by a relatively unknown research organisation or by a company not normally associated with research. In less-developed countries, the researcher needs to be aware that even government research may be biased as it may be used to support certain political postures.

> ### Researcher quote
>
> You get to know which sources to trust. It is usually a good sign if there is information about the size of the sample, response rates and the statistical significance.

2 The purpose of the research and the sponsors of the research. Understanding the motivation for the research can provide clues in assessing the quality of the data. Surveys can often be undertaken by organisations for public relations purposes, with an interesting or humorous topic being researched in order to gain wide coverage for a brand name in the media. Pressure groups such as those involved in campaigning on environmental issues or smoking may bias research and the manner in which it is undertaken to produce evidence to support their cause.

3 The number and types of respondents involved in the research. Information about the size of the sample, response rates and the statistical significance of results will also provide an indication of the rigour with which the research was undertaken. The types of respondent included in the research may also highlight whether there was any bias in the sample selection.

4 The research instrument used to collect the information. Was the research undertaken by self-completion means (i.e. responding to a postal survey or phoning a freephone number) or did the respondents get selected and screened by telephone or personal interviewers. Self-selection methods may result in bias towards only those respondents who have strong views on a particular subject.

The accuracy may be checked by using multiple sources and comparing data from one source with data from another. When the data are not consistent, the researcher should attempt to identify reasons for the differences or determine the risks in using any of the data.

Accuracy problems can also occur when using time-series data to analyse trends in data over time. The definition of the categories being measured may have been changed and therefore data from earlier time periods may not be directly comparable with current data.

Comparability

Comparability is often a problem when integrating and examining data from different sources. This is particularly the case where information is being collected from a number of countries for an international marketing research project. Differences may occur in:

1 The reliability of the information. In developing countries, where a substantial proportion of the population may be illiterate or difficult to access, population or economic data may be based on estimates, or rudimentary data-collection procedures. For example, the population census may be based on personal interviews conducted with the head of a village rather than with individual households. Even in some European countries, business statistics and income data are affected by the taxation structure and level of tax evasion. Production and sales statistics for small family businesses are often very inaccurate.

2 The frequency of studies. The frequency with which surveys are undertaken may also vary from country to country. While in the UK a population census is undertaken every ten years, in some countries it may be more than 30 years since a complete census was undertaken.

3 Measurement units. These are not necessarily equivalent from country to country. For example, in Germany the purchase of a television is included as an expenditure for recreation and entertainment, while in the US this is included as furniture, furnishing and household equipment.

4 Differences in circumstances. Even where data may seem to be comparable, there may be differences in the circumstances that lie behind the data. If a researcher were to undertake a comparison of GNP per capita data of Sweden and UK, the information might prove misleading. The high per capita income figures for Sweden, which suggest a high standard of living, do not take account of the much higher levels of Swedish taxation linked to the state's provision of social services.

Figure 3.1 sets out a flowchart that a researcher should therefore follow when evaluating secondary data.

Sources of secondary data

Internal data
Secondary data
sourced from within
the organisation
requiring the research to
be conducted.

External data
Secondary data that is
sourced from outside
the organisation
requiring the research
to be conducted.

Secondary data may be sourced from within the organisation requiring the research to be conducted (**internal data**) or from outside the organisation (**external data**). Whether it is internal or external, it should still be evaluated using the questions in Figure 3.1. Simply because information is present within the organisation does not mean it is accurate, reliable and able to be accessed in a short time scale. Data which is available in internal invoicing and accounting systems may require considerable processing before it is useful to the researcher.

However, it is always worth evaluating and collecting internal secondary data before seeking external secondary data.

Internal secondary data

Any organisation will hold information on its customers, the customers' buying behaviour and the performance of the organisation. This information may be part of an organisation's customer database or it may simply be hidden within invoicing and sales reporting systems.

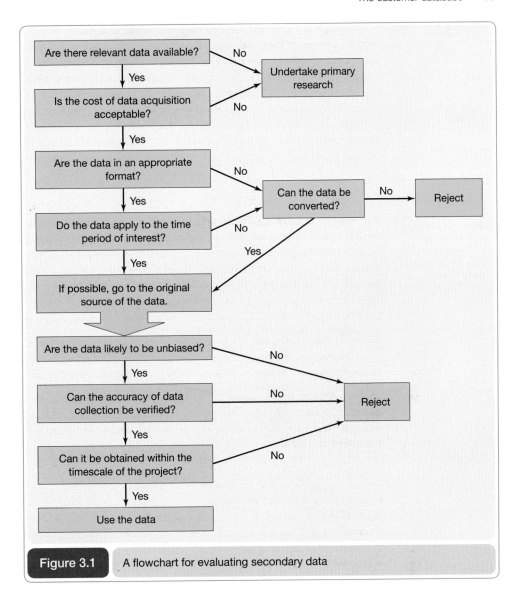

| **Figure 3.1** | A flowchart for evaluating secondary data |

The customer database

Database
A collection of related information that can be accessed and manipulated quickly using computers.

At the most basic level, a customer **database** may simply be a card index system. For example, a small opticians selling glasses and contact lenses may have a card index listing customers' names, addresses, the products purchased, the dates of their past visits to the optician and the date of their next check-up. Information about the products purchased from suppliers and costs and margins for these products may also be held within the optician's accounts and bookkeeping data.

Such basic data could be analysed in terms of:

- geographical spread of customers;
- frequency of spectacles and contact lenses replacement;
- frequency of visits;
- future trends in appointments;
- rates of retention (do customers come back after their purchase for future purchases?);
- product trends and future sales forecasts;
- price sensitivity of customers;
- profitability of individual customers and individual products.

To undertake such analyses may be time consuming where the information is spread over ledgers, computer files and paper-based files or card indexes. However, in a larger chain of opticians a computerised customer database may be held which would allow information and analysis of this type to be accessed at the touch of a few keystrokes. Such databases can be extremely complex. For example, the information gathered through loyalty cards in grocery stores such as Tesco sets out details of every individual purchase made by a cardholder, the frequency of their visits to the stores, their redemption of promotional coupons, and the typical value of their grocery shop. Such information can indicate whether individuals have pets, children, are vegetarian, their size of household and even their lifestyles (based on their purchases of convenience foods, alcohol, toiletries, etc.).

Data mining
An activity where highly powerful computers are used to dig through volumes of data to discover patterns about an organisation's customers and products.

These complex data volumes are often so large that management do not have the time or ability to make sense of the data. The solution to this is **data mining**, where powerful computers and software are used to dig through volumes of data to discover non-obvious patterns about an organisation's customers and products. For example, data mining of retail sales data may identify seemingly unrelated products that are often purchased together (i.e. sports' drinks and bananas). Data can therefore be mined to identify which products should be linked in promotional offers, which products or promotions should be offered to attract particular customers to the store, and which customers are the most profitable and worth retaining. It can also be used to identify customers for marketing research purposes. For example, if Tesco wished to test customer reactions to a new cat food product, it could use the database to identify large users of cat food who buy particular brands and flavours.

Types of customer data

There are four main types of customer data used to construct a database. These are:

1 Behavioural data. This type of data is derived directly from the actual behaviour of the customer and the interactions between the customer and the organisation. The data may come from a wide range of sources, including:

- advertising coupon responses;
- order forms;
- enquiries;
- letters;
- competition entries;
- telephone calls;
- sales order processing systems;
- accounting systems;
- payments;
- complaints.

More recently, information on online behaviour has become available and can be added to this data. The frequency with which customers access or transact Internet sites, the web pages they visit and the online enquiries they make can also be added to the database.

2 Volunteered data. These are data that customers have volunteered by filling in a form, web page or questionnaire (note that this is not a marketing research questionnaire) with the intention of updating the information that an organisation holds about them. They may do this to ensure that they get regular information about products or services that are of specific interest to them. An organisation will use such information to fill in missing fields within a database and also to provide triggers for future marketing campaigns.

3 Attributed data. Although marketing research respondents' identities are confidential and cannot be used to add to customer databases directly, the results from a marketing research study (for example, people who are in their 20s are more likely to have an MP3 player) can be extrapolated throughout the customer file. Therefore, each person within this age category will have an entry on the database saying 'high likelihood of MP3 ownership' or a score that reflects the a high probability of MP3 ownership, whereas a person in their 80s may have a very low score reflecting a very low probability of them owning an MP3 player.

4 Profile data. This is obtained by linking the data with other sources such as:

- **Social grading systems.** There are a variety of standard classification systems used in different countries to classify the population into groups. In the UK social grading is used quite extensively by the advertising industry and the marketing sector. The classification assigns every household to a grade, usually (although not exclusively) based upon the occupation and employment status of the main income earner in the household. The categories are as follows:

Occupation groups:

1 **A** (Approximately 3 per cent of the total UK population.)
   - These are professional people, very senior managers in business or commerce or top-level civil servants;
   - Retired people, previously grade A, and their widows.
2 **B** (Approximately 20 per cent of the total UK population.)
   - Middle management executives in large organisations, with appropriate qualifications;
   - Principal officers in local government and civil service;
   - Top management or owners of small business concerns, educational and service establishments;
   - Retired people, previously grade B, and their widows.
3 **C1** (Approximately 28 per cent of the total UK population.)
   - Junior management, owners of small establishments, and all others in non-manual positions;
   - Jobs in this group have very varied responsibilities and educational requirements;
   - Retired people, previously grade C1, and their widows.
4 **C2** (Approximately 21 per cent of the total UK population.)
   - All skilled manual workers, and those manual workers with responsibility for other people;
   - Retired people, previously grade C2, with pensions from their job;
   - Widows, if receiving pensions from their late husband's job.
5 **D** (Approximately 18 per cent of the total UK population.)
   - All semi-skilled and unskilled manual workers, apprentices and trainees to skilled workers;
   - Retired people, previously grade D, with pensions from their job;
   - Widows, if receiving a pension from their late husband's job.
6 **E** (Approximately 10 per cent of the total UK population.)
   - All those entirely dependent on the state long-term, through sickness, unemployment, old age or other reasons;
   - Those unemployed for a period exceeding six months (otherwise classify on previous occupation).
   - Casual workers and those without a regular income.

Although this classification is widely used in the UK, there are other social classifications used by the UK government (Socioeconomic groupings (SEG) and Socioeconomic Classes (SEC)).

- **Geodemographic profiling systems** (e.g. Super Profiles, ACORN, MOSAIC), sourced from bureaux, such as CACI and Experian. These profiling systems are based on the principle that where people live is a predictor of what people buy. Profilers have found that the neighbourhood in which you live is a good indicator of your income, size of family, stage of life and even of your interests, lifestyles and attitudes. You may argue that you are nothing like your neighbours; however, it is important to remember that the basis of these profiling products is in descriptions of groups of people, not individuals. So, it is about there being a higher likelihood of certain behaviours and lifestyles occurring in certain neighbourhoods. The neighbourhood type data is linked to database addresses via the postcode. CACI started **geodemographic profiling** with ACORN, which clusters addresses according to the census in addition to electoral roll data, consumer credit activity, the post office

Geodemographic profiling
A profiling method which uses postal addresses to categorise different neighbourhoods in relation to buying power and behaviour.

address file, the shareholders register, house price and council tax information. The census provides information on small groups of houses, which are then clustered with others according to common characteristics and given a particular ACORN label (see page 5). MOSAIC is a similar system, which has 61 postcode types in the UK constructed from 400 variables such as average time of residence, household age, occupational groups, financial data and housing standards. In an international context, Mosaic Global covers over 284 million of the world's households. Using local data from 16 countries and statistical methods, Mosaic Global identifies ten distinct types of residential neighbourhood, each with a distinctive set of values, motivations and consumer preferences, which can be found in each of the countries (see: **www.business-strategies.co.uk.**).

Lifestyle databases
Databases that consist of data derived from questionnaire responses to 'lifestyle surveys'. Such surveys make it clear to respondents that the data is being collected for the creation of a database rather than for marketing research purposes.

- **Lifestyle databases** (e.g. Claritas, Equifax Dimensions, CACI Lifestyle Database): such data are derived from questionnaire responses to 'lifestyle surveys' or product registration forms. 'Lifestyle surveys' rely on questionnaires being distributed in magazines and respondents being recruited through the offer of prizes or shopping vouchers. Such surveys should make it clear to respondents that the data are being collected for the creation of a database rather than for marketing research purposes. The product registration forms are often provided with new products and customers are invited to complete them in order to register their product for a warranty. These forms frequently ask about the purchasers' interests and lifestyle, rather than simply noting product details for warranty purposes. The information gathered in such lifestyle databases can be used to predict the behaviour or characteristics of an organisation's customers based on the extent to which their profile matches those on the lifestyle database. The main advantage of lifestyle data over geodemographic data is that it is based on individuals rather than the aggregates of individuals that exist in geodemographic data. However, it may be biased towards people who like filling in 'lifestyle surveys' or product registration cards because they have the time to do so, or are attracted by the incentives to fill them in. Geodemographic data providers claim that the official nature of the census and their other sources improves the validity of their data. However, the arguments about the various advantages and disadvantages are likely to become less important as the different approaches converge and the various data are fused together (**data fusion**).

Data fusion
Involves the fusing together of different types of information to present a more complete picture of an individual or a group of individuals.

- **Company databases** (e.g. Dunn & Bradstreet): profiling of organisations can be undertaken using information relating to number of employees or the Standard Industrial Classification (SIC), which sets out the industry sector in which the organisation is involved. Relative to the consumer profiling products, the business-to-business profiling products are still underdeveloped.

An example of profiling: Dawes Cycles

Dawes, a UK manufacturer of bicycles, produces a full range of cycles that are sold directly into independent cycle shops. Following a recent management buy-out, Dawes challenged CACI to help it to focus its limited sales and marketing resources onto those areas of greatest return.

As part of a new customer loyalty scheme, Dawes was collating customer information through cycle guarantee cards. The postcodes on these were profiled with CACI's consumer classification ACORN. Built using census data, ACORN segments the UK population into groups which share similar lifestyle and demographic characteristics.

The resulting profile enabled Dawes to determine the profile of its current consumer base and helped it to understand who its consumers were. It also helped to reshape the sales process. By analysing the catchment areas of each of the independent cycle shops using ACORN and overlaying this with typical consumer profiles and sales information, Dawes was able to rank the cycle shops to highlight those retailers that offered the greatest potential for growth. This also helped Dawes to decide on the sales team's call frequencies necessary for each cycle shop.[2]

In each European country some form of classification into social classes or socio-economic groupings has been developed. These classifications are not standardised and are based on a variety of components such as:

- the occupational status or professional position of the main income earner;
- the age at which the education of the main income earner ended;
- level of income;
- household ownership of selected products.

This makes it difficult to develop pan-European samples. Clients were seeking a better, comparable insight into European markets for the purpose of standardising products and brands, segmenting customers and targeting marketing communications. There was also a need to develop a demographic/socioeconomic classification for international bodies such as the European Commission. In order to develop a more standardised approach, the European Commission worked closely with ESOMAR to develop an ESOMAR social grade categorisation. The categorisation is constructed from:

- The occupation of the main income earner in the household (based on a range of occupation categories).
- The terminal education age of the main income earner adjusted to incorporate any further education completed following a period of employment. Five categories are defined: 21 years or older, 17–20 years, 15–16 years, 14 years, 13 years or younger.
- If the main income earner does not have an occupation then an assessment is made based on the household ownership of ten selected consumer durables (colour TV, video recorder, radio clock, a camcorder, a home computer, an electric drill, a still camera, at least two cars, a second home).

Based on these, four main classifications (which can be subdivided into eight groupings) are identified:

- AB – managers and professionals;
- C1 – well-educated, non-manual and skilled workers;
- C2 – skilled workers and non-manual employees;
- DE – unskilled manual workers and other less well-educated workers/employees.

This European approach is used by a number of organisations and it is not too different from the UK social grading scale. However, there is still a long way to go before there is industry- and government-wide agreement on a standard method of measuring socioeconomic status.

Processing data

Wherever the data originate, it is important that they are processed and stored in a methodical manner. Data capture needs to be disciplined, with data entered into prescribed fields and validated with software. The customer record is broken into fields, with each field holding an item of data such as surname, product number, time of purchase, telephone number, etc.

Any raw data being entered into a database by a call centre operator, a typist or from some external data file need to go through a number of steps before they go live on the database. These are described in the following subsections.

Formatting

Formatting aims to remove the inconsistencies and data 'noise' that appears within incoming data. Data should be in the correct sequence and length to fit within the various fields of the customer record. This may mean that punctuation and spaces may need to be removed. Lower-case data may also need to be converted to upper case. Abbreviations may also be substituted for longer or common words (e.g. *Limited* may become *Ltd*). Where the databases are international and therefore cover a number of countries, the database must take account of the different conventions in terms of addresses. For example, in France, the number of the house may be listed after the street name rather than before it, as is the case in the UK.

Validation

Software will be used to validate the accuracy of the information. Validation involves checking that the data are complete, appropriate and consistent, and may occur as the data are being entered or once the data are in the system. The database software will be able to identify fields where there are missing or invalid values. For example, the computer is likely to check name prefixes against a table of reference data such as:

01	Mr
02	Mrs
03	Master
04	Miss
05	Sir
06	Lord
07	Lady
08	Dr
09	Rev
10	Admiral
11	General
12	Major
13	Viscount
14	Hon
15	Professor

Similar tables of reference data can be used to check job titles, brands of products, models of cars, etc. Addresses are checked against the national Postcode Address File (PAF) for completeness and accuracy. The PAF in each country will hold the full postal address and postcode for each property in the country and also for large organisations that have their own unique postcode. The file can be obtained either free or for a small charge from the national post office in each country.

In the UK, the Postcode Address File (PAF) is the official Post Office file of postcodes and addresses. It includes over 26 million addresses and approximately 1.7 million postcodes. The PAF contains no data about the occupants of these addresses. It is available on CD-ROM with quarterly updates.

The data fields may also be subject to a rejection process which recognises spurious data or names given by pranksters such as Mickey Mouse and Donald Duck, although care must be taken to ensure that no real Mr M. Mouse or Mr D. Duck is wrongly branded a prankster. Software can also be used to identify consistency in the data: for example, if a file suggests that an individual does not have a mobile phone but the contact details give a mobile phone number.

Deduplication

Deduplication
The process through which data belonging to different transactions or service events are united for a particular customer. Software will be used to either automatically eliminate duplicates or identify potential duplicates that require a manual inspection and a decision to be taken.

Once the data have been entered into the database and validated, the process of **deduplication** will be undertaken. Deduplication is the process through which data belonging to different transactions or service events are united for a particular customer. Duplication may occur because address data are incomplete or entered in slightly different styles such as:

Mr David P. Jackson	Mr P. Jackson
Valley Green Gatehouse	The Gatehouse
Abbeyfield	Valley Green
Grampian	Abbeyfield
AB12 4ZT	Grampian
	AB12 4ZT
Mr & Mrs Jackson	Mr D.P. Jakson
V.G. Gatehouse	The Gatehouse
Abeyfield	Valley Green Road
Near Aberdeen	Abbeyfield
AB12 4ST	AB12

In order to maintain the integrity of a customer database, the software should either automatically eliminate duplicates or identify potential duplicates that require a manual inspection and a decision to be taken. Where the process is done automatically, the sophisticated software is adjusted to opt for overkill or underkill. *Overkill* is the technical term to describe the situation where the system removes all entries that may potentially be duplicates. *Underkill* is where the system may fail to detect duplicates as it only removes entries where the likelihood of duplication is very high. Overkill would be chosen by a credit card company to ensure a customer does not open two accounts by pretending to be two people. Underkill would be chosen where an organisation wanted to have as many prospects as possible on its database. Deduplication is more difficult in business-to-business databases as a result of organisations using multiple trading names, multiple locations, PO boxes and various abbreviations.

Deduplication needs to be undertaken each time data is added to a database and particularly when data files are merged as a result of corporate takeovers or the purchasing of external databases or mailing lists.

A database as a source of marketing intelligence

The database can provide information on the full universe of an organisation's customers rather than from just a sample as would be the case in most marketing research. The information available can be categorised into the following groupings:

- information on purchasing behaviour (products and services purchased, timing and method of purchase, trends);

- information on customer loyalty (relationship length, value, profitability);
- information on customer response (to marketing communications, new products, price changes, etc.);

However, there are weaknesses in such information:

- Database information only describes what has happened and not why. There is usually no information on why behaviour has changed or why customers have responded in the way that they have.
- Database information provides historical data and does not communicate customers' likely actions in the future. Trends that the database identifies may not continue in the future as a result of changing tastes, economic conditions, etc.
- Database information does not depict the whole market. A database only represents current customers and prospects; it provides no information on non-customers. It also provides no information on customers' behaviour with other suppliers.

Using a database for testing

Where database information has a major strength, it is in the area of tracking customer reactions to different service and product offerings. Direct marketing campaigns may have been used to obtain a direct one-to-one comparison between two marketing options, e.g. between a product with new features and an unchanged product. By presenting the two different offers to identical samples of the target audience, a measure of the selling power of each offer can be obtained.

Sample 1	New product features
Sample 2	Existing product features

The results of such a test (i.e. how many customers buy each option and what their specific characteristics are) can be stored on the customer database. It can provide an objective and measurable assessment of customers' behaviour in a true-life marketing environment. The data will show what a customer actually does when confronted by an actual proposition that has to be responded to or ignored. It can, therefore, provide an indication of what is likely to happen when a new offering is provided to the whole market.

Using a database for segmentation and targeting

The organisation that understands how different customer groups respond to different product features, prices, promotional stimuli and service support will be better able to produce product/service offerings that are better targeted at the most valuable segments of a market. The identification of these groups will enable an organisation to exploit its strengths better by selecting market segments that have requirements that are compatible with the key capabilities of the organisation. Information on customer needs and behaviour may also help to identify gaps in the market which offer new product/service opportunities. Customer databases can play an important role in the segmentation process, as they report on actual behaviour and profile data from customers rather than research data from samples of a population of potential customers. In addition, once the segments have been identified, individual customers can be allocated to a group and targeted with communications and product offerings in the most appropriate manner. This ability to work at the individual level ensures that the segmentation activity results in customer analysis that is immediately actionable.

Segmentation using a customer database is based principally on two main types of information: behavioural information and profile information. Behavioural information can enable segmentation to be done relating to purchase data and purchase behaviour, such as:

- individual products purchased (and related product needs);
- range and combinations of products purchased;
- level of repeat purchases;
- timing of purchase;
- method of purchase (online, in retail store);
- scale of purchase.

Profile information can also be used to segment customers by geodemographic, psychographic and lifestyle characteristics. For example, some banks segment by the neighbourhoods that people live in (using the ACORN profile data, see page 5), the stage of life a person is at (young married, young married with children, etc.), the level of financial sophistication (knowledge of and attitudes towards various financial products and services).

Such segmentation activity is critical to the building of relationships with customers. The primary goal of relationship marketing is to build and retain customers who are profitable for the organisation. Information from the customer database can help identify the customers who are of most value to the organisation in terms of current purchasing behaviour. The long-term value of individual customer types can also be forecast on the basis of their historical behaviour in terms of frequency of purchase, value of purchases and level of repeat purchase. This analysis is known as the customer's **lifetime value**, this will help to identify the customers on whom the organisation should focus its activities, and may also indicate the most appropriate marketing spend per customer.

For example, if a customer's lifetime value is forecast at being around £1,400 gross profit over a ten-year period, marketing expenditure of £500–£600 on that customer over that time, in terms of loyalty rewards, incentives, newsletters may be considered worthwhile. A customer with a lifetime value of around £550 gross profit over that same period would not justify such a high marketing expenditure.

> British Airways segment their loyalty card customers into blue, silver and gold card-holders based on their flight usage. Different benefits are provided to each level, with the airline's most valuable customers getting significantly better benefits, such as access to high-quality lounges, priority check-in and upgrades to first-class travel.

Linking information on usage by existing customers to any profile data on the database may also help to identify which types of new customers would be the most valuable to attract and recruit. Communications can then be targeted, highlighting products or services that are likely to be of interest to these customers.

Lifetime value analysis

Customer's lifetime value (CLV) is the present value of the estimated future transactions and resultant net income attributed to an individual customer relationship. Organisations may use their database to analyse the value of each customer in order to determine the best customers to target and to assess the most appropriate amount to be spent on recruiting and retaining these customers.

Calculating lifetime value is easier in sectors such as insurance, banking, credit cards, mobile phones, and membership organisations such as health clubs where a regular contract or payment schedule is in place. It is more difficult where products and services are purchased intermittently: for example, grocery products. In products such as computer printers the income may originally come from the sale of the printer but ongoing revenue will come from replacement ink/toner cartridges and paper products.

Lifetime value is calculated taking account of:

- the amount spent with the organisation per annum;
- the number of years a customer buys from the organisation;
- the percentage of customers remaining loyal to the organisation.

Lifetime value
The present value of the estimated future transactions and net income attributed to an individual customer relationship.

The database can provide historical information on the above variables to enable them to be predicted. The bigger the database, the more accurate the prediction. To illustrate how the database can be used, the following scenario will be considered:

A health club wishes to recruit and retain another 100 members and wants to know whether it should focus on attracting another 100 off-peak members or 100 peak members. Although peak members pay more than off-peak members, the club's database has shown that off-peak members have a much better retention rate. There is, therefore, a need to look at the lifetime value of both segments. The club's database has tracked 100 peak customers and 100 off-peak members acquired five years ago. Approximately 15 per cent of off-peak customers defect each year, which means that there is a retention rate of 85 per cent per annum. This compares with a retention rate of 65 per cent for peak members. The average income per year is £520 for off-peak members and £720 for peak members and administration costs associated with each member (membership cards, paperwork, postage, etc.) is the same for both at £60.

Calculation of lifetime revenues

In order to explain how lifetime value is calculated, the following tables will be used:

Off-peak members

Year	1	2	3	4	5
Relative sales per year	1	0.85	0.72	0.61	0.52
Direct income	£520	£442	£374	£317	£270
Indirect income	£40	£80	£68	£57	£49
Direct costs	£60	£51	£43	£37	£31
Marketing costs	£300	£34	£29	£24	£21
Net income	£200	£437	£370	£313	£267
Net present value per annum (NPV)	£400	£416	£336	£270	£219
Total lifetime value (sum of NPVs)			£1641		

Peak members

Year	1	2	3	4	5
Relative sales per year	1	0.65	0.42	0.27	0.18
Direct income	£960	£624	£403	£259	£173
Indirect income	£60	£120	£78	£50	£33
Direct costs	£60	£39	£25	£16	£11
Marketing costs	£300	£26	£17	£11	£7
Net income	£660	£679	£439	£282	£188
Net present value per annum (NPV)	£660	£647	£398	£244	£155
Total lifetime value (sum of NPVs)			£2104		

Explanation of the Tables:

Row 1: The first row sets out the ratio of first-year sales happening in each year. In the off-peak table, it reduces as the club loses 15 per cent of its original members each year. This reduction is often called the *Churn Rate*. Thus, if 100 off-peak customers are recruited in year one, there are only 52 of these remaining in Year 5.

Row 2: The second row sets out the direct income from membership subscriptions. This income falls away in the same proportion to row 1.

Row 3: The third row refers to additional sales to these members such as personalised training sessions, drinks, clothing, etc. – peak members spend more on these and expenditure in this area grows for both groups until year two and then falls away in a similar proportion to row 1.

Row 4: The fourth row sets out the administration costs associated with each member (membership cards, paperwork, postage, etc.). This does not include the fixed costs of running the health club. As the fixed costs would be incurred whether or not there are 50 or 200 members (this assumes there is no need to increase staffing or other costs with each new member).

Row 5: The fifth row sets out the marketing costs involved in attracting and retaining members. In the health club example, it may be necessary to offer discounted rates to attract new members initially (such as one month free or two memberships for the price of one). In addition, advertising and special events may need to be undertaken to attract members to consider the possibility of membership in the first place. Therefore, the cost of acquiring each new member is likely to be high and could be in the region of £300. Retention each year may require special marketing events, regular newsletters and other communications at around £40 per annum. These costs are the same for both peak and off-peak members.

Row 6: This is the total net income calculated by adding together rows 2 and 3 and subtracting rows 4 and 5.

Row 7: This gives the net present value of each year's income Net Present Value (NPV) is calculated because money today is worth more than money in the future. Inflation reduces the value of money over time. In this example, a discount rate of 5 per cent each year is used to reflect the economic conditions at the time. This means £100 in Year 2 is equivalent to £95 in Year 1 (in Year 3 it is only worth £90, in Year 4 it is £86, etc.). NPV is calculated as follows:

$$\text{Net Present Value} = \frac{\text{net income (for year x)}}{(1 + \text{the discount rate})^{X-1}}$$

In this scenario the discount rate = 5/100
The tables show that the total lifetime value over five years of the two types of customer is:

- £1641 for the off-peak customer;
- £2104 for the peak customer

Dividing these figures by 5 gives the expected return per year:

	For one new customer	For 100 new customers
Off-peak	£328	£32,800
Peak	£421	£42,100

If revenue is the only criterion, then the health club should focus their marketing efforts on peak members.

Although this is a relatively straightforward example, it demonstrates how database information can be used to analyse the retention, purchasing behaviour and ultimate value of different customer segments.

Using a database for managing promotional campaigns

The impact of past promotional campaigns can be used to forecast the outcome of future campaigns. By examining the past buying behaviour of recipients of direct mail or promotional vouchers, it may be possible to predict which segments of a database are likely to respond to similar offers in the future. Software can be used for forecasting by modelling the impact of different offerings aimed at different groups of customers. For example, software using a tree segmentation approach is frequently used to determine the specific customer characteristics on which response rate depends. Likely behaviour can often be predicted by allocating a score to each customer on the database, with scores being calculated on the basis of a formula unique to the organisation that takes account of: the frequency with which a customer makes a purchase; the date of the most recent purchase; the average value of that customer's purchases; and the product category purchased. Each customer's score is then calculated and held with the customer's record on the database. The score makes targeting easier for the marketing team by helping to predict which customers are more likely to: respond to direct mail; donate to a charity; remain loyal; make an Internet purchase.

Data mining

Data mining is the process of selecting, exploring and modelling large amounts of data to uncover previously unknown relationships and patterns of behaviour. With complex databases, it can often be difficult for managers to think up all of the possible hypotheses and questions to test with the data when looking for patterns and relationships. Data-mining software can overcome this by highlighting and reporting on all possible trends and patterns among the data elements. Such software uses probabilities and statistics to determine which relationships are least likely to have occurred by chance and can be considered as being significant. Data mining can build models to predict customer behaviour, such as the likelihood of customers renewing fitness centre subscriptions, their likely willingness to use Internet shopping for groceries and the probability of their purchasing software upgrades. The prediction provided by a model is usually called a *score*. Based on the modelling, a score (typically a numerical value) is assigned to each record in the database and indicates the likelihood that the customer whose record has been scored will exhibit a particular behaviour. For example, if a model predicts willingness to use Internet channels, a high score may indicate that a customer is likely to be very willing to use the Internet, whereas a low score indicates that the customer is always likely to prefer face-to-face transactions. After a set of customers has been scored, these numerical values can be used to identify and select the most appropriate prospects for a targeted marketing campaign. There is a danger with data mining that it can waste more time than it saves, as it can distract attention by highlighting patterns in the data that have no commercial relevance. Therefore, managers must be ruthless in determining which patterns to investigate further and which to discard.

There are five main steps in a data-mining project:

1 **Understanding requirements** – determining the purpose of the data-mining project in terms of the relevance of the outcomes to the marketing decisions that need to be taken. This ensures that time is not spent on modelling information that is of little value to decision makers;
2 **Understanding the data** – determining the nature of the data available within a dataset in terms of the nature of information held and any data quality problems (such as missing data or data that are potentially out of date);
3 **Preparing the data** – constructing the final dataset that will be used for modelling by selecting the appropriate records and attributes from the customer database as well as the transformation (i.e. changing the number or nature of codes) and cleaning of data to make them appropriate for use in the data-modelling tools;
4 **The modelling phase** – using various modelling techniques to analyse relationships between data. These techniques are principally high-level statistical techniques looking at how data is clustered, the relationships between different attributes and the behaviour that can be forecast, based on certain attributes;
5 **Evaluation of outputs** – determining whether the data mining has produced outcomes that address the original decision making. Decisions also have to be taken on the manner in which the data mining results will be used within future marketing activity.

Examples of outputs

1 Using data about health club members and using rule induction modelling techniques, a health club could generate rules that describe its loyal and disloyal members:
   - If SEX = male and AGE>41 then membership is more likely to be renewed;
   - If SEX = female and AGE<34 then membership is more likely to be renewed;
   - If PROFESSION = manager and AGE<41 then membership is more likely to lapse;
   - If FAMILY STATUS = married and AGE<41 then member is more likely to be disloyal.

2 Applying modelling involving association rule algorithms to data about the purchase of optional extras on new cars, a car manufacturer has found that 85 per cent of customers who order air conditioning also order a SatNav system, and 65 per cent order height-adjustable seating. On the basis of this relationship, the car manufacturer decides to offer these extras in a bundle, called the 'comfort pack', which increases the volume of sales of all three items and reduces the installation costs.

Data protection

In most countries and also within the European Union (EU) there are data protection laws. The key elements of EU legislation are discussed in Chapter 2. In addition to meeting the various laws relating to data protection, organisations should consider the following general principles:

An organisation should:

- never hold data about someone who does not want you to: it should give that person an opt-out;
- not write to people who do not want to be written to;
- not hold less data than it needs to be effective, nor more than is acceptable: in particular, it should avoid sensitive areas such as racial and religious data;
- make sure the data are accurate and up to date;
- make very sure that the collection methods are honest and fair – information should not be collected under false pretences (for example, claiming that information is needed for a survey when it is actually being used for a mailing list);
- allow customers to see their data at little or no charge;
- be responsible for its own data: even if it is rented out, the organisation should ensure that it is going to a reputable organisation;
- be responsible for the data that are used: even if they are rented, the organisation should ensure that they came from a reputable source;
- protect the data that it holds;
- make sure the database records the customer's permission to use the data, and when it was given (or not);
- use any scheme, such as Britain's Mailing Preference Scheme, which allows consumers to indicate a wish for a blanket suppression of direct mail from any source.[3]

Database software

In selecting software for customer databases, it is important to consider the following:

- Who will be using the database and what tasks are they likely to perform on the data?
- Will there be a single user (desktop database) or multiple users (server databases)?

- What scale of transaction data will be stored on the database?
- How often will the format of the data be modified or updated?
- What flexibility is required in terms of formats, future configurations, etc?
- What hardware is available?
- Will data access be offered over the Internet?
- Does the database need to be compatible with other software or data sources?
- What type of reports and analysis is the database expected to generate?
- What budget is available?

Answering these types of question will assist in the evaluation of specific database management systems. A desktop database system like Microsoft Access may be sufficient or, where the need is more complex with multiple users, a server platform such as SQL Server or Oracle may be required.

Marketing decision support systems

Marketing decision support system
An interactive computerised information source designed to assist in marketing decision making.

In the larger and more sophisticated organisations the customer database will only be one part of the **marketing decision support system** (MDSS) available within the organisation. The purpose of an MDSS is to combine marketing information from diverse sources into a single source which marketing staff can enter interactively to quickly identify problems and obtain standard reports as well as answers to specific analytical questions. The MDSS system may also include other internal measures of:

- sales;
- operational measures (in grocery stores these may include the speed at which items are scanned through the checkout, wastage, the frequency of products being out of stock, queue length);
- customer satisfaction scores and mystery shopping scores (see Chapter 4);
- advertising spend;
- customer complaints;
- the effectiveness of previous promotional campaigns;
- marketing research reports from studies undertaken in the past.

The MDSS will also contain external information on competitors, market trends and other environmental factors impacting on an organisation's market. A typical MDSS is assembled from three main components:

1 **Data storage:** this involves storing data from all sources in a sufficiently disaggregated way so that it can be analysed in relation to different parameters. It offers an instantaneous response to managers' requests for information without the need for a computer programmer.
2 **Reports and displays:** the capabilities of a MDSS range from simple ad hoc or regular tables and reports, to real-time delivery of information alerts to a marketing manager's computer when critical incidents happen.
3 **Analysis and modelling:** the MDSS should be able to make calculations, such as averages, develop trend data and undertake standard statistical procedures such as regression, correlation and factor analysis. The MDSS also allows modelling of 'what if' questions. For example: what are the likely implications of a 3 per cent price rise? What is the likely return from an advertising spend of 'x'? What is the ideal size for the salesforce? The models used to address these questions can range from straightforward forecasts to complex simulations representing the relationship between marketing input and output variables.

Whether internal data are held in a complex marketing decision support system or in a basic cardfile, the information that is available within the organisation should be examined first before researching external sources. The internal information may not answer the research questions, but it may provide pointers to where or how the information could be obtained through primary research or further secondary research. It may also provide lists of potential marketing research respondents as well as raising more precise information targets for the research.

External secondary information

External sources of secondary information can be obtained in hard copy format in the form of newspapers, trade journals, published reports, directories, books and government statistics. Alternatively, with the growth of the Internet, a large proportion of secondary information is now available in electronic format. Even if the information itself is unavailable electronically, the source and type of data available can frequently be identified by electronic means.

Finding secondary information on the Internet

Search engine
Internet-based tool for finding web addresses which contain collections of links to sites throughout the world and an indexing system to help you find the relevant sites. Examples include AltaVista, Yahoo! and Lycos.

If you know the web address or URL (uniform resource locator) of the website that contains the secondary data you are searching for, you can type the address into the web browser (Google Chrome and Microsoft Internet Explorer are the dominant browsers). If you do not know the specific web address, you can use a **search engine**. These can take the form of **single search engines**, each of which contains collections of links to sites throughout the world and an indexing system to help you find the relevant sites, or they can be **multiple search engines** which allow you to search several search engines simultaneously from the one site.

These search engines allow you to enter one or more key words relating to specific products, markets, countries or companies, and in return, the search engine returns a list of sites that have information relating to these key words. It is important to be as specific as possible with the key words used, otherwise the search engine may return a list of many thousands of sites. For example, if secondary information was required on the car market in Denmark, a search on Google using the key words 'cars' and 'Denmark' returns a list of over 3.5 million sites, whereas a search using the words 'cars', 'Denmark' and 'market' produces a list of 737,000 sites. Adding the words '2012 forecast', the number of sites is reduced to 66,500. This may still seem a lot, but the sites that most accurately match the key words are always listed first. To improve the relevance of your results, it may be worth using some of the searching tips shown on sites such as the Google advanced search guidelines: **http://www.google.co.uk/ help/refinesearch.html**.

Search engines

The best-known search engines

Single search engines

AltaVista
Search tool owned by Yahoo! Inc. Indexes about 250 million web pages. You can select the language of the retrieved pages (e.g. search only for pages in German). There are many localised versions of AltaVista for different countries in Europe, the Asia–Pacific region and the Americas.
www.altavista.com

Ask Jeeves

You input a question (e.g. What size is the market for family cars in Denmark?) and the engine tries to match it with a list of questions it calculates may be similar to yours, and you choose the nearest. You can see thumbnail previews of search results.
www.ask.com

Bing

Bing is the search engine from Microsoft which was launched in 2009 to compete with Google.
www.bing.com

Google

Examines over two billion web pages, and offers additional features such as automatic translation. There are many localised versions of Google for different countries in Europe, the Asia–Pacific region and the Americas.
www.google.com (to view patterns of recent search engine traffic, go to www.google.com/trends)

Lycos

Indexes about 50 million pages using Ask Jeeves search engine. There are also localised versions for many European countries, including Germany, France, the UK, Belgium, Sweden, etc. You may get routed automatically to the one with the same country code as you.
www.lycos.com

Teoma

Owned by Ask Jeeves, suggests ways to refine a search and clusters results into relevant groupings.
www.teoma.com

Web.de – *Deutschland im Internet* (German language)

Directory of German websites, which can be searched or browsed. Business section has news headlines, information from stock exchange.
www.web.de

Yahoo!

Yahoo! has local versions (e.g. Yahoo! UK & Ireland, Yahoo Deutschland, Yahoo! France, etc.).
www.yahoo.com

Multiple search engines

These are meta search engines that search a number of the most popular single search engines and retrieve the best combined results:

Apollo 7

A German meta search engine searching 11 engines, mainly German.
www.apollo7.de

Dogpile

Defaults to search LookSmart, GoTo.com, Dogpile Web Catalog, Dogpile Open Directory, Direct Hit, About.com, InfoSeek, Real Names, AltaVista, Lycos and Yahoo!.
www.dogpile.com

ixquick

Searches 12 search engines, including All the Web, LookSmart, Hotbot, Netscape and Overture. There are also localised versions for many European countries, including Germany, Denmark, the UK, Belgium, Sweden, etc.
www.eu.ixquick.com

Vivisimo
Matches responses from major search engines and automatically organises the pages into categories.
vivisimo.com

Directories of search engines

In order to identify other search engines, the following websites list available search engines as well as sources of business information:

Searchability
Describes various search engines, grouped by category.
www.searchability.com

Search Engine Watch
Links to search engines and directories with guidelines, arranged by category.
www.searchenginewatch.com

Directories

Directories
A listing of individuals or organisations involved in a particular activity. May be available in printed format, CD-ROMs or on the Internet.

In addition to search engines, there are a range of electronic **directories** available to the marketing researcher. Directories are helpful for identifying individuals or organisations relevant to a particular research study. They may be available in printed format, CD-ROMs or on the Internet. Some of the directories available on the Internet are listed below.

International directories

Dun & Bradstreet
Site includes a worldwide directory of 75 million companies and a UK Directory. Charges are made for detailed listings from the directories.
www.dnb.com

***Financial Times* company briefings**
A subscription service giving basic details plus some financials of 18,000 major companies in 50 countries.
www.ft.com

Kompass
Directory of 1.9 million companies in 70 countries worldwide. Search by product or company. You get address, phone and telephone number free for all companies, and for selected companies you can get a more detailed profile.
www.kompass.com

Telephone Directories on the web
Listing of yellow pages sites worldwide.
http://www.infobel.com

Austria: Compnet.at
Directory of 180,000 Austrian companies.
www.compnet.at

Austria: *Herold gelbe Seiten im Internet* (German language)
Austrian yellow pages directory of 290,000 firms.
www.herold.at

Belgium: Top Business (German or English language)
Directory of Belgian companies, associations and professionals.
www.topbusiness.be

Denmark: Publicom (Danish language)
Official register of Danish companies.
www.publi-com.dk

Europe: Ask Alix
Directory of 22 million companies in 15 European countries. Search by keyword, name or town. Companies that have purchased priority listings get higher ranking. Linked to multimap.com location maps.
www.askalix.com/uk

Europages: The European Business Directory (multilingual)
Includes well-established directory of basic details of 500,000 companies from 30 European countries, searchable by name or product.
www.europages.com/home-en.html

Europe: Thomas Global Register of European Manufacturers
Directory of 210,000 companies in 21 countries in Europe.
www.tremnet.com

Europe: *Wer liefert was?* (multilingual)
WLW is a directory of 340,000 firms and their products. Covers Belgium, Finland, Germany, Italy, Croatia, Luxembourg, the Netherlands, Austria, Sweden, Switzerland, the Czech Republic, Slovenia, Slovakia, the UK and France.
www.wlw.de

France: *Bottin* (French language)
Directory of French companies.
www.bottin.fr

France: *Les pages jaunes* (French or English language)
Yellow pages directory, white pages and trademark pages.
www.pagesjaunes.fr

France: *Pages Pro* (French or English language)
Directory of 600,000 businesses from France Telecom.
www.pagespro.com

Germany: *Teleauskunft* (German, French or English language)
German white pages directory and yellow pages telephone directory.
www.teleauskunft.de

Greece: Evresi
An English-language directory of Greek companies with websites.
www.evresi.gr

Greece: Greek Telephone Directories
Includes yellow pages directory in Greek or English and white pages in Greek only.
www.xo.gr

Ireland: Golden Pages
Yellow pages directory.
www.goldenpages.ie

Italy: *Pagine gialle* online (multilingual)
Directory has basic details of 3 million Italian businesses, with simple product classification. Searchable by name, address, product category, etc.
www.paginegialle.it

Netherlands: *Gouden Gids* online (Dutch language)
Yellow pages directory, including web links where available.
www.goudengids.nl

Spain: *Paginas amarillas* multimedia (Spanish language)
Yellow pages directory listing 1.6 million businesses and professionals.
www.paginas-amarillas.es

Sweden: *StorTele* (Swedish language)
Yellow pages directory of Swedish companies.
www.stortele.se

UK: Companies House
Search company database by company name or registration number.
www.companies-house.gov.uk

UK: Electronic Yellow Pages
An electronic version of BT's Yellow Pages directory, listing contact details of over 1.6 million UK businesses.
search.yell.com

UK: Kelly's
Directory of 143,000 companies in the UK and two million companies and ten million products.
http://www.kellysearch.co.uk/

UK: ThomWeb
Directory of 2 million UK firms, produced by Thomson Directories.
www.thomweb.co.uk

UK: ICC Information
Information on British and Irish companies, directors and shareholders.
www.icc.co.uk

Country information

The Internet is particularly useful for gathering information on countries. Governments provide a large amount of statistical information. In addition to general population censuses, national statistical offices produce an array of data on social conditions, consumer expenditure, industrial production, tourism, international trade, energy, agriculture, retailing and transport. The main categories of statistical information available from the UK government are:

- agriculture, fishing and forestry;
- commerce, energy and industry;
- crime and justice;
- economy;
- education and training;
- health and care;
- labour market;
- natural and built environment;

- population and migration;
- social and welfare;
- transport, travel and tourism.

A large proportion of government data can be sourced or at least identified on the government and regional websites listed in the boxes.

International information

Global information is available from the following sources:

CIA World Factbook
The CIA World Factbook is available at the Central Intelligence Agency site. The factbook has basic data on the countries of the world, produced by the CIA.
www.cia.gov/cia/publications/factbook/index.html

Europe: Eurochambres
Site of the Association for European Chambers of Commerce.
www.eurochambres.be

Europe: Market Access Database
A European Commission site, aimed at exporters. It has a database of commentary and market data on a variety of sectors in each of the European countries, together with general information about trade in the country concerned.
mkaccdb.eu.int

Europa: Public Opinion Analysis
The European Commission's monitoring survey, it is posted onto their website (with surveys on attitudes to and awareness of various topics).
europa.eu.int/comm/public_opinion

United Nations
There is free access to selected social indicators (e.g. literacy rates, unemployment) and selected reference tools and reports.
www.un.org

World Bank
Includes press releases, information on publications, and selected country and region reports.
www.worldbank.org

Country-specific information supplied by national governments

These are the official sites of the statistics departments of a number of national governments:

Australia: Australian Bureau of Statistics
Statistics available in English.
www.abs.gov.au

Austria: Statistics Austria
Statistics available in German and English.
www.statistik.at

Belgium: Statistics Belgium
Statistics available in Dutch, French, English and German.
www.statbel.fgov.be

Canada: Statistics Canada
Statistics available in English and French.
www.statcan.ca

China: National Bureau of Statistics
Statistics available in English, Mandarin and Cantonese.
www.stats.gov.cn

Denmark: Statistics Denmark
Statistics available in English and Danish.
www.dst.dk

Finland: Statistics Finland
Statistics available in English and Finnish.
www.stat.fi

France: National Institute for Statistics and Economic Studies
Statistics available in English and French.
www.insee.fr

Germany: Federal Statistical Office
Statistics available in English and German.
www.destatis.de

Greece: National Statistical Service
Statistics in English and Greek.
www.statistics.gr

Ireland: Central Statistical Office
Statistics in English.
www.cso.ie

Italy: National Institute of Statistics
Statistics in English and Italian.
www.istat.it

Japan: Statistics Bureau
Statistics in English and Japanese.
www.stat.go.jp

Netherlands: Statistics Netherland
Statistics in English and Dutch.
www.cbs.nl

Norway: Statistics Norway
Statistics in English and Norwegian.
www.ssb.no

Russia: Federal State Statistics Service
Statistics in English and Russian.
www.gks.ru

Spain: *Instituto Nacional de Estadística*
Statistics in English and Spanish.
www.ine.es

UK: Government Information Service
Links to many UK government department sites and local authority sites.
www.direct.gov.uk

UK: Official statistics
The UK Office for National Statistics site.
www.statistics.gov.uk

USA: Federal Statistics
Gateway to all US statistics.
www.fedstats.gov

Compilations of published marketing research

In addition to government data, research agencies and organisations sell reports and data on specific markets. The best known of these are listed below.

Marketing research reports

Datamonitor
Produces reports on industrial and consumer markets, worldwide but with emphasis on Europe.
www.datamonitor.com

Euromonitor
Produces reports on European markets.
www.euromonitor.com

Frost & Sullivan
Reports on industrial and consumer research, worldwide.
www.frost.com

Key Note
Produces market research reports, primarily about UK consumer markets, but with some coverage of European markets and business-to-business markets.
www.keynote.co.uk

Mintel
Produces reports on consumer markets both electronically and in print.
www.mintel.co.uk

Some agencies may also sell the data they gather from their regular audits, panels (see pages 87 and 147 for an explanation of these terms) and surveys. These can provide information on market shares, TV viewing patterns, newspaper and magazine readerships, awareness levels and purchasing behaviour. The best-known suppliers in the UK are Nielsen and BMRB, although a number of the major retailers such as Tesco and Walmart are now also offering their suppliers data about market shares within their stores.

Interview with Peter Haigh, CEO of Mintel

Ask a room full of people to name a company synonymous with market research and you're likely to get many different responses. The advertising guy might well plump for Millward Brown, while a media worker would possibly pick Nielsen Media Research or BMRB for its TGI service. And even major players, such as TNS, may find their names only trip off the tongues of those working in the FMCG sector.

Ask consumers, however, and aside from high-profile polling companies, one likely response would be 'Mintel'. On the company's website you'll find a telling testimonial from the British Library: 'Many of our users equate Mintel with market research,' it says.

For researchers this may come as something of a surprise. In preparing for this month's interview with Mintel CEO Peter Haigh, *Research* took a straw poll to gauge industry perceptions of the company.

The knowledge gained from those dozen or so phone calls was slim. A typical response was: 'I don't know that much about the company, aside from the fact that they produce a lot of reports.'

Ah, the reports: saviour of the Monday morning newspaper column-filler. You've all undoubtedly seen at least one Mintel report in your lifetimes: the distinctive yellow and black covers that open up to reveal a world of facts and figures on the state of the British consumer and the ever-evolving markets your clients work in.

Given that we visited Haigh at the company's London headquarters, it was surprisingly tricky to find enough reports to act as props for the interview photograph – a legacy, says Haigh, of the Internet and how it has changed the way market research agencies work.

Online and on-message

A lot of column inches have been devoted to how the Internet has upped the speed of the data-collection process, cut costs and improved operating margins, but its effect on data delivery – and how clients source and view vital information – has had the most impact on Mintel.

This has led to the development of Mintel's Premier service, described by Haigh as 'a suite of tools that provide data in real-time'. He believes the birth of the Internet age has provided the research industry with a 'huge opportunity to produce information more quickly to clients' – a necessity in a fast-moving world.

Adapting to this new reality has obviously been essential for Mintel and its competitors Datamonitor, Key Note and other research report publishers. After all, why would a client wait days or weeks for a research report to be published if someone else is able to provide that data online in a couple of hours.

However, it is not only clients who benefit from Internet data delivery. 'Across a typical client company,' says Haigh, 'you will find that we are working with the research department, the marketing department, the research and development department, and the boardroom. That is one of the beauties of the Internet,' he says. 'It has given us access to all those people.'

By storing data online and allowing people to access and search for relevant information, the Internet is playing an important part in fulfilling a key aim of the research industry: to have its work listened to and used throughout a client company. It's a change of tack compared to a few years back, when researchers were desperately trying to convince their clients to let them speak direct to the board. Arguably, research now stands a better chance of reaching and influencing those key decision-makers, with the Internet helping to put findings in the hands of those who want it and enabling the importance and relevance of 'insight' to filter through an organisation from the ground up.

Decisions, decisions

The relevance of the information produced by research publishers is an issue, however. Mintel, for instance, makes 70 per cent of its £30m annual revenues from published research each year. With clients constantly pushing for agencies to 'really get to know' their business, is a broad market overview – such as those found in the 550 reports produced by Mintel each year – really enough to put published research at the centre of a client's decision-making process?

'Its critical that we are a decision-making tool,' says Haigh, although he acknowledges that many clients see Mintel's reports as simply 'a starting point' for their research programme. He says he is happy with the company's revenue split of 70/30 in favour of syndicated versus customised business. 'What we are trying to do is to grow the business within those proportions,' he reveals, 'because there are only a certain amount of custom projects out there. We are comfortable with that overall percentage. It might change, but we will move with the market.'

Haigh is bullish about the usefulness of published research reports. 'I can't imagine a time where the position of someone who takes an objective view of an industry at large – and multiple industries – won't be necessary. It is critical,' he says.

'If you are just looking at what is happening within your sector or within your company, you miss what happens on the periphery and all those great ideas and great opportunities coming from outside. If anything, one has got to be looking more broadly, because each marketplace, bar none, is becoming more and more competitive, and so everybody is looking for growth opportunities.'

The critics take aim

Haigh's faith in the value of the services offered by research publishers is understandable. In our straw poll ahead of the interview, client and agency researchers broadly agreed that published research is both useful and interesting, if a tad superficial. Many described it as a teaser of what you could learn with more focused, in-depth research.

However, the way in which these reports are put together has come in for criticism. In the May 2003 edition of *Research*, Paul Charlton of Allied Bakeries took aim at 'third-party report-writers' who produce 'largely desk research, with a little cheap omnibus data so that they can claim some original research'.

This isn't far removed from how Haigh says that Mintel puts its most famous product together. The process starts, he says, with some 'trade research' – investigating the key trends and issues by scouring magazine articles, news reports and speaking to leading figures within an industry. The company's analysts will then look at secondary sources of information, before designing the consumer research questions – 'the heart of our report offering,' says Haigh.

Some may sneer at this, but it is worth remembering that these reports have earned Mintel 'business superbrand' status in the UK, putting it shoulder to shoulder with other household names, such as NatWest bank, mobile phone operator O_2 and the Royal Mail.

The company is undeniably one of the most-quoted research companies today, with regular namechecks in the national, local and trade press. It may not be home to the innovative and ground-breaking methodologies associated with some MR agencies, but it is certainly doing more than most to raise the profile and understanding of research among consumers. Given all this, it is surprising that the wider MR industry is, at best, ambivalent and, at worst, hostile towards Mintel and other research publishers of the same ilk, for there are plenty of lessons an MR agency could learn from them.

As more and more researchers are being encouraged to offer their opinions and to give clients advice based on the data – becoming what David Smith, chairman of

Incepta Marketing Intelligence calls 'trusted information advisors' – the industry could do worse than to look to the research publishers. This, after all, is their stock in trade. The opinions of their industry analysts are not only contained within their own research reports, but also appear in countless newspaper articles discussing consumer issues.

Haigh says it is important for analysts – as it is increasingly for researchers – to have the 'courage to comment on what they see'. 'It's one thing writing a report and saying this is what the facts and figures tell us. But it's another thing entirely to say: this is what it means; this is where our clients should be looking next,' he says. 'That's the fun part.'[4]

News sources

Many broadcasting companies and newspapers provide very detailed websites with press cuttings as well as information on companies and markets (see below).

Sites listing multiple sources

Google News
Gathers articles from more than 4,500 news sources worldwide, also available in national versions of Google.
www.news.google.com

Newsdirectory
Easy access to thousands of news sources, including newspapers, magazines and television stations worldwide.
www.newsdirectory.com

UN Wire
Daily free worldwide news, compiled by the United Nations; concentrates on issues such as peace, health and humanitarian issues. Provides hyperlinks, or references, to sources. E-mail delivery of headlines. Archive on website.
www.smartbrief.com

Individual sites

Belgium: *De Financieel-Economische Tijd*
Flemish-language Tijdnet ('*de website van ondernemend Belgie*'). It includes daily news from financial markets and Belgian companies.
www.tijd.be/nieuws

Europe: CBNC Europe
From NBC and Dow Jones. Recent news headlines.
www.cnbceurope.com

Europe: *Euromoney*
Has news from *Euromoney* magazine, worldwide directory of country reports.
www.euromoney.com

France: *Le Monde* and *Le Monde Diplomatique* (French language)
Free daily news stories from *Le Monde*.
www.lemonde.fr

Ireland: RTE
News from Ireland's broadcaster RTE.
www.rte.ie/news

Italy: ANSA
News from the Agenzia Nazionale Stampa Associata.
www.ansa.it

Netherlands: *NRC Handelsblad* (Dutch language)
Business news updated daily.
www.nrc.nl

Norway: *Aftenposten* (Norwegian or English language)
Economic and business news.
www.aftenposten.no

Sweden: *Affärs Världen* (Swedish language)
Business news from Sweden. Includes data on companies listed on the stock exchange.
www.afv.se

BBC News
News and business stories, with hypertext links to relevant sites. Searchable archive.
www.bbc.co.uk

Electronic *Telegraph*
From the publishers of the *Daily Telegraph*; has a City section with news stories, market prices and commentary. Searchable archive.
www.telegraph.co.uk

Financial Times
News stories, company information, country information and market reports. Current and archive information.
www.ft.com

ITN
News, including business section, from this UK broadcasting company. Also archive search available.
www.itn.co.uk

The Times and *Sunday Times*
News and business section.
www.timesonline.co.uk

Newsgroups and discussion lists

Newsgroups
Internet-based sites that take the form of bulletin boards/discussion lists on specific topics. They involve people posting views, questions and information on the site.

There are also **newsgroups** (also known as discussion lists) which function much like bulletin boards for a particular topic. With over 300,000 newsgroups currently in existence, there is a newsgroup/discussion list for almost every hobby, profession and lifestyle. Most Internet browsers come with newsgroup readers. These newsgroups involve people posting views, questions and information on the site. Then discussions may occur between two or more people on a topic. The discussions are threaded, allowing any participant to follow the thread of a discussion relating to a particular topic. Newsgroups are often useful for identifying sources of information or getting people's initial reactions to a new idea or concept. The box below provides sources for finding newsgroups.

Newsgroups

Directory of newsgroups
Provides a searchable list of available newsgroups.
www.cyberfiber.com

Google Groups
Archives approximately 80,000 usenet newsgroups and discussion fora, mostly going back to 1995 (formerly Dejanews).
www.groups.google.com

Summary and an integrated approach

Secondary information is important in the early stages of a marketing research project. It can save a lot of wasted time and effort in the primary research phase of a project. The Internet has made secondary information far more visible and accessible to the researcher. It is therefore important that the limitations of secondary data are known and care is taken in the selection of information used. This is true of both information that is available within an organisation and information that is obtained from external sources.

Customer databases can provide a significant amount of information about the behaviour and characteristics of an organisation's customers. However, they do need to be carefully designed and managed if their full value is to be realised.

In terms of integration, we have moved from a situation where marketing research was the only real source of consumer and market data to it being only one of many. Researchers, database managers and information professionals need to understand each other's activities better if organisations are to succesfully pull all these sources together, taking account of the strengths and weaknesses of each one. The manner in which organisations are addressing this through the development of Customer Insight teams is discussed in Issue 1 on page 289.

Finally, this chapter has set out the main sources of information available within and outside an organisation. The sources listed are not exhaustive and this whole area is changing rapidly; however, this chapter should certainly give an indication of what is available.

Discussion questions

1 Why should an organisation spend time gathering secondary data prior to undertaking primary research?

2 Describe the key limitations of secondary data. How can the effect of these be minimised?

3 For each of the following products and services, which industry associations would you contact for secondary data: (a) glass bottles, (b) farm machinery, (c) plumbing services, (d) photographic equipment, (e) games software?

4 What is the difference between internal and external secondary data?

5 Similar to the table of reference data on page 60, produce a table of reference data for job titles in your company or industry.

6 Describe the weaknesses of database information.

7 Enter your postcode into the **www.upmystreet.com** website and assess the accuracy of the ACORN profile for your neighbourhood that appears in the 'My Neighbours' section.

8 List the possible contents of a marketing decision support system and explain their value to a marketing decision maker.

9 Explain what data mining is and where it may be useful.

10 Use five different search engines to find 'Marketing Research: An Integrated Approach'. Which of the search engines is best at finding an information source on this book?

Additional reading

Berry, J.A. and Linoff, G.S. (2004) *Data Mining Techniques*, 2nd edn. Wiley Computer Publishing, Indianapolis.

Fletcher, K. and Peters, L. (1996) Issues in customer information management. *Journal of the Market Research Society*, **38**(2), pp. 145–60.

Jarvis, T. (2004) The Future of Fusion. *Admap*. 454, October, pp. 123–24.

Jenkinson, A. (1995) *Valuing Your Customers*. McGraw-Hill, Maidenhead.

Leventhal, B. (1997) An approach to fusing market research with database marketing. *Journal of the Market Research Society*, **39**(4), pp. 545–61.

Macfarlane, P. (2002) Structuring and measuring the size of business markets. *International Journal of Market Research*, **44**, Quarter 1, pp. 7–30.

Mort, D. (2006) *Sources of Non-official UK Statistics*, 6th edn. Gower Aldershot, England.

Stone, M., Bond, A. and Foss, B. (2004) *How to Use Data and Market Research to Get Closer to Your Customer*. Kogan Page, London.

Tapp, A. (2008) *Principles of Direct and Database Marketing*, 4th edn. FT Prentice Hall, Harlow, England.

Wills, S. and Williams, P. (2004) Insight as a strategic asset – the opportunity and the stark reality. *International Journal of Market Research*, **46**, Quarter 4, pp. 393–410.

Websites

CIO Data Warehouse Research Center: **www.cio.com/research/data**
Datawarehousing.com: **www.datawarehousing.com**
DataWarehousingonline.com: **www.datawarehousingonline.com**
The Data Warehousing Information Center: **www.dwinfocenter.org**
Teradata (examples of users of data warehouses): **www.teradata.com**

References

[1] See Key Note website for other examples (**www.keynote.co.uk**).

[2] Adapted from CACI case history on CACI website (**www.CACI.co.uk**)

[3] Adapted from Jenkinson, A. (1995) *Valuing your Customers*, McGraw-Hill, Maidenhead, p. 237.

[4] This article appeared in the April 2005 edition of *Research*, and is published with the permission of the Market Research Society.

4

Collecting observation data and monitoring online user-generated content

London Underground – observing the service

London Underground is part of Transport for London and is responsible for managing and operating the underground public transport network in and around London. Over one billion passenger journeys are made on the network each year. London Underground uses mystery shopping for monitoring and measuring the level and consistency of the underground's tangible and intangible service performance.

It uses trained independent customer service auditors (mystery shoppers) to act as anonymous travelling customers. These mystery shoppers travel around the network and follow strictly specified routes, assessing train measures and station measures relating to the following attributes:

Radius Images/Alamy

Stations	Trains
Cleanliness and environment	Cleanliness and environment
Lighting and brightness	Brightness and comfort
Temporary and short-term information	Maps and information
Permanent and long-term information	Permanent and long-term information
Electric and electronic information	Electric and electronic information
Comfort factors	Public address
Customer facilities	Staff
Ticket purchase and use	Safety
Staff	General impression
Customer mobility and access	Personal safety

The shoppers' routes are organised such that, in each quarter, a number of visits are made to each platform of the 246 London Underground stations. A typical mystery shopper's route consists of six station visits with five train assessments taking place while travelling between the stations. Each pair of shoppers is supplied with a questionnaire which includes descriptions of the rating scale to be used for each service measure together with a short statement explaining what the measure covers. The survey is designed to allow shoppers enough time to complete the train measures between station visits. When shoppers arrive at the nominated station, they move from the platform, along a routeway, through the booking hall and then exit the building. The shoppers then retrace their steps to a designated platform and move on to the next station in the assignment, carrying out a train assessment en route. All of the areas where responses are required are highly structured to minimise the impact of the shoppers' own individual preferences in terms of areas such as service or cleanliness. Shoppers are often shown videos or photographs of service environments or encounters to illustrate the appropriate rating for a specific type of encounter.

In terms of output, mystery shopping reports providing feedback on lines and individual stations are distributed after each wave of the research to over 100 users within London Underground. The majority of users are responsible for the operational management of stations and tracks. They use the mystery shopping scores for setting targets for staff and contractors as well as for developing appropriate action plans to improve performance. Line development managers and corporate planning also use the mystery shopping data to develop business cases for capital investment.[1]

Learning outcomes

After reading this chapter you should:

- understand the value of observational research;
- be aware of the different categories and types of observation research;
- in particular, understand the nature of audits and mystery shopping research;
- be aware of some of the ethical issues associated with observation research.

Key words

audit	netnography
content analysis	observation
contrived observation	one-way mirrors
ethnography	participant observation
eye-tracking	scanner-based research
hidden observation	stand-out equipment
web analytics	structured observation
mechanised observation	television viewing measurement
mystery shopping	user-generated content

Introduction

Observation is an important methodology in all forms of research into behaviour. Whether a scientist is examining the behaviour of animals or chemicals, observation using the human eye or with measuring equipment is the traditional scientific approach. The behaviour of markets, customers and organisations can also be observed. This chapter looks at how observation is used in marketing research.

Observation research defined

Observation
A data-gathering approach where information is collected on the behaviour of people, objects and organisations without any questions being asked of the participants.

User-generated content
Online material, such as comments, profiles and photographs, that are produced by end users.

Observation is a data-gathering approach where information on the behaviour of people, objects and organisations is collected without any questions being asked of the participants. The researcher becomes the witness of behaviour and events rather than the collector of information second-hand from others about their perceptions and recollections of behaviour and events. Events may be witnessed by human observers or using equipment. Monitoring people's comments in online, **user-generated content** such as on social media sites (Facebook), blogs, micro-blogs (Twitter) and video-sharing sites (YouTube) is also a form of observation. It is similar to content analysis where data in the form of verbal or visual behaviour is collected without any questions being asked of the participants.

It is important to note that observation can take a quantitative format where a large number of events or people are observed and the outputs are analysed using statistical methods similar to those discussed in Chapter 9. Alternatively, it can be small-scale and qualitative, focusing on a small number of detailed observations.

Observation only measures behaviour – it cannot investigate reasons behind behaviour, it cannot assess the participant's attitudes towards the behaviour and it cannot measure the likelihood of the participant repeating the behaviour. Also, only public behaviour is observed; private behaviour in people's homes or offices is generally beyond the scope of observation studies. The types of behaviour that can be measured are physical actions such as shopping patterns or television viewing, verbal behaviour such as conversations with customer service personnel, online behaviour on the Internet, spatial patterns such as traffic flows on roads and in-store, temporal patterns such as the amount of time spent queuing, and physical objects such as the brands of products in a consumer's bathroom cabinet (see Table 4.1).

Researcher quote

Observation tells you what people are doing but it doesn't tell you why they are doing it.

Table 4.1   Examples of what can be observed

In-store	At home	On the road	On the Internet
Arrival time in store	TV viewing patterns	Use of public transport	Comments made on review sites
Shopper's movement pattern in store	Family purchasing behaviour	Driving routes taken	Brands mentioned in blogs and on Facebook
Browsing behaviour	Brands of products owned	Behaviour while driving (e.g. use of car seat belts, mobile phones, etc.)	Links made to corporate or celebrity sites
Time spent shopping/queuing	Children's behaviour with a new toy		Products used in videos
Behaviour/expressions when queuing			Clothes worn in videos
Interaction with service personnel			Opinions expressed
Products purchased			Trends discussed
Payment methods used			

Observation allows the researcher to overcome some of the potential weaknesses of interviewing and survey research. These weaknesses include the following:

- There can be a discrepancy between real and verbal behaviour. Occasionally statements are made in interviews which are not a true reflection of the behaviour of the interviewed persons.
- Often facts are only brought to light by means of natural settings only. The interviewee is not conscious of them and they are therefore not easy to get at by questioning.
- The verbal capabilities of the interviewed person can limit the quality and quantity of information gathered.

The major advantage of observation research over surveys of respondents is that the data collected do not have distortions or inaccuracies as a result of memory error or social desirability bias. The data recorded reflect the actual behaviour that took place. For example, if a video rental outlet wanted to identify the most frequently rented videos over the last six months, in surveying its members it would find that the respondents would be unlikely to remember all the videos that they rented and/or would miss out those videos that they now feel embarrassed about having rented. The computers in the video outlet, on the other hand, could count the number of times each video is borrowed and therefore give a true representation of rental behaviour.

Observation overcomes the high refusal rates that may exist for some survey research. Respondents may be willing to provide their attitudes in a survey, but may be less willing to spend a great deal of time listing their behaviours and purchases. Much of the observation can go on without inconveniencing the participant and in certain cases without the participant being aware that it is happening.

Categories of observation

Observation studies can be categorised along the following five key dimensions:

1 natural versus contrived;
2 visible versus hidden;
3 structured versus unstructured;
4 mechanised versus human;
5 participant versus non-participant.

Contrived observation
A research approach which involves observing participants in a controlled setting.

1 Natural versus contrived observation. Consumers may be observed in their natural setting when they are going around the supermarket, queuing in banks or driving along the road. Those being observed are going about their normal activities and are unlikely to be aware that they are being observed. Alternatively, a researcher might recruit mothers with young children to be observed playing with new toys. In this case, the recruited people will know that they are participating in a study. The research may take place in a room with video cameras or one-way mirrors. It is, therefore, a contrived environment as the children may behave differently from the way they do in the natural setting (i.e. at home). However, the contrived environment tends to speed up the observation data-gathering process. The researcher does not have to wait until certain events happen; instead, the researcher can manipulate the situation and the participant to meet the research objectives.

Hidden observation
A research approach involving observation, where the participant does not know that they are being observed.

2 Visible versus hidden observation. Visible observation is where people know they are being observed, because they can see either the observer or the camera, or because a poster at a shop door may actually tell them that observation research is being undertaken in the store. If people know they are being observed, they may behave differently than normal, so hidden observation methods such as one-way mirrors and security cameras are often used for research. However, if the research is being undertaken in an environment where people would not expect to be videoed or observed, then organisations will be expected to inform them that observation research is being undertaken.

3 Structured versus unstructured observation. The recording of observations can range from being very structured to being very unstructured. At the very structured end of the scale, observers may simply count phenomena and keep a tally on a record sheet. For example, traffic counts will normally involve observers using hand-held counters and a paper record sheet. Other **structured observation** may involve the observer filling out a form similar to a questionnaire on each person being observed. Unstructured observation would involve an observer watching the actions of people either in person or on a video and making notes on behaviour.

4 Mechanised versus human observation. Where observation involves the counting of the frequency of behaviour, **mechanised observation** may be more appropriate than employing human observers. This can include automated traffic counting devices, which can count the number of cars crossing a sensor in a section of road or the number of people exiting or entering a shop, bank, museum or post office. Equipment can be installed in people's homes to monitor their television viewing patterns or to scan all the purchases that they bring home from a supermarket. In the supermarkets themselves, electronic scanners can accurately monitor the purchases being made as well as the speed at which checkout assistants are handling each item. Where the behaviour being monitored is more complex and the range of behaviour being measured is varied, the greater flexibility of human observers is required.

5 Participant versus non-participant. Where service quality and staff performance are being measured using **mystery shopping** (see the London Transport example at the start of this chapter), the observer may actually participate in the transaction that is being observed. The use of **participant observation**, where the researcher interacts with the subject or subjects being observed, stems from the field of cultural anthropology. Anthropologists would take part in a tribe's daily life in order to understand the norms, attitudes and behaviours that were neither documented nor communicable via language. In mystery shopping, the observer will communicate with the service provider as part of the transaction but will not communicate the fact that observation is being undertaken. Most other forms of observation do not involve any participation.

Specific observation methods

Audits and scanner-based research

An **audit** is an examination and verification of the movement and sale of a product. There are three main types of audit: (1) wholesale audits, which measure product sales from wholesalers to retailers and caterers; (2) retail audits, which measure sales to the final consumer; (3) home audits, which measure purchases by the final consumer.

Retail audits were introduced by ACNielsen in 1933 in the USA. They are now an international activity, with ACNielsen (www.acnielsen.com) alone undertaking regular retail audits in more than 80 countries over six continents. Originally they involved a team of auditors from a research firm visiting a representative sample of food stores every two months to count the inventory of the store and record deliveries to the store since the last visit. For each product category (including brands, sizes, package types, flavours, etc.) national and regional sales figures per store type were then produced. Additional information, such as prices, allocated display space and in-store promotional activity, would also be collected. With the growing use of electronic scanners at the checkouts of the larger multiple retailers, much of this information is now gathered electronically, with auditors only being required to visit the smaller independent stores. **Scanner-based research** has enabled data to be gathered more quickly and accurately, as well as providing the opportunity to study very short time periods of sales activity. The information from retail audits is provided to the food, household, health and beauty, durables, confectionery and beverage products industries, where it helps management

Structured observation
A research approach where observers use a record sheet or form to count phenomena or to record their observations.

Mechanised observation
A research approach involving observation of behaviour using automated counting devices, scanners or other equipment.

Mystery shopping
A form of participant observation which uses researchers to act as customers or potential customers to monitor the processes and procedures used in the delivery of a service.

Participant observation
A research approach where the researcher interacts with the subject or subjects being observed. The best-known type of participant observation is mystery shopping.

Audit
An examination and verification of the movement and sale of a product. There are three main types: wholesale audits, which measure product sales from wholesalers to retailers and caterers, retail audits, which measure sales to the final consumer, and home audits, which measure purchases by the final consumer.

Scanner-based research
Collecting sales information using electronic scanners reading barcodes at the checkouts of retailers and wholesalers. The information collected feeds into audits.

gauge product penetration, market share, overall product performance, distribution, promotion effectiveness and price sensitivity.

Wholesale audits work in a similar fashion. For example, the ACNielsen Catering Wholesale Service, a continuous tracking service, offers manufacturers detailed, weekly sales and marketing information on the wholesale sector within food service.

It offers manufacturers detailed analysis of trends by individual sector and product category, and customer segment. The customer segments include the workplace, education, health, hotels, pubs, restaurants, fast-food environments, travel and leisure. The data comes from the the largest operators in the catering wholesale sector: 3663, Brake Bros, Watson & Philips Foodservice and dbc Foodservice. Together, these operators represent up to 70 per cent of leading manufacturers' deliveries into the UK food-service market.

Home audits involve a panel of households which have been issued with a diary or an electronic scanner for installation in their kitchens to record all of their purchases across every outlet type, from warehouse clubs to convenience stores and from supermarkets to pharmacists and mass merchandisers. The diary needs to be completed on a continuous basis by the panel members and is then returned at regular intervals to the marketing research agency. Information from electronic scanners will be returned automatically overnight down the telephone line (see details of the Taylor Nelson Sofres Superpanel on page 148).

Knowledge of purchases makes it possible to analyse:

- heavy buyers and their associated characteristics;
- brand loyalty and brand switching rates;
- repeat purchases for new products.

Such information is more comprehensive than that produced from retailer's loyalty card schemes as it relates to all of the shops that a customer visits.

Television viewing measurement

In all countries where there is television advertising, the measurement of audience size is critical to the charges made for advertising slots and the scheduling of programmes. Information is required on which channels and programmes are being watched, at what time, and by what type of people.

In the UK the Broadcasters Audience Research Board (**www.barb.co.uk**) uses professional research suppliers to conduct and report on audience research. A survey takes place based on a sample of around 52,000 households per year with any UK household having an equal likelihood of being selected for interview. The questions are designed to determine patterns of television usage across the country and to ensure that the audience measurement panel is an up-to-date representation of the population.

The results of the survey, together with government census data, are then used to select a fully representative sample of homes in terms of viewing habits, TV equipment ownership, family composition, demographics, etc., to take part in the audience measurement panel. The number of homes taking part in the panel is 5,100 and each is given a nominal incentive payment for their services.

Television viewing measurement
The procedures used in the measurement of the number of viewers watching a particular television programme. In the UK around 5,100 households have electronic meters attached to their television sets to register when the set is turned on and to what channel it is tuned.

Electronic meters are attached to the television sets and register when the set is turned on and off, and which channel is tuned. In addition, each household has a control with eight numbered buttons on it, and each member of the household has his or her own number. Each person presses their number whenever they are watching the television, and again when they stop. This data is fed into the meter. The electronic meter can collect data from up to nine television sets in one household. All the information about what channel the set was tuned to and who was watching is retrieved automatically by a computer via the local telephone system.

One major challenge to **television viewing measurement** is the increasing complexity of broadcasting technology. The advent of broadcast content from non-broadcast devices such as personal video recorders (such as Sky+), Video On Demand through broadband, and PCs makes measurement more difficult, as does viewing online (BBC iPlayer) and viewing on the move (in aeroplanes, trains and on mobile phones). The changing environment has a major impact not only on the measurement technology but also on the future role of television viewing measurement (content viewed on a mobile phone may not have the same impact as that viewed on a TV at home). In the UK, Sky television operates a panel of 20,000 subscribers that have Sky+ personal video recorders (PVRs) – recording devices that allow programmes to be stored and viewed at a time suitable to the householder – to explore their viewing behaviour, while their viewing records can be directly monitored through the set-top boxes. Programmes that are watched online through catch-up TV sites such as the BBC iPlayer are monitored through monitoring Internet traffic and web analytics.

For monitoring radio listening, RAJAR (Radio Joint Audience Research Limited – established in 1992 to operate a single audience measurement system for the UK radio industry) uses diaries of radio listening that respondents are required to maintain for a one-week period. This is because the monitoring of radio listening through technology is complex, as people may listen to radios in various locations within their house, in their car, in retail stores or in their place of work. Various devices have been trialled throughout the world, but a single approach has not as yet been accepted by broadcasters, advertisers and researchers. The people-meter device is carried by members of a recruited panel and it picks up specially encoded signals transmitted by participating stations. Other devices (in the form of phones, pagers or watches) use audio matching technology that records digital snippets of sound heard by the panel member every one to two minutes. These are then matched against stored records of all broadcast material. Although technology may be perceived to be more reliable than an individual's memory of their listening habits, there are still major concerns regarding:

- **Compliance** – will the panel member keep their device with them at all times? People listen to the radio in the shower and when they are rushing to prepare to go to work or take the children to school.
- **Representativeness** – people willing to carry such a device may not be typical of the average radio listener. They may either be more interested in radio or in the specific measurement technology that they are carrying.
- **Cost** – technology of this type is expensive and the management of the data gathering is also costly in both time and money.

Monitoring Internet traffic/web analytics

Web analytics
The collection, analysis and reporting of internet data for the purposes of understanding and optimising web usage.

Web analytics is the collection, analysis and reporting of Internet data for purposes of understanding and optimising web usage. It is possible for web-based retailers and suppliers to monitor the number of times different pages on their site are accessed, what search engines brought people to the site, and what service provider browsers are using as well as tracking the peak times at which people access the site. There are many organisations that provide web analytics software and services. These analyse web traffic through either logfile analysis (reading the logfiles in which the web server records all its transactions) or page tagging, (uses JavaScript on each page to notify a third-party server when a page is rendered by a web browser). The most widely used software is Google Analytics (see Figure 4.1), which is free and available from the Google website. There are also more advanced software options available that undertake more sophisticated analysis.

With cookies, a text file is placed on a user's computer by the web retailer, making it possible to identify when users revisit the site and the sections of the site that they visit. For example, an organisation such as Amazon (**www.amazon.co.uk**) can monitor the types of book that particular customers are interested in and whether the customers spend time reading the review of the books or considering alternatives. Cookies give web retailers

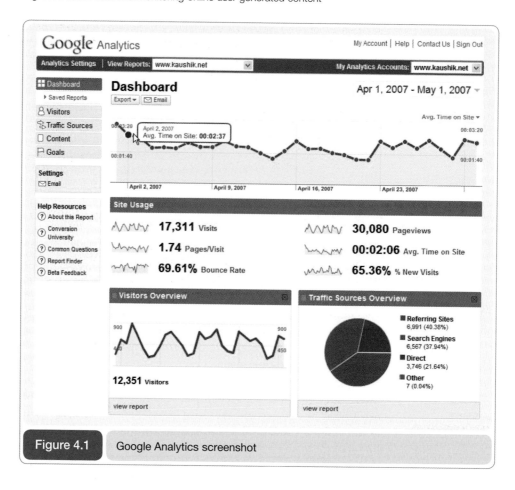

Figure 4.1   Google Analytics screenshot

an advantage over traditional retailers as they can provide information on browsers (the equivalent of window shoppers) as well as customers. Cookie deletion or the use of in-private browsing by computer users may impact on the accuracy of some of the data. For example, visitors to a site who regularly delete their cookies will inflate a site's unique visitor numbers and reduce estimates of average visitor frequency. Some sites attempt to overcome this by asking users to register each time they come to a site. Some research agencies, such as Nielsen Online (**www.nielsen-online.com**) or comScore (**www.comscore.com**), recruit panels of computer users and track their website visits through a desktop meter or through software installed on their computer. In the Netherlands, the Webmeter service tracks the panel's behaviour through a portal. In this case panellists access the Internet through a start page, which identifies the panellist and monitors their subsequent web behaviour (sites visited, length of time on each site, etc.).

One-way mirror observations

One-way mirrors
Used in qualitative marketing research to enable clients and researchers to view respondent behaviour during a discussion. Behind the mirror is a viewing room, which consists of chairs for the observers and may contain video cameras to record the proceedings.

In many focus groups used in qualitative marketing research, **one-way mirrors** are used to enable clients and researchers to view respondent behaviour during a discussion. Behind the mirror is the viewing room, which consists of chairs for the observers and video cameras to record the proceedings. An alternative to the mirror is to televise the proceedings to a separate viewing room. Examples of viewing facilities for group decisions can be seen at: **www.viewing.org.uk**

Although transcripts of what is said in a discussion are normally prepared, the one-way mirrors allow the observers to see facial expressions and non-verbal reaction to a product or concept. The way in which people handle a product in a group or the manner in which children play with a new toy can all be observed through a one-way mirror. A first-hand view of customer reaction to a product can be very useful to clients, particularly during the early development stages of a new product.

> **Client quote**
>
> The data comes alive, when you can see the people actually saying the words.

In-store observation

Observation studies within retail outlets are commonplace. The prevalent use of security cameras in stores has provided a mechanism for monitoring behaviour. That behaviour can relate to the route customers take through the store, the products that are looked at, the time spent in the store and the interaction between shoppers and sales personnel. Security cameras have all but replaced the human observers who used to follow customers around the store.

Stand-out equipment

Stand-out equipment
Sometimes known as *shelf impact testing equipment*, this is used to determine the visual impact of new packaging when placed on shelves next to competitors' products.

Stand-out equipment, or shelf impact testing, is a contrived form of observation used with new packaging to determine the visual impact of new packaging when placed on shelves next to competitors' products. Respondents are shown projected pictures (either 35 mm slides or computer-generated graphics) of shelving displays. They are asked to press a button when they see a particular brand. Measuring the elapsed time between the picture being shown and the button being pressed can provide an indication of the impact of the packaging. Different packaging colours and formats can be compared prior to the relaunch and repackaging of a product.

Eye-tracking equipment

Eye-tracking
The use of equipment in the observation and recording of a person's unconscious eye movements when they are looking at a magazine, a shop display or a website.

Eye-tracking equipment observes and records a person's unconscious eye movements when they are looking at a magazine, a shop display or a website. For example, in a magazine or on a web page it can identify what elements of a page or advertisement is viewed and the length of time a respondent spends looking at or reading the content. The equipment to do this is becoming simpler and cheaper. There is now eye-tracking technology used to explore users' reactions to a shop display that looks and feels just like an ordinary pair of glasses (see: **www.tobiiglasses.com**). In addition to evaluating new packaging or advertising, eye-tracking technology can help researchers and developers understand how customers use automated self-service facilities, operate machinery or even drive.

Mystery shoppers

Mystery shopping, a form of participant observation, uses researchers to act as customers or potential customers to monitor the processes and procedures used in the delivery of a service. In the UK mystery shopping is used quite extensively by organisations in financial services, retailing, motor dealerships, hotels and catering, passenger transportation, public utilities and government departments (see Table 4.2).

Unlike customer satisfaction surveys, the mystery shopping approach is being used to measure the process rather than the outcomes of a service encounter. The emphasis is on

Table 4.2	Major sectors using mystery shopping

Sector	Examples
Financial services	Banks, building societies, life companies, general/motor insurance, estate agents
Leisure/travel	Travel agents, tourist offices, hotels, restaurants, car hire, public houses
Transport/utilities	Airports, underground, rail, airlines, electricity, gas, water
Motoring	Motoring organisations, car manufacturers, petrol stations
Retail	Grocery, department stores, electrical, fashion, Post Office
Government departments	Benefits Agency, Vehicle Licensing, Passport Office, Inland Revenue

the service experience as it unfolds, looking at which activities and procedures do or do not happen rather than gathering opinions about the service experience. Customer satisfaction surveys on their own do not provide sufficiently detailed information to allow management to identify and correct weaknesses in the service delivery process.

Client quote

I need to know if staff are saying and doing everything according to our stated standards of quality. Only mystery shopping can tell me if this is happening.

Mystery shopping studies are used for three main purposes:

- to act as a diagnostic tool, identifying failings and weak points in an organisation's service delivery;
- to encourage, develop and motivate service personnel by linking with appraisal, training and reward mechanisms;
- to assess the competitiveness of an organisation's service provision by benchmarking it against the offerings of others in an industry.

Mystery shopping aims to collect facts rather than perceptions. These facts can relate to basic enquiries, purchases and transactions covering topics such as:

- How many rings before the phone was answered?
- How long was the queue?
- What form of greeting was used?

They can also relate to more complex encounters such as in the purchase of a mortgage where the procedures adopted in a two-hour, fact-finding meeting can be assessed in terms of service quality and financial compliance.

In terms of any research approach, the reliability of a technique can be defined as the extent to which similar observations made by different researchers would provide the same results. This is a very important issue if mystery shopping results are to be taken seriously

Table 4.3	Rating scale used by London Underground

Politeness of staff	
Score	**Comment**
10	Excellent – very courteous
9	–
8	Good – polite
7	–
6	–
5	Acceptable – business like
4	–
3	–
2	Poor – brusque
1	–
0	Unacceptable – short or rude

and particularly if staff are to be rewarded on the results. Attempts are made to maximise the reliability of mystery shopping through the use of objective measurement and the careful selection and training of the shoppers.

Objective measurement is clearly possible in verifying whether an activity did or did not happen (e.g. whether the customer's name was used), and also where attributes can be counted (e.g. the number of checkouts that are open and queue length). However, judgements on the appearance of the premises and staff as well as the actions of staff in terms of politeness, product knowledge and helpfulness are slightly more subjective. Users and agencies attempt to minimise this subjectivity by using rating scales with descriptive labels (Table 4.3). This is often supported by verbatim comments from shoppers to justify their rating selection.

All of the areas where responses are required are highly structured to minimise the impact of the shoppers' own preferences in terms of areas such as service or cleanliness. Shoppers are often shown videos or photographs of service environments or encounters to illustrate the appropriate rating for a specific type of encounter.

An encounter involves interaction, and the quality of that interaction is as dependent on the customer as it is on the service provider. How does mystery shopping reduce the impact of the shopper's personal characteristics such as sex, age, accent, looks, ethnic background and personality? Great care is taken in the selection of mystery shoppers. The shoppers must match a customer profile that is appropriate for the scenario that they are being asked to enact. This becomes more important and more difficult as the encounter becomes more complex. Selecting passengers for public transport may require less rigorous procedures than selecting a customer for a mortgage or investment product. For these complex products, the agencies are of the opinion that the shopper should invent the absolute minimum by using their own financial details and personal circumstances. This can clearly cause difficulties, particularly where a customer's details are entered onto a centralised computer (e.g. during a fact-find for a financial product). That shopper may not be able to approach the financial organisation again, and with the use of credit scoring agencies there may also be problems when approaching other financial institutions. Similar problems occur in purchasing an item such as a car, in that a shopper cannot enter a showroom and ask about a sports car, then reappear weeks later and enquire about a family car. Therefore agencies have to continually recruit and maintain a bank of credible shoppers. This can be difficult – one car manufacturer cancelled a mystery shopping programme because the agency was having difficulty continually recruiting new and credible car purchasers. Credibility may require shoppers to be existing customers of the organisation, and where the purchase is normally a joint purchase, husband and wife teams may need to be recruited.

Selection is also important with regard to the personality of the shopper. Most situations require the shopper to adopt a neutral rather than an aggressive or defensive approach in the service encounter. In traditional marketing research, a field supervisor would be able to check the suitability of an interviewer by accompanying and observing them during their first interviews. With the exception of situations where the shopper is relatively anonymous, such as in a train or a grocery store, it is difficult to accompany and supervise the shopper. Each encounter may vary, so a repeat visit will not be able to verify the accuracy and reliability of the shopper's observations. Agencies have to rely on edit checks of completed evaluation forms, looking at the trends of a particular shopper's observations as well as checking the logic of the evaluation.

Training is also important, particularly with regard to the briefing of shoppers on their circumstances and needs but also in terms of data-collection skills. Shoppers receive a detailed briefing on the scenario that they are to enact, focusing on their personal characteristics, the questions they should ask and the behaviours they should adopt. They are then tested on these elements to ensure that the service encounter is realistic and to reduce the opportunity for the true identity of the mystery shopper to be detected by the service personnel.

Researcher quote

We want 'natural' encounters; we don't want to use mystery shoppers who simply want to play the part of an awkward customer.

The training of data-collection skills focuses on identifying the elements of the service to be observed as well as the retention and recording of the information. Retention and recording of information is particularly important, as the shoppers cannot complete an assessment form during the service encounter. Therefore shoppers receive memory testing and training. In certain situations they may be able to use *aides-mémoire* to record and retain data (e.g. writing on a shopping list or making notes about a holiday or financial product) but otherwise the information must be memorised until the encounter is complete and the shopper has left the premises. On a two-hour, fact-finding interview for an investment product, there can be a large amount to remember.

In traditional survey research, the reliability of a research approach is often judged on sample size. In mystery shopping, an outlet may only be shopped once or possibly twice in any wave of the research. For example, if a hotel chain undertakes a mystery shopping exercise three times per year, during each phase of the research, individual hotels will receive an assessment based on one visit from a mystery shopper. Where an outlet offers a range of different types of product, slightly more visits may be necessary (e.g. a bank branch may receive three or four separate visits and telephone enquiries about mortgages, savings products and transaction products). The service organisations justify such limited numbers of visits by stating that every service encounter is critical and the quality of service delivery should be identical in each encounter. This has an implication for the results generated from these studies. An organisation may find that the average mystery shopping score for all of its outlets may follow a certain trend but the scores for individual outlets may fluctuate from month to month depending on the specific circumstances at the time of the visit. The aim of the service companies is to standardise the quality of all service encounters; the fluctuations provide a measure of the extent to which standardisation of service is being achieved.

Integration	An international perspective

International service organisations, such as airlines, hotels and retail stores, monitor their service delivery worldwide by integrating the data from their mystery shopping programmes with a variety of other data such as:

- number and type of complaints;
- number of transactions;
- value of transactions;
- customer loyalty/repeat purchase data;
- customer satisfaction scores;
- staff satisfaction scores.

Organisations, such as British Airways, Hilton Hotels and The Body Shop, aim to provide a consistent level of service throughout the world. The combination of these measures provides the organisation with an assessment of their service delivery in each country and an understanding of the geographic areas or outlets that need to improve their performance. Improvements can then be made in aspects such as staff training, internal communications and reward mechanisms. The impact of these improvements can be monitored through further waves of integrated data collection and analysis.

Content analysis

Content analysis
The analysis of any form of communication, whether it is advertisements, newspaper articles, television programmes or taped conversations. Frequently used for the analysis of qualitative research data.

Content analysis involves the analysis of the content of any form of communication, whether it is advertisements, newspaper articles, television programmes, Web pages or taped conversations. For example, the content of advertisements might be investigated to evaluate their use of words or themes or characters. Equal opportunity groups may carry out a study to look at the number of times women or ethnic minorities appear in mass media advertising. Companies may study the images or messages used by competitors as an input to the design of their own promotional materials. The content of annual reports, corporate statements and speeches can all be analysed in the same manner. Study of the content of communications can be more sophisticated than simply counting the items – the communication is broken into meaningful units using carefully applied rules. Further discussion of this technique is covered in Chapter 5, as it is a method that is frequently used for analysing qualitative data.

Ethnography

Ethnography
A form of participant observation that involves the study of human behaviour in its natural setting. For example, a researcher may accompany consumers (sometimes with a video camera) as they engage in a wide range of activities such as going on a shopping trip with friends. It involves the researcher exploring the interactions between group members, their reaction to various events and experiences, how they consider different courses of action and take decisions.

Ethnography involves the study of human behaviour in its natural setting. It is a form of participant observation which has its roots in the academic discipline of anthropology and the activities of social anthropologists, who imersed themselves in the day-to-day lives of tribes or communities where they recorded the norms, values and behaviours that shaped the group's existence. As academic ethnography has moved more towards the study of modern rather than primitive society, commercial organisations have become interested in its use for marketing research purposes. This involves a form of participant observation where a researcher accompanies consumers (sometimes with a video camera) as they engage in a wide range of activities such as students having an evening out or groups of female friends shopping for clothes. It involves the researcher exploring the interactions between group members, their reaction to various events and experiences, how they consider different courses of action and take decisions. The language they use and the seriousness with which they approach an issue or a purchase can assist organisations with advertising and communication campaigns. For example, health promotion campaigns aimed at reducing young people's consumption of alcohol need to understand the context (emotions, motivations, peer pressure) in which young people consume and talk about alcohol.

For ethnographic research to be effective, researchers need to spend as much time as possible understanding the group that they are to observe before starting fieldwork. This not only allows them to assimilate better but allows them to make more informed deductions about the reasons behind the actions of group members. It is important to note that, in comparison with traditional ethnographic approaches used in anthropology, ethnography in market research is, by its very nature, less rigorous. Researchers spend only a limited amount of time with their subjects and are unlikely to have been fully trained in the social science theory and practice of ethnography. The analysis of the participant's actions and the reasons behind them may also be more subjective. However, even without such rigour, ethnography can still provide richer, deeper insights into consumers. More specifically, it can be used to develop more valid language and measures in consumer surveys as well as to develop a better understanding of any patterns that emerge in other qualitative or quantitative data.

To be an effective ethnographic researcher, one needs to have an ability to quickly develop confidence and trust with people from a variety of backgrounds. This is particularly important as respondents are expected to reveal things about themselves in a variety of situations. Respondents need to feel comfortable with the researcher and comfortable with the situation. It is therefore advisable to tell them as much about the purpose of the research as possible. What are the objectives, who are the researchers involved and what will be done with the information collected? Obviously the ethnographic researcher wants the respondent to act naturally, but it is not uncommon for people initially to want to emphasise certain behaviours and hide others while they are being observed. The combination of time and the skill of the ethnographic researcher frequently results in respondents losing their inhibitions and reverting to their natural behaviours. This is made all the easier if the researcher can:

- use the same terminology and language of the respondent;
- wear similar types of clothing;
- give an impression of having an affinity with the respondent's interests and lifestyle;
- combine an ability to immerse themselves in an experience while maintaining an external observer's viewpoint.

It is usual for ethnographers to work in pairs or in teams, although only one or two of the researchers may come into contact with the respondents. The others help in the interpretation of the data at points during the data-collection phase and also once all of the data have been collected. Unlike pure observation, there will be interaction with the respondents which can provide the reasons behind certain behaviours (why did they only spend two minutes in this shop? Why did they choose that programme on their washing machine?) Therefore, a large quantity of data may be collected and reported. These may take the form of handwritten notes in field diaries, audio notes on voice recorders, digital photographs, video clips and physical evidence (such as magazines, tickets, receipts and packaging). Visual material such as video reports are particularly useful at communicating information to client organisations.

Ethnography is relatively small scale, with many studies involving fewer than 12–15 respondent cases. It provides cultural understanding insights into consumers and their thinking processes and behaviours. All of the material is integrated into site case reports, which can then be examined by topic area and customer-type. Information can then feed into brainstorming sessions with client managers looking for inspiration in terms of new concepts and ideas. It is inherently exploratory in nature and is likely to lead to further qualitative and quantitative research being needed to test any findings before any new products, services or advertisements are developed.

Monitoring user-generated content

User-generated media has the potential to allow researchers to listen in on consumer conversations. Millions of consumer comments, reviews, discussions and ideas now appear on review sites, message boards, blogs and social networks. People in the past may have had to be asked before they gave their views; these views are now expressed in public and recorded for others to measure, track and interpret.

The challenge is to trawl through these Web-based comments, views and opinions and analyse only that which is relevant and of value. There are many cheap, automated blog search tools, such as Google blog search (**http://blogsearch.google.com**) or technorati (**http://technorati.com**), as well as user generated media-tracking solutions (sometimes known as Listening platforms) developed by providers, such as Cision (**http://uk.cision.com**) and Radian6 (**www.radian6.com**), which simply identify all information appearing about a brand or company. These all have the following strengths and weaknesses:

1 Strengths:
   - they are relatively inexpensive to use;
   - they sometimes provide sophisticated dashboards with easy-to-use reporting features;
   - they can facilitate early detection of problematic issues which could negatively affect an organisation;
   - they can provide a feel of customer or public opinion on a wide range of issues and metrics.
2 Weaknesses:
   - they are automated systems, and they are not always accurate in processing the varied language, abbreviations or text-speak used on these sites;
   - they do not capture everything that is relevant;
   - they do not understand the context in which things are being said;
   - they need to be supplemented by human analysis.

As a result of these weaknesses, many agencies such as TNS Media Intelligence, Millward Brown Precis and Nielsen's BuzzMetrics offer services that employ human analysts to examine the information that is collected, verify the material, determine the relevance and assess what it means. Cleaning and relevance checking is particularly important with user-generated content, as the automated systems struggle with inaccurate spelling, grammar and punctuation.

Companies may also monitor independent review sites, for example, dealing with travel: tripadvisor (**www.tripadvisor.com**), or cars: what car (**www.whatcar.com**) or parenting issues: mumsnet (**www.mumsnet.com**), as well as sites set up by disgruntled customers (**www.lhatestarbucks.com**).

In addition to these hands-off type monitoring approaches, organisations may use their own social networking or websites to create a community that will attract user-generated content. For example, Mystarbucksidea (**www.mystarbucksidea.force.com**) is a site run by Starbucks to generate ideas, opinions and feedback from customers. British Airways have their own Facebook site and post new initiatives and their advertisements on this site to get customer reactions to them. Car manufacturers such as Ford use their visual vehicle configurator on their website to monitor how customers prefer to configure their ideal car from a choice of specifications and accessories.

Monitoring of user-generated content can therefore be seen as a form of observing and listening. Some academics argue that monitoring of this type should really be seen as secondary research rather than observation. However, it is not static material, it is constantly changing and there are possibilities for participant observation through interacting or experimenting with the posting of ideas, advertisements and through the establishment of online user communities.

Netnography, sometimes known as online *ethnography* or *webnography*, is the ethnographic study of communities on the World Wide Web. It generally involves a researcher participating fully as a member of the online community. Communities which are relevant to the topic being researched (i.e. computer game players) or communities where there are high levels of interaction and comments being posted are likely to provide the richest sources of information. These may lead to new ideas for the design of new products such as games consoles or software development.

Netnography
Sometimes known as *online ethnography* and *webnography*, netnography is the ethnographic study of communities on the World Wide Web. It generally involves a researcher fully participating as a member of the online community.

Data may be collected by copying transcripts from the forum itself or by the researcher taking notes on observations of interactions. There are ethical issues that stem from this type of research, however, particularly around the issue of researchers taking an active part in the discussions/conversations of a community. In such situations it is generally accepted that the researcher should fully disclose his or her presence, job function, and research intentions to online community members during any research assignment.

Customers may speak more freely within their online community than when they are taking part in traditional marketing as they possibly don't feel that they are under as much scrutiny. However, balanced against this is the concern that they may not be posting their views accurately, but may instead be posting comments that enhance their own reputation or reinforce the online persona that they are trying to create. Therefore, although this area of observation and monitoring is likely to grow significantly over the next five to ten years, there are still many questions that need to be addressed in order to better understand the user-generated content and its value to research, such as:

- What motivates people to post comments and other materials?
- Do people post to create an image or persona of themselves, to get accepted by others or to challenge others?
- Are their comments influenced by the opinions of those who have already posted?
- Does the nature of the site influence the content of the material posted (for example: Facebook as opposed to a site hosted by Ford or Starbucks)?
- How much do these posts influence customers and potential customers?

Ethical issues in observation research

Observation methods introduce a number of ethical issues. The use of cameras and other hidden observation methods impact upon the respondent's right to privacy. Chapter 2 details the manner in which the marketing research codes of conduct deal with observation. However, the general rule of thumb is that consumer behaviour can only be observed and videotaped without the participant's permission when the behaviour occurs in a public place (e.g. in a street or a retail store). If the observation is undertaken in any other location or where the participant would not expect to be observed by others, then permission must be sought. Therefore in any contrived environment or interviewing situation (e.g. focus groups), the participants must be told that they will be observed or videotaped. Deception is not an acceptable practice.

Summary and an integrated approach

Observation is an important marketing research tool. It allows the researcher to overcome some of the potential weaknesses of interviewing and survey research by providing a more detailed and accurate record of behaviour. The researcher is not dependent on the willingness or the memory of respondents to recall factual information.

However, observation only measures behaviour – it cannot identify reasons for behaviour or respondents' attitudes towards the behaviour. It can answer questions such as what, where, when and how but it cannot determine why someone behaves in the way that they do.

Observation can take many forms and can be categorised according to the following key dimensions:

- natural versus contrived;
- visible versus hidden;

- structured versus unstructured;
- mechanised versus human;
- participant versus non-participant.

Observation does not necessarily have to focus on the behaviour of customers: mystery shopping examines the performance of organisations and their service personnel. Mystery shopping, a form of participant observation, has become a major activity of the marketing research industry as a result of the increasing emphasis being put on service quality and service standards.

In addition, the long-established observation methods such as audits, traffic counts, television viewing measurement, one-way mirrors, eye tracking, content analysis, ethnography and stand-out equipment have been augmented as a result of improved technology by the more recent developments in scanner-based research, web analytics, video recording, and the monitoring of user-generated content. With more and more enquiries and purchases being handled online and by telephone call centres, mechanical or technological methods of observing behaviour are likely to become even more important. In addition, the growth in user-generated content on social media sites, customer review sites, blogs and video-sharing sites offers great opportunities to the researcher but also challenges the researcher to identify what is useful and valid in this fast changing area.

Observation research should not be seen as a substitute for other research methods. In fact, combining observation with database and other qualitative or quantitative research techniques is often a very powerful approach to obtaining a deeper understanding of consumers.

Discussion questions

1. What are the biggest limitations of observation research?
2. What advantages does observation research have over interviewing and survey research?
3. In what type of situations would contrived observation be more appropriate than natural observation?
4. In the past week, how many of your actions or behaviours do you think have been observed mechanically?
5. What advantages does mystery shopping have over sending a manager around various service outlets to see what is happening?
6. Describe the workings of a retail audit.
7. How do web-based retailers and suppliers monitor your actions on their sites?
8. What attempts are made to make mystery shopping as objective as possible?
9. What training do you need to become a mystery shopper?
10. Is observation for marketing research purposes ethical? Justify your answer.

Additional reading

Atkinson, P., Coffey, A., Delamont, S., Lofland, J. and Lofland, L.H. (2007) *Handbook of Ethnography*. Sage, London.

Cooke, M. and Buckley, N. (2008) Web 2.0, Social Networks and the Future of Market Research. *International Journal of Market Research*, **50**(2), pp. 267–92.

Dawson, J. and Hillier, J. (1995) Competitor mystery shopping: methodological considerations and implications for the MRS Code of Conduct. *Journal of the Market Research Society*, **37**(4), pp. 417–27.

Desai, P. (2010) Get real: from the viewing facility to the real world. *International Journal of Market Research*, **52**(1), pp. 136–38.

Green, A. (2010) *From Prime Time to My Time: Audience Measurement in the Digital Age.* WARC Publishing, London.

Grove, S.J. and Fisks, R. (1992) Observational data collection methods for services marketing: an overview. *Journal of the Academy of Marketing Science*, **20**(3), pp. 217–24.

Hine, C.M. (2000) *Virtual Methods: Issues in Social Research on the Internet.* Berg Publishers, UK.

International Journal of Market Research (2007) – special issue on ethnography, **49**(6).

Morrison, L.J., Colman, A.M. and Preston, C.C. (1997) Mystery customer research: cognitive processes affecting accuracy. *Journal of the Market Research Society*, **39**(2), pp. 349–62.

Mariampolski, H. (2006) *Ethnography for Marketers: A Guide to Consumer Immersion*, Sage, London.

Phillips, A. (2010) Researchers, snoopers and spies – the legal and ethical challenges facing observational research. *International Journal of Market Research*, **52**(2), pp. 275–78.

Wilson, A.M. (1998) The use of mystery shopping in the measurement of service delivery. *Service Industries Journal*, **18**(3), pp. 148–63.

Wilson, A. and Gutmann, J. (1998) Public transport: the role of mystery shopping in investment decisions. *Journal of the Market Research Society*, **40**(4), pp. 285–94.

Reference

[1] Adapted from Wilson, A. and Gutmann, J. (1998) Public transport: the role of mystery shopping in investment decisions. *Journal of the Market Research Society*, **40**(4), pp. 285–94.

5 Collecting and analysing qualitative data

The Police – understanding the public

The Police in the UK are required to collect data on citizen satisfaction levels from people who have been the victims of crime, covering action taken, ease of contact, keeping people informed, treatment and overall satisfaction. The Police force responsible for the Surrey area of England serving a population of just over a million people has regularly found, over a number of years, that satisfaction levels of black and minority ethnic groups have been consistently below that of the white population. A programme of qualitative research was therefore commissioned to find out about the nature of this citizen satisfaction gap and to identify what could be done to narrow or eliminate it.

The research consisted of 33 depth interviews with respondents of differing ages and gender from different ethnic groups. These were undertaken in 23 different locations to explore any differences between urban and rural areas. The second stage of the project involved running seven focus groups, involving six to eight participants from white British, south Asian and black African populations in each group.

One of the key findings from the research was that, although differences existed between different ethnic groups, there were also significant differences between members of higher and lower socio-economic groups, as well as across different age groups, in the accuracy of perceptions regarding the police service and its activities.

Jack Sullivan/Alamy

There was also felt to be a need for police training so that officers have a greater understanding of the dynamics of different black and minority ethnic communities. Training would also need to cover social hierarchies, gender differences, age seniority and how these factors impact on interaction between police officers and the public.

Some of the other ideas suggested to improve communications included a need for a free or low-cost, non-emergency phone number for those in lower socioeconomic groups, and the importance of a smooth handover when changes in police personnel take place, so that the social relationship between the police and the people they serve is maintained.

These and many other ideas from the research project have been fed into Surrey Police's equality, diversity and human rights strategy. In addition, the findings, some of which have national policy implications, have also been shared with other police forces in England and Scotland.[1]

Learning outcomes

After reading this chapter you should:

- be able to identify the types of research most suited to qualitative research;
- be aware of the key characteristics of individual depth interviews;
- understand the key tasks involved in undertaking group discussions;
- appreciate the main types of projective technique;
- be aware of the influence of technology on the future of group discussions;
- understand the processes and procedures involved in analysing qualitative data.

Key words

accompanied shopping	online group discussions
animatics	paired interviews
brand mapping	participant validation
brand personalities	photo sorts
cartoon completion	projective questioning
chat rooms	projective techniques
coding	role playing
concept boards	screening questionnaire
content analysis	sentence completion
content analysis software	spider-type diagrams
cut-and-paste method of analysis	stimulus materials
data display	storyboards
data validation	tabular method of analysis
discussion guide	text analysis software
focus groups	topic list
grounded theory	transcripts
group discussion	triangulation
group dynamics	video conferencing
group moderator	viewing rooms
individual depth interview	word association tests

Introduction

This chapter is designed to introduce you to the principal methods used to gather qualitative data. It discusses the two most commonly used qualitative research approaches, these being the individual depth interview and the group discussion (also known as the *focus group* or *group depth interview*). Techniques such as projective techniques that are used to enhance the productivity of the qualitative approach will also be discussed.

Qualitative research defined

Qualitative research can be defined as research which is undertaken using an unstructured research approach with a small number of carefully selected individuals to produce non-quantifiable insights into behaviour, motivations and attitudes. Taking the key components of this definition:

- the data-gathering process is **less structured** and more flexible than quantitative research and does not rely on the predefined question and answer format associated with questionnaires;
- it involves **small samples** of individuals who are not necessarily representative of larger populations;
- although the sampling process may lack the statistical rigour of more representative studies, great **care is taken in the selection of respondents** owing to the time and effort that will be spent on researching the views of each of them;
- the data produced is **not quantifiable** and is not statistically valid – qualitative research is concerned with understanding things rather than with measuring them;
- the researcher obtains **deeper and more penetrating insights** into topics than would be the case with a questionnaire or a more structured interview.

It is a mistake to consider qualitative and quantitative research as two distinctly separate bodies of research – many studies encompass both approaches, with qualitative research being used to explore and understand attitudes and behaviour, and quantitative research being used to measure how widespread these attitudes and behaviours are.

Researcher quote

A study which combines qualitative and quantitative methods gives you depth of understanding as well as information about the general representativeness of that understanding.

Types of research most suited to qualitative research

There are three main areas where qualitative research is most commonly used; these are exploratory research, new product development and creative development research.

Exploratory research

Exploratory research will be used when an organisation's management wishes to increase its understanding of customer attitudes, emotions, preferences and behaviours. As such, qualitative research may be required to obtain an initial understanding of:

- **Consumer perceptions of a product field.** For example: *Do consumers consider muesli bars as competing in the biscuit market, the cake market or the confectionery market? Is flavoured fromage frais exclusively a children's product?*
- **Consumer segments.** For example: *How should users of mobile phones be segmented? How can beer drinkers be segmented?*

- **Dimensions which differentiate brands.** For example: *Why do consumers buy Coca-Cola rather than Pepsi? What training shoe brands are considered to be suitable for the sports enthusiast rather than the fashion conscious?*
- **The decision-making process.** For example: *What do consumers think about when selecting birthday cards? How do people go about planning their annual holiday?*
- **Product usage patterns and behaviour.** For example: *What emotions do different decor and colour schemes in a hotel trigger? What would make customers change their mobile phone network?*
- **Identifying service or product improvements.** For example: *What improvements would customers like to see in the service they receive from a bank? How could the design of railway carriages be improved?*

Such exploratory research will assist in determining whether an organisation should undertake further research, and will also help to define the objectives, information targets and sample for a programme of more extensive research.

New product development

Qualitative research is particularly suited to obtaining reactions to new product concepts and designs where consumers are presented with an idea or innovation that they have not experienced before. During the new product development process there is usually a stage where a concept has been developed in a communicable form but no tangible usable product is available for testing. Qualitative research can help to determine if the concept warrants further development and provide guidance on how it might be improved and refined. By exposing people to the concept and getting their reactions, it is possible to identify:

- perceived benefits of the concept;
- weaknesses in the concept;
- likely interest in the concept;
- potential target market for the concept;
- suggested improvements or developments of the concept.

Qualitative research can also be used in the later stages of the product development process to assess reactions to mock-ups or prototypes of new products and their packaging.

Client quote

Qualitative research can give you confidence that the product concept you are creating is as exciting as you think it is.

Creative development research

Qualitative research can assist in the development of the message and creative execution of advertising and promotional activity. It can also be used to pre-test the chosen execution to determine whether it achieves an organisation's communication objectives.

During the development stage, qualitative research can enable 'the creatives' from an advertising agency to understand the consumer's relationship with the product group and individual brands. All promotion involves the encoding of a message to accomplish an organisation's communication objectives. Encoding is the process of translating messages into a symbolic form through the use of words, symbols and non-verbal elements that have meaning for and can be interpreted by the target audience. Qualitative research can assist in this process of encoding by providing information on the language that consumers use when talking about products, the lifestyles that they associate with different brands and the perceived value they place on different product attributes during brand selection.

Qualitative research also plays a role in the pre-testing of promotional material before it is launched to ensure that it is communicating the intended message to the target audience. The intention is not to judge whether the respondents like the advertising or promotional material but is instead aimed at analysing the campaign's effectiveness at correctly communicating the intended message.

The individual depth interview

Individual depth interview
An interview that is conducted face-to-face, in which the subject matter of the interview is explored in detail using an unstructured and flexible approach.

Individual depth interviews are interviews that are conducted face-to-face, in which the subject matter of the interview is explored in detail using an unstructured and flexible approach. As with all qualitative research, depth interviews are used to develop a deeper understanding of consumer attitudes and the reasons behind specific behaviours. This understanding is achieved through responding to an individual's comments with extensive probing. The flexibility of this probing sets this interview approach apart from other questionnaire-type interviews. Although there is an agenda of topics (topic list) to be covered, the interviewers will use their knowledge of the research objectives, the information gained from other interviews and the comments of the respondent to select which parts of the dialogue with the respondent to explore further, which to ignore, and which to return to later in the interview. Not only is the depth interview flexible, it is also evolutionary in nature. The interview content and the topics raised may change over a series of interviews as the level of understanding increases.

Researcher quote

You really obtain an understanding of a subject when you listen to people in depth.

Key characteristics

Length

Depth interviews tend to be longer than traditional questionnaire-based interviews, with many lasting in the region of 60–90 minutes. The research industry also undertakes mini-depth interviews, which are less wide ranging in the areas covered and tend to last up to a maximum of 30 minutes. Mini-depth interviews are often combined with other research techniques such as hall tests (see page 144) or tests in places where respondents may not be available for a longer period (e.g. at an airport or railway station).

Information collection

Almost all depth interviews are tape recorded. This enables the conversation to flow, eye contact to be maintained and interaction to occur. On some occasions video recording may be undertaken, particularly where the style of the individual respondent and/or non-verbal reaction to a subject is required.

Topic list

Topic list
Sometimes known as an *interviewer guide*. It outlines the broad agenda of issues to be explored in an individual depth interview or group discussion. It may also indicate the points at which stimulus material or projective techniques should be introduced.

A **topic list** or interviewer guide is used which outlines the broad agenda of issues to be explored and indicates at which points stimulus material or projective techniques should be introduced. It must be stressed that a topic list contains a list of topics or issues and does not consist of predetermined questions. The format of a topic list is similar to the group discussion guide shown in Figure 5.2 (page 112).

Location

Interviews are normally undertaken in the respondent's own home or office, although this can sometimes result in interruptions from telephones, children or work colleagues. However, this threat of interruption has to be balanced against the opportunity for the interviewer to experience the context of the respondent. From an office it may be possible to determine the seniority of the respondent and the extent to which the respondent uses technology, such as computers, as well as the nature and size of the respondent's employer. In the home, the neighbourhood, the street, the house and the interior will help to provide background on the lifestyle of the respondent.

Using the respondent's premises also allows the researcher to access additional materials for the interview such as files and brochures in an office, or bills and the contents of the kitchen cupboard at home. Alternatively, interviews can be undertaken in central locations such as hotels, cafés and bars where the number of possible interruptions can be reduced and refreshments can be provided to put the respondent at ease. Overall, interviews are carried out wherever it is convenient for the respondent and may include retirement homes, prisons, airports, etc.

Paired interviews

Paired interview
A depth interview involving two respondents such as married couples, business partners, teenage friends or a mother and child.

Although many depth interviews involve one respondent, it may be necessary to undertake the interview with a pair of people such as a married couple, a mother and child, two business partners or even teenage friends. **Paired interviews** allow the interviewer to assess how the two respondents influence each other's attitudes and behaviour. However, they should only be used where both individuals are jointly involved or where each has an influence on the actions of the other in the area under investigation; for example:

- **married couple:** purchasing mortgages, electrical white goods, DIY products, contraception methods, etc.;
- **mother and child:** purchasing clothes, toys, confectionery; television viewing habits;
- **teenage friends:** attitudes towards music, fashion, entertainment activities;
- **business partners:** attitudes towards financing arrangements, technology, government support.

The development of rapport

The development of rapport is critical to the success of a depth interview: respondents will only open up and express their true feelings and opinions if they feel comfortable with the interviewer. Rapport is not automatic and has to be worked at during an interview. Interviewers can attempt to ensure that they dress in a manner which is not too dissonant from the respondent – for example, dressing smartly when interviewing a businessperson or dressing casually when interviewing students or young people.

Researcher quote

If people aren't relaxed, they won't open up and it can feel like an interrogation rather than a conversation.

Body language

Frequently, the interviewer may mirror the body language of the respondent in terms of posture, hand movements and expressions. This is similar to our own actions when we meet friends, and assists in the building of rapport. As long as it is done in a relatively natural manner, it should put the respondent at their ease. A depth interviewer needs to demonstrate visually an interest in what the respondent is saying through behaviours such as nodding agreement, smiling and maintaining eye contact. Silence can be used to demonstrate an interviewer's willingness to learn by allowing the respondent to think rather than filling a pause in the interview with further questions.

The skills of the interviewer

The flexibility of the depth approach means that the skill of the interviewer is critical to the quality of information obtained from the interviews. A standard fieldforce interviewer is trained to administer questionnaires in a relatively mechanical manner by asking questions accurately and quickly. This is very different from the conceptual thinking required of a depth interviewer, who has to establish a rapport with the respondent while keeping his or her own opinions concealed and encouraging the respondent to develop points and summarise his or her views. Where a questionnaire-based interview can often seem like an interrogation, a depth interview should seem like a free-flowing conversation. The Qualitative Research Study Group (1979) suggested that a good qualitative interviewer needs to demonstrate the following qualities:

- intellectual ability plus common sense;
- imagination plus logic;
- conceptual ability plus an eye for detail;
- detachedness plus involvement;
- neutral self-projection plus instant empathy;
- non-stereotypical thinking plus a capacity to identify the typical;
- expertise with words plus a good listener;
- literary flair/style plus capacity to summarise concisely;
- analytical thinking plus tolerance of disorder.[2]

Researcher quote

The quality of the research output depends on the research input and that input is the interviewer. The skills of the qualitative interviewer will determine the level and depth of information obtained.

Specialised depth interviews

Accompanied shopping
A specialised type of individual depth interview, which involves respondents being interviewed while they shop in a retail store and combines observation with detailed questioning.

Accompanied shopping is a specialist type of depth interview, which involves respondents being interviewed while they shop in a retail store, and combines observation with detailed questioning. The interviewer obtains the agreement of respondents to accompany them on a shopping trip. Purchases and the selection process are then observed, with the interviewer asking how certain decisions and purchases are arrived at as they occur. This enables the interviewer to witness the impact of displays, packaging and point-of-sale material on *real behaviour* rather than recalled behaviour. Owing to the time and cost involved, the number of accompanied shops is usually small. There are also concerns among some researchers that the interviewer's presence may bias behaviour, with respondents choosing healthier or more environmentally friendly products when they are being observed.

Group discussions

Group discussion
Also known as *focus groups* or *group depth interviews*. These are depth interviews undertaken with a group of respondents. In addition to the increased number of respondents, they differ from individual depth interviews in that they involve interaction between the participants.

Focus groups
see Group discussions.

Group dynamics
The interaction between group members in group discussions.

Group discussions (also known as **focus groups** or *group depth interviews*) are depth interviews undertaken with a group of respondents. In addition to the increased number of respondents, they differ from individual interviews in that they involve interaction between the participants. The views or contribution of one person may become the stimulus for another person's contribution or may initiate discussion, debate and even arguments. The interaction between group members, commonly called **group dynamics**, is critical to their success and is their principal asset. Group discussions developed out of the group therapy approach used by psychiatrists to tackle areas such as addiction and behavioural problems in patients. Psychiatrists found that patients were more willing to talk about a topic if they were aware that other people had similar experiences and attitudes as themselves. They would also talk about a topic in more detail if they were in discussion with other group members than if they were to respond to direct questioning. This is the case whether the subject matter relates to psychologically oriented problems such as alcohol dependency or to marketing research issues relating to brand image, new packaging and advertising messages. Group discussions can provide the researcher with a richer and more detailed knowledge of a subject. It can also highlight the dynamics of attitudes, by showing how participants change their opinions in response to information or stimulus introduced by others. Information about the triggers that change opinions is of particular importance to advertisers.

Group discussions were first used for marketing research in the mid-1950s, when they were termed *motivational research*. Since then, their use has grown dramatically, not only for research on commercial products but also for governments and political parties. They take the form of a moderator holding an in-depth discussion with 8–12 participants on one particular topic. However, this description belies the complexity of the tasks involved in managing and running a successful focus group. The following subsections set out the detail of the tasks involved.

Recruitment of participants

Recruitment involves ensuring that appropriate respondents are identified, invited to participate and ultimately turn up, prepared to take part in the group discussion. Recruitment is a very critical element of group discussions and has long been a major quality-control issue in the UK marketing research industry. Group discussions are unlikely to achieve their research objectives if the wrong types of participant are recruited, all of the invited participants do not turn up, or they turn up with erroneous preconceptions or expectations.

The research proposal will set out the type of participants required for a group discussion and, on the basis of this, the research manager will produce a specification for the recruiting interviewers. For example, if Colgate is researching a new type of toothpaste for sensitive teeth, the specification may request adults between the ages of 18 and 45 who regularly purchase and use specific brands of toothpaste for sensitive teeth. Care must be taken to ensure that the specification is not so tightly defined that it becomes a very difficult task to find appropriate participants within the short time scales that are frequently imposed. The participants would normally be recruited in street interviews or in doorstep interviews, although telephone interviews or interviews in stores (or in this case, in dentists' waiting rooms) could also be used. Members of the public will be screened for their appropriateness using a **screening questionnaire** similar to the one set out in Figure 5.1.

Screening questionnaire
A questionnaire used for identifying suitable respondents for a particular research activity, such as a group discussion.

In addition to assessing appropriateness to the topic, a screening questionnaire will be used to screen out those potential participants who work in or have some connection with toothpaste manufacturers or the marketing research industry. It will also aim to identify and

Name:		Date:	
Address:		Phone:	
Time:		Interviewer:	

Good morning/afternoon,

I am _____ from _____ Marketing Research Services. We are planning a group discussion on the topic of toothpaste and sensitive teeth. Would you be interested in participating in such a session on _____ at _____

(IF 'NO', TERMINATE AND TALLY)

1   Do you regularly purchase any of the following brands of toothpaste? (SHOW LIST OF TOOTHPASTE BRANDS)

    YES................   1 CONTINUE
    NO ....   2 TERMINATE AND TALLY

2   Are you between the ages of 25 and 64?

    YES................   1 CONTINUE
    NO ....   2 TERMINATE AND TALLY

3   Do you live in the Glasgow area?

    YES................   1 CONTINUE
    NO ....   2 TERMINATE AND TALLY

4   Do you or any member of your family work for an advertising agency, a marketing research firm or a company that makes, sells or distributes toothpaste?

    YES................   1 TERMINATE AND TALLY
    NO ....   2 CONTINUE

5   When, if ever, did you last attend a marketing research group?   _____
    (IF LESS THAN 6 MONTHS AGO, TERMINATE AND TALLY)

Figure 5.1	Sample screening questionnaire to recruit group participants

screen out 'the professional group discussion participant'. These are individuals, sometimes members of the recruiter's family or friends who can often be co-opted by less than professional recruiters into groups on a regular basis to make up the numbers and ease the scale of the recruiter's task. However, through attending many group discussions they become atypical and respond differently to stimuli, and therefore do not accurately reflect the attitudes and behaviours of the market segment under investigation. The increase in respondent refusal rates can tempt recruiters to co-opt these tame participants. It is, therefore, important that screening questionnaires are used to ensure that appropriate standards of recruitment are maintained. However, it is also important that the researcher makes the recruiter's job as straightforward as possible by keeping the screening questionnaire short and simple rather than trying to use it to gather large amounts of additional material on each of the potential participants.

> ### New 'group discussion' concerns
>
> A significant number of group discussion participants are repeat attendees, according to a new study that raises questions over how some groups are recruited. The BMRB survey found that one in ten people who had taken part in a group over the past 12 months had done so at least three times that year, while one in 100 had clocked up 16 or more visits. The findings suggest that almost one-third of an eight-person group will have attended at least four groups in the past year, with one person having attended at least 16. The figures may be overly high, BMRB said, as they suggest more groups are being run in Britain than current estimates. However, they still raise concerns over repeat attendance, the firm added.[3]

If a respondent meets the criteria on the screening questionnaire, they will then be invited to participate in the group discussion, which may take place anything up to a week after recruitment. If the recruit accepts the invitation, they will often be given an invitation card setting out the venue, time, contact numbers, etc. However, this does not guarantee that the recruit will attend the group. One of the biggest problems in undertaking group discussions is the high incidence of 'no-shows'. People say they will attend, but then fail to appear because they have something more interesting to do, or experience 'cold feet' about attending the group. Why does this happen? In trying to understand people's attitudes towards why they do or do not take part in a group discussion, it is useful to consider the typical negative attitudes that a potential participant may have:

- I am worried that it is all a con-trick.
- I won't have anything useful to say.
- I am going to feel embarrassed.
- I am worried that they are going to try and sell me something.
- I don't know anybody there and I don't know what is going to happen.
- Why should I spend my valuable time helping with research?
- It will probably be very boring.
- I did one before and I didn't enjoy the experience.
- I might be the only person there.

It is the role of the recruiter to reassure the potential participant that it is vitally important that they attend, as their input will be crucial to improving the particular product or service in question. Incentives of financial rewards or gifts and vouchers will frequently be offered to demonstrate the value put on the participant's contribution in both input and time. This would be promised at the recruitment stage and given to the participant when they attend the group discussion. Recruiters should also explain what will happen, the typical number of people attending and the type of relaxed atmosphere that will exist. The legitimacy of the exercise can be communicated through explaining the links of the recruiter to professional bodies such as the Market Research Society and through using a respectable or high-profile venue.

Selection of group discussion venue

Viewing rooms
Specialist facilities/ locations for group discussions. They are set out in the form of a boardroom or living-room setting with video cameras or a large one-way mirror built into one wall. Some are owned by research agencies, but the majority are independent and available to anyone willing to pay the hourly room-hire rates.

Traditionally, group discussions were held in locations where participants felt most comfortable, such as individual homes located in the same area as the respondents or hotels for business people. These locations have no special facilities apart from the researcher using an audio tape recorder. Although the majority of group discussions are still undertaken in such venues, there are also a growing number of specialist **viewing rooms** or viewing facilities in cities and large towns throughout Europe. Some are owned by research agencies, but the majority are independent and available to anyone willing to pay their hourly room-hire rates.

These specialist facilities are set out in the form of a boardroom or living-room setting with video cameras or a large one-way mirror built into one wall. Behind the mirror or in a room linked to the video cameras there is a viewing room, which holds chairs and note-taking benches or tables for the clients and researchers. The participants' comments, body language and reactions can be watched from these rooms without inhibiting the activities of the group discussion participants. This is not the only opportunity that the clients or researchers have, as the action is also videotaped or audio taped for later viewing or analysis. However, live viewing does allow the marketing, research and advertising people to view together and discuss the implications of what they see and hear. It also allows young researchers to observe and learn about group dynamics, content, structure and the role of the moderator.

The group discussion participants will be told that they are being watched or taped but this rarely inhibits them, particularly after the discussion has been running for a few minutes. Refreshments and food or snacks will also be commonly provided to assist in relaxing the atmosphere.

Scheduling and the number of group discussions

In scheduling group discussions, the needs of the participants, the research team and the clients must be considered. For the participants, it relates to times at which the people in the target group are likely to be available, e.g. outside working hours, around school times for parents, times of available public transport, etc. For the research team, if multiple group discussions are being undertaken with more than one moderator, the logistics of moving videos and other support material between the groups as well as travel times need to be considered. For clients, if they want to attend, the timing of group discussions must fit with their diaries and availability.

With regard to the number of groups, three or four group discussions are sometimes sufficient, particularly if there is consensus in the findings obtained from each group. The moderator tends to learn a great deal from the first two discussions. Frequently the third and fourth sessions only help to confirm the findings of the first two, as much of what is said in these groups has been said before. More groups may be needed if the researcher is seeking information about regional differences or differences between different segments of the target population. Undertaking only one or two groups can be dangerous as there is always the chance that you get a group whose views are atypical of the target population.

Creation of a discussion guide

Discussion guide
see Topic list.

Similar to the topic list in individual depth interviews, a **discussion guide** is used which outlines the broad agenda of issues to be explored and indicates at which points stimulus material or projective techniques (see pages 114 and 115) should be introduced. The discussion guide is generated by the research team based on the research objectives and client information needs. The guide tends to break the group discussion into three phases:

1 The introduction phase includes:
   • the objectives of the session;
   • explanation of the nature of a group discussion;
   • the general agenda of topics to be followed;
   • prompts for the participants to introduce themselves.
2 The discussive phase includes:
   • general topic areas to be discussed;
   • potential prompts and stimulus material.
3 The summarising phase includes:
   • prompts for summarising what has been discussed;
   • thanks to participants.

Indicative timings are often placed on the various phases of the discussion. These are not aimed at controlling the discussion but are simply used to provide the moderator with a guide as to the approximate weighting to give to each part of the discussion in order to meet the project's research objectives.

Figure 5.2 shows an actual discussion guide used by a moderator to explore hotel guests' attitudes towards the various attributes provided by a hotel during a weekend break.

Introduction (10–12 minutes)

❑ Welcome and explain nature of group discussions
❑ Explanation of research project, objectives, sponsors, etc.
❑ Format of session
❑ Introductions: first name, home town, length of stay
❑ Reasons for coming to this (a) destination (b) hotel

Ease of obtaining information/booking prior to arrival (10 minutes)

❑ Type and source of information used and required prior to booking
❑ Means of contact: telephone/answering machines/Internet/correspondence/coupon response/travel agent
❑ Expectations of a brochure – what can make it useful/useless
❑ Central reservations versus individual establishment versus travel agent
❑ Information required over the telephone and with confirmation
❑ Ask for examples of good contact and examples of disappointing contact

Quality of accommodation (40 minutes)

What makes a good impact/bad impact (obtain examples):

1 **On arrival and prior to entering hotel**

2 **On entering the reception area**

3 **The bedroom**

   ❑ What makes a bedroom comfortable?
   ❑ If not mentioned, ask about bathroom, bed, bedding, cleanliness, control of temperature, television, radio, lighting, mini-bar, cupboard space, telephone, decor, security, tea/coffee facilities, toiletries, etc.)
   ❑ Expectations of room service
   ❑ Provide examples of bedrooms that have failed to reach or exceeded expectations

4 **Dining and bar facilities**

   ❑ What enhances/spoils the experience?
   ❑ Cover areas such as:
      ❑ service (efficiency versus friendliness)
      ❑ decor/ambience
      ❑ quality of offering
      ❑ range of offering
   ❑ Do these vary according to the meal being taken (e.g. breakfast versus dinner)
   ❑ Provide examples of good and bad experiences

Figure 5.2   Discussion guide on hotel attributes

5   **Leisure facilities**

　　❐   Importance of leisure facilities – what is required and service expected/level of use

6   **Departure**

　　❐   Obtain good and bad experiences of checking out – summarise important issues

7   **Other features relating to accommodation**

Overall value for money (10 minutes)

❐   Perceptions of what this means
❐   Understanding of hotel grading system (crowns/commended, etc.)

Summary of satisfaction criteria (10 minutes)

❐   So overall what are the key things that affect satisfaction (prerequisites versus desirables)?
❐   Check to see if anything was left unsaid that is important

Thanks for your participation

Figure 5.2	*Continued*

Moderating the group

Group moderator
The interviewer responsible for the management and encouragement of participants in a group discussion.

The skill of the **group moderator** is critical to the success of a group discussion. The moderator has to bring together a group of strangers, build a rapport between them, focus their discussions on the appropriate topics, and ensure that they all have an equal opportunity to contribute, while also restraining any participants who would like to dominate the group. They must do all of this in a supportive rather than a dominating manner – the client does not want to hear the moderator's views: instead, he or she wants to hear what the participants have to say.

Researcher quote

Every group is different, you don't know how it is going to go. You need to stay alert and be ready to react to every situation.

No two group discussions run in exactly the same manner, as the personalities of the participants are different in each group. Some groups work well with a great deal of cooperation, participation and a willingness to listen to each participant's point of view. Others can result in tension, defensiveness and general hostility. It is important for a moderator to understand the thinking process of the group participants.

1 Seeking understanding: many participants will turn up in a slightly anxious state, unsure about what is going to happen and possibly uncertain about the exact topic, the length of time they will be there and what is expected of them. This will make them defensive and relatively quiet and subdued until they can work out what is going on. This situation can be eased partially by the recruiter and also by the interviewer in the introduction phase of the group discussion. The recruiter should be clearly informing the participants about the topic area, the nature of a group discussion and the time that they will need to set aside for the exercise. The moderator should reinforce this in the early stages of the group discussion. It is also important for the moderator to share the broad agenda for the discussion, so that the participants have some knowledge of what is likely to be discussed next rather than being anxious about what or how much is yet to come. The moderator may also wish to 'surface' any anxieties by asking the group during the introduction phase what they expected to happen prior to arriving at the venue.

2 Wish to feel included: a participant will be anxious until they make a contribution to the discussion. This anxiety will increase, the longer the period of non-contribution. It is important for the moderator to involve all participants at a very early stage in the group discussion. Getting participants to introduce themselves, should not be seen as addressing this issue. Although introductions help, particularly where participants introduce the person sitting next to them rather than themselves, there is a need for some input on the topic from each participant early on in the discussion. Projective techniques, discussed on page 115, may be one way of doing this.

3 Seeking to communicate my status/experience: it is quite normal, particularly in the early stages of a group discussion, for participants to try to communicate their status relative to the others in the group. This may take the form of communicating their extensive experience or knowledge of the topics being discussed (e.g. 'I have a brother who works in the car industry and he says . . .'); alternatively, they may communicate an air of aloofness (e.g. 'I don't have time when I go shopping to notice the type of packaging on a product'). This is all to do with positioning within the groups and will tend to die down as the group discussion progresses. If it does get out of hand, with one individual attempting to dominate the discussion, the moderator may need to interrupt and ask what the others in the group think about a particular topic.

4 Wish to relate to others: once members have established their status within the group, they will tend to settle down to cooperate on the tasks of the group, telling of experiences, anecdotes, attitudes, etc. The body language of the group becomes much more positive, with participants mirroring each other's language and gestures. They are willing to listen to each other and agree or accept each other's viewpoints. At this stage the moderator should play a very passive role, becoming involved only to maintain the discussion on relevant subject areas. The moderator should be happy to allow silences rather than filling them with a battery of questions; it is even possible to offer up the silence for discussion: 'That seems to have killed the discussion. Any thoughts about why?'.

5 Wish to be seen as having valuable opinions/views: throughout a group discussion, participants are keen to see that people are listening to them and what they are saying. The moderator's role is to show that he or she is listening by maintaining eye contact, nodding, and smiling or frowning at appropriate times, probing for further information and mirroring the body language of the contributor.

6 Wish to leave: the moderator must realise that the participants are unlikely to be as interested in the topic as the research team, so it is important to bring the group to an end before the participants start becoming edgy and thinking about things they are going to be doing after the group has finished. It is therefore good practice, when fidgeting occurs, to 'signpost' to the group that it is almost time for winding up. Participants are then more likely to remain committed to the activity if they know that there is not much longer to go. The last few minutes should allow the participants to add any comments that they feel should have been covered in the discussion.

Stimulus materials
Materials used in group discussions and individual depth interviews to communicate the marketer or advertiser's latest creative thinking for a product, packaging or advertising to the respondents.

Good moderators need to develop an awareness of the changing moods and feelings in a group as the discussion progresses. Such an awareness can help in the planning and handling of each group discussion.

Stimulus material

Stimulus material is used to communicate the marketer's or advertiser's latest creative thinking for a product, its packaging or its advertising. Using such material, it is possible to get the participants' reactions to the creative ideas. The material may take many forms, ranging from complete advertisements on video to a set of concepts sketched out on a flipchart or board. Care must be taken in interpreting participants' reactions to **stimulus materials**, as the setting and the semi-complete state of the materials may result in participants being more critical of the concepts. The most common types of stimulus material are:

- **Concept boards:** a set of boards on which different product, advertising or pack designs or attributes are illustrated.
- **Storyboards:** key frames for a television advertisement are drawn consecutively, like a comic strip. Storyboards can also be presented on different pages of a flip chart – to avoid group participants reading ahead.
- **Animatics:** key frames for a television advertisement are drawn or computer generated and then filmed with an accompanying sound track. Actual photographs can also be used to improve the presentation.
- **Mock-up packs or products:** a 3D mock-up of a new packaging or product design.
- **Completed advertisements:** these may be in the form of videos, press ads, etc.

Concept boards
A type of stimulus material which uses a set of boards to illustrate different product, advertising or pack designs.

Storyboards
A type of stimulus material where key frames for a television advertisement are drawn consecutively, like a comic strip.

Animatics
A type of stimulus material where key frames for a television advertisement are drawn or computer generated with an accompanying sound track.

Projective techniques

Projective techniques
Techniques used in group discussions and individual depth interviews to facilitate a deeper exploration of a respondent's attitudes towards a concept, product or situation.

Projective techniques are techniques used in group discussions and individual interviews to facilitate a deeper exploration of a respondent's attitudes towards a concept, product or situation. They involve respondents projecting their feelings into a particular task or situation, enabling them to express attitudes that they find difficult to verbalise. A projective technique may gather 'richer' data than do standard questioning and discussion. Although the results of projective techniques are sometimes difficult to interpret, they provide a useful framework to get respondents to start exploring and talking about a subject in more depth.

> ### Researcher quote
>
> Projective techniques really get the respondents talking and laughing . . . but you need that to get to the bottom of a subject!

There is a very wide range of potential techniques, although the most frequently used for marketing research are *projective questioning, word association, brand personalities, brand mapping, photo sorts, sentence completion, cartoon completion* and *role playing*. Other well-known techniques such as the Thematic Apperception Test (TAT), the Rorschach inkblot test and psychodramas are more common in the field of pyschoanalysis than in marketing research.

Projective questioning

Projective questioning
Sometimes known as *third-party technique*, this is a projective technique that asks the respondent to consider what other people would think about a situation.

Projective questioning, sometimes known as *third-party technique*, is probably the most straightforward of projective techniques. It involves putting the respondent 'in somebody else's shoes' and asking questions such as:

- 'What do you think the average person thinks about when selecting a bank for a savings account?'
- 'What do you think people in your street would think if they saw a BMW parked in your driveway?'
- 'A lot of people seem very negative about McDonald's fast food. Why do you think that is the case?'

Answers to such questions will usually reflect the opinions of the respondent without causing them any embarrassment at having to express their own feelings overtly. Examples such as the McDonald's question may also help to reassure the respondent that other people have opinions similar to themselves. By looking at something from a different perspective, respondents may identify attitudes or concerns that they were not aware they had.

Word association tests

Word association tests
A projective technique that involves asking respondents what brands or products they associate with specific words. In addition to the direct outputs regarding brand imagery, it is also a very useful technique for building rapport within a group discussion and getting everybody contributing and involved.

The clinical application of **word association tests** in psychoanalysis dates back to the late nineteenth century when they were used to analyse the human thinking process. In marketing research, word association is typically used in conjunction with brand names or celebrity endorsers. With brand names it highlights not only the products with which the brand is associated, but also identifies the values associated with a particular brand or corporate identity. This can assist marketers in developing communication objectives and strategies to position or differentiate their brands from those of competitors. Similarly, in selecting a celebrity to endorse a product in an advertising campaign or in a sponsorship deal, it is useful to determine what values are associated with the celebrity.

Examples of word association tests

What is the first thing that comes to mind when I say 'chocolate'?
Write down the first ten things that come to mind when I say 'IBM'.
What is the first thing that comes to mind when I say 'Tiger Woods'?

Answers can either be reported verbally or written down. The moderator would not stop after the respondents have identified one word but instead would probe respondents for further words. So for 'chocolate', respondents might give answers such as 'Cadbury's', 'biscuit', 'bar', 'treat', 'luxury', 'temptation', etc.

Respondents can then be asked why they associate chocolate with each of these words. For example: what is the link between chocolate and temptation? The answer may help in the development of advertisements similar to the ones used for Cadbury's Flake.

In addition to the direct outputs of word association, the technique is also very useful as a way of warming up a group by getting everybody contributing and involved. Most people find it fun and it is a very straightforward task for respondents to undertake.

Brand personalities

Brand personalities
A projective technique which involves respondents imagining a brand as a person and describing their looks, clothes, lifestyles, employment, etc.

Brand personalities involve respondents imagining a brand as a person and describing their looks, clothes, lifestyles, employment, etc. For example: 'If Nokia was a person, what type of person would he or she be?' might result in answers such as:

A modern, relatively young slightly quirky male, who is small in size, reasonably attractive and interesting to know. Probably into pop music and outdoor pursuits.

This could compare with Philips:

A slightly older family-oriented person who is pretty dependable and slightly boring. Probably into classical music and golf.

Alternatively, respondents can also be asked to imagine the brand as another product: for example: 'If British Airways was a car what type of car would it be and how would this compare with SAS or easyJet?' Whichever approach is taken, developing brand personification can help to verbalise the imagery and vocabulary associated with the brand.

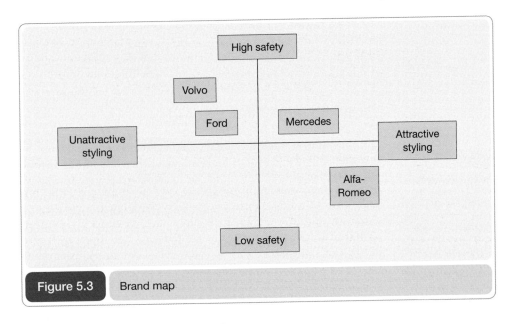

Figure 5.3   Brand map

Brand mapping

Brand mapping
A projective technique which involves presenting a set of competing brand names to respondents and getting them to group them into categories based on certain dimensions, such as innovativeness, value for money, service quality and product range.

Brand mapping involves presenting a set of competing brand names to respondents and getting them to group them into categories based on certain dimensions, such as innovativeness, value for money, service quality and product range. This can be done by giving out the names verbally and allowing the respondents to use a flip chart, or by putting them on cards and allowing the respondents to sort the cards into groups. Sometimes axes relating to different dimensions (see Figure 5.3) are provided to enable direct comparisons to be made between different groups and respondents.

Brand mapping is a useful technique for discovering how consumers segment a market and also for understanding a brand's positioning. Respondents can also be shown new advertising or packaging designs to see if this changes the positioning of the brand in any way.

Photo sorts

Photo sorts
A projective technique which uses a set of photographs depicting different types of people. Respondents are then asked to connect the individuals in the photographs with the brands they think they would use.

Photo sorts can be done either by using a set of photographs on individual cards or by using a collage of photographs on a display board or flip chart. The photographs tend to depict different types of people of varying ages, lifestyles, employment types, etc. Respondents are then asked to connect the individuals in the photographs with the brands they think they would use. For example, in research undertaken for Manpower recruitment, respondents had to match pictures of different types of office staff with different temp agency brands. In a similar way to brand mapping, photo sorts allow the researcher to understand how consumers perceive a brand and its positioning.

Sentence completion

Sentence completion
A projective technique which involves providing respondents with an incomplete sentence or group of sentences. Respondents are then asked to complete them.

In **sentence completion**, the respondent is given an incomplete sentence or group of sentences and is then asked to complete them. This helps to highlight attitudes that lie just below the surface. Examples of incomplete sentences are as follows:

- 'People who eat Pot Noodle are . . .'
- 'I think people who buy products from mail order catalogues are . . .'
- 'Tesco, as a supermarket, is . . .'

Once a respondent has completed the sentence, they can then be probed to find out why they said what they did. In many ways, sentence completion is similar to word association, although it can enable researchers to put the respondent's thinking process into a proper context.

Cartoon completion

Cartoon completion
A projective technique which involves a cartoon that the respondent has to complete. For example, the cartoon may show two characters with balloons for dialogue. One of the balloons sets out what one of the characters is thinking or saying, while the other is left empty for the respondent to complete.

Cartoon completion is a pictorial version of sentence completion. The cartoon usually shows two characters with balloons for dialogue or thoughts similar to those seen in comic books. One of the balloons sets out what one of the characters is thinking or saying, while the other is left empty for the respondent to complete. An example is shown in Figure 5.4. The faces of the figures are usually expressionless so that the respondent is not influenced to respond in a particular manner. A variation on this approach is to have a cartoon of a character using a particular brand or facing a particular situation and asking the respondent to verbalise what the character is thinking.

| Figure 5.4 | Cartoon completion |

Role playing

Role playing
A projective technique which involves a respondent being asked to act out the character of a brand.

Role playing is another route of obtaining information about brands without directly asking questions of the respondent. Respondents are asked to act out the brand. For example, a lawn mower manufacturer needed information on consumer perceptions of differing competitor brands. In the group discussions, respondents were asked to move across the room as different brands of lawn mower (e.g. as an Atco, as a Flymo, as a Black & Decker). Such role playing can often be difficult to interpret, although respondents are generally asked to explain what they are doing and why. Respondents can also be asked to play the part of a particular brand and sell themselves to other members of the group (for example, an instruction may be: 'Play the part of Huggies nappies and try to persuade a new mother why she should buy you rather than a competitor'). As role play involves an element of exhibitionism, it will only work with people who are relatively extrovert and relaxed.

Technological developments in qualitative research

The arrival of the Internet and improvements in telecommunications have led to agencies and companies experimenting with alternative ways of running and viewing group discussions. In terms of viewing, there is the potential for clients to watch a group discussion over their company's in-house broadcasting network or through video streaming on the Internet. This can allow more people to be involved in observing the research, particularly if it is being carried out in a different region or country. Pieces of the video broadcast can also be incorporated into e-mails or PowerPoint presentations to demonstrate the points being made.

In terms of running groups, improved telecommunications have enabled groups to be run by **video conferencing**. This has tended to be used with businesspeople who may find it difficult to attend a group discussion in one location as they are situated in various locations throughout the world. The screen facing each participant can be split so that they can view the facial expressions of the moderator and all of the other participants. This is an expensive way of running group discussions but may be appropriate for subjects such as high-value industrial products or first-class air travel.

A cheaper version is **online group discussions** or private **chat rooms** where a group is recruited who are willing to discuss a subject online usually using text. Participants are recruited by phone, e-mail or through an online special interest group. They react to questions or topics posed by the moderator and type in their perceptions or comments taking account of other participants' inputs. As people are typing in responses, it can often be difficult to develop any real group dynamics and it is impossible to see people's non-verbal inputs (facial expressions, etc.). Even with webcams, the video picture is usually so poor, interpretation of body language can be difficult. In some cases, respondents are asked to use emotion indicators such as smiling faces (☺) or different fonts or colours to reflect the way they feel; however, these do not truly capture the full breadth of emotion. The ability to type fast is also quite critical, particularly if interaction is sought. Participants may also be distracted by events within their own office or home, as the environment is not under the control of the moderator. However, such chat rooms may be useful for discussing high technology topics or with people who would be unwilling to attend a group discussion because of their geographical dispersal or their introverted nature. The current widespread use of software such as MSN Messenger in the under-25 age group is also likely to mean that a growing number of people will be accustomed to this form of interaction. In addition, improvements in modems, bandwidth and computer connections may also offer greater opportunities to use webcams and voice in online group discussions.

Video conferencing
The bringing together of a group of individuals using a video link and telecommunications. Can potentially be used for group discussions, particularly where the respondents are located in various parts of the world.

Online group discussions
These are group discussions or private chat rooms where a group is recruited who are willing to discuss a subject online usually using text (webcam and microphone are sometimes used). Participants are recruited by phone, e-mail or through an online special interest group. They react to questions or topics posed by the moderator and type in their perceptions or comments taking account of other participants' inputs.

Chat rooms
An Internet-based facility that can be used for online focus groups where individuals are recruited who are willing to discuss a subject online usually using text.

Researcher quote

Online groups can be easier to recruit, but are far more difficult for the moderator to control – it is sometimes difficult to involve all the participants, particularly if you have one or two who are dominating the interaction.

One area where the Internet is starting to make an impact in qualitative research is in the use of blogs, interactive discussion boards and online communities. Participants may be set the task of writing a blog over several days on topics of interest to the researcher. A blog (derived from the term 'web log') is a website maintained by an individual with regular entries of commentary, descriptions of events, or other material such as graphics or video. Although this may seem like data collection through an electronic diary, it provides topics and strands for further discussion and dialogue between the researcher and the participant online or offline. Blogs also provide a researcher with a view of how people lead their lifes and the thought processes they go through. When participants upload videos and photographs, we can observe how a family interacts when eating a meal, watching television advertisements, etc.

Interactive discussion boards involve a group of 10–15 participants responding to questions, prompts or stimuli online over a three- or four-day period. Once they submit their response, they get to see everyone else's comments and can choose to respond to them. As they respond, the next question becomes available for them to answer, but only after they have answered the previous question, while the respondent only sees the rest of the group's answers once they have provided a response. Respondents can take part in the boards from any location at any time that suits them and can return to previously answered questions to join the debate at any stage. Such an approach is useful for looking at new product development or for brainstorming new ideas.

Online communities on Facebook and Bebo may not be used to undertake the qualitative research, but may be used to recruit research participants or to maintain contact with a small panel of respondents that are taking part in qualitative research on an ongoing basis for an agency.

Analysis of qualitative data

As the researcher is often intimately intertwined with the gathering of qualitative research, it may be assumed that he or she will be able to analyse and interpret the data as it is collected. However, there are difficulties in attempting to short-cut the analysis in this manner. While the data is being gathered, the researcher is often more concerned with the process of doing the research rather than the detail of the content. The content that is generally recalled is the content that supports the researcher's or the client's own point of view. The comments of particularly vociferous or articulate respondents may be recalled more easily than others.

Content analysis
The analysis of any form of communication, whether it is advertisements, newspaper articles, television programmes or taped conversations. Frequently used for the analysis of qualitative research data.

Taking stock at the end of the project is therefore preferable as the researcher can be re-immersed in all of the data gathered and can organise the content into a form that directly answers the research objectives. This type of analysis is called **content analysis** because it analyses the content of the tapes and transcripts that represent the output of the qualitative research. Content analysis involves two main components:

1 organisation of the data: the structuring and ordering of the data using manual or computerised procedures;
2 interpretation of the data: determining what the data says with regard to the research objectives.

Organisation of the data

Transcripts
Detailed 'word-for-word' records of the depth interview or group discussion setting out the questions, probes and participant answers.

The data from qualitative research will take the form of audio or video recordings of the depth interviews or group discussions. Although some researchers may undertake analysis directly from these media, the majority obtain typed **transcripts** of the interviews or discussions to work from, as it is extremely difficult to analyse segments of different interviews and groups when the researcher is having to move back and forth between different sections of different recordings. The recordings should not be discarded, as they will be useful in highlighting different points to clients at the end of the study and they also help to determine the strengths of respondents' feelings through highlighting the expressions and tone of voice used when certain points were made.

The transcripts provide a detailed 'word-for-word' record of the depth interview or group discussion setting out the questions, probes and participant answers. They are the foundation upon which the analysis is based and significant care should be taken in their preparation. Transcribing the material is a slow process, particularly for group discussions where there are many participants with some speaking more clearly than others. Sometimes the transcriber has to go back and forward throughout the recording to clearly understand and capture what has been said.

Coding
The procedures involved in translating responses into a form that is ready for analysis. Normally involves the assigning of numerical codes to responses.

Reducing the data

Reducing or **coding** the data involves processing the data into discrete chunks and creating a reference and categorisation mechanism for these chunks of data so that they can be easily

Table 5.1	Participant responses

Attitudes towards the restaurant experience	Respondent Identifier
It was really noisy, you couldn't have a conversation.	Resp 1.
There was a real buzz in the air	Resp 2.
Service was awful	Resp 3.
The staff were overworked	Resp 4.
The music was good	Resp 5.
It had a very limited choice of food	Resp 6.
The soup was cold	Resp 7.
That was the best steak I have had far a long time	Resp 8.
It had weird decor	Resp 9.
The staff were very friendly	Resp 10.
The food was good	Resp 11.
The food was expensive	Resp 12.

retrieved for analysis. This referencing and categorisation is done through the researcher assigning labels or codes to the data relevant to the objectives of the research project. Codes are essentially labels that assign meaning to the data collected. These can sometimes be colour coded to highlight commonalities between different transcripts more clearly. Participant answers to a question may be coded in a number of ways and, in certain cases, multiple codes may be given to the same piece of data. This can be demonstrated using Table 5.1, which shows a variety of responses to questions and probing relating to a recent restaurant experience.

In categorising these responses, the researcher could create codes such as 'positive comments' and include the comments from respondents 5, 8, 10 and 11 or codes such as 'negative comments' (respondents 1, 3, 4, 6, 7, 12) or comments relating to 'noise/music' (1, 2, 5) or 'the restaurant environment'(1, 2, 5, 9) or 'the service' (3, 4, 10) or 'the food' (6, 7, 8, 11, 12) or the 'quality of the food' (7, 8, 11) or 'range of food' (6) or 'price of food' (12). If all of these categories were used, a comment such as 'the food was expensive' would have three codes allocated to it, indicating that it was a negative comment, relating to food and in particular relating to the cost of food.

There are many different ways in which the data can be categorised. This is a decision for the researcher to make on the basis of the research aims and objectives. The examples in the table related to very short statements, but sometimes longer comments and statements need to be kept intact and coded to reflect the true meaning of the points being made. As a researcher works through the transcripts, it may emerge that important themes are not fully reflected in the codes being used and, therefore, it may be necessary to develop new codes or revise the existing ones.

Coding is a time-consuming process, but it forces a researcher to focus upon the key elements appearing in the data. To understand the meaning of these elements and their interrelationships, it is necessary to display the elements of the qualitative data in an accessible and abbreviated format.

Data display

Summarising and presenting of information in order that relationships or connections can be identified and conclusions can be drawn.

Data display

Data display involves the summarising and presenting of information in order that relationships or connections can be identified and conclusions can be drawn. Data display also allows

	Users	Non-users
Attitudes towards quality	'The quality is fine – it is certainly no worse than any of the other brands' 'Good quality' 'Reliable/dependable'	'I feel less confident about the build quality of the product' 'Adequate – not impressive'
Attitudes towards price	'It is quite a bit cheaper than the competing brands' 'Good value for money'	'It is cheaper but that reflects the quality' 'Cheap'
Attitudes towards typical users	'The average person' 'Sensible not flash'	'Downmarket – somebody concerned about price more than style' 'Somebody who shops at a discount store'

Figure 5.5 An example of a tabular approach to qualitative analysis

others to view the logic behind the manner in which the relationships and conclusions have been reached. The most common manual approaches for doing this are:

- the tabular method;
- the cut and paste method;
- spider-type diagrams;

The tabular method

Tabular method of analysis
A method for analysing qualitative research data using a large sheet of paper divided into boxes.

The **tabular method of analysis** normally takes the form of a large sheet of paper divided into boxes (similar to a very large Excel spreadsheet) with the two or three most important respondent characteristics (users, non-users; smokers, non-smokers; male, female) being put in the column headings. The row headings are the most important issues relating to the research objectives for the project (see Figure 5.5). The researcher then transfers the content (in the form of verbatim quotes, interpretation or a précis of behaviour and attitudes) into the relevant boxes. When all the groups or depth interviews are structured in this manner, it becomes easier to compare and contrast the data collected.

This form of tabular approach ensures that each transcript is treated in the same way and therefore can allow two or more researchers to undertake the task simultaneously. This is very important, as it can take a considerable amount of time to go through each transcript, particularly when it relates to a group discussion of up to two hours in length.

On the negative side, it has the disadvantage of being inflexible, in that information which does not fit into the framework is often ignored even though it may be valuable in another manner to the research and the client. It can also be quite a laborious exercise copying over material into the grid of boxes.

Cut-and-paste method of analysis
A method for analysing qualitative research data where material is cut and pasted from the original transcript into separate sections or tables relating to each topic. Cutting and pasting can either be done physically using scissors or using a word-processing computer package.

The cut-and-paste method

The **cut-and-paste method of analysis** is similar to the tabular approach except, rather than data being copied across to a grid, the material is cut and pasted from the original transcript into separate sections or tables relating to each topic. This can be done either by physically cutting up copies of the transcript and sticking them onto separate sheets relating to a range of separate categories or, alternatively, by computer. Most word-processing packages will allow such cut and paste activities to be undertaken in a virtual form without scissors and glue before printing out the recategorised data.

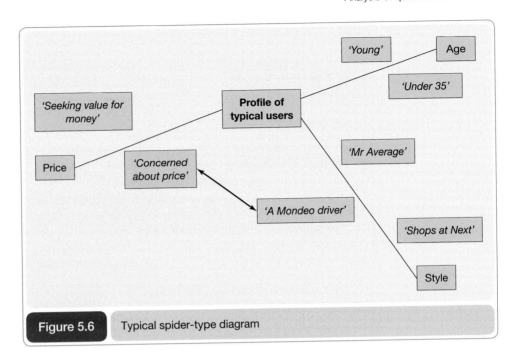

Figure 5.6   Typical spider-type diagram

Spider-type diagrams

Some researchers may use **spider-type diagrams** (also known as *Mind Mapping*®) to organise the data. These set out each of the issues at the centre of a diagram with the key responses emanating from the centre like a spider's web, highlighting the links between different issues (Figure 5.6). The interconnections are therefore much clearer to the researcher and the client than is the case in the tabular format. However, it is often difficult for more than one researcher to undertake the task simultaneously as they are unlikely to categorise the linkages in the same manner.

Data validation

A researcher needs to demonstrate that the explanations and conclusions drawn from the qualitative data are not just a reflection of their own views. It is very possible that a researcher's previous opinions about a situation or behaviour may (often unintentionally) influence the way that they interpret the data. **Data validation** attempts to address this through the verification of the appropriateness of the explanations and interpretations drawn from qualitative data analysis. Two of the most commonly used validation approaches for qualitative research are triangulation and participant validation.

Triangulation

As stated in Chapter 1, the term **triangulation** is borrowed from the disciplines of navigation and surveying, where a minimum of three reference points are taken to check an object's location. In marketing research, comparing information from different kinds of data and different methods allows a researcher to seek corroboration for the qualitative research findings. A researcher may consider using published data or undertaking a programme of quantitative research or even observations and photographs to validate the qualitative findings.

Participant validation

Participant validation involves taking the findings from the qualitative research back to the participants/respondents that were involved in the study and seeking their feedback. If the feedback verifies the explanations and conclusions, then the researcher can be more confident about the validity of the findings.

Computerised programs

Data analysis programs can also be used to categorise and order the data. Computers can assist with the sheer volume of data that can be collected. The two main broad groups of programs are content analysis software and text analysis/theory building software.

Content analysis software

Content analysis software
Software used for qualitative research which basically counts the number of times that pre-specified words or phrases appear in text.

Content analysis software basically counts the number of times that pre-specified words appear in text: for example, the number of times that 'efficiency' is mentioned in interviews about selection criteria for choosing process equipment. The software can often do various operations with what it finds, such as marking or sorting the text found into new files and the production of text-frequency distributions. The text-frequency distributions that are produced can provide initial comparisons between transcripts to determine the main topics or themes that they share. However, analysis of this type is very crude and is only of value in giving a broad first feel of the data rather than any form of detailed analysis.

Text analysis/theory building software

Text analysis software
Software used for data analysis in qualitative research. Such software helps segment the data and identify any patterns that exist.

Text analysis software packages, such as QSR NUD*IST, The Ethnograph and QSR NVivo,[4] help the researcher divide the data into chunks or segments, attach codes to the segments and then find and display all of the segments with a given code (or combination of codes). For example, the word 'efficiency' may not be mentioned directly, but segments of text on 'cost effectiveness', 'speed of production', etc. could all be categorised within the same coding. The researcher can then retrieve data where one category or topic is discussed in relation to another. Patterns and relationships within the data may then be identified through using the software's system of rules and hypothesis testing features, which are frequently based on formal and Boolean searching logic. (Boolean requests relate to 'and/or/not' requests; for example, cost effectiveness AND production, effectiveness OR production, effectiveness NOT production.) Some programs will search for overlapping or nested segments. For example, they would find where a segment coded 'efficiency' overlaps with 'speed of production'. NUD*IST, which stands for Non-numerical Unstructured Data Indexing Searching and Theorising, is a programme which allows the researcher to build up a complex categorisation system to classify the data. The software allows the researcher to build up tree displays of categories which can be continually altered as the researcher refines the categories and the relationships between them.

In selecting software for qualitative analysis, the following factors should be taken into consideration:

1 **Data entry:** does the program allow the researcher to format text in any format or does the text need to be formatted along strict rules relating to numbers of characters per line and delineation of blocks of text?
2 **Data storage:** can the data be stored in the original word-processed format or does it need to be split into separate files, making it difficult to change or add to the text?
3 **Coding:** can the coding be done on-screen or does it require the researcher to work with a hard copy to assign the codes before entering them into the computer? How complex can the coding be? Does it allow multiple codes or nesting of codes on a single block of text? Does it allow the researcher to make marginal notes and annotations? (This is particularly important when a team of researchers is involved in doing the analysis as it ensures that the reasons given for assigning specific codes are made explicit.)
4 **Search and retrieval:** how fast can the package search for and retrieve appropriate strings of data? (This may relate as much to computer hardware as it does to software.) What information does it display on the results of searches (the text only or the text and details about the context in which the text appears)? Does it maintain a record of all searches done?

Interpretation of the data

Although some of these computer packages and content analysis procedures can be very sophisticated, it should be noted that they are only capable of organising the data: they do not interpret what it means. The researcher needs to interpret what was said, determine what it all means and identify the implications for marketing decisions. The researcher needs to think through the manner in which things were said to determine what messages the respondents were trying to communicate, either consciously or subconsciously. A researcher's understanding of this increases with experience of qualitative research but also from personal experience of socially interactive situations in everyday life. In our day-to-day social interactions, we do more than listen to others: we interpret their commitment, belief and enthusiasm in what they are saying. We notice inconsistencies, uncertainty, fear and incomprehension. We can often recognise the boasting, bluffing and disguising that people do to cover up their true opinions and behaviour. Combining these intuitive skills with an understanding of the literature on group dynamics can go a long way to providing the researcher with the necessary toolkit to understand respondents in qualitative research. Such understanding will make it possible for the researcher to determine the implications for the research objectives and ultimately for the marketing decisions that have to be made.

Another approach to qualitative data analysis – grounded theory

Grounded theory
A set of analysis techniques that were developed in the 1960s by two medical sociologists, Glaser and Strauss (1967). It is more commonly used by academic researchers rather than marketing research practitioners in areas where little is known about a subject or where a new approach to understanding behaviour is required. It is a systematic method of generating theory and understanding through qualitative data collection and analysis.

Grounded theory is a set of analysis techniques that were developed in the 1960s by two medical sociologists, Glaser and Strauss[5] (1967). It is more commonly used by academic researchers than by marketing research practitioners in areas where little is known about a subject or where a new approach to understanding behaviour is required. It is a systematic method of generating theory and understanding through qualitative data collection and analysis.

Unlike other qualitative research where the data are collected and then analysed, grounded theory researchers collect data and analyse them simultaneously from the outset. The researcher will start with a broad area of interest such as car buying, and will use preliminary interviewing to open up this area. The researcher will then examine the initial information and participant views to develop further questions around these views and seek out further participants who could potentially elaborate on the topics/views identified. This is repeated many times with the researcher refining the emerging themes and conclusions as they go along. The individual researcher needs, therefore, to be involved at each stage of the data collection and analysis. The data analysis that is ongoing throughout the period of data collection and afterwards has four main components:

1 Coding data – although similar to the coding discussed earlier in this chapter, it tends to be far more detailed and guides further data gathering as the project proceeds. It starts with open coding, undertaken on a line-by-line basis, where everything is coded in order better to understand the issues and concepts. This is followed by selective coding which focuses on the core variables identified by the data (and not variables that have been determined beforehand and forced on to the data).

2 Memo writing – involves the writing of notes, arguments and ideas that come about as the researcher goes through the data. The process produces a bank of ideas on concepts, meanings and ideas about what is emerging from the data and may also identify gaps and missed opportunities in earlier data collection.

3 Theoretical sampling – this relates to further data gathering driven by the ideas and concepts emerging from the coding and memo writing. The aim is to seek out other situations or participants that may assist in discovering variations in the concepts and theories identified. Thinking about concepts should become more precise with further research inputs.

4 Integrating analysis and sorting – the various memos are then sorted, which may result in new ideas emerging that are recorded in further memos. The emphasis at this stage is very much on connections with the focus being on how ideas fit together. This results in a collection of explanations that explains the subject of the research

Undertaking a grounded theory approach is a very time-consuming activity and it is very difficult to predict how long a study will take. It is, therefore, acceptable for academic research but may be inappropriate for marketing research that has to meet client-determined timescales.

Summary and an integrated approach

Qualitative research provides researchers with detailed information on the behaviour, motivations and attitudes of respondents. It is most commonly used for exploratory research, new product development and creative development. The main approaches in qualitative research are the individual depth interview and the group discussion. The interactive nature of both of these approaches means that their success is dependent on the skills of the interviewer or the moderator. The relative merits of each approach are set out below.

Advantages of depth interviews over group discussions:

- The respondent is the centre of attention and can therefore be probed at length to explore remarks made which may provide critical insights into the main issue. The respondent cannot hide behind other people's comments or discussions and does not have to compete for time to talk.
- Group pressure is eliminated, so the respondent reveals what he or she actually thinks rather than what is acceptable to the rest of the group.
- Respondents may be willing to talk about sensitive topics that they would hesitate to discuss in front of other people.
- Recruitment is a less complex process.
- Group facilities are not required and the interviews can be undertaken in the respondent's home or office.
- Depth interviews are necessary where group participation is difficult because respondents are geographically dispersed or have very busy diaries.

Advantages of group discussions over depth interviews:

- Depth interviews are more expensive than focus groups when viewed on a per-interview basis.
- Depth interviews are more time consuming. A typical depth interviewer will undertake a maximum of four interviews per day, whereas a moderator could do two groups involving a total of 16–20 people in the same time scale.
- Group discussions allow interaction between participants, providing a stimulus to each participant.
- Group discussions highlight the dynamics of attitudes by showing how participants change their opinions in reaction to the views of others.

Projective techniques such as word association and sentence completion can be used to enhance the quantity and quality of material produced by both individual depth interviews and group discussions.

At the end of a qualitative project the researcher needs to be re-immersed in all of the data gathered and organise the content into a form that directly answers the research objectives.

This type of analysis is called *content analysis* and involves the twin activities of data organisation and data interpretation.

Finally, it is important to reiterate that it is a mistake to consider qualitative and quantitative research as two distinctly separate bodies of research: many studies incorporate both approaches. Used in combination, they can provide a far clearer picture of a market and its characteristics.

Discussion questions

1 Describe the skills that you think a moderator of a group discussion should have.

2 In the Screening Questionnaire (Figure 5.1), the interviewer is asked to tally the people who are rejected. Why do you think this is?

3 Why are group discussions widely used in the development of advertising?

4 Why is qualitative research particularly suited to the early stages of new product development?

5 Describe the key characteristics of an individual depth interview.

6 Why is the development of rapport so critical to qualitative research?

7 The interviewer or moderator is critical to the success of qualitative research. Discuss.

8 What is a projective technique?

9 Why would you run a group discussion by video conferencing or over the Internet?

10 Explain the most common approaches to the analysis of qualitative data.

Additional reading

Bruggen E., Willems, P. (2009) A critical comparison of offline focus groups, online focus groups and e-Delphi. *International Journal of Market Research*, **51**(3), pp. 363–82.

Catterall, M. and Maclaran, P. (1998) Using computer software for the analysis of qualitative market research data. *Journal of the Market Research Society*, **40**(3), pp. 207–22.

Cowley, J.C.P. (1999) Strategic qualitative focus group research – define and articulate our skills or we will be replaced by others. *International Journal of Market Research*, **42**(1), pp. 17–38.

Ereaut, G., Imms, M. and Callingham, M. (2002) *Qualitative Market Research: Principle and Practice*. Sage Publications, London.

Goulding, C. (2002) *Grounded Theory: A Practical Guide for Management, Business and Market Researchers*. Sage Publications, London

Gordon, W. (2000) *Goodthinking – A Guide to Qualitative Research*. Admap Publications, London.

Gordon, W. and Langmaid, R. (1988) *Qualitative Market Research: A Practitioner's Guide*. Gower, London.

Krueger, R.A. (1998) *Analysing and Reporting Focus Group Results*. Sage, Newbury Park, CA.

Keegan, S. (2009) *Qualitative Research: Good Decision Making Through Understanding People, Cultures and Markets*. Kogan Page, UK.

Marks, L. (2000) *Qualitative Research in Context*. Admap Publications, London.

Robson, S. and Foster, A. (eds) (1989) *Qualitative Research in Action*. Arnold, London.

Silverman, D. (2009) *Doing Qualitative Research*, 3rd edn. Sage Publications, London.

References

[1] Carey, S. (2010) Helping them with their enquiries. *Research*, August, pp. 32–3.

[2] Market Research Society, R&D Society Sub-Committee on Qualitative Research (1979) *Qualitative Research – A Summary of the Concepts Involved.*

[3] Cervi, B. (2001) New 'focus groupie' concerns. *Research*, January, p. 8.

[4] QSR NUD*IST and QSR NVivo: **www.qsrinternational.com**. *The Ethnograph*: **www. scolari.co.uk.**

[5] Glaser, B.G. and Strauss, A.L. (1967) *The Discovery of Grounded Theory.* Aldine, Chicago, USA.

6 Collecting quantitative data

The National Readership Survey

The UK National Readership Survey is funded by the Institute of Practitioners in Advertising (IPA), the Newspaper Publishers Association (NPA) and the Periodical Publishers Association (PPA). The survey is aimed at assessing the effectiveness of different types of printed media for advertisers, advertising agencies and publishers. This large-scale programme of quantitative research is contracted out to the research agency Ipsos-MORI Ltd and costs over £4 million to undertake. The research is carried out continuously throughout the year with over 36,000 respondents interviewed each year. The computer-assisted personal interviews (CAPI) are carried out by interviewers using laptop computers. Interviewers visit houses

Jack Sullivan/Alamy

selected using a multi-stage probability sample derived from the Postcode Address File, and one individual is selected for interview within each household based on a strict sampling selection process.

Respondents are asked about over 250 publications using visual prompts on an electronic screen radio-linked to the interviewer's laptop computer. Respondents are shown a sequence of around 50 screens shots, each of which carries the titles of six publications (the order in which the screens are shown is rotated – the order in which the titles are shown on the screen is also rotated). For any of the publications that they have seen in the last year, they are asked specific questions about the recency and frequency of readership, using further visual prompts. Results are weighted to produce estimates of the number and type of readers in the general population for each of the publications. Organisations which subscribe to the NRS can obtain detailed information on the readers of each publication covering aspects such as demographics, shopping behaviour, income levels, household composition, house ownership, ownership/usage of various forms of technology, leisure pursuits, education, TV viewing habits, etc. Advertisers can use such information to improve the placing of advertisements to match the target audience that is being sought. Also publishers use it to determine what rates to charge and optimal advertisers to sell space to.[1]

Learning outcomes

After reading this chapter you should:

- be aware of the characteristics of the main quantitative survey methods;

- appreciate how technology is being used to undertake these methods;

- understand the application of these methods within omnibus surveys and experimental techniques (hall tests, placement tests and simulated test markets).

Key words

CAPI
CATI
e-mail surveys
executive interviewing
face-to-face surveys
hall tests
in-home/doorstep interviewing
Internet panel
kiosk-based surveys
mixed-mode studies

omnibus surveys
online surveys
panel research
placement testing
postal surveys
quantitative research
self-administered surveys
simulated test markets
street interviewing
telephone interviewing

Introduction

This chapter is designed to introduce you to the principal methods used to gather quantitative data. To be quantifiable, data needs to be collected in an ordered and structured manner. The most popular structured approach to data collection in marketing research is the survey method. There are as many forms of survey method as there are different forms of communication. The advent of online surveys has added to the more traditional survey forms of telephone and personal interviews. This chapter will look at the various survey methods available, as well as at the application of these approaches within the specialist areas of omnibus surveys, hall tests, placement tests, simulated test markets and panels.

Quantitative research defined

Quantitative research
A structured research approach involving a sample of the population to produce quantifiable insights into behaviour, motivation and attitudes.

Quantitative research can be defined as research which is undertaken using a structured research approach with a sample of the population to produce quantifiable insights into behaviour, motivations and attitudes. Taking the key components of this definition:

- the data gathering is **more structured** and less flexible than qualitative research as it tends to use predefined questions that are consistently used with all respondents;

- the research tends to involve **larger samples** of individuals than would be used in qualitative research. While some quantitative studies may involve as many as tens of thousands of respondents, many involve samples in the region of 100 to 200 individuals;
- in comparison with qualitative studies, quantitative studies can be **more easily replicated** and direct comparisons can be made between the results;
- the data gathered provides answers that can **quantify the incidence** of particular behaviours, motivations and attitudes in the population under investigation;
- analysis of quantitative studies will tend to be **statistical** in nature and will commonly be undertaken with the help of computer software.

However, in considering quantitative research, it is important to re-emphasise the point made on page 127 – that is, many studies encompass both qualitative and quantitative approaches, with qualitative research being used to explore and understand attitudes and behaviour and quantitative research being used in a conclusive or confirmatory manner to measure how widespread these attitudes and behaviours are.

Survey methods

Surveying involves the structured questioning of participants and the recording of responses. These tasks can be undertaken verbally, in writing or via computer-based technology. An interviewer may be used to administer the survey or the respondent may complete the survey on his or her own. These second type of survey are known as self-completion or self-administered surveys. Interviewer-administered questionnaires are generally undertaken over the telephone or through face-to-face contact in the home, street or place of work. They may involve the use of paper-based questionnaires or computer terminals (laptops and notepads). Self-completion surveys can be delivered and collected from respondents by post, by hand, by fax, online, by e-mail or potentially by SMS messaging on a mobile phone. The various survey methods are shown in Figure 6.1.

Face-to-face methods

Face-to-face surveys
Research which involves meeting respondents face-to-face and interviewing them using a paper-based questionnaire, a lap-top computer or an electronic notepad.

Face-to-face surveys, or personal interviewing methods, can be categorised into in-home/doorstep, executive and street. They involve meeting the respondent face-to-face and interviewing them using a paper-based questionnaire, a lap-top computer or an electronic notepad. Face-to-face contact of this type has the following advantages over more remote approaches, such as telephone and self-completion methods, because it is generally easier to:

- motivate a respondent to take part and answer difficult questions when there is direct face-to-face interaction;
- convince the respondent that the research and the interviewer are genuine;
- check and ensure respondent eligibility before the interview is conducted;
- assist a respondent with a more complex questionnaire or set of questions;
- judge the interest, impatience and the seriousness with which a respondent is answering a questionnaire;
- improve understanding of the interviewer and the respondent through non-verbal communication;
- control the visual elements of the questionnaire (showcards and photographs will be shown at the correct point in the questionnaire, unlike self-completion methods where everything is seen at once, or the telephone where visuals are impossible to use).

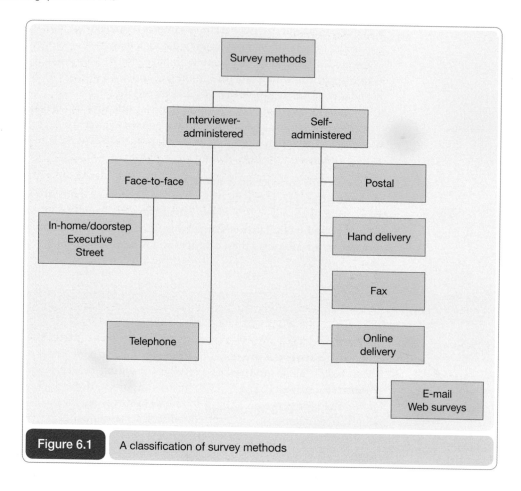

| Figure 6.1 | A classification of survey methods |

To be balanced against this are the drawbacks of personal interviewing:

- It is generally seen as being a more costly and time-consuming approach.
- Interviews need to be clustered within specific geographical areas (e.g. cities, town centres, etc.) if interviewers are to be used efficiently. People in more remote locations are less likely to be interviewed.
- The training and briefing of interviewers can be more difficult as a result of their geographical dispersal.
- Quality control is more difficult as supervisors have to travel around a dispersed set of interviewers to ensure that proper interviewing standards are being met.
- It is more difficult to motivate interviewers than is the case in a centralised call centre.

Interviewer bias can also be more prevalent in personal interviewing and can take various forms. It can bias who is interviewed, with interviewers choosing houses or respondents that they feel more comfortable about approaching. It can also happen as a result of the way the interviewer asks a question and also the manner in which the interviewer responds facially and verbally to an answer. Finally, it can happen as a result of the manner in which the interviewer records the answer. All of these elements of bias are more difficult to monitor when an interviewer is in somebody's house/office or is in the street, in comparison with being in a centralised telephone call centre.

In-home/doorstep interviewing
Face-to-face interviews undertaken within the home of the respondent or on the doorstep of their home.

In-home/doorstep interviewing

In-home/doorstep interviewing undertaken at the respondent's place of residences, either within the house or more often on the doorstep of the house, was the traditional form of interviewing undertaken in consumer markets. Questions about grocery products, soap powders and the like were regularly asked of housewives by interviewers with clipboards. In many developed countries, this form of interviewing has declined significantly as the increase in the number of working women has resulted in fewer women being at home during the day when interviewers call. This makes interviewing more time consuming, particularly as many interviewers are unwilling to go around knocking on doors outside daylight hours. The increased time it takes to get the interviews and the larger number of houses requiring to be visited has resulted in these home-based interviews becoming significantly more expensive than street or telephone-based interviews. However, they are still used where the type of house or neighbourhood is critical to the research design. In developing countries, they may be the only way of getting to respondents, particularly where telephone ownership is low. They also have the advantage of being able to put the respondents at their ease in a familiar environment as well as enabling the interviewer to use visual material (e.g. pictures or lists of names) to speed up the interview and improve data quality.

> ### Researcher quote
>
> It is becoming more and more difficult to get the desired sample from doorstep interviews as there are some inner-city areas where interviewers are unwilling to go after 5 p.m. and there are also a growing number of people (particularly the elderly) who are unwilling to open their doors to strangers.

Executive interviewing

Executive interviewing
Quantitative research interviews with business people, usually undertaken at their place of work, covering subjects related to industrial or business products and services.

Executive interviewing is the business-to-business version of in-home/doorstep interviewing. This type of survey involves interviewing businesspeople at their place of work about industrial or business products and services. The term 'businesspeople' should be seen in its broadest sense as it may involve interviewing factory managers about lubricants or machinery, office managers about stationery and photocopiers, architects about building materials, shopkeepers about delivery services, doctors about pharmaceuticals, farmers about tractors, and teachers about books.

Interviewing of this type is expensive, because the interviewer needs to be more skilled to remain credible and successfully undertake interviews in these areas where they may have little detailed knowledge or understanding in comparison with doing research on consumer products. It is also more expensive, because the process of interviewing is more complex. First, the individuals responsible for purchasing or specifying the products need to be identified and located. This usually involves phoning organisations and being passed around many departments and individuals until the correct person is found. Sometimes lists can be obtained, but these are not always accurate or up to date. Once the correct person has been identified, it is necessary for the interviewer to get them to agree to be interviewed. If the interviewer can speak to the target respondent directly then this may not be too difficult. However, when he or she is shielded behind secretaries and receptionists, the task can become time consuming and difficult.

> ### Researcher quote
>
> Receptionists come out with: 'he's busy', 'he's in a meeting', 'she doesn't do marketing research', 'she wouldn't have time to see you', 'phone back in a couple of months'. However, when you do eventually manage to get hold of the target you usually find that they are really keen to talk to somebody about topics related to their work.

An appointment must then be made for the interview and the interviewer needs to travel to the respondent's workplace to undertake the research.

Street interviewing

Street interviewing
Interviews where respondents are approached and recruited while they are shopping or walking in town centres. In North America, these are known as *mall intercept interviews*.

Street interviewing, known as *mall intercept interviewing* in North America, involve respondents being approached while they are shopping in town centres. They are then interviewed on the spot or asked to come to a **hall test** (see page 144).

In Europe, unlike North America, most street interviews are undertaken in the open air rather than in shopping malls or centres, as many shopping centre managers view interviewing as an unnecessary nuisance to shoppers. Some shopping centres do allow interviews but charge a fee and must be booked in advance.

Interviewing in the open air can adversely affect the quality of the data obtained. A respondent being interviewed in wet, cold or even very hot weather may not be as attentive to the questions being asked as would someone located in the comfort of their own house or even a shopping mall. Distractions from passers-by, traffic and the general noise of a busy shopping street can make interviewing very difficult. There may also be difficulties in recruiting respondents as shoppers frequently avoid interviewers holding clipboards because they are in a hurry or are preoccupied with their shopping activities. Street interviewing also severely limits the length of the interview as it is unlikely that a respondent will be willing to answer questions for more than ten minutes while standing holding shopping bags in a busy main street.

> **Researcher quote**
>
> There is nothing worse than standing in the rain with your questionnaires watching people crossing the road to avoid you!

Even with these difficulties, street interviews are still very popular as they are significantly less expensive than in-home interviews. Interviewers do not need to spend time visiting houses where no one is at home, as the respondents come to the interviewer rather than the other way around.

Derivatives of street interviews are exit surveys where respondents are interviewed as they exit an exhibition or venue (e.g. a sports centre, a tourist attraction, a theme park) about their attitudes towards the facilities and their experiences within the venue. Major retailers and transport operators also carry out this type of research within their outlets, asking questions about their brand of products or services.

> British Airports Authority, which owns airports in the UK, interviews travellers within its airports about customer satisfaction levels with check-in procedures, retail outlets, car-parking, restaurant and toilet facilities. Questions will relate to the range of facilities, ease of use, speed of service, cleanliness, helpfulness of staff, clarity of signage, etc. Interviews are carried out with travellers as they wait in lounges and as they browse the airport shops.

CAPI
Computer-assisted personal interviewing. Where lap-top computers or pen-pad computers are used rather than paper-based questionnaires for face-to-face interviewing.

Computer-assisted personal interviewing (CAPI)

More and more large marketing research agencies are using **CAPI** (computer-assisted personal interviewing) methods for their personal interviewing rather than paper-based questionnaires.

This either involves using a laptop computer for indoor (in-home or executive) interviewing or a 'penpad' for outdoor use (a touchscreen computer where an 'electronic pen' is used to point at answer boxes and which has the ability to write directly onto the screen for verbatim responses) for outdoor use. Computers of this type allow direct data entry, doing away with the need for the collection of paper-based questionnaires from all of the interviewers and the laborious task associated with transferring the information from the questionnaires to a computer. The computer also routes the interviewer through the questionnaire, showing one question at a time in response to the answers given to previous questions. This results in interviews that flow more smoothly as interviewers no longer have to shuffle through the questionnaire to find the next appropriate question. The computer also edits the input for incorrect and incompatible replies; instructions are then given to the interviewer to reduce any inconsistencies. At the end of a day's interviewing, the data can be downloaded to the researcher's central computer, allowing for immediate analysis.

Telephone interviewing

Telephone interviewing
Quantitative research where the interviewing is undertaken over the telephone.

Telephone interviewing is used for business-to-business and consumer-type research. The majority of the interviews are undertaken from a centralised call centre location, although a small number involve interviewers using their own home-based telephones. The main benefit of the centralised location is control. The interviewers can be briefed and trained in one location. Their calls can be monitored using unobtrusive monitoring equipment that allows supervisors to listen in on interviews and correct or replace interviewers who are interviewing incorrectly. Quality control checks can be done on the questionnaires immediately after they have been completed. The cost of calls can also be logged accurately. Finally, interviewers need to clock in and out of work, allowing control of the timing of the interviews and ensuring that interviewers work sufficient hours regularly.

Unlike personal interviews, the interviewers do not need to be located near the respondents and the need for interviewer travelling time and expenses is eliminated. Interviews can be undertaken nationally or internationally from one central location, with many of these locations being situated outside major cities where office rental costs and staff costs are much less. Some of the interviewer bias that may exist with personal interviewers is also reduced: first, through the tighter supervision, which ensures that questions are asked correctly and responses are recorded accurately, and second, through the interviewer's selection of respondents being dictated by the names and/or numbers supplied rather than the approachability of different types of respondent. The telephone also has the advantage of reaching people who otherwise may be difficult to reach through any other means, such as businesspeople travelling around or people who live in flats with entry-phones.

The other major benefit of telephone interviews is speed. Interviewers can be briefed and be conducting interviews within hours of the questionnaire being developed. It would take much longer to brief a team of personal interviewers. This speed can mean that interviewing can be timed to happen immediately after a specific event. For example, an advertisement or an electioneering party political broadcast may appear on television at 7 p.m., and interviewers can then be phoning viewers to seek their attitudes towards the broadcast by 7.05 p.m.

The telephone survey does have some inherent disadvantages. The biggest relates to respondent attitudes towards the telephone. Over the past 15 years there has been a major growth of telephone usage for telemarketing purposes throughout Europe. Home improvement companies, financial service organisations, catalogue marketers and even charities use the telephone to generate sales/funds, either directly or by arranging for a sales representative to visit prospective purchasers. Many are persistent and relatively aggressive callers, and in certain situations some disguise their approach as being marketing research. This activity is called 'sugging' (selling under the guise of research) by the marketing research industry. As a result, many members of the public are confused about the difference between marketing research, where the confidentiality of the respondent is maintained, and telemarketing, where names and data will be used for selling purposes, either directly or by selling the information onto other companies. Refusal rates are therefore increasing, and consumer concerns in certain countries have led to legislative controls on unsolicited calls for telemarketing or telephone research (e.g. in Germany and parts of the USA). Consumers are also using equipment such as answering machines to screen their calls before answering them. The Market Research Society in the UK provides a freephone service for respondents to phone in order to check that the research is bona fide. However, this is only of benefit to those who are willing to spend time checking on the credentials of the agency and the research; many respondents will take the easier option of simply refusing to take part.

Researcher quote

You get home improvement companies who phone up saying they are doing marketing research. They usually only ask one question about whether the respondent has double glazing. If the respondent says no, they proceed immediately into a sales pitch. They make telephone surveys so difficult for the rest of us!

Although some telephone interviews can last 25–30 minutes, they are normally much shorter and certainly shorter than face-to-face interviews. Respondents lose interest more quickly when they only have their sense of hearing stimulated (no visual or tactile cues to occupy the other senses) and it is easy for them to hang up the phone when they become bored. Certain types of question such as complex ranking questions or questions with a large number of multiple-choice responses are also more difficult to undertake over the phone.

Integration — An international perspective

In international telephone surveys there may be specific problems in undertaking interviews. One of these relates to low levels of telephone ownership, particularly in many of the developing countries in Africa and Asia. This can result in telephone samples in these countries being biased towards particular types of consumer (especially in the professional classes). Even in developed countries there may be problems relating to the coverage of telephone networks owing to the growth of the use of mobile phones and people choosing to rely solely on mobile rather than landline networks (e.g. students, people on low incomes, professional-type people, countries with poor public networks). Even if respondents can be accessed through the telephone network, different cultures will react differently towards a telephone survey. For example Mediterranean and Arabic peoples are reluctant to divulge personal details over the telephone, whereas North Americans and northern Europeans are more open towards providing information over the telephone.

Computer-assisted telephone interviewing (CATI)

In the mid- to late-1980s telephone research agencies were starting to provide interviewers with a computer so that they used a paper-based questionnaire to ask questions but typed the responses directly into the computer. This was superseded by computer software, which put the questions on the monitor, allowing the interviewer to enter the response for each question, with the computer automatically routing the interview to the next appropriate question. For example, a 'Yes' answer to one question may lead to a further set of questions, whereas a 'No' answer should be routed onto the next topic area.

CATI also allows for customisation of questionnaires. For example, at the start of an interview, we might ask respondents their name and the age of their children. Later in the interview, questions might be asked about each child. This may appear on the screen as follows: 'Mr Wilson, regarding your 10-year-old son, what breakfast cereal does he eat?' Other questions about this child and other children would appear in similar fashion. In international research, questionnaires can be switched to different languages. Many CATI systems also allow for the direct recording of verbatim comments given to open-ended questions.

Such systems also eliminate inconsistencies in responses. For example, if a respondent states that he does not drive but later answers that he has a car, the computer would ask the interviewer to clarify this.

In terms of managing the interviewing process, today's CATI systems are frequently linked to the telephone dialling process so that as soon as one interview is finished, the computer is dialling the next number. Such dialling can also be set up so that it predicts (predictive dialling) when an interview is likely to finish and starts dialling before the previous questionnaire is fully completed. ISDN technology allows the equipment to detect busy signals and no answers, immediately dialling other respondents to minimise interviewer waiting time.

In the USA a number of organisations are experimenting with completely automated telephone interviews (CATS) which use interactive voice technology. Instead of a human interviewer, questions are asked by the recorded voice of an interviewer with respondents answering the closed-ended questions using their touch-tone phone. It is proving to be more successful with in-bound calls where respondents are recruited through a mail shot and are then asked to phone a freephone number to complete the survey. Such an approach can be useful for basic customer satisfaction research and limited research linked to specific loyalty programmes, warranty registration, etc.

CATI
Computer-assisted telephone interviewing. CATI involves telephone interviewers typing respondent's answers directly into a computer-based questionnaire rather than writing them on a paper-based questionnaire.

Self-administered surveys

Self-administered surveys
Surveys where the respondent completes the questionnaire with no help from an interviewer. The questionnaire can be delivered to the respondent via the mail (postal surveys), by hand, by fax or online (e-mail, web surveys).

Self-administered surveys differ from the above methods, in that no interviewer, either live or recorded, is involved. Although this means that there is no interviewer available to bias or influence the data gathered from the respondent, it also means that there is no interviewer available to clarify questions or responses. The survey form or questionnaire must be able to clearly communicate the questions being posed and provide a straightforward approach to respond. It must also be able to motivate the respondent to complete all of the questions. The design of self-administered questionnaires is discussed in Chapter 7. Their delivery can be accomplished via the mail (postal surveys), by hand, by fax or online (e-mail, online surveys) or using SMS.

Postal surveys

Postal surveys
Self-administered surveys that are mailed to pre-selected respondents along with a return envelope, a covering letter and possibly an incentive.

In **postal surveys**, questionnaires are mailed to pre-selected respondents along with a return envelope, a covering letter and possibly an incentive. The respondents complete and return the questionnaire. Although postal surveys have been around for many years, their importance has grown as a result of the prevalence of customer databases and customer satisfaction measurement.

Postal surveys are superficially attractive on account of their cost relative to other methods using interviewers, but this has to be balanced against the low response rates associated with postal surveys. Response rates associated with postal surveys are variable and depend on the respondents' level of interest in the subject, the relationship between the respondent and the researching firm, the accuracy of the mailing list and the incentive offered. Typical response rates for well-executed surveys are around 40–50 per cent (i.e. for every 1,000 questionnaires, only 400–500 completed questionnaires are returned). However, it is not uncommon for some surveys to receive less than a 20 per cent response rate.

> ### Researcher quote
>
> In designing a good postal survey, you have to look at the survey from the respondent's point of view. Why will they bother replying?

Response rates may be improved by addressing the following:

- **Accuracy of the mailing list:** the accuracy of the mailing list and the extent to which it can be segmented into the most relevant targeted groups is critical to the success of postal surveys. The source of the list is therefore important: lists that relate to customers who are regularly interacting with an organisation are likely to be more accurate and detailed than lists relating to customers who have only made a one-off purchase or lists that have been purchased from an external list-broker.
- **Pre-contact:** prior contact with the research organisation, where respondents have taken part in previous research and have agreed to being recontacted, usually results in a higher response rate. There is also some evidence to suggest that pre-notification of the survey by telephoning, e-mailing or writing to potential respondents also improves the response rate.
- **Part of an existing relationship:** postal surveys are also more likely to be effective when there is some form of relationship between the researcher and the respondent (e.g. between companies and their customers, account holders, subscribers or loyalty card members). Relationships such as these are likely to mean that the respondent is more interested in the subject and has at least a perception that taking part in the survey will improve the relationship or service received in the future.
- **The covering letter:** The letter which accompanies the questionnaire needs to sell the benefits of the survey to potential respondents and should encourage them to respond. Generally, the letter should be personalised and should help to reassure recipients that the research is genuine and will follow research industry guidelines. The Market Research Society in the UK has a symbol which can be put on the letter. In addition, the letter should cover the following:
  - the purpose of the research;
  - reasons why people should respond;
  - the ease of completion and the short time needed to complete;
  - an assurance of confidentiality;
  - the manner in which recipients were selected;
  - a contact number for more information;
  - the time scale for return and the manner in which it should be returned;
  - a thank-you.

  The envelope in which the covering letter and questionnaire is despatched should also look distinct from a typical direct mail envelope. An official-looking envelope is likely to be taken more seriously. There are conflicting views about whether the return envelope should have a stamp or a pre-paid format. Respondents may feel obliged to return an envelope with a stamp; however, this should be balanced against the increased cost of putting postage stamps on every envelope, as the use of the pre-paid format only involves paying the postage for envelopes that are actually returned.
- **Incentives:** incentives such as an entry into a prize draw can be effective in increasing response rates; they may also speed up the response if a closing date is given. Other incentives such as discount vouchers can also be used. The impact of sending pens and pencils

with the questionnaire has dropped as a result of many charities sending these items with their fundraising mail shots.

- **Reminders:** sending out reminders around ten days after the questionnaire is posted out is quite effective, and telephone calls can also be used as a second or final follow-up. This raises the cost of the survey. It may also mean that questionnaires will need to be numbered so that the researcher can recognise who has and has not responded. This may lead to fears of loss of anonymity on the part of the respondent – the covering letter may need to reassure respondents about the purpose of any such numbers or identification marks.
- **Questionnaire design:** questionnaire design also has an important influence on response rates. This is discussed further in Chapter 7.

Advantages and disadvantages of postal surveys

Advantages

- **National and international coverage:** can be sent to a geographically dispersed sample.
- **Low cost:** for each completed questionnaire from a geographically dispersed sample, postal surveys are likely to be around one-third of the cost of a typical telephone survey and less than a ninth of the cost of a typical face-to-face interview.
- **No interviewer bias.**
- **Respondent convenience:** the respondents can complete the questionnaire at their own speed when they want. They can confer with other members of their household or refer to files, documents, etc.
- **Piggybacking:** the questionnaire can piggyback on the back of other correspondence such as bank statements, warranty registrations and newsletters, reducing the cost further.

Disadvantages

- **Low response rate.**
- **Biased response:** those who respond may not be representative of the population. It may be that only those who have strong opinions or have links with the organisation being researched take the time and effort to complete the questionnaire.
- **Lack of control of questioning:** it is difficult to control the manner in which the questionnaire is completed. As a result sections may be left blank.
- **Lack of control of respondent:** it is difficult to ensure that the named recipient answers the questions. It is not unknown for managers to get their secretaries or parents to get their children to complete the questionnaires.
- **Limited open-ended questions:** it is difficult to get respondents to write down full answers to open-ended, verbatim-type questions. Therefore, most questions should simply involve ticking boxes, and open-ended questions should be limited to a very small proportion of the total.
- **Pre-reading of questionnaire:** care must be taken in designing the questionnaire as the respondent can read the whole questionnaire in advance of completing it. This has implications for awareness and attitude type questions.
- **Response time:** from time of despatch, it can take two to three weeks until all completed questionnaires are returned. There may even be the odd questionnaire drifting in up to ten weeks after the survey was despatched. Postal or telephone reminders may be needed to get respondents to return questionnaires.

Hand delivery of survey

Self-administered questionnaires may be handed to potential respondents or left for their collection rather than posted. Where the audience is captive such as in an aeroplane, in a hotel, in a car hire office or in a restaurant, this approach is inexpensive and can produce a high response rate. In an aeroplane the cabin crew hand out the questionnaire to passengers in selected seats during a flight and collect them before the plane lands. In hotels, questionnaires about service delivery are traditionally left in the bedrooms for guests to complete. However, research has shown that response rates tend to be higher when the questionnaire is personally handed to guests by reception staff. Some restaurants also have a brief questionnaire on the back of their bills. If staff rewards are tied in with the responses to these questionnaires, care must be taken to ensure that real customers rather than staff are completing them – it is not unknown for staff to pretend they are customers to improve their own situation.

> ## Researcher quote
>
> If you leave a questionnaire in a hotel room to be completed, the average person won't fill it in. You need to hand it to guests or you will only hear feedback from those who are very dissatisfied or very satisfied.

Kiosk-based surveys
Surveys often undertaken at an exhibition or trade show using touch-screen computers to collect information from respondents. Such computers can be programmed to deliver complex surveys supported by full-colour visuals as well as sound and video clips. They can be much cheaper to administer in comparison with the traditional exit survey undertaken by human interviewers.

Kiosk-based surveys

Kiosk-based surveys can be undertaken at exhibitions and trade shows using touch-screen computers to collect information from respondents. At the 2005 British Open Golf Championships, spectators were invited to use freestanding computer terminals to report on their satisfaction with the event and their requirements from future tournaments. Such computer terminals can be programmed to deliver complex surveys supported by full colour visuals as well as sound and video clips. They can be much cheaper to administer in comparison with the traditional exit survey undertaken by human interviewers.

Fax surveys

E-mail surveys
Self-completion surveys that are delivered to pre-selected respondents by e-mail. The questionnaire can take the form of text within the e-mail or can be sent as an attachment (either as a word-process document or as a piece of software which runs the questionnaire).

There are now very few surveys delivered by fax as they have almost all been replaced by online surveys or surveys sent out attached to e-mails. In their day, fax surveys were only appropriate for business or professional respondents. They were only effective when potential respondents were pre-warned by telephone or e-mail and their agreement was sought prior to sending. However, the quality of the presentation of the questionnaire varied dramatically depending on the quality of the potential respondent's fax machine. Missing pages and questions appearing on a curled up thermal paper roll were not user friendly and resulted in relatively poor response rates.

Online surveys

Online surveys
Self-completion questionnaires which are delivered via the Internet. They may appear on the computer screen as a standard questionnaire where the respondent scrolls down the page completing each question. Alternatively, they can take the form of an interactive questionnaire with questions appearing on the screen one at a time.

The two main online methods available to researchers are **e-mail surveys** and **online surveys**. They can both deliver a questionnaire to potential respondents through desk-based PCs but also through portables, digital television and Web-enabled mobile phones. E-mail surveys are similar in many ways to postal surveys with the exception that they are delivered electronically. Online surveys on the other hand are the equivalent of taking a postal survey and turning it into a computer-assisted research tool.

E-mail surveys

There are two main types of e-mail survey: those where the questionnaire appears as text within the e-mail and those where the questionnaire is sent as an attachment (either as a word-processed document or as a piece of software which runs the questionnaire).

Where the questionnaire appears in the text with tick boxes and spaces for responses, the respondent simply scrolls down the e-mail entering text or checking boxes and then sends the questionnaire back to the researcher by using the 'reply' facility. If the questionnaire is produced by one of the many specialised Windows-based software tools that are available, then the system will automatically collate the data and produce tables and graphs. The questionnaire will also look like a traditional self-completion survey. However, if it is produced on standard e-mail software, the questionnaire will look far less professional and the researcher will need to transfer responses to a data processing package manually.

If attachments are used, these can simply be word-processed documents that the potential respondent can open with their own software, enter responses and return. Care must be taken to ensure that the document is compatible with the various versions of software that potential respondents are likely to have. Alternatively, executable e-mail questionnaires are questionnaire programs sent as a file attachment. Once received, the respondent clicks on the attachment, the first question appears on the screen and the program routes the respondent through a series of questions depending on the answers given. The attachment is then e-mailed back on completion. This has the advantage that a more complex questionnaire can be used than is the case with the other e-mail approaches. However, its complexity also means that the file size of the attachment can be quite large and can cause problems when sending by e-mail. As a result, this type of approach is more commonly used for staff surveys within organisations using the company's intranet network.

Whichever e-mail method is used, the research will tend to be cheaper and faster to implement than is the case for postal surveys. Respondents may also give more detailed responses to open-ended questions than with postal surveys as they have a keyboard in front of them and are used to producing short, structured responses using the e-mail medium. Against this there are the difficulties in developing a representative sample when using e-mail as, first, there is no comprehensive list of e-mail addresses and second, there are still large segments of the population who do not have access to the Internet and do not have an e-mail address.

The amount of spam (unsolicited 'junk' e-mails) being sent to computer users is growing, which may make it difficult for e-mail surveys. The sending out of unsolicited surveys should therefore be avoided and a prenotification should be sent first, inviting respondents to take part. Researchers should also be aware that respondents may be concerned about confidentiality as the returned questionnaire is likely to have the respondent's e-mail address attached. It is important that the researcher emphasises that the confidentiality of the respondent will be protected.

Online surveys

Online surveys take a number of forms, but the most common are the standard questionnaire format and the interactive questionnaire. The standard questionnaire format has the questionnaire appearing on the page as it would on paper. The respondent scrolls down the page, completing each question. In general, this has been superceded by the interactive online questionnaire which is similar to those used in CAPI and CATI systems, with questions appearing on the screen one at a time. The respondent submits their answer and then the computer shows a new question dependent upon the answer to the previous questions. The fact that the interactive questionnaires download questions one at a time means that the respondents' answers will not be influenced by their seeing the full set of questions; however, this may be extremely annoying for users with slow modems as they wait for each question to download. Respondents also have to complete all questions correctly before they are allowed to proceed and their answers are submitted, which can infuriate respondents who do not want to answer a particular question or have an answer that does not match those on a predefined list.

Online surveys are growing in importance as the number of Internet and, particularly, broadband users increase. The fact that respondents are all Internet users may mean that they are not typical of all consumers groups; however, this may not matter for research aimed at specific target groups such as technology users, Internet shoppers, young people or companies. Potential respondents can be invited to take part through e-mails or by a link through a company's website or intranet site. When they appear on a website, they are often called 'pop-up' surveys, as they typically appear in a new browser window that appears to pop out of the screen. They are often used as a way of sampling website users to determine profiles and/or satisfaction. Once again, this may mean that the sample is particularly biased towards e-mail users and those with an interest in the specific company and web pages. Pop-up surveys have also had difficulties as a result of the widespread adoption of pop-up blocking software being installed by users to block pop-up advertising (although technical solutions do exist to get around this issue). To overcome this, many online surveys invite potential respondents through a web-link sent out in an e-mail or appearing on a social media site. In such cases, the e-mail or social media site will set out the rationale and objectives of the research as well as providing assurances regarding confidentiality and ethics before inviting potential respondents to proceed via the highlighted web-link to the survey.

Overall, online surveys have the following advantages;

- **Reduced costs** – Using the Internet rather than telephone interviews can cut costs dramatically as there are no personnel involved in administering the questionnaires and there are no call charges. The costs are even likely to be less than for a postal survey where there are photocopying and postage costs.
- **Fast delivery** – There are a growing number of online survey software packages and survey hosting sites that make the design and analysis of online surveys very straightforward. Therefore, online surveys can be designed, despatched to thousands of potential respondents and analysed very quickly. Clients can also frequently view the interim results as they arrive.
- **Easily personalised** – Similar to CATI and CAPI surveys, online surveys can be personalised with only the most relevant questions being asked of each respondent. In addition, respondents can pause and resume the survey at their convenience. To ensure that respondents do not complete the survey more than once, unique passwords are provided to potential respondents when they are invited to participate. These passwords permit only one set of questions to be completed.
- **Penetrating different target groups** – Online surveys can access business people and wealthy individuals who may be difficult to reach through the telephone, post or face to face. By locating an online survey on their website, an organisation can potentially reach a wide and varied audience if their site has a large number of visitors. Organisations also frequently use their in-house intranet to undertake staff surveys or surveys with distributors or sub-contractors.
- **Can include images and video** – Online surveys can include a variety of multi-media components including images, audio and video clips. This can make the survey more interesting for respondents and can be used to test reactions to advertisements or view the products that they are being asked about.

There are two main ways of developing and conducting online surveys:

1 Online survey software: Software packages such SNAP (included with this book) and SPSS (**www.spss.com**) can produce online surveys in the same manner that they produce paper and computer-assisted questionnaires. These are then put on an organisation's web server which is linked to a database that receives and stores the responses. The database can be analysed by the software packages in the normal manner. There are also a number of specialised software packages (such as surveypro(**www.apian.com**) or confirmit(**www.confirmit.com**)) that are specifically designed for online questionnaire production and delivery. They consist of a questionnaire design tool, web server, database and data delivery program.

2 Survey design and web-hosting sites. There are a number of websites (for example: **www. surveymonkey.com**, **www.zoomerang.com** or **www.qualtrics.com**) that allow researchers to design an online survey without loading any design software. The survey is administered on the web-hosting site's server, and tabulations and data files are made available to the researcher. The sophistication of the questionnaires and the analysis will vary depending on the fees charged by the site. However, some of the sites offer very basic questionnaires and their analysis for free.

> ### Researcher quote
>
> In the future, online surveys will replace a significant number of postal surveys.

Mobile phone surveys

With the growth in mobile phones and particularly smart phones, such as Apple's iPhone and Google's Nexus, it is hardly surprising that attempts have been made to harness these devices for marketing research purposes. However, uptake of mobile surveys using SMS messaging has tended to be relatively limited as the costs are generally greater than for online surveys and the limit on the size of text messages make them relatively inflexible. They can. however, be useful for getting immediate responses to an event or service. For example, a hotel guest could be sent a text immediately after leaving the hotel, asking them about customer satisfaction and attitude ratings for service delivery. Similarly, a passenger on a train could be sent a series of short questions about the train service in real time as the journey progresses. However, the number of questions is limited to probably no more than 3–5 and each question has to be very short and simple. It is also likely that the growth in smart phones with Internet capabilities will mean that more online surveys will be completed on mobiles at the expense of any growth in SMS-based surveys. There are also apps appearing for Apple iPhones and iPads that enable survey data to be collected through Internet connections.

Omnibus surveys

Omnibus surveys
A data-collection approach that is undertaken at regular intervals for a changing group of clients who share the costs involved in the survey's set-up, sampling and interviewing.

Omnibus research is a data-collection approach that is undertaken at regular intervals for a changing group of clients who share the costs involved in the survey's set-up, sampling and interviewing. Basically, **omnibus surveys** consist of series of short question sets, with each set belonging to a different client. For a fee, each client purchases space on the survey's questionnaire, either on a one-off basis or regularly each time the survey operates. A number of research agencies in the UK and across Europe undertake omnibus surveys with a particular type of respondent on a regular timetabled basis. Some of the best-known omnibus surveys include:

- **TNS Face-to-Face Omnibus**, operated by TNS,[2] interviews up to 4,000 different adults aged 16+ twice per week. The sample is selected to be nationally representative, and is interviewed face-to-face in the respondents' own homes using CAPI multi-media pen technology. Tabulate results available within two days of fieldwork.
- **CAPIBUS**, operated by Ipsos MORI,[3] uses CAPI in a weekly omnibus survey covering a high-quality sample of 2,000 adults aged 15+ each week of the year in the UK (and 1,000 in France, Germany, Spain and Italy), with results available in just ten days.
- **Telebus**, operated by GfK NOP,[4] undertakes a computer-assisted telephone interview omnibus of 1,000 UK adults each week. If clients deliver the questions to the agency by Friday, the results are returned to the client on Monday.

There are also specialist omnibus surveys, such as **Motorbus** (GfK NOP), which interviews 500 motorists each weekend, and the **Business Omnibus** (BDRC Continental Research), which interviews managers in 500 businesses bi-monthly.

These are just a few of the many omnibus surveys that are available; they enable companies to get fast results to a small number of questions from a relatively large sample at a relatively low cost. The charges for inclusion in a survey normally consist of a joining fee, a cost per individual question, a cost per coded answer and a charge for any special analysis required. For a small number of questions, these charges will be significantly cheaper than undertaking an ad hoc survey to reach the same size of sample. This is unlikely to be so where the number of questions is large and the type of questions is complex.

In addition to using omnibus surveys to obtain a 'snapshot' of awareness, attitudes or behaviour, a client can subscribe to a survey on a regular basis, enabling these attributes to be tracked over time. This is particularly useful for monitoring the effectiveness of promotional activities such as advertising or sponsorship.

There are two drawbacks to omnibus surveys. The first of these is inflexibility – a client cannot change the nature of the sample being interviewed as this would adversely affect other clients who are using the survey as a tracking study. There is also inflexibility in the type and number of questions that any client can ask within a particular wave of the survey. Questions have to be relatively straightforward with no one subject or product area being allowed to dominate the questionnaire. Clients also tend to be concerned about the position in which their questions appear in the questionnaire. They have two basic fears: (1) that other questions will bias the answers to their own questions and (2) that the respondent will lose interest nearer the end of the questionnaire. Many would like to have their questions appear at the beginning of the questionnaire, but this would be impossible to do for all clients, so similar sets of questions tend to be grouped together (e.g. questions about grocery products, then questions about financial services, then holidays and travel, etc.).

There are many omnibus surveys available; clients need to select carefully, taking account of the following considerations:

- population covered;
- method of data collection;
- frequency of fieldwork;
- reputation of supplier for quality research;
- pricing;
- speed of reporting;
- sample composition and size.

Hall tests

Hall tests
Research undertaken in a central hall or venue commonly used to test respondents' initial reactions to a product, package or concept. Respondents are recruited into the hall by interviewers stationed on main pedestrian thoroughfares nearby.

Hall tests are so called because they involve hiring a hall, hotel room or other venue in a central location, usually next to a shopping area. Respondents are recruited into the hall by interviewers stationed on the main pedestrian thoroughfares nearby. They are screened in the street to ascertain their suitability relative to the sample required (usually a quota sample) before being taken or directed to the hall. In the hall, researchers test respondent's initial reactions to a product or package or concept. They may be asked to taste a new drink, smell a new perfume, look at a new design for a car, or open and close a new form of packaging for milk. The emphasis is very much on people's initial reactions to these aspects as they will only be in the hall for a very short period of time (10–20 minutes). Hall tests are not very appropriate for evaluating the longer-term usage of a product. For example, a hall test may show people's initial reactions to the look of a new vacuum cleaner, but attitudes towards the cleaning ability of the cleaner could only be gauged by testing in people's homes (placement tests).

However, many products, such as groceries, are selected in retail stores on the basis of first impressions; analysing these impressions is therefore very important to marketers.

In planning hall tests there is a need for care and common sense. For example, the type of venue and the time of day may adversely influence the test. Undertaking a taste test for alcohol in a church hall or very early in the morning may provide very different results than if the test was undertaken in the evening in the function room of a hotel or bar.

Products can be tested on their own (a monadic test) but are more frequently tested against one or two other products (a multiple test). Some packaging tests may include all the competitors' products within a given range. Having tasted, smelt, touched or looked at the product, respondents will be interviewed by an interviewer using a structured or semi-structured questionnaire. Such research is normally quantitative, although some studies may require a qualitative dimension to be added. To satisfy this, depth interviews may be undertaken with a subsample of respondents who complete the main questionnaire.

In terms of scale, it is usual to carry out hall tests in a number of locations to overcome regional bias, with samples of around 100–400 people being interviewed in a typical project. The throughput at each venue will depend on the number of interviewers, the complexity of the quota of respondents being sought and the number of people shopping, but a target of between 50 and 100 respondents per day per hall is not uncommon. Clients can often attend the hall to observe respondents' reactions and obtain a feel for the likely results.

Placement tests

Placement testing
The testing of reactions to products in the home and where they are to be used. Respondents are given a new product to test in their own home or in their office. Information about their experiences with and attitudes towards the products are then collected either by a questionnaire or by a self-completion diary.

Not all products are appropriate for testing in halls. Products that need to be tested over a period of time, such as vacuum cleaners, cars, photocopiers and anti-dandruff shampoos, are better tested where they are used: that is, in the home, in the office or on the road. Home testing is also appropriate where products need to be prepared by the consumer, such as a cake mix, or where the whole family is involved with the product (e.g. a new type of tomato sauce). Testing of products in the home and where they are to be used is called **placement testing**.

In placement testing, respondents who match the target population are recruited, often from omnibus surveys or street interviews. They are then given a new product to test in their own home or in their office. Information about their experiences with and attitudes towards the products are then collected by either a questionnaire (self-completion or interviewer administered) or by a self-completion diary. The diary involves completing information on specific question areas about the product on a daily or weekly basis. The information is then sent back to the researcher by post or by electronic means.

Products may be tested in this way for anything from three weeks for a new electrical product to 6–12 months for a new car or office equipment. Ford gets a sample of organisations that have company car fleets to test new models for periods of up to 12 months before launching a new car in the market place. There is a risk that competitors will see the product during the test, but that may be less of a problem than launching a product that does not meet customer needs.

Researcher quote

It is amazing what you find out when real people in their own homes test a product rather than it being tested by R&D people in a lab.

Placement tests can be expensive to organise and undertake, as sufficient numbers of products in their finished format need to be produced for testing. More respondents may also need to be recruited than are actually required, since people may drop out of the exercise before the test is complete, either because they do not like the product or because they lose interest in filling out the diary.

Simulated test markets

Simulated test markets
A research approach used to predict the potential results of a product launch and to experiment with changes to different elements of a product's marketing mix. Rather than testing in retail stores, simulated test markets rely on simulated or laboratory-type testing and mathematical modelling.

Simulated test markets or store tests were traditionally used to assist marketers in predicting the potential results of a product launch and to experiment with changes to different elements of a product's marketing mix. Using different commercial television transmission areas, it was possible to compare a control area where the product offering remained unchanged against an area where a new product, a new promotional campaign or a new pricing policy was introduced. Products would appear on retail shelves beside competing products and the consumers would be unaware that a test was being undertaken. The thinking behind such a test was that national sales could be extrapolated from a test area that was representative (in miniature) of the national market and where the marketing activities could be undertaken without interference or contamination from external variables. The television transmission areas were important because the advertising seen in a local area could be controlled and changed. This is more difficult with the advent of satellite and cable television, where the population may be watching multiple national and international channels. This change, along with the following difficulties associated with attempting to control the many variables in a test area, has resulted in the virtual disappearance of traditional area and store testing in favour of simulated test marketing:

- **Isolation:** increasing difficulty in isolating an area with overlapping television regions, newspaper circulation areas, satellite and cable TV advertising, as well as the growth in national retailers and people commuting longer distances to work and shop.
- **Timing:** to be accurate, test markets may need to run for periods of up to six months. It is becoming more difficult to control variables for that length of time with rapid changes occurring in market conditions and competitor activity. Test markets of this length also enable competitors to prepare their own plans to tackle the new product.
- **Competitor spoiling:** it is not uncommon for competitors to spoil a test market by flooding an area with their own products or promotions. In certain circumstances, they may buy up the new products to give a false impression of their success.
- **Area selection:** it is often difficult to identify areas that truly reflect the demographic make-up of a nation.
- **Cost:** running a test market with associated advertising and finished products can be a very expensive activity.

As traditional test markets have declined, there has been a corresponding increase in the use of simulated test markets. Simulated test markets rely on simulated or laboratory-type testing and mathematical modelling. A typical simulated test market involves the following steps:

1 Recruiting participants using street, doorstep or telephone interviews. Participants would be screened to ensure that they were members of the target population (for example, in a programme of research prior to the launch of the round tea bag, Lyons Tetley sought participants who were heavy tea drinkers; see page 204).
2 Those who qualify are exposed to the product concept or prototype and in many cases the packaging, promotion and advertising for the new product. This is frequently done at the same time as the participants are exposed to competing products and advertising.
3 Participants are then given an opportunity to buy a product from the product range under investigation (i.e. the new product and competing products) from the researcher or interviewer. Frequently this is done using a catalogue of the products with respondents being given freedom of choice.

4 If the product is one that is consumed and repurchased (e.g. a food or soap powder), respondents would be asked to buy only this type of product from the researcher. Researchers would then visit each week over a period of time and the respondents would be asked to repurchase from the catalogue of products available. Customers would use their own money when purchasing. Questionnaires may also be used to examine participants' experience of using their chosen product and the reasons for purchasing it.

5 The trial and repeat purchase information developed from these activities would be used as the input to a computerised simulation program that is used to project share or volume for the product if it were distributed on a national basis.

Undertaking tests on this basis is quicker and requires no complex negotiations with local retailers and media suppliers. Competitors are also less likely to adversely impact on a test and are less likely to know that a test is being conducted. On the negative side, participants may still be influenced by the national media and advertising that they are exposed to. Some participants may also alter their behaviour as a result of being part of the test (e.g. they do not buy the cheapest product as they normally do but instead buy products in order to impress the researcher with their expensive or cosmopolitan taste). However, having said this, most simulated test markets are seen as being as accurate if not more accurate than the traditional store testing.

Panels

A panel (sometimes known as a *longitudinal survey*) is a form of survey from which comparative data is collected from the sampling units on more than one occasion. Panels can consist of individuals, households or organisations, and can provide dynamic information on:

- broad trends in a market (e.g. are people moving from buying white bread to brown bread? Which television programmes are more or less popular than previously?);
- case histories of specific respondents (e.g. level of repeat purchases, brand switching, reaction to special offers and advertising);
- attitudes and reactions over time to particular products or services (a placement test is a type of panel where people's reaction to a new type of vacuum cleaner or car can be measured over time);
- Voting intentions in relation to national and local government elections using online panels (see: **www.yougov.com**).

Information may be gathered by questionnaire, telephone interviews, diaries (documents where the respondent records their behaviour and purchases over a period such as a week or a month), barcode readers or through the Internet. The best-known examples of **panel research** are the consumer purchase panels monitoring individual or household buyer behaviour in the areas of grocery, food and drink, and toiletries. However, the retail audits described in Chapter 4 are produced from panels of retailers.

Although panel research design is similar to that of any quantitative survey design in terms of sampling, data collection and data analysis, it is different in that it has to be designed for long-term consistency. Purchasers of trend data from panel research need data series (possibly stretching back over many years) that are reliable and that have not been affected by methodological problems or changes. Ongoing control is therefore critical in panel research. Such control is particularly important with regard to the recruitment and maintenance of panel members. The key tasks involved are:

- **Recruitment of a representative sample of the population that is willing and capable of doing the task:** panels require more of a commitment from their members than is the case with one-off surveys. Ease of recruitment will vary depending on the perceptions of

Panel research
A research approach where comparative data is collected from the same respondents on more than one occasion. Panels can consist of individuals, households or organisations, and can provide information on changes in behaviour, awareness and attitudes over time.

potential respondents towards the commitment required in terms of both time and effort, balanced against their perception of the value of the research and any specific incentives or rewards offered. For example, a computer expert may require little reward and be quite willing to regularly spend time filling in a questionnaire on new software and technology, whereas a busy household may require significant prizes or payments to regularly report on their grocery shopping. Recruitment also requires panel member training as the success of the research is dependent on the skill of the panellists in completing the task (e.g. noting purchases made, using a barcode scanner on their purchases or completing a diary).

- **Maintaining the members of the panel once recruited:** the goal is to hold onto as many panel members as possible in order to maintain consistency of reporting and also to get the full return from the costs of recruitment and training. Panellists will be offered incentives to undertake their tasks and also to encourage longer panel membership. This usually involves some kind of loyalty reward scheme similar to a loyalty card for a supermarket, where points can be saved for a future purchase or product discount. Newsletters, prize draws, mystery gifts and regular telephone calls are also frequently used to maintain the link between the research agency and the panellist and to sustain their interest in the task.

- **Replacing panel members who leave with similar respondents to maintain consistency:** there will always be some level of turnover of panel members, although hopefully this will be kept to a minimum. People move house, their circumstances change or they lose interest in taking part in the research. Researchers must always have a group of trained-up panellists to replace them. Replacement is on a like-for-like basis, not only in terms of demographic subgroup but also in terms of behavioural characteristics. For larger panels, recruitment of panel members is often an ongoing activity, with recruits being put onto a back-up or substitute panel for a period of time before being brought into the main panel as replacements. Their performance as potential panellists can therefore be monitored before they go live and impact on the 'real' panel data.

- **Quality control:** computer software is frequently used to check on the consistency of data coming from a panel member. Are the panellists undertaking the correct task when they should and are they doing it consistently? Abnormal purchasing patterns or potential errors in data entry can be identified and queried with the panellist.

As refusal rates in other forms of marketing research increase, panels of committed respondents may become more important in the gathering of market information. Panels are obviously advantageous as they provide measurement of change over time. The increased commitment of the panellists can also enhance the quality of the data collected. On the other hand, panel members may not be totally representative of the population as a whole in the fact that they are interested in the topic being investigated and are therefore willing to spend time and effort noting their purchases and behaviour. They may also alter their behaviour because they know that their behaviour is being recorded (e.g. they may buy less chocolate, ready prepared meals, discount items, etc.).

Taylor Nelson Sofres (TNS) Superpanel (www.tnagb.com)

The TNS Superpanel provides purchasing information on British grocery markets and consists of 15,000 households which are demographically and regionally balanced to offer a representative picture of the market place. Data are collected twice weekly via electronic terminals in the home, with purchases being recorded via home scanning technology. The sample is drawn from all individuals aged 5 to 79 who are resident in domestic households on mainland Great Britain and the Isle of Wight and who are in telephone-owning households. Recruitment involves the main shopper in a selected household being contacted by telephone and then having the Superpanel service described to them, together with an outline of the personal task involved, the characteristics of the equipment used and the incentivisation package. If the household agrees, a complete package is despatched to them, including the electronic terminal, instructions and a demonstration video, so that the household can install the equipment themselves. All household members, including children, record details of their purchases and the shops visited by scanning on-pack barcodes using a specially designed computerised scanner together with a code book. The code book is used for non-barcoded fresh food products. The data is transferred by a modem overnight to the TNS headquarters. Panellists receive monthly incentives and six-monthly bonuses for taking part. These can be accumulated and redeemed for a selection of gifts from a catalogue. A monthly newsletter is also sent out to maintain communication and announce winners for monthly prize draws.[5]

Internet panels

Internet panel
A panel of people recruited through the Internet for marketing research purposes. Based on the profile of each individual participant, the panel operator sends out personalised e-mail alerts identifying surveys that they would like the participant to complete. For each completed survey, the participant's will either be credited with a cash sum or will be entered into a prize draw.

For many online surveys, Internet-recruited panels are frequently used. An **Internet panel** is established through web-based advertising or posting and offers cash payments or other rewards for participation in online studies. A potential participant visits the panel operator's site and sets up a membership account by providing demographic details. The collection of such data is important not only for profiling potential respondents but also to gauge the staying power of respondents. If a person is unwilling to answer a number of demographic questions during sign-up, then they are unlikely to complete an online survey regularly. Using the profile of the participant developed from this detailed demographic information, the panel operator sends out personalised e-mail alerts identifying the surveys that they would like the participant to complete. For each completed survey the participant's account will either be credited with a cash sum or will be entered into a prize draw. An example of such a panel can be found at (**www.yougov.com** or **www.lightspeedpanel.com**). A typical participant may complete between three and four surveys per month. The challenge for the operators is to keep panel members motivated. The number of surveys, the level of rewards and the sameness of the surveys all impact on motivation levels. Overall, the churn rate tends to be quite high as unmotivated respondents move onto other panels, lose interest or fail to provide details on changed email addresses.

Mixed-mode studies

Mixed-mode studies
Research studies that use a variety of collection methods in a single survey (e.g. using the same questionnaire online and face-to-face) in order to improve response rates.

The growing costs involved in undertaking research combined with a reduction in response rates has resulted in the number of mixed-mode (also known as *multi-mode*) studies increasing. **Mixed-mode studies** involve using several different fieldwork methods in a single research survey. It may be achieved through using a combination of computer-assisted personal and telephone interviews with an online survey. It may also involve allowing respondents to switch modes part-way through an interview (for example: starting with a telephone interview and completing the study online). Mixed-mode can be particularly beneficial in international multi-country research studies, where the method most suited to each individual country's culture can be used (for example, undertaking one study using online data collection in North America, telephone in Europe and face-to-face in the Middle East).

Mixed-mode does tend to improve response rates; however, as discussed in Issue 8 on page 316, there are concerns about the comparability of the types of respondent across the different methods and also the comparability of response collected by different survey types. People do respond differently to complex scaling questions or open-ended questions, if they are involved in a personal interview in comparison to a web-based survey. The critical element is keeping the questionnaire as simple and straightforward as possible in order to reduce these differences. As response rates continue to decline, particularly in telephone research, it is expected that the research industry will see a greater propensity of multi-mode studies.

Summary and an integrated approach

This chapter has set out the wide range of quantitative techniques that are available to marketing researchers. Survey research is the most popular marketing research technique and can be implemented through interactive methods, such as personal or telephone interviewing, or with no direct contact through self-administered methods delivered by post, by hand, by telephone or by electronic means. Where interaction occurs, it is critical to stress the importance of the interviewer. In telephone and personal interviews, the interviewers are the main interface with respondents and are, therefore, a vital link to consumer cooperation. With refusal rates increasing, good interviewer training and induction programmes are critical to the future success of these methods. Computers are assisting the interviewing process through computer-assisted personal and telephone interviews (CAPI and CATI) and to a lesser extent through completely automated telephone surveys (CATS).

Postal surveys and surveys that are handed to respondents have traditionally made up the bulk of self-administered surveys. However, the advent of the Internet has resulted in the development of e-mail and online surveys. These have the advantages of being fast and cheap with the potential of reaching a large number of people. The surveys can also incorporate multimedia graphics and potentially audio. Currently, web users are not representative of the population as a whole, but this is changing, with digital television and web-enabled phones offering potential access to an even wider audience.

Some of the key factors that determine the broad choice of survey method are set out in Table 6.1 for each of the approaches. However, each method should not be considered in isolation, as many projects may require multiple methods and could possibly combine with data collected through qualitative research and database information.

This chapter has also described derivatives of these survey methods. Omnibus surveys, which can be face-to-face or telephone, are surveys that are undertaken at regular intervals for a changing group of clients who share the costs involved in the set-up, sampling and interviewing processes. They can provide access on a continuous or ad hoc basis to a large sample in a very short time scale for a client who wishes to ask only a limited number of questions. Survey methods can also be used within the testing of new products, new product attributes and new packaging. Such testing can take the form of hall tests, where initial reactions are assessed, placement tests, where products that need to be tested over a period of time are assessed, or simulated test markets, where the likely impact of a product launch is assessed. These testing or experimentation methods are all generally quantitative in nature and rely on survey-type instruments and sampling procedures to collect data.

	Face-to-face	Telephone	Self-administered	
			Off-line	**Online**
Low cost	☺	☺☺	☺☺☺	☺☺☺
Time required to complete study	☺☺	☺☺☺	☺	☺☺☺
Suitability for geographically dispersed sample	☺	☺☺☺	☺☺☺	☺☺☺
Control over interviewing process	☺☺	☺☺☺	☺☺	☺☺
Suitability for long questionnaire	☺☺☺	☺☺	☺☺	☺☺
Greater diversity of question-types	☺☺☺	☺	☺☺	☺☺
Positive public perceptions	☺☺	☺	☺☺☺	☺☺☺
Ability to motivate respondents	☺☺☺	☺☺	☺	☺☺
Suitability for sensitive or taboo subjects	☺☺	☺	☺☺	☺☺
Ability to probe and clarify	☺☺☺	☺☺☺	☺	☺☺
Response rates	☺☺☺	☺☺	☺	☺

Table 6.1 A comparison of survey approaches

Discussion questions

1 How does quantitative research differ from qualitative research?

2 What advantages does personal interviewing have over telephone interviewing?

3 What does interviewer bias mean and how can it impact on personal interviewing?

4 What are the advantages of using computers to assist in the undertaking of personal or telephone interviews?

5 Why are response rates for telephone interviewing on the decline?

6 How can the response rates of postal surveys be improved?

7 Discuss the proposition that online surveys will soon replace all postal surveys.

8 Describe the workings of an omnibus survey and explain why a client may use one.

9 In what circumstances would you use a placement test rather than a hall test?

10 Describe the workings of a panel and explain why a panel may be used instead of a one-off survey.

Additional reading

Blyth, B. (2008) Mixed mode: the only 'fitness' regime. *International Journal of Market Research*, **50**(2), pp. 241–66.

Brennan, M., Benson, S. and Kearns, Z. (2005) The effect of introductions on telephone survey participation rates. *International Journal of Market Research*, **47**(1), pp. 65–74.

Bronner, F. and Kuijlen, T. (2007) The live or digital interviewer: a comparison between CASI, CAPI and CATI with respect to differences in response behaviour. *International Journal of Market Research*, **49**(2), pp. 167–90.

Cobanoglu, C., Warde, B. and Moreo, P.J. (2001) A comparison of mail, fax and web-based survey methods. *International Journal of Market Research*, **43**(4), pp. 441–52.

Curasi, C.F. (2001) A critical exploration of face-to-face interviewing vs. computer mediated interviewing. *International Journal of Market Research*, **43**(4), pp. 361–75.

Dommeyer, C.J. and Moriarty, E. (1999) Comparing two forms of an e-mail survey: embedded vs. attached. *International Journal of Market Research*, **42**(1), pp. 39–50.

Kellner, P. (2004) Can online polls produce accurate findings? *International Journal of Market Research*, **46**(1), pp. 1–22.

Mehta, R. and Sivadas, E. (1995) Comparing response rates and response content in mail versus electronic mail surveys. *Journal of the Market Research Society*, **37**(4), pp. 429–39.

Manfreda, K.J., Bosnjak, M., Berzelak, J., Haas, I. and Vehovar, V. (2008) Web surveys versus other surveys: a meta-analysis comparing response rates. *International Journal of Market Research*, **50**(1), pp. 79–104.

Okazaki, S. (2007) Assessing mobile-based online surveys: methodological considerations and pilot study in an advertising context. *International Journal of Market Research*, **49**(5), pp. 651–75.

Sparrow, N. and Curtice, J. (2004) Measuring the attitudes of the general public via internet polls: an evaluation. *International Journal of Market Research*, **46**(1), pp. 23–44.

Taylor, H. (1999) Does Internet research work? *International Journal of Market Research*, **42**(1), pp. 51–63.

Tse, A.C.B. (1998) Comparing the response rate, response speed, and response quality of two methods of sending questionnaires: e-mail vs. mail. *Journal of the Market Research Society*, **40**(4), pp. 353–61.

Vicente, P., Reis, E. and Santos, M. (2009) Using mobile phones for survey research: a comparison with fixed phones. *International Journal of Market Research*, **51**(5), pp. 613–34.

Weible, R. and Wallace, J. (1998) Cyber research: the impact of the Internet on data collection. *Marketing Research*, **10**(3), pp. 19–31.

Wilcox, S. (2000) Sampling and controlling a TV audience measurement panel. *International Journal of Market Research*, **42**(4), pp. 413–30.

References

[1] For more information see **www.nrs.co.uk**.

[2] For more information see **www.tns-ri.co.uk**.

[3] For more information see **www.ipsos-mori.com**.

[4] For more information see **www.gfknop.com**.

[5] For more on the TNS Superpanel, see **http://superpanel.tns-global.com/superpanel/**.

7 Designing questionnaires

The Target Group Index

The Target Group Index (TGI) is a subscription service operated by Kantar Media Research Group in 60 countries for advertisers, advertising agencies and media owners. It is aimed at improving the effectiveness of promotional activity by identifying and describing target groups of consumers and their media exposure. Each year 24,000 people in the UK complete a self-administered questionnaire on their purchasing behaviour, media exposure and lifestyles. Respondents are recruited through personal interview and then given the questionnaire to complete and send back. The effective response rate is 60 per cent of those who are recruited. That high level of response is dependent on the time and effort put into developing and testing of the questionnaire, not only to ensure that it collects accurate data but also that it is attractive, clear and interesting to potential respondents.[1]

Bon Appetit/Alamy

Learning outcomes

After reading this chapter you should:

- understand the sequential stages involved in designing a questionnaire for quantitative research;
- be aware of the three main types of question (open, closed and scaled response) and their usage;
- understand the most commonly used scaling approaches (constant sum, Likert, semantic differential, stapel and purchase intent scales);
- be aware of the guidelines regarding the wording, sequencing, layout and pilot testing of questionnaires.

Key words

closed questions	pilot testing
coefficient alpha	purchase intent scale
constant sum scales	questionnaire-design process
construct validity	reliability of scales
content validity	scaling questions
dichotomous questions	semantic differential scale
end-piling	split-half reliability
funnel sequence	stapel scale
Likert scale	test-retest reliability
multiple-choice questions	validity
open-ended questions	

Introduction

In survey research, a questionnaire is the research instrument designed to generate the data necessary for accomplishing a project's research objectives. It standardises the wording and sequence of questions in order that each respondent is asked to provide information in exactly the same manner. This control ensures the validity of any comparison being made between different respondents' answers, as well as providing data in a form that can easily be analysed. Questionnaires provide the critical communication link between the researcher and the respondent. A questionnaire must:

1 communicate to the respondent what the researcher is asking for;
2 communicate to the researcher what the respondent has to say.

The primary objective of questionnaire design is to try to reduce the 'noise' or distortion in that two-way communication, in order that each party correctly understands what the other is saying (Figure 7.1). Questions that are difficult to interpret or answers that are either incomplete or confusing are examples of the noise that can hinder clear communication. Creating a questionnaire that provides a good communication vehicle is a difficult task, one that requires a structured and systematic approach. This chapter identifies the critical activities involved in each stage of a questionnaire's design. As part of this the different types of questioning and scaling approaches will be discussed.

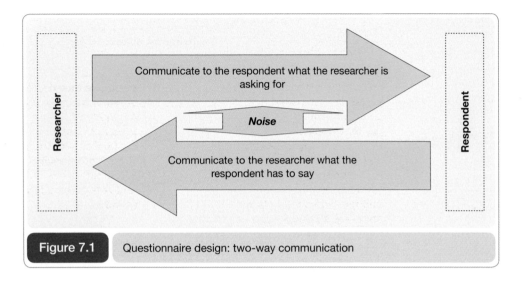

| Figure 7.1 | Questionnaire design: two-way communication |

The questionnaire-design process

Questionnaire-design process
A stepped approach to the design of questionnaires.

If you have never considered the **questionnaire-design process** before, you may think it is simply a matter of writing down questions similar to those that you would have in a normal conversation. However, in conversations misunderstandings are commonplace. People answer questions that are different from those that are asked. People use facial expressions, hand actions and clarifying words to further explain their questions or answers. People also interrupt each other to clarify misunderstandings, yet people talking at cross-purposes is still a common phenomenon. Therefore, clarity of communication is not as simple an activity as it seems. Another example of this is illustrated by the following question from a recent survey about student finance:

Do you encounter any difficulties in paying the rent for your accommodation?

Yes_____ No_____

The researcher was looking at the financial difficulties that students were facing and, at face value, there appears to be little wrong with the question. However, many students answered the question in relation to the *process* of paying rent rather than the difficulties associated with the actual *raising of the finance* to pay rent. The question therefore attracted more 'No's than expected, because people found payment simple since they paid by direct debit or standing order or because the landlord came round regularly for the money. One respondent even stated that he had no difficulties because his landlord lived in the flat upstairs from him. This demonstrates that people can read different meanings into questions. Therefore questionnaire design should not be taken lightly, since improper design can lead to inaccurate information and incomplete data and may result in research moneys being wasted. It is therefore advisable to adopt the stepped approach outlined in Figure 7.2 for the questionnaire-design process.

Although these steps are shown as sequential, one should not see them as totally discrete. The steps are interrelated, as questionnaire design is an interactive process, with many drafts of a questionnaire being produced before a final version is complete. Changes in one of the later steps may result in the researcher having to make changes to elements involved in one of the earlier steps. For example, a proposed change in the layout and appearance may require a researcher to rethink response formats or question sequence. Problems identified when

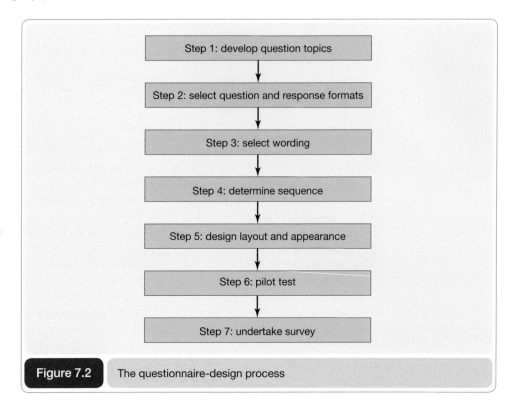

Figure 7.2   The questionnaire-design process

the questionnaire is pilot tested may also impact on any of the preceding steps. So, although the tasks should be tackled in the sequence shown, each step will remain incomplete until the final questionnaire is approved for use on the survey.

The tasks involved in each of these interrelated steps will now be described in detail in the following sections.

Step 1: develop question topics

In developing the question topics, researchers should take account of the project's research objectives, the findings of any exploratory qualitative research undertaken and the characteristics of the respondents.

Research objectives

The research objectives should be seen as the key driver of questionnaire design. Which topics need to be included to provide the required information to fully satisfy the research objectives? Which topics are of critical and which of secondary importance? What level of detail is required? What classification information is needed about the respondent? How will the results from the research be presented and used? Answers to these types of question will help to determine the topics to be covered, the weighting to be given to each topic and the broad manner in which the information should be collected. They will also help in determining which information is truly needed in comparison to information that is simply 'nice to know'. Such 'nice to know' information may add significantly to the length of a questionnaire, resulting in higher refusal/non-response rates among respondents.

Qualitative research findings

If a programme of exploratory primary research has been undertaken prior to the quantitative research, the findings can be used to clarify what should be asked and also the best ways of tackling each topic. The qualitative research should also help in determining the most relevant wording for questions and the statements to be used in rating scales.

Characteristics of respondents

Respondents must be able and willing to provide the information requested. Ability is based on the respondents having knowledge of the subject in question: will they be able to recall how many shoes they tried on the last time they visited a shoe retailer? (*It is unlikely unless they visited a shoe retailer very recently.*) Will they be able to recall accurately how long they stood in the supermarket queue during their last visit? (*They will probably only remember if the length of time was excessive or something unusual happened.*)

In determining the topics, the researcher needs to put him/herself in the position of the respondent and determine which subjects the respondent is likely to have sufficient knowledge or memory of. Even where the respondents have knowledge, they may be unwilling to answer questions on a particular topic, either because they think it is a sensitive and private matter or because they find the subject boring or uninteresting. Private subjects may relate to areas such as financial matters, earnings, personal hygiene products or contraceptives for consumers, or profits, future plans or supplier details for organisations. The researcher needs to consider how much information is needed in such areas and how the specific subjects should be tackled.

The level of interest respondents have in a subject is likely to have an impact on the potential number of questions that can be asked in a survey. If the respondents perceive the topic as having limited relevance to them, they may fail to complete self-administered questionnaires, hang up during a telephone interview or simply give any set of answers in order to finish the interview. The environment in which the respondent is interviewed can exacerbate this further. For example, it may be very difficult to maintain the attention of a respondent in an uninteresting subject during a street interview where there may be many other distractions. Therefore, in determining the topics, care must be taken to identify how they can be made to seem interesting and relevant to potential respondents. There is a need to look at the topics from the respondent's perspective: are they concise, relevant and interesting?

Having taken these three inputs into account, the researcher should develop a rough set of topics/question areas to be addressed that can then be fitted into specific question formats.

Step 2: select question and response formats

There are basically three main forms of questions based on their format for capturing responses. These are open-ended (response) questions, closed (response) questions and scaling (response) questions.

Open-ended questions
Questions that allow respondents to reply in their own words. There are no pre-set choices of answers and the respondent can decide whether to provide a brief one-word answer or something very detailed and long. Sometimes known as *unstructured questions*.

Open-ended questions

Open-ended questions (sometimes known as *unstructured questions*) are those in which the respondents can reply in their own words. There are no preset choices of answers, and the respondent can decide whether to provide a brief one-word answer or something very detailed and long. In the examples below, one-word answers may be all that is required (e.g. for question 1); however, for the other questions, more detailed answers may be more useful. Respondents may need to be encouraged to elaborate on a short answer by the use of probes such as: 'Is there anything else?', 'In what way?', 'Can you expand on that?'

Typical open-ended questions

1 *Which country do you come from?*_____
2 *What did you enjoy most about your flight?*_____
3 *Why did you choose to fly by British Airways?*_____
4 *What is your opinion of the proposed merger between British Airways and Airline X?*

Open-ended questions are frequently used because the range of potential answers is very wide (for example, question 1 above), or where the research team feel that they lack sufficient knowledge about the subject to provide an exhaustive list of potential answers. Open-ended questions may uncover reasons why people fly British Airways that researchers had not recognised before. Such questions can provide researchers with a large amount of information that would not be available from a predetermined list of responses. The respondents answer from their own frame of reference using their own phrases and terminology. Such information may be particularly useful for copywriters designing advertising copy using the consumers' language.

Open-ended questions may also help to explain the answers to other types of question appearing in a questionnaire. For example, attitude rating scales may show a person's dissatisfaction with an organisation, but an explanation for this may only come from an open-ended question about reasons for satisfaction/dissatisfaction. Answers may be more honest in open-ended questions instead of simply being appropriate and matched to the set of responses provided.

Open-ended questions do have their drawbacks. One of the most significant is their analysis and interpretation. This involves editing and coding, where editing involves the reduction of the many responses into a number of categories and then coding each of the answers into one of these categories (see Table 7.1). If there are too many categories, it may be difficult to identify patterns or determine the relationships with answers given to other questions; too few categories lead to the categories being too broad and relatively meaningless. This is a time-consuming process and generally has to be undertaken manually even if the data has been collected using computer-assisted interviewing. Unusual or complex answers may need to be interpreted by the researcher and forced into a category that does not exactly match (e.g. where should the researcher put: 'I have had bad experiences flying Lufthansa on that route regarding reliability').

Table 7.1	Coding of open-ended responses

3 Why did you choose to fly by British Airways?_____

Category	Code
Executive Club member	1
Times of flights	2
In-flight catering	3
Service	4
Price	5
Connections	6
Out of habit	7
No choice	8
Other	9

The depth of information may vary dramatically between respondents, depending on the ability of the interviewer to fully probe the subject and also the ability of the respondent to articulate their views. Shy or inarticulate respondents may provide the bare minimum of information. Open-ended questions are particularly difficult in self-administered or online questionnaires where the respondents do not have an interviewer to probe further. When respondents are on their own, they frequently write brief, incomplete answers which are of limited value to the researcher. However, it should be stressed that not all interviewers are good at recording answers verbatim and many simply summarise what respondents say, potentially missing out key points.

Some of these problems can be partially overcome in interviewer-administered question-naires by pre-coding (before the interviews) rather than post-coding (after the interviews) potential responses. Although the question will still be asked in an open-ended manner, a list of answers will appear on the questionnaire along with an 'other' category for non-conforming answers. Interviews then tick the pre-printed answer that most closely matches what the respondent says. This makes the recording of the answers straightforward and reduces the analysis time. However, it loses the detail of the phrases and terminology used by respondents and it requires the researcher to have sufficient knowledge of the subject to anticipate most of the potential answers. It should be noted that pre-coded, open-ended questions are different from closed or multiple-choice questions; although probing may occur, the list of answers is never read out. Respondents can respond in any way that they think fit. In contrast, multiple-choice questions require the alternative answers to be read or shown to the respondent.

Closed questions

Closed questions
Questions that require the respondent to make a selection from a predefined list of responses. There are two main types of closed questions: dichotomous questions with only two potential responses and multiple response questions with more than two.

Closed questions are ones that require the respondent to make a selection from a predefined list of responses. There are two main types of closed questions: dichotomous questions with only two potential responses and multiple response questions with more than two. With each, the question is asked and the response alternatives are read out (or read by the respondent) before the most appropriate response is selected. Unlike open-ended questions, all respondents provide the same level of depth and interviewers only need to tick the selected box instead of summarising or recording responses verbatim. Analysis and the data entry process are also far simpler.

Dichotomous questions

Dichotomous questions
questions with only two potential responses (e.g. Yes or No).

Dichotomous questions are the simplest form of closed question as the respondent is limited to two fixed alternatives.

---

1 *Have you shopped at Tesco before?*
   Yes   1
   No   2

2 *Each week, are you visiting this Tesco store more often or less often than last year?*
   More often   1
   Less often   2

Some respondents may have difficulty choosing between the two options so a 'don't know' category is often added to address such situations. Dichotomous questions do not provide much detail. For example, question 1 tells us nothing about how frequently the respondent visits the store nor whether their most recent visit was yesterday or five years ago. Question 2 does not distinguish between those who are visiting much more often and those who are visiting only slightly more often. Respondents may also have difficulty in answering a question with polarised alternatives. For example, a respondent who visits Tesco with the same frequency as last year may have difficulty answering question 2. However, even with these weaknesses, dichotomous questions are useful as screening-type questions to determine whether a respondent should be asked further questions on a particular topic.

Multiple-choice questions

Multiple-choice questions
Questions that provide respondents with a choice of predetermined responses to a question. The respondents are asked to either give one alternative that correctly expresses their viewpoint or indicate all responses that apply.

Multiple-choice questions provide respondents with a choice of potential responses to a question. The respondents are asked either to give one alternative that correctly expresses their viewpoint or to indicate all responses that apply.

The responses available to the respondent need to be mutually exclusive and collectively exhaustive.

Mutually exclusive means that each of the responses should be distinct, with no overlap between the categories. Problems are often seen with this in multiple-choice questions that relate to numerical values.

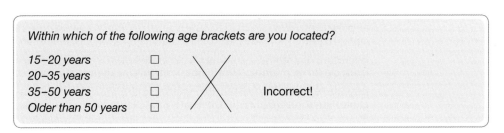

With this question where do respondents who are 20, 35 or 50 place their tick? The categories are not mutually exclusive. This causes confusion and results in the collection of incorrect data.

Collectively exhaustive means that all potential responses are listed. This means that the researcher needs to know all or most of the answers during the questionnaire-design phase. This is relatively straightforward for factual information (such as newspapers read, brands of dog food purchased, European countries visited) where there is a relatively finite list. It is more difficult for factors relating to attitudes and opinions (although a qualitative research phase that has been undertaken prior to the quantitative research or a previous research study may help). Even where the research team think they know all the potential answers, it is often best to include an 'other' category enabling an alternative answer to be written in.

> *Which national newspaper do you read on a regular basis?*
>
> The Times ☐
> Daily Telegraph ☐
> Financial Times ☐
> Guardian ☐
> Sun ☐
> Daily Express ☐
> Daily Mirror ☐
> *Other (please specify) _____*

The optimum number of response categories in a question will be dependent on the manner in which the questionnaire is to be administered. Too many categories in a self-administered questionnaire will add to the overall length of the questionnaire, impacting on response rates and also potentially on mailing costs for postal surveys. In such cases the list should be limited to those responses that are considered to be most likely, supporting these with an 'other' category. In telephone and personal surveys, where the various categories need to be read out to respondents, long lists can increase interview time and try respondent patience. Respondents may also have difficulty remembering all of the categories by the time the interviewer gets to the end of the list. In personal interviews this can be overcome by putting the list on a 'show-card'. Rather than the interviewer reading out the options, the respondent is given the show-card and asked to select from it. In telephone interviews, where no visual options are available, the list may need to be reduced similar to self-administered questionnaires. If long lists of response category are essential to the research, personal interviewing may be the only option.

> ### Researcher quote
>
> It frequently takes longer to generate the response categories than it does to design the questions.

The researcher must also consider how many responses per participant will be accepted for a question. If only a single response is required (i.e. from this list, which factor is most important?), software such as that used in computer-assisted interviewing or online surveys will be set to accept only one answer. When a tickbox is clicked, the answer becomes selected; if another tickbox is then clicked, it is then selected and the previously selected answer is unselected. It is important to ensure that the software has been set to single or multiple response during the questionnaire-design phase, otherwise the findings may be limited in a manner that wasn't anticipated.

The ordering of potential responses is important as it can influence a respondent's choice, especially when they are slightly unsure as to what answer to give. This is particularly the case when the responses are in the form of words, phrases and statements rather than numbers. Research has shown that respondents are more likely to choose the statements at the beginning or end of a list rather than those appearing in the middle. To reduce the impact of this, interviewers are frequently asked to rotate the sequence of categories from one questionnaire to the next. So, for the question on newspapers set out above, the interviewer would start the list of potential responses with *The Times* for respondent 1, with *Daily Telegraph* for respondent 2, and so on. If this is done systematically, each response category will occupy various positions within the sequence, reducing the impact of position bias when considered across all respondents. This may be difficult in paper-based, self-administered questionnaires, as many versions of a questionnaire would need to be produced, adding to the costs of the survey. However, online survey software does allow rotation in an online questionnaire.

Scaling questions

Scaling questions
Questions that ask respondents to assign numerical measures to subjective concepts such as attitudes, opinions and feelings.

Scaling questions in marketing research normally refer to procedures for the assignment of numerical measures to subjective concepts such as attitudes, opinions and feelings. The assignment of numbers enables the information from different groups of the population to be more easily compared and summarised. Statistical techniques can also be used to manipulate and analyse the data obtained. In designing scales there are a number of different dimensions that need to be considered: unidimensional versus multidimensional assessment; graphic versus itemised rating formats; comparative versus non-comparative; forced versus non-forced scales; balanced versus unbalanced scales. Design issues also exist with regard to the number of scale positions and the labelling/pictorial representation of positions.

Unidimensional versus multidimensional assessment

Scales can be unidimensional or multidimensional. Unidimensional scaling focuses on only one attribute: for example, satisfaction. Respondents would be asked to rate their satisfaction with a particular product or service. Multidimensional scaling looks at a variety of dimensions, so a questionnaire about an overnight stay in a hotel may look at attitudes towards a range of items such as the comfort of the bedroom, the quality of the food, the helpfulness of reception staff, the range of amenities, etc.

Graphic versus itemised rating formats

Graphic rating scales (sometimes known as continuous rating scales) present respondents with a continuum, in the form of a straight line anchored between two extremes:

Respondents are asked to place a tick or cross on the line to represent the level of quality that they associate with the product under investigation. With regard to analysis, a score is assigned by dividing the line into categories and assigning the score based on the category within which the mark has been placed. For example, if the line was 15 cm long, each 2.5 cm could equal one category starting at 0 for low quality to 6 for high quality. A potential drawback of a graphic rating scale of this type is that coding and analysis takes a significant amount of time as physical distances have to be measured and interpreted for each attribute being assessed. Also, respondents may find it difficult to translate their feelings into distances on a line. To overcome this, some scales provide more structure to the respondent by assigning numbers along the scale while still allowing the respondent to mark the line at any point between the values identified:

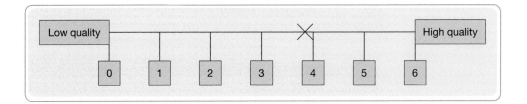

Although graphic rating scales suggest greater precision than other forms of scale, the precision is generally considered to be spurious owing to the difficulties respondents have in visualising attitudes as a distance along a line and in determining the fine distinctions between different points on the line. As a result, graphic rating scales are used significantly less frequently than are itemised rating scales.

Itemised rating scales have a finite set of distinct response choices. The respondent chooses the rating or score that best reflects their view of the subject. These can take a variety of numerical and non-numerical forms, as can be seen in the following example from customer satisfaction questionnaires for hotel guests.

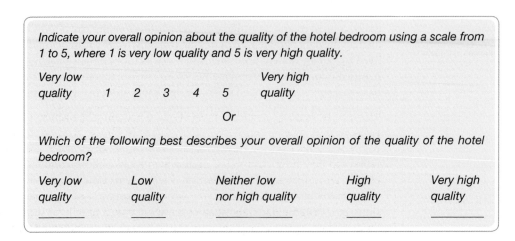

Respondents tend to find that itemised rating scales are generally easier than graphic rating scales. They are also much easier to analyse.

Comparative versus non-comparative assessments

Comparative rating scales ask respondents to compare the organisation or issue in relation to a common frame of reference. Everybody is comparing like with like. In contrast, a non-comparative rating scale does not provide a standard frame of reference and allows respondents to select their own frame of reference or even to use no frame of reference at all. For example, respondents in the following question may be comparing Asda eggs with eggs from other supermarkets, or with eggs they had as a child, or eggs they had in France on holiday or with eggs that they buy from the local farmers' market.

Non-comparative rating scale

Rate the quality of the eggs that you have previously purchased from Asda using a rating scale where 1 is very poor quality and 5 is very high quality.

Very poor quality	1	2	3	4	5	Very high quality

This compares with the following questions, which provide a frame of reference within which the respondent positions the eggs from Asda.

Comparative rating scales

1 *In comparison to the eggs that you have previously bought from Tesco, rate the quality of the eggs from Asda using a rating scale where 1 is significantly lower quality and 5 is significantly higher quality.*

Much lower quality than Tesco	Lower quality than Tesco	About the same quality	Higher quality than Tesco	Significantly higher quality than Tesco
1	2	3	4	5

2 *Rank the following retailers for the quality of their eggs by placing a 1 beside the best, a 2 beside the store you think is second best, and so on.*

Tesco	____
Asda	____
Sainsburys	____
Marks & Spencer	____
Morrisons	____

The first of these questions compares one object directly against another, so the frame of reference is Asda eggs compared with Tesco eggs. The second uses a rank-order scale, which places the items (in this case, stores) in order. Rank-order scales are attractive because they reflect the way most people look at items, suppliers, etc., by placing them in an order (first choice, second choice, third choice, etc.) rather than attaching scores to things. Ranking and comparative rating scales in general do have the disadvantage that they are dependent on the respondent having knowledge of the subject with which the comparison is being made. Some Asda egg buyers may never have tasted Tesco eggs and therefore would have difficulty answering question 1 and they would only be able to partially complete question 2. The second specific problem with rank-order scales is that the researcher only receives ordinal or order data. Nothing is known about the relative difference between the factors being ranked. Do the retailers' eggs only vary slightly in quality or are one or two retailers significantly better than the others? This makes it difficult for a company to know how much they need to improve to alter their ranked position. This may not be an important weakness where the research is trying to assess aspects such as purchasing priorities. For example, a ranking approach may be very useful for a car manufacturer trying to identify customers' priorities in terms of standard and optional car features.

Overall the choice of comparative versus non-comparative formats is dependent on both the likely breadth of knowledge held by respondents, which may or may not enable them to make comparisons, and the specific purpose for which the client organisation wants the data.

Forced versus non-forced scales

A forced-choice scale does not allow respondents the option of selecting a neutral rather than a positive or negative view about an attribute. In general, a rating scale with an even number of categories is forced, whereas an odd number of categories allows for a middle/neutral option.

Example of forced-choice scale

Indicate your overall opinion of the cost of IKEA furniture by ticking one of the following categories.

Very inexpensive   Inexpensive   Expensive   Very expensive

_____   _____   _____   _____

Example of non-forced-choice scale

Indicate your overall opinion of the cost of IKEA furniture by ticking one of the following categories.

Very inexpensive	*Inexpensive*	*Neither expensive nor inexpensive*	*Expensive*	*Very expensive*
_____	_____	_____	_____	_____

There is no clear agreement on whether forced-response choices provide information that is superior to scales where a neutral option is available. Forcing respondents to take a positive or negative view when they do not have any significant opinion on a subject may result in a set of spurious data. On the other hand, providing a neutral option may result in certain respondents selecting it in order to hide their true feelings or because they simply do not want to put the effort into examining what they do think. It is certainly the case that the majority of scales used in marketing research in the UK use an odd number of positions, which incorporate a neutral response. However, forced scales should not be rejected out of hand but should be considered for subjects where the researcher feels that there are likely to be very few people with neutral attitudes. For example, if an airline was to ask their passengers about the comfort of their seats, the appropriateness of including a neither comfortable nor uncomfortable category is questionable.

Balanced versus unbalanced scales

End-piling
A situation where almost all responses appear in a few categories at one end of a measurement scale.

A balanced scale is one that has an equal number of positive and negative response choices. Most scales are balanced, as there is a danger of biasing respondents to answer in a certain manner if there are more positive than negative categories or vice versa. The only exception to this is where **end-piling** is expected; that is, where almost all responses appear in a few categories at one end of a measurement scale. This can occur if a scale is looking at the importance of features in a product. For example, motorists could be asked to rate the following car attributes: fuel efficiency, comfort, safety, ease of handling. All of these are unlikely to be considered as unimportant; however, their relative importance may vary. An unbalanced scale in which a majority of the choices favour one side, such as the one below, may be more effective at determining the relative differences in importance.

Unimportant	Important	Very important	Critical
( )	( )	( )	( )

The number of scale positions

The number of categories to include in a rating scale is linked to the forced/non-forced and balanced/unbalanced issues. It is a topic that is controversial, with different researchers preferring different numbers, in many cases with limited justification for their choice. The majority of surveys use rating scales with typically between 5 and 9 categories. Sometimes scores out of 10 are used as people have tended to become accustomed to this type of scoring while progressing through their formal education at school. At face value, the larger the number of categories, the more precise the measurement. However, this will only be the case if respondents are able to make the fine distinctions between the categories when assessing what is being measured. What is the actual difference between a 7 and an 8 on a 9-point scale? Therefore, the capabilities of the respondents should be considered when selecting the number of positions, as should the method of administering (fewer positions in telephone interviews) and the nature of the attribute being examined (it may be easier to use more categories when looking at an attribute such as performance in comparison to looking at satisfaction).

Labelling and pictorial representation of positions

Most rating scales will have a pair of anchor labels that define the extremes of a scale. However, researchers will often put intermediate labels in the form of words and numbers on the scales. There are no hard and fast rules as to the number or form these labels should take. However, it is generally better to leave a category unlabelled than to make up a label that does not fit with the other labels. Labels tend to become more difficult to develop when there are more than five or six in a scale (for example, what category does one put between 'good' and 'very good' or between 'poor' and 'very poor'). So, generally in scales involving more than seven categories, a number of the categories will be unlabelled.

Very weak	Weak			Neither weak nor strong	Strong			Very strong
(1)	(2)	(3)	(4)	(5)	(6)	(7)	(8)	(9)

Picture labels can also be used to help respondents understand the categories and distinguish between them. These can be particularly useful in surveying children or people from different ethnic backgrounds. McDonald's uses faces similar to the ones overleaf to assess customer satisfaction with its service.

Commonly used scaling approaches

Constant sum scales

Constant sum scales require the respondent to divide a given number of points, usually 100, among a number of attributes based on their importance to the individual (Figure 7.3). This has advantages over a standard rank-order scale in that the researcher not only obtains the ranked importance of each attribute but also the scale of difference that the respondent perceives as existing between the different variables. Two attributes can also be awarded equal values, which may be difficult in a ranking question. The principal weakness of this approach is that the number of attributes has to be relatively limited otherwise the respondents have difficulty allocating the points to total 100. Ten is most commonly seen as being the maximum number as respondents generally have difficulty in dividing by any number greater than 10.

> *Below are five characteristics of food processors. Please allocate 100 points among the characteristics in a manner that represents the importance of each characteristic to you. The more points that you allocate to a characteristic, the more important it is to you. If a characteristic is totally unimportant, you should allocate 0 points to it. Please make sure the total points that you allocate add up to 100.*

Characteristics of food processors	Number of points
Has many accessories	
Is made by a well-known manufacturer	
Is easy to clean	
Is stylish	
Is quiet to operate	
	100 points

Figure 7.3   A constant sum scale used in a food processor study

Likert scale

The **Likert scale** is based on a format originally developed by Renis Likert in 1932. The scale involves respondents being asked to state their level of agreement with a series of statements about a product, organisation or concept. The scores are then totalled to measure the respondent's attitude. The number of statements included in the scale may vary from study to study, depending on how many characteristics are relevant to the subject under investigation. Each statement expresses either a favourable or unfavourable attitude towards the concept under study. The respondent indicates agreement by selecting one of the following descriptors: strongly agree, agree, neither agree nor disagree, disagree, strongly disagree. Figure 7.4 presents eight illustrative statements that a mobile phone manufacturer can use to measure attitudes towards one of its products.

As Figure 7.4 shows, a typical feature of Likert scales is that there is normally a good balance of statements that are favourable and unfavourable towards the product or concept. Such a

I would now like to find out your attitudes towards this model of phone. Therefore, for each of the following statements, please tell me if you strongly agree, agree, neither agree nor disagree, disagree, or strongly disagree.

	Strongly agree	Agree	Neither agree nor disagree	Disagree	Strongly disagree
The phone is easy to use					
The phone's design is stylish					
The keys are too small					
The phone is better than the one I currently use					
The functions and commands are confusing					
I would look good with a phone like this					
The phone looks as if it is built to last					
I don't need a phone like this					

Figure 7.4   An example of Likert scale items

mix of statements will reduce the chances of respondents simply agreeing with all statements. After the scale has been administered, numbers are assigned to the responses, usually using the numbers 1 through to 5 (occasionally the number set −2, −1, 0, +1, +2 is used). As some of the statements will be favourable and others unfavourable, the allocation of numbers will have to vary accordingly. With favourable statements, 1 would be allocated to strongly disagree, 2 to disagree, 3 to neither agree nor disagree, 4 to agree and 5 to strongly agree. The allocation of numbers would be reversed for unfavourable statements. Then each respondent's overall attitude is measured by summing his or her numerical ratings on the statements making up the scale. On a 20-item scale, the maximum favourable score would be 100. Therefore, a person scoring in the 80s or 90s would be considered as having a positive attitude to the product or company being assessed. However, in addition to the summing of the scores, it is important to look at the components of the overall attitude as respondents with the same total may rate individual attributes differently. Some respondents may be positive about the functionality of the mobile phone, whereas others may be more positive about its style. Information such as this may explain why a phone is or is not selling and may also identify what attributes are attractive to particular market segments.

The overall value of the Likert scale depends on the care with which the statements making up the scale are selected. Designing a good Likert scale involves generating a large pool of statements (possibly up to 100 statements for a final scale of 20) and then sifting through these to arrive at the final statements used in the survey. The sifting process is usually undertaken using a pre-test of the statements with a small sample of the population to be researched. Statements are rejected if respondents consider them to be unclear or ambiguous. They are also rejected if they fail to discriminate between respondents with differing attitudes. This is determined by comparing respondents' scores for each individual statement with their total score for all statements. The statements on which the respondents' scores correlate positively or negatively with the respondents' total scores are better indicators of attitudes and are hence more useful for inclusion. Therefore, of the original pool of statements, the 20 or 30 statements that are unambiguous and have the highest correlations with the total attitude scores will be selected. Care taken in the selection and sifting of the statements is critical if the Likert scale is to be considered reliable and sensitive. Of all of the scales available, the Likert scale is probably the one that is most commonly used in commercial marketing research.

Semantic differential scale

Semantic differential scale

A scaling approach which requires the respondent to rate a brand or concept using a set of bipolar adjectives or phrases (e.g. helpful and unhelpful; friendly and unfriendly). Each pair of adjectives is separated by a seven-category scale with neither numerical nor verbal labels.

Although the **semantic differential scale** plays a similar role to a Likert scale, its construction is more complex. The researcher selects a set of bipolar adjectives or phrases (e.g. helpful and unhelpful; friendly and unfriendly) that could be used to describe the product, company, brand or concept. Each pair of adjectives is separated by a seven-category scale with neither numerical nor verbal labels. Respondents are asked to rate the brand or concept for each pair of adjectives (Figure 7.5).

The location of the positive statements should be randomly placed on the right and left of the scale, in order to force the respondents to think about the adjectives before responding, otherwise respondents may simply go down the attributes giving the same rating to all. Care is also required in selecting the pairs of adjectives/phrases and these should be chosen in a systematic manner similar to that used for Likert scales.

Now consider your attitudes towards Adidas. Listed below are pairs of statements that could describe a sports brand. For each pair, mark an X between the two statements in a position that best reflects your view of Adidas.

Expensive	:___:___:___:___:___:___:	*Inexpensive*
The choice of professionals	:___:___:___:___:___:___:	*The choice of amateurs*
Old-fashioned	:___:___:___:___:___:___:	*Modern*
A market leader	:___:___:___:___:___:___:	*A market follower*
High quality	:___:___:___:___:___:___:	*Low quality*

Figure 7.5 An example of a semantic differential scale

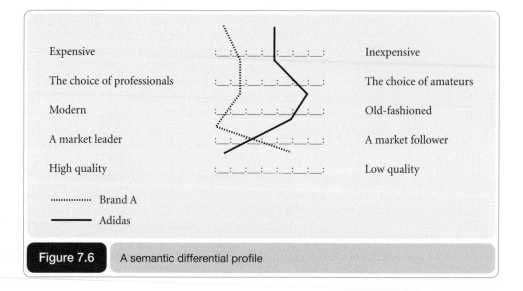

Figure 7.6 A semantic differential profile

In terms of analysis, the seven categories can be numerically coded using a scale of 1, 2, 3, 4, 5, 6, 7 or −3, −2, −1, 0, 1, 2, 3 and overall attitude scores can be obtained for the combined attributes as well as the individual descriptors (making sure that negative descriptors are reversed). Commonly a pictorial profile of semantic differential results is produced (see Figure 7.6). Note that to facilitate interpretation of the information, all of the favourable descriptors are placed on the same side of the profile.

Such a profile can provide a quick and efficient means of identifying differences between different brands, companies, concepts, etc. According to Figure 7.6, Adidas has a higher rating for quality than brand A but in all other respects brand A has a superior image. Such ease of comparison has resulted in semantic differential scales being regularly used for corporate image research.

Stapel scale

Stapel scale
A scaling approach which is a variation of the semantic differential scaling approach. It uses a single descriptor and 10 response categories with no verbal labels.

The **stapel scale** is a variation of the semantic differential scale which uses a single descriptor rather than a pair of opposite descriptors. The scale is a forced-choice scale with ten response categories and no verbal labels (Figure 7.7).

The data obtained from stapel scales can be analysed in much the same way as for the semantic differential scale with overall attitude scores and pictorial profiles based on the mean scores.

The principal advantage of the stapel scale is that the researcher does not have to go through the arduous task of identifying bipolar adjective pairs. However, the layout of the scales can sometimes make it difficult for all respondents to understand what is required of them. It also takes up more space in a questionnaire, adding to questionnaire length and refusal rates. As a result, the stapel scale is used to a much lesser extent in commercial marketing research than either semantic differential or Likert scales.

Purchase intent scales

Purchase intent scale
A scaling approach which is used to measure a respondent's intention to purchase a product or potential product.

The **purchase intent scale** is used to measure a respondent's intention to buy a product or potential product. It is frequently viewed as a multiple-choice question rather than a scale. However, as it attempts to quantify a subjective measure, it will appear here as a scaling technique. The purchase intent scale is generally asked during the concept testing stages of new product development and also when companies are considering revisions to their products or services. The scale is very straightforward – consumers are simply asked to make a subjective judgement about their buying intentions (see Figure 7.8).

For the following statements relating to freight transport, indicate with your first impression how accurately the statements on the left-hand side represent Railfreight.

The more accurately you think the word describes Railfreight, the larger the plus number you should choose. The less accurately you think a phrase describes Railfreight, the larger the minus number you should choose. You can select any number from +5 for words you think are very accurate to −5 for words you think are very inaccurate.

	+5		+5		+5		+5
	+4		+4		+4		+4
	+3		+3		+3		+3
	+2		+2		+2		+2
Reliable	+1	*Competitive*	+1	*Fast transit*	+1	*Good record for*	+1
deliveries	−1	*in price*	−1	*times*	−1	*loss and damage*	−1
	−2		−2		−2		−2
	−3		−3		−3		−3
	−4		−4		−4		−4
	−5		−5		−5		−5

Figure 7.7   A stapel scale used for assessing attitudes towards Railfreight

---

1 *If new product X sold for £2.75 and was available in the stores where you normally shop, would you:*

Definitely buy product X [SKIP to Q3]	*1*
Probably buy	*2*
Probably not buy [ASK Q2]	*3*
Definitely not buy [ASK Q2]	*4*

2 *What if the product was priced at £1.99? Would you:*

Definitely buy product X	*1*
Probably buy	*2*
Probably not buy	*3*
Definitely not buy	*4*

Figure 7.8 A purchase intent scale

Many companies use the purchase intent scale to make go/no-go decisions in product development by adding together the definitely buy and probably buy categories and comparing this total against a predetermined go/no-go threshold (say, for example, 70 per cent of respondents answering in these categories). Using past data from previous product launches, some organisations may be able to forecast the expected market share based on patterns of purchasing intentions.

Evaluating the validity and reliability of scales

To ensure the adequacy and **reliability of scales**, they should be examined in terms of their reliability and validity.

Reliability

Reliability refers to the extent to which a scale produces consistent or stable results. Stability is most commonly measured using test-retest reliability and consistency is measured using split-half reliability.

Test-retest reliability measures the stability of scale items over time. Respondents are asked to complete scales at two different times under as near identical conditions as possible. The degree of similarity between the two measurements is determined by computing a correlation coefficient (see Chapter 9). The higher the correlation coefficient, the greater the reliability. The time interval between the two measurements is critical if this measure is to be meaningful. The gap between the two tests must be long enough to ensure that responses in the second test are not influenced by the participants' memory of the first test. However, the interval shouldn't be so long that the underlying attitudes change between the tests. There is no agreed view as to the optimal time interval, but two to four weeks is normal practice.

Split-half reliability measures the internal consistency of a summated scale and refers to the consistency with which each item represents the overall construct of interest. For example, how consistently do items such as 'I like driving a Ford' and 'Ford offers value for money' measure consumer attitudes towards Ford cars. The method involves randomly dividing the various scale items into two halves (so a scale of ten items would be broken into two scales of five items) and the resulting halves are correlated (see Chapter 9). High correlations between the two halves suggest internal consistency in what is being measured. Of course, this may be influenced by how the random halves occur, so researchers will usually try to consider all possible combinations of split halves. This can be done using a statistical test, **coefficient alpha** or Cronbach alpha which considers all possible split-half coefficients resulting from different splittings of the scale. This coefficient varies between 0 and 1 with any value greater than 0.6 indicating satisfactory internal consistency-reliability.

Reliability of scales
Refers to the extent to which a rating scale produces consistent or stable results. Stability is most commonly measured using test-retest reliability and consistency is measured using split-half reliability.

Test-retest reliability
This measures the stability of rating scale items over time. Respondents are asked to complete scales at two different times under as near identical conditions as possible. The degree of similarity between the two measurements is determined by computing a correlation coefficient.

Split-half reliability
This measures the internal consistency of a summated rating scale and refers to the consistency with which each item represents the overall construct of interest. The method involves randomly dividing the various scale items into two halves. High correlations between the two halves suggests internal consistency of what is being measured.

Coefficient alpha
see Cronbach alpha

Validity
Whether the differences in the subject to be measured were actually measured by the research scale.

Content validity
A subjective yet systematic assessment as to how well a rating scale measures a topic of interest. For example, a group of subject experts may be asked to comment on the extent to which all of the key dimensions of a topic have been included.

Construct validity
An analysis of the underlying theories and past research that supports the inclusion of the various items in the scale. It is most commonly considered in two forms, convergent validity and discriminant validity.

Validity

The **validity** of a scale relates to whether the differences in the scores on the scale reflect true differences in what is being measured. The most common ways of measuring validity are content validity and construct validity. If a scale is not reliable then it isn't a valid scale; however, a reliable scale may not necessarily be valid and therefore its validity should be assessed.

Content validity involves a subjective yet systematic assessment as to how well the scale measures the topic of interest. A scale should consist of all of the dimensions of the construct or topic. For example, a staff satisfaction scale that doesn't include any dimensions on salary or rewards is unlikely to be a valid measure of overall staff satisfaction. A group of subject experts may be asked to comment on the extent to which all of the key dimensions have been included. As this type of evaluation is very subjective, it is often supplemented by considering construct validity.

Construct validity looks at the underlying theories and past research that supports the inclusion of the various items in the scale. It is most commonly considered in two forms, convergent validity and discriminant validity. **Convergent validity** is a measure of the extent to which the results from a scale correlate with those from other scales or measures of the same topic/construct. **Discriminant validity** assesses the extent to which the results from a scale do not correlate with other scales from which one would expect it to differ. For example, you would expect results from a scale looking at people's attitudes towards sports cars to correlate with scales looking at attitudes towards speed (convergent validity) and not correlate with scales looking at fuel efficiency (discriminant validity).

Step 3: select wording

Whatever form of question or scaling technique is used, care must be taken in the words that are used and the phrasing that is adopted. The complexity and style of the wording will be specific to the topic and the respondents involved. The overriding principle should be that wording and phrasing should be as simple and straightforward as possible. There are certain errors that researchers should be aware of and avoid. These are discussed in the following subsections.

Ambiguous questions

Respondents and researchers may read different meanings into questions, resulting in inappropriate or unexpected answers.

In a survey with children:

When will you leave school?

To this question, should they answer with the age when they leave school for good or should they give the time of day that the school closes?

In a survey for a paint manufacturer:

What did you decorate last?

One respondent gave the reply: 'the Christmas tree'.

To avoid such confusion and surprises, questions should be tested with a small group of potential respondents to check that their understanding of the questions is similar to that of the researcher.

> ### Researcher quote
>
> It always amazes me how many different meanings people can read into a very simple, straightforward question.

Double-barrelled questions

Double-barrelled questions are questions where two topics are raised within one question. Such questions can cause difficulty for the respondent because they do not know which of the topics to address, particularly if they have different views about each one. They also cause difficulty for the researcher team, as they are unclear as to which topic the respondent is addressing. For example:

> *Have you seen an improvement in the quality of this hotel's food and accommodation?*
>
> *Yes_____ No_____ Don't know_____*

This relates to the two separate issues of accommodation and also food. A 'no' response from the respondent could mean:

(a) there has been no improvement in either food or accommodation;
(b) there has been an improvement in food but not in accommodation;
(c) there has been an improvement in accommodation but not in food.

Only the respondent will know what he or she means. This type of problem can be overcome by breaking the question into two or more questions and rewording the questions to focus on only one issue at a time (i.e. one focusing on food and the other focusing on accommodation).

Leading or loaded questions

Leading or loaded questions are questions that tend to steer respondents towards a certain answer, particularly where the respondents are unsure as to their true feelings. For example:

> **1** *Don't you think smoking is antisocial?*
>
> *Yes___ No___*
>
> **2** *How often do you buy goods from cheap or discount-type stores such as TK Maxx?*
>
> *Very frequently   ___*
> *Frequently   ___*
> *Occasionally   ___*
> *Never   ___*
>
> **3** *Do you think students like government policies?*
>
> *Yes___ No___ Don't know___*

Because of the phrasing, 'Don't you think . . . ?', respondents are more likely to answer 'yes' to question 1. Also, emphasising the 'cheap or discount' aspect of the TK Maxx store in question 2 may make respondents less willing to say 'frequently' or 'very frequently'. In question 3, does the answer 'no' mean that the students dislike government policies or does it mean that they do not have any strong views about government policies? This question is one-sided in its current format; if the answers are to have any value it should be written as:

> *Do you think students like or dislike government policies?*
>
> *Like___ Dislike___ Neither like nor dislike____ Don't know____*

Although leading questions are sometimes used by unethical groups to gain feedback to further their particular cause or ideas, the majority are developed unknowingly by researchers who have not maintained a totally objective viewpoint throughout the questionnaire design process. Researchers must therefore take care to construct questions in as neutral a fashion as possible.

Implicit assumptions

Questions with implicit assumptions are questions where the researcher and the respondent are using different frames of reference as a result of assumptions that both parties make about the questions being asked. These have similar outcomes to ambiguous questions; the difference is that the question is clear and it is the assumptions that underlie it that are ambiguous.

> *Do you use the memory keys on your phone when making calls?*
>
> *Yes___ No___*

This question makes several implicit assumptions. First, it is not clear whether the researcher is asking about the respondent's mobile phone or landline phone (or even a phone at work). The answer is likely to vary depending on what the respondent assumes. The researcher also assumes that the respondent's phone has memory keys and that the respondent knows what they are. It is necessary to state the frame of reference with more clarity or ensure that the respondent is qualified to answer the question by using one or more filter questions. A filter question is a question that tests to see whether a respondent qualifies for or has experience relevant to a subsequent question. The following filter questions could be used to ensure that the same frame of reference is being used for the above question:

> 1 *Do you own a mobile phone?*
>
>   *Yes___ No [GO TO Q4]___*
>
> 2 *Does your mobile phone have memory keys to store telephone numbers?*
>
>   *Yes___ No [GO TO Q4]___ Don't know [GO TO Q4]*
>
> 3 *Do you use the memory keys on your phone when making calls?*
>
>   *Yes___ No___*

Filter questions are particularly important at the start of a questionnaire to screen out respondents who are inappropriate to the study being undertaken. Care must be taken with the number of filter questions as they can unnecessarily add to the length of the questionnaire and can sometimes try the patience of the respondent. In some cases it may be more appropriate to place a 'not applicable' response category in a question rather than adding an additional question as a filter.

Researcher quote

I was always told to be careful about making assumptions. If you **assume**, it can make an **ASS** of **U** and **ME**!

Integration   An international perspective

When undertaking international research, the wording may need to be changed for each country, not only because of language differences but also owing to cultural and environmental factors. Direct translation of a questionnaire may not communicate the same meaning to different nationalities of respondents. The questionnaire should be adapted to the individual environments in which it will be used, and should not be biased in terms of any one culture. For example, the interpretation of scaling questions is different with different nationalities. In many Asian cultures people are unwilling to give negative ratings about individuals or organisations. Assumptions should not be made about purchasing behaviour, as the role and position of women, family members and retailers may differ significantly. Literacy rates may also vary, resulting in difficulties with open-ended questions or complex wording.

Step 4: determine sequence

In sequencing questions in a questionnaire, it is often best to approach it from the respondent's point of view: what sequence will respondents perceive as being interesting and logical? If respondents feel that they are jumping from subject to subject, the questioning can feel more like an interrogation than a relaxed marketing research survey. Therefore, questions on similar topics should be clustered together within the questionnaire, allowing respondents to maintain their train of thought on one topic before moving on to the next.

One of the most controversial issues in sequencing is the positioning of classification questions and whether they should appear at the start or end of a questionnaire. Classification questions are questions that appear in almost all questionnaires and are concerned with gathering data on the respondent's personal or demographic characteristics. Such classification questions may be located at the start of a questionnaire if they are needed to screen (accept or reject) people for interview. For example, this may be necessary where respondents are being selected to meet the specific requirements of a quota sample.

However, in all other circumstances classification questions should be located at the end of a questionnaire. Interest and rapport must be established at the start of a questionnaire if the respondent is to complete the questions in a thorough and thoughtful manner. Questions at the start of the questionnaire should therefore be interesting and relatively straightforward both in terms of content and question format. Classification questions and questions on sensitive subjects (potentially embarrassing or private topics) should be avoided until nearer

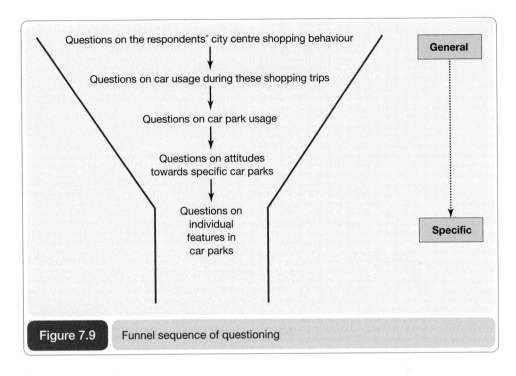

Questions on the respondents' city centre shopping behaviour

General

Questions on car usage during these shopping trips

Questions on car park usage

Questions on attitudes towards specific car parks

Questions on individual features in car parks

Specific

Figure 7.9	Funnel sequence of questioning

the end when rapport and interest have been established. Respondents may also feel more obliged to answer these questions at the end because they have already taken time and effort to answer all of the earlier questions.

Funnel sequence
A sequence of questioning that moves from the generalities of a topic to the specifics. Funnel sequencing is particularly critical where answers to earlier specific questions could bias the answers to later questions. It is also important where the researcher wishes to ensure that respondents are only asked questions that are specifically relevant to them.

Questions should follow a **funnel sequence**, moving from the generalities of a topic to the specifics. For example, if a survey was looking at attitudes towards shoppers' car parking facilities in a city centre, the funnel approach would probably move through the order shown in Figure 7.9.

Funnel sequencing is particularly critical where answers to earlier specific questions could bias the answers to later questions. It is also important where the researcher wishes to ensure that respondents are only asked questions that are specifically relevant to them. Some of the general questions at the start of the funnel sequence may act as skip questions that determine what specific questions are asked of a particular respondent further down the funnel. For example, if the respondent in the car-parking questionnaire stated that he or she only used one particular car park, then the respondent would only be asked about the features that relate to that car park. Traditionally, skip patterns involving respondents being asked different numbers of questions in different sequences needed to be as straightforward as possible if interviewers or self-administered respondents were not to become confused. This is less of a problem where computer-assisted interviewing is used as the computer package can be programmed to move around the virtual questionnaire in any way that the researcher feels to be appropriate.

Step 5: design layout and appearance

The layout and appearance of the questionnaire is particularly important in self-administered and postal questionnaires. Response rates are likely to be higher if the questionnaire looks attractive, uncluttered and easy to understand. Even where interviewers are involved, the care and attention the interviewer gives to recording the responses is likely to be influenced by the layout and appearance of the questionnaire.

The key elements are:

- **Spacing:** attempting to make a questionnaire look shorter can result in researchers using smaller typefaces and squeezing as many questions as possible onto a page. This is counter-productive – respondents and interviewers find the questionnaire difficult to use, and as a result response rates are reduced and poorer quality data is obtained. The questionnaire should look uncluttered, with plenty of space between questions and for responses to open-ended questions. In multiple-choice and scaling questions, the potential answers should be sufficiently far apart for the interviewer or respondent to be able easily to pick the proper row or column. Splitting a question or its responses over different pages to save space should also be avoided. The typeface should be clear and of a sufficient size, with instructions to the respondent or interviewer printed in capitals or bold face type to differentiate them from the questions.

- **Quality of production:** a questionnaire that is poorly reproduced on poor quality paper may prove less expensive but can give the impression that the survey is unimportant. As a result, the quality and number of responses will be adversely affected. Questionnaires can be made to look more professional by high-quality printing and paper and by stapling the pages into the form of a booklet rather than simply a sheaf of A4 paper. This is particularly important for self-administered or postal questionnaires.

- **Variety:** a questionnaire that uses similar question formats or has large banks of scaling questions can look intimidating to the respondent. So, the sequencing and layout of the questionnaire should seek visual variety in the look of the questions and the questionnaire. Colour, typefaces, borders and arrows can also be used to delineate different sections of questions or different skip patterns through the questionnaire.

- **Coding/analysis requirements:** although design and layout decisions are critical to effective data collection, those who will be involved in the coding and analysis of the questionnaires should also be consulted about the best layout and design requirements for efficient data processing.

Specific design issues for online surveys

In online surveys, there are a number of specific design issues. The most significant are:

- **Headings and progress information:** in order to motivate respondents to continue and complete a survey, researchers use a combination of page headings, section introductions and progress bars. Headings and introductions are important whenever a questionnaire changes context, highlighting the end of one section before moving onto another topic. Not only does this keep the respondent informed, but it also gives them a sense of momentum as they move through the survey. Many research industry guidelines also recommend progress bars that tell the respondent, using a moving bar or a percentage completed chart, how far through the survey they are.

- **Forced completion:** many web survey software programs can be configured to force respondents to answer every question. Forcing completion should result in the researcher obtaining the data they want without any missing sections. However, forced completion can also result in lower response rates, suggesting that respondents may prefer to abandon a survey rather than be forced to answer a question that they don't want to answer or where they don't agree with any of the options available to them. Best practice is to keep open-ended questions unforced, with closed questions being forced with a 'prefer not to say' option added to particularly sensitive questions.

- **The first page:** the first page of the online survey should be welcoming and provide a brief outline about the nature of the survey and the expected length of the survey. There should also be important information regarding privacy policy: confirmation that the survey is operated in accordance with the MRS Code of Conduct, together with details of who is conducting the research and how they can be contacted. If there is a prize draw or other reward, this should be stated on the first page with a link to a separate terms and conditions (and the terms and conditions should have a 'Print' function so that the respondent can make their own copy).

- **The last page:** the last page should thank the respondent and ask for any final comments on the research topic or the survey. If the study includes a prize draw or if the survey offers the respondent the opportunity to take part in further activity, such as joining an online panel, then the survey should seek contact details on this last page.
- **Multimedia:** it is possible to incorporate images (logos and pictures of products), audio, video (using Flash technology), animated and interactive components (sliders to enter rating scales; drag and drop options) in online surveys. However, they may not work properly on certain types of PC, web browsers or at different download speeds. Audio clips may not be practical where the PC is being used at work or in a public place. The researcher needs to ensure that the use of multimedia enhances the research instrument rather than creating so much variability that the research results become questionable. There is also a need to consider people who may have difficulty with multimedia, such as those with a visual impairment. A number of countries employ legislation and initiatives aimed at ensuring that as many people as possible can view and use a website. No respondent should be discriminated against, and this is particularly the case for studies undertaken by government or public organisations.

Software for questionnaire development

There are many computer packages that can help in the design and layout of traditional and web-based surveys. In the UK examples of such software include **Snap** (an evaluation copy is included in this book), QPSMR, MerlinPlus, Confirmit and Visual QSL. In a package such as the **Snap** package from Mercator, the researcher only needs to type in the questions to be asked and the package will produce the layout for the questionnaire, including instructions and scaling questions, in an attractive and clear manner. Following the completion of the interviews, the data can be fed back into the same package for analysis. A particular benefit of these packages is that the question-and-answer text and data definitions from the questionnaire can be taken over into the analysis and tabulation of results without requiring to be rekeyed into the computer. If you wish to try using software to develop a short questionnaire, the evaluation version of Snap accompanying this book allows you to create short questionnaires (a maximum of 10 questions and 25 respondents per survey). The quick guide in the Appendix provides tutorial guidance on how to do this.

Step 6: pilot test

Pilot testing
The pre-testing of a questionnaire prior to undertaking a full survey. Such testing involves administering the questionnaire to a limited number of potential respondents in order to identify and correct flaws in the questionnaire design.

Pilot testing (sometimes known as *pre-testing*) involves administering a questionnaire to a limited number of potential respondents in order to identify and correct design flaws. The potential respondents for the pilot test and for the full survey should be drawn from the same populations. The questionnaire should also be administered in the same manner as that planned for the full survey. Where interviewers are involved, they should be able to identify errors in the format and nature of questions, judge respondent reaction to the questionnaire, measure the time taken to complete the questionnaire, and determine the overall appropriateness of the questionnaire to the target population. However, where the questionnaire is self-administered, a researcher should be present during the pilot test when respondents are completing the questions. Some respondents are then asked to voice their thoughts as they attempt to answer each question. Others will be asked to complete the questionnaire in a normal fashion so that the time for completion can be noted and then they will be asked to explain their experiences with the questionnaire.

Normally, the pilot test sample is relatively small, varying between 10 and 40 respondents, depending upon the heterogeneity of the target population. It is better to test the questionnaire systematically with detailed probing of a small sample rather than doing superficial testing with a large one.

If significant changes are made to the questionnaire following the pilot test, it is recommended that the pilot test be repeated with the revised questionnaire.

Researcher quote

Pilot testing is critical if you want to make sure that the questionnaire is going to fully address your information targets.

Step 7: undertake survey

Following the pilot test, the managers who will be using the information from the research should always be asked to finally approve a questionnaire before it goes 'live' with the respondents. This ensures that there will be no disputes at the end of the project about incorrect or inappropriate questions being asked. Once the approval has been received, the data collection can commence.

Summary and an integrated approach

This chapter has examined the sequential stages involved in designing a questionnaire for quantitative research. The process consists of the following:

1 develop question topics;
2 select question and response formats;
3 select wording;
4 determine sequence;
5 design layout and appearance;
6 pilot test;
7 undertake survey.

Specific emphasis was placed on describing the three main types of question (open, closed and scaled response) and their usage. The different types of each were explained, including the most commonly used scaling approaches (constant sum, Likert, semantic differential, stapel and purchase intent scales). Guidelines were also provided regarding the wording, sequencing, layout and pilot testing of questionnaires.

Questionnaire design has a major influence on the quality of data gathered in any survey. It also has a major impact on the response rates in self-administered studies. Therefore, it is critical that a systematic and careful approach is taken to questionnaire design if research money is not to be wasted.

In terms of integration, there is little point in replicating information that may already be available on customer databases, since asking respondents to confirm details about their buying behaviour, product ownership or service usage simply lengthens the questionnaire, resulting in frustrated respondents and added costs. Frustrated respondents give poor-quality responses and are less willing to take part in future research projects.

Discussion questions

1 Explain the concept of 'noise' in questionnaire design.

2 What factors should a researcher consider when developing question topics?

3 Why would a researcher choose to use an open-ended question?

4 What factors are critical in the development of multiple-choice questions?

5 Explain the difference between comparative and non-comparative rating scales.

6 Explain the difference between forced and non-forced rating scales.

7 What are the main differences between a Likert scale and a semantic differential scale?

8 In wording questions, what are the main faults that a researcher should attempt to avoid?

9 Explain what is meant by the funnel sequence of questioning.

10 What are the main elements that should be considered in designing the layout and appearance of a questionnaire?

Additional reading

Albaum, G. (1997) The Likert scale revisited. *Journal of the Market Research Society*, **39**(2), pp. 331–48.

Albaum, G., Roster, C., Yu, J.H. and Rogers, R.D. (2007) Simple rating scale formats: exploring extreme response. *International Journal of Market Research*, **49**(5), pp. 633–50.

Brace, I. (2004) *Questionnaire Design: How to Plan, Structure and Write Survey Material for Effective Market Research*. Kogan Page, London.

Dawes, J. (2008) Do data characteristics change according to the number of scale points used? An experiment using 5-point, 7-point and 10-point scales. *International Journal of Market Research*, **50**(1), pp. 61–77.

Gendall, P. (2005) The effect of covering letter personalisation in mail surveys. *International Journal of Market Research*, **47**(4), pp. 367–82.

Lietz, P. (2010) Research into questionnaire design: a summary of the literature. *International Journal of Market Research*, **52**(2), pp. 249–72.

Likert, R. (1932) A technique for the measurement of attitudes. *Archives of Psychology*, 140. Also in Summers, G.F. (ed.) (1970) *Attitude Measurement*. Rand McNally, Chicago, IL, pp. 149–58.

Moskowitz, H.R. and Martin, B. (2008) Optimising the language of email survey invitations. *International Journal of Market Research*, **50**(4), pp. 491–510.

Oppenheim, A.N. (1992) *Questionnaire Design, Interviewing and Attitude Measurement*. Pinter Publishers, London.

Reynolds, N., Diamantopoulos, A. and Schlegelmilch, B.B. (1993) Pre-testing in questionnaire design: a review of the literature and suggestions for further research. *Journal of the Market Research Society*, **35**, April, pp. 171–82.

Sudman, S. and Bradburn, N.M. (1983) *Asking Questions*. Jossey Bass, San Francisco, CA.

Reference

[1] For more information see **www.tgisurveys.com**.

8 Sampling methods

Television audience measurement

Television audience measurement is about providing estimates of the number of people watching television. It exists in almost all countries where commercial television broadcasting occurs and the estimates it provides are very important to:

CreativeAct – Technology series/Alamy

- *commercial and public broadcasting companies* who make and schedule programmes – to understand how much to charge advertisers and understand what programmes are popular with whom and at what time;
- *advertisers* who want to select slots that are likely to be seen by the target audience that they are interested in;
- *organisers of events*, such as the World Cup – as the audience statistics can be used to estimate the price they should charge for broadcasting rights around the world;
- *companies* such as Ford that sponsor events such as the UEFA Champions league football tournament who want to know how many people are seeing their brand associated with the event.

In the UK, television viewing estimates are obtained from a panel of television-owning private homes representing the viewing behaviour of the 26 million TV households within the UK. The panel is selected to be representative of each ITV and BBC region, with predetermined sample sizes. Each home represents, on average, about 5,000 of the UK population. Each home has a peoplemeter, which is a box about the size of a paperback book with a display screen that sits near or on top of the television. The meter comes with a remote control, and each member of the household is assigned an individual button which they are asked to press every time they enter or leave the room while the television is on. All the devices in a home are connected to a central unit which is polled by the research company's computer each night through the panel member's telephone line. If the TV is turned on and no viewer identifies himself, the meter flashes to remind them to press their button.

Appropriate sampling is critical, if the estimates are to be of value and are to be trusted. Panel homes are selected via a multistage, stratified and unclustered sample design so that the panel is representative of all television households across the UK. A range of individual and household characteristics are deployed to ensure that the panel is representative. The prime characteristics are a 20-cell matrix, made up of means of TV reception, life stage (pre-family, young family, older family, post-family and retired) and social grade. As information on the large majority of characteristics is not available from census data, it is necessary to conduct an Establishment Survey to obtain this information.

The BARB Establishment Survey has the aim of measuring the characteristics of UK households (demographics, viewing equipment, etc.), producing universes for panel control and weighting purposes. It is carried out on a continuous basis and involves some 53,000 interviews per annum. It is a random probability survey, which means that every private residential household within the UK has a chance of being selected for interview. Interviews are conducted face-to-face using Computer Assisted Personal Interviewing (CAPI) and take, on average, 20 minutes to complete. The survey ensures that any changes taking place in the population can be identified so that the television viewing panel can be updated and adjusted to ensure that it continues to reflect the television-owning population. In addition to being the prime source of television population information, the Establishment Survey also generates the supply of addresses as the sample frame from which the viewing panel is recruited.[1]

Learning outcomes

After reading this chapter you should:

- be aware of the steps involved in the sampling process;
- understand the concepts of population and sampling frame;
- be aware of the different types of probability and non-probability sampling techniques;
- be aware of some of the problems involved in sampling for Internet surveys;
- be able to explain how to determine the sample size for a survey;
- understand the concepts of sampling and non-sampling error.

Key words

access panels
area sampling
census
cluster sampling
confidence levels
convenience sampling
data errors
disproportionate stratified random
    sampling
Interviewer Quality Control Scheme (IQCS)
judgement sampling
multi-stage sampling
non-probability sampling
non-response errors
non-sampling errors

normal distribution
population of interest
probability sampling
proportionate stratified random sampling
quota sampling
sample
sampling
sampling error
sampling frame
sampling frame error
simple random sampling
snowball sampling
stratified random sampling
systematic sampling
weighting

Introduction

In quantitative marketing research, it is very unlikely that a researcher will be able to survey every person in the target market or population of interest. Constraints of time and money restrict researchers to seeking a sample of respondents that is representative of that population. The selection of that sample is critical to the accuracy with which the data that are collected reflects the reality of the behaviour, awareness and opinions of the total target market. In any study, researchers need answers to questions such as:

- What type of people do we want to survey?
- Where do we find these types of people?
- How do we select the individuals involved?
- How many individuals do we need to survey?
- How representative is the information we collect?

This chapter sets out the process involved in answering these questions through the development of a sampling plan. The major sampling approaches that are available to the marketing researcher will also be discussed, as will the sampling and non-sampling errors associated with quantitative research.

The sampling process

Sampling
The selection of a sample of respondents that is representative of a population of interest.

The process involved in developing a **sampling** plan can be summarised in the six steps shown in Figure 8.1. The remainder of this chapter will discuss each of these steps in detail.

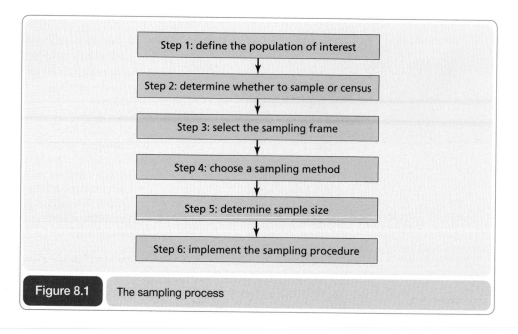

Step 1: define the population of interest

Step 2: determine whether to sample or census

Step 3: select the sampling frame

Step 4: choose a sampling method

Step 5: determine sample size

Step 6: implement the sampling procedure

Figure 8.1   The sampling process

Step 1: define the population of interest

Population of interest
The total group of people that the researcher wishes to examine, study or obtain information from. The population of interest will normally reflect the target market or potential target market for the product or service being researched. Sometimes known as the *target population* or *universe*.

The **population of interest** (sometimes referred to as the *target population* or *universe*) is the total group of people that the researcher wishes to examine, study or obtain information from. The population of interest will normally reflect the target market or potential target market for the product or service being researched. However, accurate delineation of the population of interest is the key foundation step in the sampling process. For example, a researcher conducting a study into the potential market for an updated model of the VW Golf may need to consider a wide range of categories as potential delineators before coming to a clear definition of the population he or she is interested in.

Possible categories

- All car drivers.
- Current owners of VW Golfs.
- Current owners of mid-size hatchbacks.
- People who have previously sought information on VW Golf models.
- Those who are likely to purchase cars in the next 24 months.
- Those who are likely to purchase mid-size hatchbacks in the next 24 months.

Final definition of population

- Car drivers who are current owners of mid-size hatchbacks who are likely to purchase a replacement mid-size hatchback in the next 24 months.

It is then up to the researchers to provide explicit instructions about the qualifications for inclusion in the target population to interviewers or those responsible for developing a mailing list for a postal survey. Screening questions will then be developed to qualify which respondents should or should not be included in the research. Certain groups of the population of interest may be excluded for obvious reasons (e.g. employees of car manufacturers or dealerships may be excluded as they may work for competitors or have atypical opinions). There are no specific rules or guidelines for defining the population of interest – it simply requires careful, logical thinking about the characteristics of the target market or target audience.

Researcher quote

You should always take time to carefully think through the nature of the population of interest.

Step 2: determine whether to sample or census

Census
Research which involves collecting data from every member of the population of interest.

A **census** occurs when data is obtained from every member of the population of interest. For example, the UK government population census, which takes place every ten years, requires every adult in the UK to provide information about characteristics such as employment, travel patterns, family relationships, etc. This is a very large, complicated and expensive data-gathering exercise, which may partially explain why it can only be done on a ten-yearly basis. Censuses in marketing research are also very rare. Many populations of interest may consist of thousands or even hundreds of thousands of people. The cost, time and effort that is required to interview every single person is prohibitive for marketers and marketing researchers. The value of interviewing every person may also be questionable, as the data are likely to be only marginally better than data obtained from a carefully designed sample.

Censuses are occasionally used for research involving specialised industrial products or services where the number of customers is very small. For example, a research project looking at the use of specialised chemicals in the paper-making industry may be able to gather information from all of the paper mills in the country or region being investigated. However, it should be stressed that this is only appropriate where the market is very small and specialised; for most studies a **sample** of the population of interest will be sought.

Sample
A subset of the population of interest.

Step 3: select the sampling frame

Sampling frame
A list of the population of interest from which the researcher selects the individuals for inclusion in the research.

The **sampling frame** is a list of the population of interest from which the researcher selects the individuals for inclusion in the research. It can be a list of names and telephone numbers for telephone surveys, a list of addresses for mail or doorstep interviews, or a map showing local housing. It is unlikely that the list will match the population of interest exactly. If we wanted to interview every household within a town, we could use the town's telephone directory as our sample frame. However, people may have moved or died recently; some may not have their telephone number listed in the directory; some may prefer to use a mobile phone and some may not have any phone at all. The researcher will need to determine whether the residents included in the telephone directory are likely to differ markedly from those who are not included. The answer will probably be yes, as those without telephones are likely to be in the poorer than average category, those using mobiles will be younger than average and those likely to be unlisted will be more affluent than average. This difference means that a sample based on the telephone directory will have **sampling frame error**. The nature of this will be discussed in more detail in the section on sampling and non-sampling error later in the chapter.

Sampling frame error
A bias that occurs as a result of the population implied by the sampling frame being different from the population of interest.

To reduce sampling frame error, a number of lists may be added together to create the sample frame. There may be a wide range of lists available, which may relate to mailing lists of homeowners, magazine subscribers, people who have responded to previous direct mail campaigns, retail loyalty cardholders, members of clubs, etc. Similar lists exist of manufacturers, distributors, service organisations and retailers in the business-to-business research sector.

Where no lists exist, it may be necessary to use a general list of the population. Potential respondents would then be selected based on their answers to a number of filter questions which would screen them either into or out of the research. In telephone research the procedure of random digit dialling can be used, where the numbers to be telephoned are selected using random number-generation software. This selects numbers in a random manner similar to the numbers being chosen for the national lottery.

Access panels
A database of individuals who have agreed to be available for surveys of varying types and topics. Rising rates of refusals and non response, make it more difficult to recruit for a single survey, therefore sampling from a pool of potentially willing marketing research respondents can be seen as an appropriate way of saving time and money.

A growing trend in the market research industry is the use of **access panels** as the sample frame for predominately online surveys but also for telephone and face-to-face surveys. An access panel is a database of individuals who have agreed to be available for surveys of varying types and topics. Rising rates of refusals and non-response make it more difficult to recruit for a single survey; therefore, sampling from a pool of potentially willing marketing research respondents can be seen as an appropriate way of saving time and money. Many agencies have built an access panel in order to avoid the challenges involved with random recruitment and the potential inaccuracies and unpredictability of other databases. The various sampling procedures that are discussed later in this chapter can generally be applied to a sample frame constructed from an access panel, although care must be taken to ensure that the same respondents are not selected all of the time, otherwise respondent fatigue and boredom can set in, impacting on response rates and the quality of the data. Strict panel management is required, and relationships need to be developed with panel members in order to build loyalty and a willingness to complete surveys when requested.

Overall, whichever sample frame is used, it is generally unlikely that it will be a perfect fit for any particular study. It is therefore important for the researcher to be aware of any short-comings in the sample frame in order to make adjustments in the remaining steps of the sampling process.

Integration | An international perspective

How do you achieve true representativeness and comparability across 12,000 interviews in countries as diverse as Russia, Nigeria, Egypt, Kenya and Tanzania? And which do not even have accurate or recent census data?

When the BBC first approached Ipsos MORI about running a large-scale audience measurement survey across such diverse countries, the international research team knew that, in addition to the usual issues of faithful local language translation and practical time differences, the project would require additional planning and training in two areas: first, sample design and, second, questionnaire administration and content.

In this survey, the BBC World Service needed to ensure proper coverage of those people who rely on the radio as a source of information – the poor in remote areas (who do not even have a TV as a source of information).

Second, in terms of questionnaire design and administration, many of the required non-urban population are unable to read or write, so different interviewing skills and procedures are needed. And with a typical interview taking one hour in English, longer in local languages, the ability to maintain cooperation levels (without incentives – a UK phenomenon) was critical.

Ipsos MORI's involvement in this survey first started in 13 countries in 2004 and was repeated in 2005 in the above six countries. Using its own research network and recommendations from the BBC World Service, Ipsos MORI has evolved and developed its working relationship over time with regional offices and partnering organisations across countries to successfully carry out the fieldwork requirements each year.

In 2005, the lead team in London completed full personal briefings with the local countries to ensure the survey's objectives and nuances were clear, as well as to raise suggested solutions for any possible obstacles they could run into during the fieldwork process. This also gave executives working on the project invaluable insight into these markets and helped to solidify established working relationships with regional partners – and a trusted regional coordination hub approach has been selectively used. For example, to manage the fieldwork in each of the three African nations being studied in 2005, Ipsos MORI used a central point of contact in South Africa to liaise with the local agencies in Kenya, Tanzania and Nigeria.

With no universal telephone access and limited communications infrastructure, the best way to get in touch effectively with the desired universe in varied economic infrastructures, climates and living situations is face-to-face. Face-to-face interviews were the natural fit for this type of audience measurement and attitudes survey, and interviewers in the field had to deal with problems in tracking down respondents whose living arrangements were very varied and also in which a significant proportion lived outside the main cities in extremely rural areas. One major challenge was to reach and interview enough illiterate respondents to achieve a nationally representative sample, and to ensure these participants were not turned off from completing the survey by the amount of time and extra steps needed to complete it without reading.

Because the questionnaire included sections in which respondents' answers were based on cards held up by the interviewers, illiterate respondents took significantly more time to complete the full survey (one hour for literate English respondents), as the interviewer needed to read out the possible answers on each card. While face-to-face interviewing and working with illiterate respondents proved laborious, it is the most effective way to achieve a truly random sample in countries without a modern tele-communications infrastructure in place.

Achieving uniformity in the questionnaire was a challenge from the start. For example, in 2005 this had to be translated into Russian, Arabic, two divergent versions of Kiswahlili for the Tanzanian and Kenyan surveys, and Igbo, Yoruba, Hausa – all native languages spoken in different regions of Nigeria. To ensure the questionnaire was well translated and would be accepted in each of the very different local cultures being surveyed, the lead Ipsos MORI team guided translations by local agency contacts, with regional offices and the executives working on the project in each participating country reviewing the language for consistency with local dialect and custom. An independent review of the translations was made before they were put in the field. Managing accountability and communication between regional offices and the lead team and client can be a challenge on any international project. Notwithstanding the varying resources available in each of the countries in this 2005 study, the lead London team was bridging seven timelines and, due to client internal reporting deadlines, had to ensure the progress and completion by country was kept close together even though the sample size varied from 1,000 to 3,000 per country. With both Ipsos MORI and the BBC World Service having conducted similar projects around the globe in the past, both the client and agency knew to set clear schedules and to manage internal expecta-tions by allowing sufficient flexibility in to the timeline to allow for the type of problems known to arise – from a government declaring unexpected national holidays to regional uprisings!

(Source: Ipsos Mori broadcasts its solution to the BBC World Service. *Research Business*, 2006 – reproduced here with the permission of the Market Research Society)

Step 4: choose a sampling method

Sampling methods can be grouped under two headings, probability and non-probability sampling.

Probability sampling methods

Probability sampling
A set of sampling methods where an objective procedure of selection is used, resulting in every member of the population of interest having a known probability of being selected.

These comprise samples in which an objective procedure of selection is used, resulting in every member of the population of interest having a known probability of being selected. In **probability sampling** the researcher specifies some objective and systematic procedure for choosing potential respondents from a population. Once the procedure has been set out, the selection of potential respondents is independent of any arbitrary, convenient or biased selec-tion by the researcher. This systematic approach enables probabilities to be assigned to (a) the likelihood of each member of the population being surveyed and (b) the extent to which the values obtained in the survey can be projected to reflect the true values held by the population as a whole. This second area relates to sampling error (the difference between the sample value and the true value of a phenomenon for the population being surveyed), which can be stated in mathematical terms: usually the survey result plus or minus a certain percentage.

Probability sampling methods

Advantages

- The survey results are projectable to the total population (plus or minus the sampling error) – the data is definitive rather than indicative.
- The sampling error can be computed.
- The researcher can be sure of obtaining information from a relatively representative group of the population of interest.

Disadvantage

- The rules for respondent selection and sample design significantly increase the researcher/interviewer costs, time and effort.

Non-probability sampling methods

These comprise samples in which a subjective procedure of selection is used, resulting in the probability of selection for each member of the population of interest being unknown. A large proportion of marketing research studies use **non-probability sampling** methods, as they can be executed more quickly and easily than probability samples.

Non-probability sampling
A set of sampling methods where a subjective procedure of selection is used resulting in the probability of selection for each member of the population of interest being unknown.

Non-probability sampling methods

Advantages

- The cost is significantly less than probability samples to undertake.
- The less stringent procedures required in potential respondent selection mean that they can be conducted reasonably quickly.
- Sample sizes tend to be smaller.
- The researcher can target the most important respondents.

Disadvantages

- Indicative rather than definitive results.
- Sampling error cannot be computed.
- The researcher does not know the degree to which the sample is representative of the population from which it is drawn.
- The researcher needs to make certain assumptions about the groupings within the population of interest.

The most commonly used sampling methods are shown in Table 8.1.

Table 8.1	Most commonly used sampling methods

Probability sampling methods	Non-probability sampling methods
Simple random sampling	Convenience sampling
Systematic sampling	Judgement sampling
Stratified random sampling	Quota sampling
Cluster sampling	Snowball sampling

The types of probability sampling

Simple random sampling

Simple random sampling
A probability sampling method where every possible member of the population has an equal chance of being selected for the survey. Respondents are chosen using random numbers.

In **simple random sampling**, every possible member of the population has an equal chance of being selected for the survey. If a list of the population is available, we can number each of the members of the population and select the sample either on the basis of random numbers generated by a computer or a published table of random numbers.

> For example, if we wanted five potential respondents from a population of 25, the random number generator may select the following five people: numbers 3, 9, 14, 15, 24. These are the people we would approach for interview.

For a simple random sample, the probability of a population member being picked is calculated using the following formula:

$$probability\ of\ selection = \frac{population\ size}{sample\ size\ required}$$

For example, if the population is 1,000 and the sample size is 200, then the probability of selection is 1 in 5. Each member of the population has a 1 in 5 chance of being selected (5 = 1,000/200).

If a complete listing of the population is available, simple random samples live up to their name and involve a very straightforward procedure. However, a complete, up-to-date population listing is extremely difficult to obtain and therefore tends to be limited to two specific situations:

1 Where a company is selecting people from a population that is defined as its own database of customers. Computer programs can then select random samples from the database.
2 Where random digit dialling is used for telephone interviews. So, in a survey of fixed-line telephone users being carried out in Glasgow the area code would remain constant but a computer would randomly generate all the remaining digits in the telephone number.

Researcher quote

> Simple random sampling is only possible when we can get a complete, up-to-date listing of the population of interest.

Systematic sampling

Systematic sampling
A probability sampling approach similar to simple random sampling but which uses a skip interval (i.e. every nth person) rather than random numbers to select the respondents.

Systematic sampling produces samples that are almost identical to those generated by simple random sampling. However, it is considered to be easier to implement, as it does not involve random number generation or tables for selection of all potential respondents.

It does require a full listing of the population, as in simple random sampling, but these do not need to be numbered. Instead a **skip interval** is calculated and the names are selected on the basis of this skip interval.

The calculation can be computed using the following formula (which is the same as the one used for calculating the probability of selection set out above):

$$skip\ interval = \frac{population\ size}{sample\ size}$$

For example, using the earlier example, if the population is 1,000 and the sample size is 200, then the skip interval is 5 and so every fifth name from a list would be selected for the sample. A random starting number should be drawn to determine where the skip pattern should start. For example, the random starting point may be 4. Combining this with a skip pattern of 5 results in the following names being used in the sample: 4th, 9th, 14th, 19th, . . . 999th.

The systematic sample is far easier to construct using this approach than is the case for simple random sampling. As a result, the time and cost involved in sample design is less. There is a remote possibility that there are certain patterns in the listing of the population and by taking every *n*th person, the sample is not representative of all groups in the population. For example, selecting respondents on an aeroplane using a systematic sampling method and seat numbers may always include bulkhead and emergency exit rows, which may bias any measurement of attitudes relating to leg room. It is, therefore, always worthwhile to examine the selected sample to ensure that there are no obvious anomalies.

Stratified random sampling

Stratified random sampling
A probability sampling procedure in which the chosen sample is forced to contain potential respondents from each of the key segments of the population.

Stratified random sampling is a probability sampling procedure in which the chosen sample is forced to contain potential respondents from each of the key segments of the population.

It is created by first dividing the population of interest into two or more mutually exclusive and exhaustive subsets, and then taking random samples (either simple random or systematic sampling) within each subset. Subsets may relate to different age ranges in the population, gender, ethnic backgrounds, etc.

In many cases, stratified samples are used rather than simple or systematic random sampling because of their statistical efficiency. The sampling error (i.e. the difference between the survey result and the value for the population as a whole) is likely to be smaller for a stratified sample than for a simple or systematic random sample. This can be shown by the following example:

The following grid represents the population of interest (50 individuals, 40 per cent of whom are male (M) and 60 per cent female (F)). The researcher requires a sample of 10. A systematic sample starting at person 3 with a skip interval of 5 would select the people who are shaded (7 males and 3 females). If the purchasing behaviour of males and females is significantly different then the data from the sample will not reflect the situation within the overall population.

M	F	M	F	F	F	M	M	M	F
F	F	M	M	M	F	F	F	F	F
F	F	F	F	F	M	M	M	M	M
F	F	M	F	M	F	F	M	M	F
F	F	M	F	F	F	M	F	F	M

With a stratified sample, the population can be split into, say, the two subsets of males and females, and the importance of each can be reflected in the sample. This can be done in one of two ways: proportionate and disproportionate stratified random sampling.

Proportionate stratified random sampling

Proportionate stratified random sampling is where the units or potential respondents from each population subset are selected in proportion to the total number of each subset's units in the population. For the example above, that would mean 60 per cent of the sample would be female and the remaining 40 per cent would be male. Although this approach has better statistical efficiency than simple random samples, it does have problems where a subset makes up only a small percentage of the total population. This can result in the sample for that subset being very small, making it very difficult for the researcher to do any specific analysis that focuses on that subset alone or where comparisons are to be made between subsets.

Disproportionate stratified random sampling

Disproportionate stratified random sampling is where the units or potential respondents from each population set are selected according to the relative variability of the units within each subset. This approach provides one of the most efficient and reliable samples. There are two steps involved. First, the number of units/potential respondents to be taken from each subset are determined in the same manner as for a proportionate sample. Then the numbers are adjusted to take relatively more units from those subsets that have larger standard deviations (more variation) and relatively fewer units from those subsets having smaller standard deviations. This allocates more units to the subsets where the potential for sampling error is greatest. A potential difficulty in this procedure is that the researcher may not know in advance the level of diversity that exists within each subset. Consequently, proportionate, rather than disproportionate, random sampling is more commonly used. However, if there is variability and researchers are also concerned about small subsets, they may adopt the procedure of drawing samples of equal rather than proportionate size from each subset.

Cluster sampling

An adequate sampling frame may not be available to allow the researcher to adopt the random sampling approaches that have been discussed thus far. Where this is the case, **cluster sampling** is often used.

With cluster sampling, the researcher does not need to produce a complete sample frame for the total population, but instead only needs to develop sample frames for the clusters that are selected. This makes the sampling process shorter and potentially less complicated. Each of the clusters should ideally represent the total population in microcosm. This means that the make-up of each of the clusters is similar with similar levels of variability within each cluster. This is very different from the subsets in stratified random sampling, where the subsets had to be homogeneous and significantly different from each other. However, the ease of sample selection in cluster sampling must be balanced against the potential difficulty in forming clusters that truly reflect the total population in miniature. Cluster sampling, therefore, tends to be limited to situations where the population can be easily divided into representative clusters. One of the most common approaches is using names in a membership directory or telephone directory.

Proportionate stratified random sampling
A form of stratified random sampling (*See* **Stratified random sampling**) where the units or potential respondents from each population subset are selected in proportion to the total number of each subset's units in the population.

Disproportionate stratified random sampling
A form of stratified random sampling (*See* **Stratified random sampling**) where the units or potential respondents from each population set are selected according to the relative variability of the units within each subset.

Cluster sampling
A probability sampling approach in which clusters of population units are selected at random and then all (one-stage cluster sampling) or some (two-stage cluster sampling) of the units in the chosen clusters are studied.

> A directory holds 50,000 names listed alphabetically on 500 pages with 100 names on each page. If the researcher wants a cluster sample of 1,000 names, he or she can randomly select ten pages and take all of the names from these pages as the sample. As the names are listed alphabetically, the sample should be representative of the total directory. This may not be the case if the area of study is influenced by ethnic factors, as certain sections of the directory may be biased towards certain ethnic groups, e.g. names starting with Mc and Mac (Scottish), or common names such as Patel (Asian) or Smith (English).

There are a number of different approaches to cluster sampling:

- **One-stage cluster sampling** (sometimes known as *simple cluster sampling*): once the clusters have been selected by random selection, data are collected from all of the units/ people in the selected clusters.
- **Two-stage cluster sampling:** once the clusters have been selected by random selection, a random sample is taken of the population units in each of the selected clusters. The two-stage approach tends to be used when the clusters are relatively large.
- **Area sampling:** a type of cluster sampling in which the clusters are created on the basis of the geographic location of the population of interest. **Area sampling** is probably the most widely used version of cluster sampling. A researcher undertaking a door-to-door survey may divide an area into neighbourhoods, housing blocks or streets and choose a random sample of these. After selecting the geographical clusters to be included, a sample of potential respondents will be approached in each cluster area. No sample frame is needed for the geographical clusters that are not selected. There is the possibility with area sampling that sections of the population could be excluded because the areas are not totally representative of the population as a whole. This is particularly the case when one considers that inhabitants of a particular neighbourhood are more likely to be like each other than like people in other neighbourhoods. To compensate for this and to reduce sampling errors, researchers are advised to use a large number of small clusters rather than a small number of large clusters.

Area sampling
A type of cluster sampling in which the clusters are created on the basis of the geographic location of the population of interest.

Multi-stage sampling

When sampling national populations, a representative sample will be necessary but researchers may also require interviews to be concentrated in convenient areas. To achieve this, a multi-stage approach in developing a sample may be needed. As the name suggests, the sample selection process involves a number of successive sampling stages before the final sample is obtained.

For example, a sample of households in the UK may be developed using the following steps:

1 List the postcode areas in the UK. The postcode areas are selected from the list so that each postcode area has a probability of being selected proportionate to the number of addresses each contains (for example, G, the Glasgow postal area, may be chosen at this stage).
2 Within each postcode area selected, all postcode districts would be listed in order of number of addresses each contains. Selection of postcode districts would also be proportionate to their number of addresses (for example, the district G4 may be selected at this stage).
3 Within each selected postcode district, individual postcode locations would be chosen proportionate to the number of households within each postcode cluster (usually around 15 homes).
4 One household would be chosen from the selected locations using systematic random sampling procedures.

Multi-stage sampling
A sampling approach where a number of successive sampling stages are undertaken before the final sample is obtained.

This example of **multi-stage sampling** can be seen as a combination of stratified sampling, cluster sampling and systematic sampling. By using this combination of methods, the researcher does not need to have a full list of all the households in the UK; instead, all that is required is a list of households for each of the selected postcodes.

The types of non-probability sample

Convenience sampling

Convenience sampling
A non-probability sampling procedure in which a researcher's convenience forms the basis for selecting the potential respondents (i.e. the researcher approaches the most accessible members of the population of interest).

Convenience sampling is a procedure in which a researcher's convenience forms the basis for selecting the potential respondents. The researcher approaches the most accessible members of the population of interest. This may mean stopping people in the middle of a shopping street, interviewing employees that are present in an office, interviewing customers as they exit a service outlet or selecting names from a company's database. This may seem to be very biased and unprofessional. However, if the composition of the selected sample is reasonably similar to the population of interest, it can provide useful information, particularly for exploratory research purposes. Where a client is seeking an indication of what is going on in the market place, a convenience sample may provide the answers. However, care and time should be taken in thinking through the appropriateness of the particular sample to the study and the population of interest (for example, asking people waiting in a railway station about public transport may not be appropriate if the researcher is interested in the views of the population as a whole).

Judgement sampling

Judgement sampling
A non-probability sampling procedure where a researcher consciously selects a sample that he or she considers to be most appropriate for the research study.

Judgement sampling (sometimes known as *purposive sampling*) refers to any procedure where a researcher consciously selects a sample that he or she considers to be most appropriate for the research study. This is different from convenience sampling, where a researcher may consider the appropriateness of a sample but will not exert any effort to make it representative of the population of interest. Judgement samples involve the deliberate choice of each sample member. For example, in business-to-business or industrial markets, certain companies may be selected to appear in the sample because they are typical of the purchasers in a particular segment (for example, Shell and BP may be included as being typical of large oil companies). In consumer research, certain neighbourhoods may be selected as representing the typical mix of the population of interest. Judgement samples are particularly appropriate where the sample size for a research project is relatively small. In small samples, a carefully chosen judgement sample may be better able to represent the mix of potential respondents in a population than even a probability sample as you can balance your sample to be in keeping with known market characteristics.

Quota sampling

Quota sampling
A non-probability sampling procedure which involves the selection of cells or subsets within the population of interest, the establishment of a numerical quota in each cell and the researcher carrying out sufficient interviews in each cell to satisfy the quota.

Quota sampling involves the selection of cells or subsets within the population of interest. A numerical quota is established for each cell and interviewers are asked to carry out sufficient interviews in each cell to satisfy the quota. For example, a sample of 100 adults may be constructed with the following quotas covering eight sample cells:

Age (years)	Male	Female
20–29	10	10
30–44	10	10
45–59	25	25
60 or over	5	5

Quota samples and stratified samples are often confused; however, there are two significant differences between the two approaches. First, potential respondents for a quota sample are not selected on a random basis, as they need to be for a stratified sample. In quota samples the potential respondents are selected on a subjective basis, with the only requirement being that a designated number are interviewed in each cell. Second, the factors used for determining the subsets must be selected on the basis of a correlation between the factors and the topics being investigated. In quota samples, the factors used for selecting the quotas are selected on the basis of researcher judgement only. Quota samples do allow the researcher to define the cells using a number of characteristics (e.g. sex, age, location, socioeconomic group, product use, etc.) in combination rather than the one (or occasionally two) in stratified random sampling.

If the control characteristics used in designing the cells are relevant to the research questions, then quota sampling is superior to judgement and convenience sampling in terms of sample representativeness. However, care must be taken to ensure that the definitions of the cells are not so complicated (e.g. having a cell that requires ten respondents who are 20–25 years old, have an income in excess of £28,000, live in Manchester, and who have purchased a house in the last two years) that the time and effort needed to fill the cell is beyond the value of the information gained.

Snowball sampling

Snowball sampling
A non-probability sampling procedure where additional respondents are identified and selected on the basis of referrals of initial respondents. It tends to be used where the population of interest is small or difficult to identify.

Snowball sampling tends to be used in low-incidence populations that make up a very small percentage of the total population (e.g. people with certain disabilities, people with unusual hobbies or interests, specialist manufacturers). It involves a sampling process where additional respondents are identified and selected on the basis of referrals of initial respondents. Where the potential respondents (e.g. people who keep reptiles as pets) are difficult to find and where screening members of the general population to identify these individuals would be prohibitively expensive, the snowballing technique may be used. It is far more cost effective to identify a small number of the low-incidence group and ask them to identify other potential respondents similar to themselves.

However, researchers need to note that the final sample is likely to be biased, because individuals are likely to recommend contacts and friends who generally hold similar ideas and views to themselves.

Sampling for Internet and e-mail-based surveys

Sampling of potential respondents for Internet and e-mail-based surveys generally takes the form of convenience samples. It is clearly accepted that respondents on the Internet do not accurately reflect the general population, as there are large sections of the public who do not currently have access to the relevant technology. However, even for those who do have access, the problem of representativeness is exacerbated by the fact that there is no comprehensive and reliable sample frame of e-mail addresses. Reasons for this relate to people constantly changing their Internet service providers and their e-mail addresses, people having multiple e-mail accounts, and people being cautious about publishing their e-mail addresses in case they get spammed with junk mail. As Internet shopping and other usage increases, this problem may be reduced. Certainly well-established Internet retailers such as Amazon or Dell and travel companies such as Expedia already have reasonably reliable e-mail listings from which they can construct samples. Some researchers attempt to recruit samples of consumers via Internet bulletin boards. However, it is unlikely that these potential respondents will be representative of anything other than membership of the bulletin board in question. An alternative approach is to interrupt visitors when they visit a a particular website with a 'pop-up' window which invites them to participate in a survey. In convenience sampling, every visitor is intercepted, although recruitment may be made more representative by imposing quotas relating to certain types of visitor. Alternatively, a random sampling approach can be adopted where the software selects the recipients of the 'pop-up' at random. Using a random approach improves representativeness and discourages multiple response from the same respondent.

However, the most common approach used by research agencies involved in Internet research is the development of panels of online individuals who have agreed to be involved in research projects. They are recruited from a variety of sources: banner ads on targeted sites, e-mail marketing, partnerships with high traffic sites such as Google and recruitment through other research activities such as omnibus surveys. However, these people are self-selected, meaning that they are only representative of people who respond to requests for research volunteers and are willing to spend time completing electronic questionnaires. This may make them very different from the true population of interest, in terms of being more technically oriented or being a type of 'Internet junkie'. Agencies try to minimise this by obtaining detailed profiles of each panellist through an initial questionnaire that they are asked to complete. Such profile information is typically used to develop quota samples for each study that is undertaken. To maintain the reliability of the sample, participants are provide with a password that is unique to their e-mail address. The password has to be used at the start of the survey, allowing the software to ensure that respondents undertake the survey only once.

Step 5: determine sample size

One of the most difficult decisions for any young researcher is the determination of the most appropriate size of sample for a study. The process of determining sample size relates to financial, managerial and statistical issues. Although a bigger sample may reduce the sampling error associated with a project, this has to be balanced against the increased cost and time involved in the data-collection process. Research costs and interviewing time are likely to increase in direct proportion to any increase in sample size (a 50 per cent increase in the size of the sample will result in a 50 per cent increase in cost and interviewer time). However, sampling error tends to decrease at a rate equal to the square root of the relative increase in sample size (so a sample that is increased by 100 per cent (i.e. doubled) is only likely to reduce its sampling error by 10 per cent). Research managers and clients need to determine the relative importance of precision against time and cost considerations. There are a number of ways in which sample size is determined.

Budget available

Frequently the sample size is determined by the amount of money that is available for the project. A marketing manager may state that he or she is willing to spend £15,000 to examine a particular aspect of a market. After making allowances for questionnaire design, data processing, analysis, etc., the remainder determines how many interviews can be undertaken. Although this may seem unscientific, it is realistic, as the resources available for marketing research in a company have to compete against budgets for promotional activity, new product development, etc. Researchers and marketers therefore need to carefully consider the value of reliable information in relation to its cost.

Sample sizes used in similar studies

Many researchers will rely on their past experience to determine an appropriate sample size. Previous studies covering similar research objectives may guide the researcher to select a particular sample size. These will give an indication of:

- **The homogeneity of the population of interest:** if there are likely to be significant differences in the views or behaviours of the population, a larger sample will be required.
- **The likely response rate:** if refusal rates within a particular population of interest are likely to be higher than the norm, then the sample of potential respondents will need to be larger.

- **The incidence rate of the characteristic being investigated:** where the characteristic being investigated is common among those in the sample frame, the sample will be smaller than will be the case if the characteristic is rare. (For example, a research study on televisions will need to approach fewer households to find TV owners than if the study was on home computers.)
- **The number of subgroups of data that are to be analysed:** the larger the number of sub-groups of the sample that the researcher wishes to analyse separately, the larger the required total sample size. Individual subgroups of the sample will have larger sampling errors than the total sample. It may be difficult to determine whether there are real differences between the results from two subgroups or whether the difference is simply a reflection of sampling error.

Statistical methods

For probability samples, statistical methods are generally used to determine sample size (these are not appropriate for non-probability samples). The statistical methods require three pieces of information:

1 an estimate of the standard deviation for the population;
2 the acceptable level of precision expressed as sampling error;
3 the desired confidence level that the result of the survey will fall within a certain range (result +/− sampling error) of the true result of the population.

There are a number of different formulas for calculating simple random samples, stratified samples and cluster samples. Although the general principles of sample size calculation are similar, the formulas for stratified and cluster samples are more complicated and are beyond the scope of this particular text.

With simple random sampling, the formula chosen depends on whether the researcher is trying to measure averages (e.g. the average weekly expenditure on grocery shopping; the average number of nightclub visits made by students per month) or is trying to measure proportion (e.g. the percentage of households that have purchased a television in the last two years).

Studies involving averages (means)

The formula for calculating sample size for studies that involve the estimation of the mean or average value in a population is as follows:

$$N = \frac{Z^2 \sigma^2}{E^2}$$

where Z is the level of confidence expressed in standard errors, σ is population standard deviation and E is the acceptable level of precision expressed as sampling error.

Considering each of the variables in the formula with regard to a study looking at average weekly expenditure on grocery shopping:

1 Specify the level of precision: the client and researchers will need to decide on the level of precision that is acceptable. This is influenced by the available budget and time scales. For determining weekly shopping expenditure, a value that is within +/−£5 ($\sigma = 5$) may be acceptable, whereas in the concept testing of a new product, greater precision may be needed as significant investment decisions will be dependent on the results.

2 Determine the acceptable confidence interval: the acceptable confidence interval is also influenced by budget and time constraints. To understand the concept of **confidence levels** it is important to consider the **normal distribution**.

Confidence levels
The probability that the true population value will be within a particular range (result plus or minus sampling error).

Normal distribution
A continuous distribution that is bell-shaped and symmetrical about the mean. This means that in a study, 68.27 per cent of the observations fall within plus or minus one standard deviation of the mean, approximately 95.45 per cent fall within plus or minus two standard deviations, and approximately 99.73 per cent fall within plus or minus three standard deviations.

The normal distribution

Scientists who observed that repeated samplings of the same population fitted within a common distribution of results first identified the properties of the normal distribution or normal curve in the eighteenth century. This distribution is bell-shaped and symmetrical about the mean value (see Figure 8.2). This means that in a study, 68.27 per cent of the observations fall within plus or minus one standard deviation of the mean, approximately 95.45 per cent fall within plus or minus two standard deviations and approximately 99.73 per cent fall within plus or minus three standard deviations. The exact areas contained by the normal distribution are to be found in special Z scale tables (see Table 1 in Appendix 1) in most statistical textbooks. The most frequently used values in surveys are for the 95 per cent (Z value = 1.96) and 99 per cent (Z value = 2.58) confidence limits.

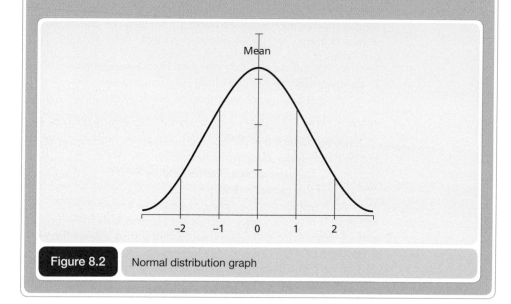

| Figure 8.2 | Normal distribution graph |

Sampling error
The difference between the sample value and the true value of a phenomenon for the population being surveyed. Can be expressed in mathematical terms: usually the survey result plus or minus a certain percentage.

So Z equals the level of confidence that the true mean of the sample falls into the interval defined by the sample mean plus or minus the acceptable level of E, the **sampling error**. For the study of grocery shopping, the researcher may decide that he or she needs to be 95 per cent confident that the true population mean falls into the interval defined by the sample mean plus or minus £5. A total of 1.96 standard errors are required to provide for 95 per cent of the area under a normal curve. Therefore the value for Z in this example will be 1.96.

3 Estimate the standard deviation for the population: It is impossible to know the standard deviation before undertaking a survey, therefore the researcher has to rely on an estimate when calculating sample size. The estimate can be based upon:

● Results from a previous study: if a study has been undertaken on a similar subject with a similar population, it may be possible to use the results of the previous study as an estimate of the population standard deviation.
● Use secondary data: secondary data may be available to assist in the estimation.
● Conduct a small pilot survey: a pilot survey could be used to develop an estimate of the population standard deviation. Such a pilot survey could also be used to test the appropriateness of questions in the questionnaire.
● Judgement: using judgement to determine the likely standard deviation.

In the grocery purchases study, the standard deviation was estimated as being £40.80. Once the survey has been completed and the true sample mean and standard deviation have been calculated, the researcher can make adjustments to the initial estimates of the confidence interval and determine the precision level actually obtained.

For the grocery purchases example the overall calculation would be as follows:

$$N = \frac{Z^2 \sigma^2}{E^2}$$

$$N = \frac{(1.96)^2 \times 40.8^2}{5^2}$$

N = 256 (rounded to the next highest number)

Therefore the sample size is 256.

Studies involving proportions

Where studies relate to proportions rather than averages or means, a different formula is used, which uses estimates of likely proportions rather than standard deviations. The formula is as follows:

$$N = \frac{Z^2[P(1-P)]}{E^2}$$

where Z is the level of confidence expressed in standard errors, E is the acceptable amount of sampling error and P is the proportion of the population having a certain behaviour or characteristic.

If a researcher is looking at purchasing behaviour of televisions over the last two years, then the following values could be substituted: in a similar way to the previous example, an acceptable sampling error level is set. For example, an error level of plus or minus 5 per cent (written as 0.05) is set. A Z value of 1.96 is established relating to a 95 per cent confidence level. Finally, P is the estimated percentage of the population that have bought televisions over the last two years, say 25 per cent (written as 0.25).

The resulting calculation identifies that a random sample of 289 respondents is required:

$$N = \frac{(1.96)^2[0.25(1-0.25)]}{0.05^2}$$

$$N = 289$$

Therefore the sample size is 289.

Once the survey has been conducted and the actual proportions or sample means/standard deviations (for studies involving means) have been calculated, the researcher can assess the accuracy of the estimates used to calculate sample size. At this stage, adjustments can be made to the levels of sampling error based on the sample size and the actual sample measurements.

Adjustment of sample size for larger samples

Generally there is no direct relationship between the size of the population and the size of sample required to estimate a characteristic with a specific level of error and a specific level of confidence. The only area where sample size may have an effect is where the size of the sample is large in relation to the size of the population. The normal assumption in sampling is that sample elements are drawn independently of one another. Although it is safe to assume this when a sample is less than 10 per cent of the population, it is not when the sample is bigger than 10 per cent. An adjustment is therefore made to the sample size. This adjustment is called the **finite population correction factor**. The calculation used to reduce the required sample involves the following formula:

$$N^1 = \frac{nN}{N + n - 1}$$

where N^1 is the revised sample size, n is the original sample size and N is the population size.

For example, if the population has 1,200 elements and the original sample size is 250, then:

$$N^1 = \frac{250 \times 1200}{1200 + 250 - 1}$$

$$N^1 = 208$$

Based on this adjustment using the finite population correction factor, a sample of 208 is required in comparison with the original 250.

Step 6: implement the sampling procedure

Once the sample size has been determined and the sampling procedure has been selected, the researcher can start selecting the members of the sample and begin the survey. However, the purpose of conducting a survey based on a sample is to make inferences about the population of interest rather than simply reporting on the characteristics of the sample. It is therefore important to know why the characteristics of a sample may differ from those of the population.

Sampling and non-sampling error

A certain level of sampling error will always exist in studies that involve collecting data from only a part of the population. Sampling error merely reflects the extent of random chance in selecting respondents with different views and behaviours. It says nothing about the accuracy of the data collected from probability samples – it simply reflects the accuracy of estimates about the total population that can be made from that data. The higher the sampling error, the wider the confidence interval estimate for the population parameter will be. The amount of sampling error can be reduced by using a sampling procedure that has high statistical efficiency and/or increasing the sample size.

Non-sampling errors
Errors that occur in a study that do not relate to sampling error. They tend to be classified into three broad type: sampling frame error, non-response error and data errors.

In addition to sampling error, there are a number of other errors that can occur and impact on the accuracy of survey data. These other errors are called **non-sampling errors** as they consist of any error in a research study other than sampling error. They tend to be classified into three broad types: sampling frame error, non-response error and data error. While sampling errors can be estimated using statistics, non-sampling error results in bias that is difficult, if not impossible, to estimate. However, if researchers are aware of the potential non-sampling errors, they can take steps to minimise them.

Sampling frame error

Sampling frame error is a bias that occurs as a result of the population implied by the sampling frame being different from the population of interest. For example, a telephone directory may be used to generate a list of people in a geographic area. This may differ significantly from the overall population as it will exclude people who are unlisted, people who only use mobile phones (e.g. students) and people who do not have access to a telephone. The researcher must determine whether excluding these groups of people is likely to produce significantly different results than would be the case if they were included. In other words, do the members of the population included in the telephone directory differ significantly from those not included? If they do, there may be a need to look at modifying the sampling frame or adopting an alternative sampling approach. The researcher may need to supplement the sampling frame with names from another source such as the electoral roll or may need to use an alternative sampling approach such as area sampling combined with doorstep interviews.

Non-response errors

Non-response errors
Errors in a study that arise when some of the potential respondents do not respond. This may occur due to respondents refusing or being unavailable to take part in the research.

Non-response errors arise when some of the potential respondents included in a sample do not respond. The primary reasons for non-response are:

- **Refusals:** includes members of the population who fail to respond to postal surveys or who refuse to be interviewed on a subject, either because the timing is inconvenient or because of resistance to the survey. Efforts can be made to reduce refusal rates by:
  - *In postal/self-completion questionnaires*: making the questionnaire and questions short, interesting and attractive, offering incentives, sending out reminders, including reply-paid envelopes.
  - *In telephone and face-to-face surveys*: making contact at times convenient to the respondent, using well-qualified interviewers, offering incentives, providing information to guarantee the authenticity of the research, careful questionnaire design.

- **Non-availability of respondents:** may result from people being on holiday when a postal questionnaire arrives or being away from home when an interviewer calls, either at the door or on the telephone. Some interviewers may be tempted to substitute another respondent for the one that is unavailable, but in probability samples there is the danger that this may cause bias because the people who are actually available are in some way different from those who are unavailable. For example, a programme of telephone interviews undertaken in the early evening may miss those who do not answer their phones because they are feeding young families at that time, they work late or commute long distances, they work shift patterns, they undertake social or hobby interests in the evening, or they are watching their favourite television programme at that time. By omitting any of these groups, researchers may be missing an important segment of the population from their sample and as a result may be biasing the survey results. Call-backs (phoning or returning to a potential respondent's address at a similar or different time) are more effective in reducing non-response error than the substitution of available respondents. Call-backs obviously add to the cost of a study, however. Many researchers will attempt three calls on a potential respondent (one original and two call-backs) to complete the interview. Only then would substitution with available respondents be used.

Non-response error can be reduced, but it cannot be eradicated from surveys. Researchers need to consider the implications of non-response for their research findings and should indicate the level of non-response in the final research report. This will enable the report's audience to take account of this when interpreting the research findings.

Data error

Data errors
Non-sampling errors that occur during data collection or analysis that impact on the accuracy of inferences made about the population of interest. The main types of data error are respondent errors (where respondents give distorted or erroneous answers), interviewer errors and data analysis errors.

Data errors are any errors that occur during data collection or analysis that impact on the accuracy of inferences made about the population of interest. They can be classified into three main types:

- **Respondent errors:** respondents may inadvertently or intentionally give distorted or erroneous responses. Respondents may give erroneous answers because they fail to under-stand a question and do not want to admit their incomprehension. This is difficult to control, although the guidelines for questionnaire design outlined in Chapter 7 may help to reduce this by ensuring that questions are as simple as possible and are pre-tested with representatives of the population of interest before they are used in a full survey. Even where questions are clearly expressed, respondents may give socially acceptable answers or may give answers that they think will impress or shock the interviewer or researcher. For example, respondents may inflate their level of earnings, reduce the number of cigarettes they smoke, increase the number of sexual encounters they have had, or reduce the number of incidences that they break the speed limit when driving. The respondents' distortions may be altered according to age, sex and appearance of the interviewer. Distortions of this type are far more difficult to detect and measure. Their reduction is attempted through the placing of sensitive questions nearer the end of an interview once rapport and trust have been established between the respondent and the interviewer. Rather than using open-ended questions on subjects where distortions are likely to occur, multiple-choice questions are used (see the example below). This highlights the types of answer that the interviewer is expecting rather than leaving the respondent to judge how the interviewer will respond to a particular answer. Respondents frequently do not want to embarrass themselves by giving an inappropriate or unusual answer.

Open-ended question:

What is your annual salary before tax?

£_____

Multiple-choice question:

Within which of the following categories does your annual salary (before tax) fall?

Less than £12,000	___
£12,000–£14,999	___
£15,000–£19,999	___
£20,000–£29,999	___
£30,000–£39,999	___
More than £40,000	___

Using a range of different types of interviewer may also balance out the impact of respondents answering to please or impress the interviewer. Beyond these measures, it is very difficult to influence respondents who are determined to distort their answers.

- **Interviewer errors**: errors can also occur as a result of interviewers recording answers incorrectly. This may be particularly evident for open-ended questions, where some interviewers may try to summarise the respondent's answer rather than writing it verbatim. A small minority of unprofessional interviewers may also partially fill out questionnaires by themselves rather than asking bona fide respondents. The keys to reducing such errors are selection, training and supervision. In the UK the quality of these inputs is being improved through the **Interviewer Quality Control Scheme (IQCS)**. The Market Research Society, the Association of Market Survey Organisations, the Association of Users of Research Agencies and a number of leading research companies jointly run this scheme. Agencies subscribing to the scheme are visited by quality control inspectors who audit the research operations with the objective of maintaining and raising the standards of fieldwork. Those agencies that satisfy the inspectors are able to use the IQCS logo. Some clients will only use agencies that are approved to the IQCS standard. **Validation** of the completed interviews is also important in exposing any falsification of information by unscrupulous interviewers. After all the interviews are completed, the research agency recontacts a small percentage of the respondents surveyed by each interviewer. This is done to check on the following:

1 Was the person actually interviewed?

2 Did the person meet the sampling requirements of the survey? (e.g. If the survey related to people of a certain age range, is the respondent within that age range?)

Interviewer Quality Control Scheme (IQCS)
A quality control scheme for interviewers in the UK. The scheme is aimed at improving selection, training and supervision of interviewers and is jointly run by the Market Research Society, the Association of Market Survey Organisations, the Association of British Market Research Companies, the Association of Users of Research Agencies, and a number of leading research companies.

3 Was the interview conducted in the correct location and in the required manner? (e.g. Was it undertaken in the predefined street or did the interviewer recruit people in a shopping centre or café? Were the proper showcards used?)

4 Did the interviewer ask all of the questions in the survey or did they only ask certain parts of the questionnaire? (Respondents may need to be asked a number of sample questions to verify this.)

5 Was the interviewer courteous? (e.g. Is there anything that the respondent was unhappy about?)

Such checks on the validity of the interview process are critical to ensure that the results are truly representative of the respondents interviewed.

In addition to validating the questionnaire with the respondent, the questionnaires will be checked to ensure that (1) there is consistency in the answers provided (if somebody has two children at the start of the questionnaire, then later questions also relate to two rather than three children), (2) answers are recorded for all questions and (3) appropriate skip patterns have been followed. This checking is part of the **editing** process carried out prior to the data entry and analysis of the questionnaires. Where computer-assisted interviewing has been used, this will have been done automatically by the computer during the interview process.

- **Data analysis errors**: errors can occur when data is transferred from the questionnaires to computers by incorrect keying of information. Such errors can be identified and reduced by checking a sample of questionnaires against the computerised data. This will identify any keying errors. Computers can also be used to check for unexpected codes in the data and test for the consistency of data on each respondent.

Researcher quote

Non-sampling error can be reduced but it is impossible to totally eradicate it.

Using weightings

Sample results are used to generalise about the population surveyed. If the sample is not representative of that population because of sampling errors or non-response, then these generalisations will be flawed. Equally, if some groups have been over-sampled, it will be necessary to adjust the data to reflect the proportions found in the population. This process is called **weighting**. There are various approaches to weighting but the simplest is to apply known proportions to the findings. For example:

Weighting
The process of adjusting the value of survey responses to account for over- or under-representation of different categories of respondent. Weighting is used where the sample design is disproportional or where the achieved sample does not accurately reflect the population under investigation.

	Percentages across	
	Men	**Women**
Population	49%	51%
Sample achieved	42%	58%
Weight applied	1.17	0.88

As long as demographic information about the population is known or can be reliably estimated, then weighting can help considerably to improve estimates, provided that the disparities found between the sample and the population do not arise from a lack of coverage of significant parts of the population. However, when weighting is used, researchers must always provide a full description of the weighting procedures.

Summary and an integrated approach

In marketing research it is very rare that a researcher will be able to undertake a census of every member of a particular population. Therefore a subset or sample of the population needs to be selected and surveyed. This chapter has taken you through the main steps in the sampling process. These steps can be summarised as follows:

1 **Define the population of interest:** this is the total group of people that the researcher wishes to examine and will normally reflect the target market or potential target market for the product or service being researched.
2 **Determine whether to sample or census:** as stated above, the major part of marketing research is undertaken with a sample rather than a census of the population of interest.
3 **Select the sampling frame:** obtain a list of the population of interest, from which the researcher selects the individuals for inclusion in the research.
4 **Choose a sampling method:** either a probability or non-probability sampling method can be used. Probability sampling includes the following types: simple random sampling, systematic sampling, stratified random sampling, cluster sampling and area sampling. Non-probability sampling includes convenience sampling, judgement sampling, quota sampling and snowball sampling. Selection is based on the sample frame available, budgets, time scales and the precision with which the survey results can be projected to reflect the true values held by the population under investigation.
5 **Determine sample size:** the process of determining sample size relates to financial, managerial and statistical issues.
6 **Implement the sampling procedure.**

Both sampling error and non-sampling error impact upon the accuracy of survey results. Sampling error reflects the accuracy of estimates about the total population that can be made from the data. For probability samples, this can be expressed as the confidence interval that is placed on the estimate of the population parameter. Non-sampling errors relate to any error in the survey findings other than sampling error, and are usually classified as sampling frame error, non-response error and data error.

In terms of integration, customer databases incorporating address, telephone and online contact information as well as behavioural and profile information can obviously play an important part in the design of sampling frames for a marketing research study. Often poor response rates in surveys are a result of inadequate sample frames created from poorly maintained and out-of-date customer records on client databases. So, the reliability and integrity of the sampling process is often inextricably linked to the reliability and integrity of the organisation's database.

Discussion questions

1 Explain the term 'population of interest'.

2 Why does the marketing research industry undertake so few censuses?

3 What are the differencs between probability and non-probability sampling errors?

4 Explain the similarities and differences between simple random samples, systematic samples and stratified random samples.

5 Why do some studies require a multi-stage sampling approach?

6 Explain the differences between quota samples and stratified samples.

7 Discuss the proposition that the determination of sample size is simply a matter of guesswork.

8 Identify the different types of sampling frame error and suggest ways in which each of them can be reduced.

9 What is the purpose of the Interviewer Quality Control Scheme (IQCS)?

10 Discuss the problems of establishing representativeness for Internet and e-mail-based surveys.

Additional reading

Bradley, N. (1999) Sampling for Internet surveys: an examination of respondent selection for Internet research. *Journal of the Market Research Society*, **41**(4), pp. 387–95.

Corlett, T. (1996) Sampling errors in practice. *Journal of the Market Research Society*, **38**(4), pp. 307–18.

Nancarrow, C. and Cartwright, T. (2007) Online access panels and tracking research; the conditioning issue. *International Journal of Market Research*, **49**(5), pp. 573–94.

Research Development Foundation (1999) Business co-operation in market research. *Journal of the Market Research Society*, **41**(2), pp. 195–225.

Schillewaert, N., Langerak, F. and Duhamel, T. (1998) Non-probability sampling for WWW surveys: a comparison of methods. *Journal of the Market Research Society*, **40**(4), pp. 307–22.

Sparrow, N. (2006) Developing reliable online polls. *International journal of Market Research*, **48**(6), pp. 659–80.

Reference

[1] For more information see **www.barb.co.uk**.

Tetley and the round tea bag

To counter a loss in market share in the tea market to super-markets' own branded products, Lyons Tetley developed a round tea bag as a possible replacement for their traditional square bag. The problem for the company was that the risk of changing shape would be very high – the brand turned over around £80 million at that time. In addition, new packaging machinery would cost several million pounds and take some time to obtain and install, and the relaunch would cost several million more. The three key questions were:

1 Would roundness increase the share of Tetley by attracting sufficient non-users to Tetley to compensate for any Tetley users who would be lost because of the change?
2 Was the novelty of roundness likely to wear out in a relatively short period of time?
3 Would the gain in share be sufficient to pay for the cost of the relaunch?

Creative Element Photos/Alamy

Tetley used a simulated test market to answer these questions. A panel of 240 heavy buyers of tea were recruited using the following qualification criteria:

1 the household used at least 80 tea bags in a two-week period;
2 the household regularly used one of four major national brands (Tetley, Typhoo, Quick Brew or PG Tips).

The qualified panel members were asked to attend a local briefing session at which the research project was explained to them and they were shown the packaging and a TV advertisement for round bags in the setting of packaging and advertising for the familiar principal brands. The panel was then operated by interviewers calling each week with an illustrated brochure of tea brands and sizes with the lowest prices prevailing in the best of three local supermarkets that week. Tetley's round bags was one of the brands included in the brochure. To induce trial, the round bag was offered at a promotional price over the first two weeks.

In the total panel, 46 per cent of participants tried round tea bags and made at least one repeat purchase. Thus 76 per cent of trialists liked it sufficiently to make at least a second purchase. People preferred the product because of their perception of its improved flavour (note: the tea was the same as in the square bag; it was only the shape of the bag that was different).

The panel was originally planned to run for 12 weeks, by which time stable repeat purchasing rates had emerged. Lyons Tetley was still sufficiently concerned about possible novelty wear-out that it ran the panel on for a further eight weeks. However, there was no perceptible erosion of the repeat purchase rate after over four months' exposure to the brand.

Analysing the purchasing patterns in detail and using the results to forecast potential sales patterns, Lyons Tetley decided to relaunch using the round tea bag. In spite of considerable competitive activity at the time of the launch, the relaunch was a major success. As a result, many competitors have developed their versions of round tea bags, pyramid tea bags and drawstring tea bags.[1]

Learning outcomes

After reading this chapter you should:

● understand the key steps in data entry and analysis;
● have an understanding of the statistical techniques used most frequently in marketing research.

Key words

chi-square
cluster analysis
coding
conjoint analysis
correlation
cross-tabulations
data cleaning
data entry
descriptive statistics
factor analysis
frequency distributions
holecounts
hypothesis testing
interval data

measures of central tendency
measures of dispersion
multiple discriminant analysis
multiple regression analysis
multivariate data analysis
nominal data
ordinal data
perceptual mapping
ratio data
regression
statistical significance
t test
Z test

Introduction

Once data collection has been completed and the validation and editing (described on page 200) has been undertaken, the researcher moves on to the stage of data entry and analysis. This chapter is designed to introduce you to the three main steps involved in this phase of the research process. These are:

● Step 1: coding
● Step 2: data entry
● Step 3: tabulation and statistical analysis.

More and more components of these three steps are undertaken automatically by computers through questionnaire analysis or statistical software packages. However, researchers need to develop an awareness and understanding of these activities and statistical techniques if they are to both understand the data and present the findings in an accurate and confident manner. This chapter aims to provide that awareness and understanding.

Coding

Coding
The procedures involved in translating responses into a form that is ready for analysis. Normally involves the assigning of numerical codes to responses.

Coding is the first step and involves translating responses into a form that is ready for analysis. To understand coding, it is necessary to understand how research responses are held in a computer file.

A computer file consists of all the responses relating to all of the respondents in a study. It is made up of a series of records, with each record containing all of the responses from one respondent. Each record is organised in the form of a number of fields, with each field representing a question in the questionnaire. Codes are the numerical data in each field representing the respondent's answer to a particular question. This is shown in the following example (Table 9.1) of a computer file relating to four respondents answering a questionnaire consisting of five questions.

Coding therefore involves the assigning of numerical codes to responses so that they can be (1) recognised by the computer, (2) stored in the data fields and (3) interpreted and manipulated for statistical and tabular purposes. For example, in a dichotomous question with a yes/no response format, 'yes' could be assigned the code 1 and 'no' could be assigned the code 2. This could then be stored for each respondent in a manner similar to that shown for field 1 in Table 9.1.

With many of the computer packages used to design questionnaires, the codes for closed questions (i.e. dichotomous questions, multiple-choice questions, rating questions) will be established prior to the questionnaire being used. Such questions are described as **pre-coded**. For open-ended questions where the responses are not known in advance, the codes are applied after the data collection phase and are therefore described as **post-coded**.

The process of post-coding responses to open-ended questions involves the following steps:

1 **Developing a list of responses:** the researcher prepares lists of the actual responses to each open-ended question. This may involve listing the responses from all of the questionnaires or doing so for a sample if the number of questionnaires is very large. Some questionnaire software packages such as Snap (see the list of software packages at the end of the chapter) allow the researcher to enter the data verbatim before providing a computer listing of all the responses.

2 **Categorising responses:** a number of responses will essentially have the same meaning even though different words may have been used. These responses can be consolidated into a single category. So thousands of responses may be consolidated into a maximum of, say, 10–12 categories. For example, answers such as: inexpensive, moderate price, reasonable price, fair price, appropriate price, affordable, correct price, etc., may all be consolidated into a category entitled 'acceptable price'. There may need to be some subjective assessment, on the part of the researcher, to determine whether an answer fits into a category or whether a new category is required.

Table 9.1	An example of data in a computer file				
	Field 1 *Question 1*	**Field 2** *Question 2*	**Field 3** *Question 3*	**Field 4** *Question 4*	**Field 5** *Question 5*
Record 1 (respondent 1)	1	5	245	1	2
Record 2 (respondent 2)	2	3	356	3	2
Record 3 (respondent 3)	2	6	32	5	3
Record 4 (respondent 4)	1	2	243	3	2

3 **Assign and enter codes:** a numeric code is assigned to each of the categories. The codes are then entered into the computer file for analysis.

In the future, such post-coding may become easier as software for automated coding becomes more common and reliable. Such software uses algorithms to search open-ended responses for keywords, phrases and patterns in order to categorise responses and assign codes. However, the reliability of such software needs to improve, as you will know from the incorrect word associations that occur when you use an Internet browser to find websites.

Data entry

Data entry
The transfer of data from a questionnaire into a computer, either directly in computer-assisted interviewing, or by an operator copy-typing the responses from questionnaires or the optical scanning of printed questionnaires.

With computer-assisted interviewing and web-based surveys, **data entry** is done automatically. In all other situations, data have to be transferred from the questionnaire either by:

1 an operator typing the responses from the questionnaires into the computer;
2 the optical scanning of questionnaires.

This can be done using appropriate scanning equipment and questionnaires that have an appropriate layout. Scanning has significantly moved on from the time when computers could only read the data if respondents used pencils to fully shade an entire square next to their response choice.

Data cleaning
Computerised checks made on data to identify inconsistencies and to check for any unexplained missing responses.

Once the data have been entered, computerised checks will be made to check that there are no inconsistencies and to identify if there are any unexplained missing responses. This task is called **data cleaning**. Inconsistencies may include out-of-range data values (e.g. a code of 8 on a five-point (1–5) scale), extreme values (where one respondent has a very different response from all other respondents) or logical inconsistencies (where a respondent answers a question about a service that he says he does not use). 'Missing value' is the term used to describe situations where no response to a question is recorded. These may be expected as particular respondents will have legitimately skipped certain questions; however, others may result from keying errors. Where these problems exist, the computer can be programmed to print out details of the questionnaire, record number, field number and the offending value or missing value.

Tabulation and statistical analysis

Once the data are stored in the computer and free of errors, the researcher needs to select the most appropriate approach to tabulation and statistical analysis. Tabulation involves laying out data in easy-to-understand summary tables, while statistical analysis is used to examine the data further and identify or confirm patterns that are difficult to see or interpret. The selection of approach will be determined by the objectives of the research (what questions/problems do the research findings need to address?) and the type of measurement data that has been collected. There are four basic types of measurement data:

Nominal data
Numbers assigned to objects or phenomena as labels or identification numbers that name or classify but have no true numeric meaning.

1 **Nominal data.** The word 'nominal' means 'name-like' – in other words, the numbers assigned to objects or phenomena that name or classify but have no true numeric meaning. They are simply labels or identification numbers (see the examples below) that partition data into mutually exclusive and collectively exhaustive categories and as such they cannot be ordered, added or divided.

> Gender: Male (1) Female (2)
> Type of transport used: Car (1), Coach (2), Train (3)

The only calculation or quantification possible with nominal data is the counting of the number and percentages of objects in each category; for example, 50 car users (37 per cent) and 26 train users (19 per cent). Only a limited number of statistics, all of which are based on frequency counts, are possible. These include the mode, chi-square and binomial tests (all of which are explained later in this chapter).

Ordinal data

Numbers that have the labelling characteristics of nominal data, but also have the ability to communicate the rank order of the data. The numbers do not indicate absolute quantities, nor do they imply that the intervals between the numbers are equal.

2 **Ordinal data**. This stems from ordinal scales and has the labelling characteristics of nominal data, but also has the ability to communicate the order of the data. The numbers do not indicate absolute quantities, nor do they imply that the intervals between the numbers are equal. Ordinal scales are used strictly to indicate rank order – the numbers are void of any meaning other than order. Here is an example of an ordinal scale.

> Please rank the following car makes from 1 to 5, with 1 being the make which offers the best value for money and 5 being the one that offers the least value for money:
>
> Ford ____
> Renault ____
> Fiat ____
> BMW ____
> Toyota ____

If Fiat is ranked 4 and BMW is ranked 5, there is no indication as to whether Fiat has much better or only slightly better value for money than BMW. Common arithmetical operations such as addition or multiplication cannot be used with ordinal scales. As such, it is inappropriate to calculate a mean; instead modes and medians are used.

Interval data

Similar to ordinal data with the added dimension that the intervals between the values on a scale are equal. That means that when using a scale of 1 to 5, the difference between 1 and 2 is the same as the difference between 4 and 5. However, the ratios between different values on the scale are not valid (e.g. 4 does not represent twice the value of 2).

3 **Interval data**. This is similar to ordinal data with the added dimension that the intervals between the values on a scale are equal. This means that when using a scale of 1 to 5, the difference between 1 and 2 is the same as the difference between 4 and 5. However, in an interval scale, the zero point is not fixed; instead, it is an arbitrary point. This can be demonstrated in the example below, where 1 does not represent a particular level of cost effectiveness that can be defined, but simply provides an evaluation of cost-effectiveness relative to the elements being compared. For example, a respondent's ratings may be allocated differently if the list of cars were to change (for example, if Skoda was added to the list). As a result, calculating the ratios between different values on the scale is not valid. In other words, a manufacturer receiving a rating of 4 does not represent twice the value for money of a manufacturer that has a rating of 2.

> Please rate the following car makes on a scale of 1 to 5, where 1 represents very poor value for money and 5 represents very good value for money.
>
> Ford 1 2 3 4 5
> Renault 1 2 3 4 5
> Fiat 1 2 3 4 5
> BMW 1 2 3 4 5
> Toyota 1 2 3 4 5

Unlike nominal and ordinal data, arithmetic means and standard deviations can be calculated using interval data. Correlation coefficients and many statistical tests, including *t* tests, can also be used with interval data.

Ratio data

Actual 'real' numbers that have a meaningful absolute or zero. All arithmetic operations are possible with such data.

4 Ratio data. This consists of actual, 'real' numbers that have a meaningful absolute zero or origin. Actual characteristics of a respondent or a situation, such as age, height, level of expenditure, number of products purchased and time taken are all examples of ratio-scale variables. Not only is the difference between 4 and 6 the same as the difference between 58 and 60, but 60 is 10 times the size of 6. The nature of ratio data means that all arithmetic operations are possible.

It should be noted that nominal and ordinal data are sometimes referred to as **non-metric data**, whereas interval and ratio data are sometimes referred to as **metric data**.

Tabulations

Holecounts and frequency distributions

Holecounts

The number of respondents who gave each possible answer to each question in a questionnaire. Sometimes known as *frequency distributions*.

Frequency distributions

See Holecounts.

Researchers often attempt to get a first feel of the data they have by producing a **holecount**. This name originates from the days when punched cards were used to enter data into computers and holes in the cards represented the responses to each of the questions. Holecounts, sometimes known as **frequency distributions**, communicate the number of respondents who gave each possible answer to each question. Figure 9.1 sets out an example of a frequency distribution about transport usage. In addition to frequencies, such a table will typically indicate the percentage of those responding who selected each response. These percentages are normally calculated using the number of people asked as the base figure. However, unless the number of non-responses (people who refused or chose not to answer a particular question) has a bearing on the research objectives, it is often more sensible for the base to relate to the number of people asked less the number who did not respond. So, using the example in Figure 9.1, a more accurate base would be 1995 (2000 − 5).

Sometimes, researchers will print out a questionnaire with the holecount numbers appearing next to each response on the questionnaire. This helps the researcher to obtain a very quick overview of the pattern of responses and may influence the next steps in terms of tabulation and analysis.

Researcher quote

Holecounts give an indication of what types of further analysis are likely to be useful.

Q17 What method of transport did you use to travel to the theme park today?

	Total
Total respondents asked	2,000 (100%)
Car	1,735 (87%)
Coach/bus	206 (10%)
Train	54 (3%)
No response	5 (−%)

Figure 9.1   An example of a frequency distribution

Method of transport by number of children

	Total	0	1	2	3	4	More than 4
				Number of children			
Total asked	2,000 (100%)	200 (100%)	229 (100%)	422 (100%)	365 (100%)	568 (100%)	216 (100%)
Car	1,735 (87%)	72 (36%)	123 (54%)	402 (95%)	358 (98%)	567 (100%)	213 (99%)
Coach/bus	206 (10%)	88 (44%)	96 (42%)	17 (4%)	3 (1%)	0 (0%)	2 (1%)
Train	54 (3%)	40 (20%)	8 (3%)	3 (1%)	1 (0%)	1 (0%)	1 (0%)
No response	5 (0%)	0 (0%)	2 (1%)	0 (0%)	3 (1%)	0 (0%)	0 (0%)

Figure 9.2　An example of a cross-tabulation

Cross-tabulations

Cross-tabulations
Tables that set out the responses to one question relative to the responses to one or more other questions.

Cross-tabulations are both simple to use and provide a powerful analysis technique. They examine the responses to one question relative to the responses to one or more other questions. Figure 9.2 shows a simple cross-tabulation that explores the relationship between the method of travelling to a theme park and the number of children within the group/party. Interestingly, the figure shows that the larger the number of children, the more likely it is that the party will have travelled by car. Three different percentages may be calculated for each cell in a cross-tabulation table: column, row and total percentages. Column percentages (used in Figure 9.2) are based on the column total, row percentages are based on the row total, and total percentages use the table total as the base.

Many statistics, spreadsheet and questionnaire packages, such as Snap, Excel and SPSS, can generate cross-tabulations at the press of a button. It is also possible to cross-tabulate data in an almost endless number of ways within a survey. However, it is important for the researcher to exercise judgement to determine which cross-tabulations are appropriate in order to (1) meet the research objectives and (2) show differences that indicate patterns in the data that are significantly different from what is likely to have occurred by chance.

In addition to cross-tabulations, data can be presented in a variety of graphical formats using pie charts, line graphs, bar charts and pictograms. Like cross-tabulations, these can also help in the communication of results and patterns in data. These graphical approaches are described and explained in Chapter 10.

Descriptive statistics
Statistics that help to summarise the characteristics of large sets of data using only a few numbers. The most commonly used descriptive statistics are measures of central tendency (mean, mode and median) and measures of dispersion (range, interquartile range and standard deviation).

Descriptive statistics

Descriptive statistics help to summarise the characteristics of large sets of data using only a few numbers. The most commonly used descriptive statistics are measures of central tendency (mean, mode and median) and measures of variability (range, interquartile range and standard deviation).

Measures of central tendency

Measures of central tendency
Measures that indicate a typical value for a set of data by computing the mean, mode or median.

Measures of central tendency indicate a typical value for a set of data by computing the mean, mode or median.

The mean

The mean is probably the most commonly used average in marketing research. It is the arithmetic average and is calculated by summing all of the values in a set of data and dividing by the number of cases. It can only be computed from interval or ratio (metric) data.

The mode

The mode can be computed with any type of data (nominal, ordinal, interval and ratio) and represents the value in a set of data that occurs most frequently. One problem with the mode is that any data set may have more than one mode (i.e. a number of categories/values may all be equal and each share the highest frequency).

The median

The median can be computed for all types of data except nominal data. When all of the values in a data set are put in ascending or descending order, the median is the value of the middle case in a series (if the number of values is an even number and therefore no single middle value exists, the two middle values are added together and divided by two). The median has as many cases on the higher side as on the lower side. The measure offers the advantage of being unaffected by extreme cases at one end or the other of the data set. It may, for example, be appropriate where a few extreme values may impact adversely on representativeness of the arithmetic mean.

The mean, median and mode for a set of ages are shown below.

Mean, median and mode

Ages of ten respondents:
42, 45, 43, 46, 48, 49, 39, 42, 45, 42.
Mean = 44 years   Mode = 42 years   Median = 44 years

Measures of dispersion

Measures of dispersion
Measures that indicate how 'spread out' a set of data is. The most common are the range, the interquartile range and the standard deviation.

Measures of dispersion indicate how 'spread out' a set of data is. The **range** is probably the simplest measure and is found by calculating the difference between the largest and smallest values in the data. As such, the range is directly affected by any extreme values. The range for the ages in the example above would be $(49 - 39) = 10$. The **interquartile range** reduces the impact of any extreme values by measuring the difference between the 75th and 25th percentile. To compute these percentiles, the data is arranged in order of magnitude, and the 75th percentile is the value that has 75 per cent of the data values below it and 25 per cent (i.e. $100 - 75$) above it. The 25th percentile is identified in the same manner and is then subtracted from the value of the 75th percentile to obtain the interquartile range.

The most commonly used measure of dispersion is the standard deviation of a data set. It is calculated by taking the square root of the sum of the squared deviations from the mean divided by the number of observations minus 1. The formula is shown below. Basically it tells the researcher what is the average distance that the values in a data set are away from the mean. The standard deviation of different sets of data can be compared to see if one set of data is more dispersed than another.

$$s = \sqrt{\frac{\sum_{i=1}^{n}(x_i - \bar{x})^2}{n-1}}$$

where n is the number of units in the sample, x_i is the data obtained from each sample unit i, and $\bar{x}$ is the sample mean value, given by $\sum_{i=1}^{n}\frac{x_i}{n}$.

Statistical significance

In marketing research it is common for statistical inferences to be made which attempt to make generalisations about population characteristics from sample results. However, in statistical inference it is possible for numbers to be different in a mathematical sense but not significantly different in a statistical sense. For example, a sample of 1,000 car drivers is asked to test drive two cars and indicate which they prefer. The results show that 52 per cent prefer one car and 48 per cent prefer the other. There is a mathematical difference in the sample results but in statistical terms what is the likelihood that this difference would also be evident in the general population? The difference is probably smaller than the level of accuracy with which we can measure attitudes in the general population using a sample of 1,000 car drivers. To understand this, it is important to consider the meaning of the following two concepts:

1 **Mathematical differences.** It is obviously a fact that where numbers are not exactly the same, they are different (e.g. 8 can be seen to be different from the number 10). This does not, however, suggest that the difference between the two numbers is either important or statistically significant.

2 **Statistical significance.** If a particular difference is large enough to be unlikely to have occurred due to chance or sampling error, then the difference is statistically significant.

Statistical significance
If the difference between two statistical measures is large enough to be unlikely to have occurred due to chance or sampling error, then the difference is considered to be statistically significant.

> ### Researcher quote
>
> It is important to understand the difference between mathematical differences and statistical differences.

Various approaches for testing whether results are statistically significant are discussed in the following section. It should be noted, however, that tests of sample precision are based on an assumption of random sampling. These tests cannot be applied to non-random samples.

Hypothesis testing

A **hypothesis** can be defined as an assumption or proposition that a researcher makes about some characteristic of the population being investigated. The marketing researcher needs to determine whether research results are significant enough to conclude something about the population under investigation. For example:

- Research undertaken ten years ago suggested that a typical family's weekly expenditure in a supermarket was €76. However, a recent survey suggests an expenditure of €82. Considering the size of the samples used, is the result significantly higher?
- The marketing manager of a leisure centre believes that 60 per cent of his customers are younger than 25. He does a survey of 250 customers to test this hypothesis and finds that, according to the survey, 51 per cent are under 25. Is this result sufficiently different from his original view to permit him to conclude that his original theory was incorrect?

Hypothesis testing
Testing aimed at determining whether the difference between proportions is greater than would be expected by chance or as a result of sampling error.

These situations can both be evaluated using a statistical test. In **hypothesis testing**, the researcher determines whether a hypothesis concerning some characteristic of the population of interest is likely, given the evidence. To do this, the researcher needs to establish the hypothesis and then select an appropriate technique to test it.

1 Establish the hypothesis: Hypotheses are stated using two basic forms: the null hypothesis H_0 and the alternative hypothesis H_1. The null hypothesis is always the hypothesis to be tested and is the statement of the status quo where no difference or effect is expected, whereas the alternative hypothesis is the one in which some difference or effect is expected (i.e. a difference that could not occur simply by chance). The null and alternative hypotheses complement each other; they are mutually exclusive (i.e. they cannot both be true at the same time). For example, a marketing manager for a chain of retail grocery stores believes that the value of an average customer's shopping basket is less than €80. She conducts research based on 1,000 customers passing through the checkouts and finds the average value to be €94. For this example, the null hypothesis and the alternative hypothesis might be stated as:

Null hypothesis H_0: *Mean value of shopping basket is less than €80.*

Alternative hypothesis H_1: *mean value of shopping basket is €80 or more.*

A statistical test with these hypotheses can have one of two outcomes: that the null hypothesis is rejected and the alternative hypothesis is accepted or that the null hypothesis is not rejected based on the evidence.

2 Select an appropriate statistical technique to test the hypothesis: There are many statistical tests available but this book concentrates on the three most commonly used tests, the chi-square test, the Z test and the t test. Before describing these tests, it is necessary to explain three concepts that impact on the tests:

(a) **Degrees of freedom:** many of the statistical tests require the researcher to specify degrees of freedom in order to find the critical value of the test statistic. Degrees of freedom (d.f.) are defined as the number of observations (i.e. the sample size) minus one. Therefore a sample (n) has $n - 1$ degrees of freedom.

(b) **Independent versus related samples:** the selection of the appropriate test statistic may require the researcher to consider whether the samples are independent or related. Independent samples involve situations in which the measurement of the variable of interest in one sample has no effect on the measurement of the variable in the other sample. In the case of related samples, the measurement of the variable of interest in one sample may influence the measurement of the variable of interest in another sample.

> If, for example, 20–30-year-olds and 50–60-year-olds were interviewed in a survey regarding their frequency of attending the cinema, the samples would be considered to be independent, as the response of the younger group is unlikely to have an impact on the responses of the older group. However, in a tracking study using a panel of respondents where awareness or attitudes are measured over time, measurements during each wave of the research may be contaminated by respondents thinking differently about a subject having taken part in a previous wave of the research. The samples in each wave are therefore not independent.

(c) **Errors in hypothesis testing:** hypothesis tests are subject to two general types of error, which are generally referred to as Type I and Type II errors. A Type I error involves rejecting the null hypothesis when it is actually true. This may occur as a result of sampling error (see Chapter 8). The probability of committing a Type I error is referred to as the alpha (α) level. The alpha level needs to be selected for each test and is commonly set at 0.05 (meaning that there is a 5 per cent chance of a Type I error occurring). Reducing the alpha level below 0.05 increases the probability of a Type II error occurring. A Type II error involves failing to reject the null hypothesis when it is actually false. The alpha (α) level selected should be a function of the relative importance of the two types of errors. If there are major consequences of rejecting the null hypothesis (e.g. in a clinical trial of a new drug), then the alpha level should be low (e.g. 0.01). However, for most marketing research scenarios, there is no real difference between the impact of a Type I and a Type II error and therefore an alpha (α) level of 0.05 is commonly used.

Testing goodness of fit: chi-square

Surveys regularly produce frequency tables and cross-tabulations. Researchers need to ask whether the number of responses that fall into different categories differ from what is expected. The chi-square (χ^2) test enables the researcher to test the 'goodness of fit' between the observed distribution and the expected distribution of a variable.

Chi-square test of a single sample

Consider the example of a bank that selects three bank branches of equal size for refurbishment. A different design is used in each outlet and the number of product enquiries is monitored over a three-month period and is shown below:

	Number of enquiries
Branch 1	11,154
Branch 2	10,789
Branch 3	11,003

Chi-square
A statistical test which tests the 'goodness of fit' between the observed distribution and the expected distribution of a variable.

The marketing manager needs to know whether there is a significant difference between the number of enquiries being made at each branch. The **chi-square** (χ^2) one-sample test is used to answer this question:

1 Specify the null and alternative hypotheses:

   Null hypothesis H$_0$: *The number of product enquiries in the different branches is equal.*

   Alternative hypothesis H$_1$: *There is a significant difference in the number of product enquiries in the various branches.*

2 Determine the number of product enquiries that would be expected in each category if the null hypothesis were correct. This would mean the same number of product enquiries in each of the branches (calculated by totalling the number of product enquiries and dividing by three [$(11{,}154 + 10{,}789 + 11{,}003)/3 = 10{,}982$]. Under the null hypothesis, each of the branches should have expected 10,982 product enquiries. (Note: chi-square should not be used if (a) more than 20 per cent of the categories have expected frequencies of less than 5 or (b) any of the expected frequencies are less than 1.)

3 Calculate the chi-square value using the following formula:

$$\chi^2 = \sum_{i=1}^{k} \frac{(O_i - E_i)^2}{E_i}$$

   where O_i is the observed number in the ith category, E_i is the expected number in the ith category and k is the number of categories.

   For the banking example:

$$\chi^2 = \frac{(11{,}154 - 10{,}982)^2}{10{,}982} + \frac{(10{,}789 - 10{,}982)^2}{10{,}982} + \frac{(11{,}003 - 10{,}982)^2}{10{,}982} = 6.13$$

4 Select the level of significance (α). If the 0.05 (α) level of significance is selected, the χ^2 value with 2 degrees of freedom ($k - 1$) is 5.99 (see Table 2 in Appendix 1).

5 As the calculated χ^2 value (6.13) is higher than the table value, the null hypothesis should be rejected. The researcher can then conclude with 95 per cent confidence that customer response to the branch designs was significantly different. In other words, the variation among the branches is greater than would be expected by chance. However, although it confirms a difference, it does not confirm whether any design is significantly better than the others are.

Chi-square test of two independent samples

The chi-square test is also used by researchers to determine whether there is any association between two or more variables. For example, the following research results on bank branch visits appeared in a cross-tabulation:

Number of visits per month	Male	Female	Totals
1–4	180	80	260
5–8	100	180	280
More than 8	20	40	60
Totals	300	300	600

The expected frequency for each cell is calculated as follows:

Number of visits per month	Male	Female	Totals
1–4	$300 \times 260/600 = 130$	$300 \times 260/600 = 130$	260
5–8	$300 \times 280/600 = 140$	$300 \times 280/600 = 140$	280
More than 8	$300 \times 60/600 = 30$	$300 \times 60/600 = 30$	60
Totals	300	300	600

The value of χ^2 is calculated using the following formula:

$$\chi^2 = \sum_{i=1}^{r} \sum_{j=1}^{k} \frac{(O_{ij} - E_{ij})^2}{E_{ij}}$$

where O_{ij} is the observed number in the ith row of the jth column and E_{ij} is the expected number in the ith row of the jth column.

$$\chi^2 = \frac{(180 - 130)^2}{130} + \frac{(80 - 130)^2}{130} + \frac{(100 - 140)^2}{140}$$

$$+ \frac{(180 - 140)^2}{140} + \frac{(20 - 30)^2}{30} + \frac{(40 - 30)^2}{30} = 67.99$$

The tabular χ^2 value at 0.05 level of significance, and $(r - 1) \times (k - 1) = 2$ degrees of freedom is 5.99 (see Table 2 in Appendix 1). Because the calculated $\chi^2 = 67.99$ is more than the tabular value, the null hypothesis is rejected and the researcher can conclude that there is a significant difference between males and females in terms of the frequency of visits to bank branches.

Hypotheses about means and proportions

Where sample data produces a mean (for example, the average value of a weekly grocery shop) or a proportion (59 per cent of the sample prefer butter), researchers may wish to test a hypothesis relating to these figures. To do this, either a Z test or a t test is used. A Z test is used if the researcher is aware of the population's mean and variance (actual or assumed) and the sample size is larger than 30. A t test is appropriate when the mean and variance of the population are not known or where the sample size is less than 30. The *t* test tends to be used more frequently by marketing researchers.

Z test

A mobile phone manufacturer undertook a survey of 1,000 mobile phone users examining attitudes towards different brands of phone. Each phone was rated for quality using a 1–5 rating scale. The mean rating for Nokia was 3.6. The sample standard deviation was 1.8. The client company wants to determine whether Nokia's rating is significantly higher than the average score for all of the brands of phone (3.1).

Z test

A hypothesis test about a single mean where the sample size is larger than 30.

A **Z test** for hypotheses about one mean is used with the null hypothesis (H_0) being: Nokia's quality rating is equal to or less than 3.1. The alternative hypothesis states that Nokia does have a higher rating than 3.1.

At the 0.05 level of significance, the tabular value of *Z* (critical) = 1.64 (see Table 3 in Appendix 1 – the table for *t* is used because *t* holds the same value as *Z* when the sample is greater than 30). The tabular value of *Z* at any level of significance depends on whether a one-tailed or two-tailed test is involved. If an evaluation is required to determine whether something is more or less than something else (as is the case here), then a one-tailed test is appropriate. If an evaluation is required to test whether something is the same as something else, then a two-tailed test is appropriate.

The first step is to calculate the estimated standard error of the mean, using the formula:

$$\text{Standard error} = \frac{\text{Standard deviation}}{\sqrt{\text{Sample size}}} = \frac{1.8}{\sqrt{1,000}} = 0.06$$

$$Z = \frac{(\text{Sample mean} - \text{Population mean})}{\text{Estimated standard error}} = \frac{3.6 - 3.1}{0.06} = 8.3$$

As 8.3 is larger than the critical *Z* value (1.64), the client company can infer with 95 per cent confidence that Nokia's quality is higher than the average value of quality.

Alternatively, proportions may be involved. Say, for example, a survey of 300 customers found that 67 per cent of them disliked a new flavour of a well-known snack product. Before withdrawing the product, the brand manager wants to determine whether the true percentage is greater than 60 per cent. The null and alternative hypotheses are specified as:

H_0: The proportion of the population who dislike the product is equal to or less than 60 per cent.

H_1: The proportion of the population who dislike the product is more than 60 per cent.

Step 1 involves calculating the estimated standard error using the following formula:

$$S_p = \sqrt{\frac{P(1-P)}{n-1}}$$

where *P* is the proportion specified in the null hypothesis and *N* is the sample size.

$$S_p = \sqrt{\frac{0.6(1-0.6)}{300-1}} = 0.028$$

Calculate the *Z* value using the following formula:

$$Z = \frac{(\text{Observed proportion} - \text{Proportion under null hypothesis})}{\text{Estimated standard error } (S_p)} = \frac{0.67 - 0.6}{0.028} = 25$$

At the 0.05 level, the table value of *Z* = 1.64 (see Table 3 in Appendix 1 – value for *Z* where d.f. = infinity, 0.05 significance, one-tail). On this basis the null hypothesis is rejected because the calculated *Z* value is larger than the critical *Z* value. The brand manager can then withdraw the product as he can conclude with 95 per cent confidence that more than 60 per cent of customers dislike the new flavour.

If the proportions in two independent samples are to be compared – for example, to determine whether the number of people disliking one flavour of snack product in the UK survey is significantly different from the number disliking the flavour in a separate study in France – the procedure is similar to the test above except that the following formula is used:

$$S_{P_{a-b}} = \sqrt{P(1-P)\left(\frac{1}{n_a} + \frac{1}{n_b}\right)}$$

where

$$P = \frac{n_a P_a + n_b P_b}{n_a + n_b}$$

P_a is the proportion in sample a, P_b is the proportion in sample b, n_a is the size of sample a and n_b is the size of sample b.

t test

t test
A hypothesis test about a single mean if the sample is too small to use the *Z* test.

Although the *Z* test is generally used for large samples with a sample size of more than 30, some statistical computer packages use the *t* **test** for all sample sizes. The procedures for using the *t* test are similar to those for using the *Z* test. The different formulas are as follows:

For a mean and one sample:

$$t = \frac{\text{Sample mean} - \text{Mean under null hypothesis}}{\text{Estimated standard error of the mean}}$$

For comparing means in two samples:

$$t = \frac{(\text{Mean from sample 1}) - (\text{Mean from sample 2})}{\sqrt{[(\text{Standard error for sample 1})^2 + (\text{Standard error for sample 2})^2]}}$$

In addition to *t* tests and *Z* tests, there are a number of other tests depending on the nature of the data and the comparisons made. For example with ordinal data, the tests listed in Table 9.2 are used.

Table 9.2	Statistical tests used with ordinal data	
Test	**Data type**	**Sample type**
ANOVA (analysis of variance)	Interval and ratio data	Testing the means of two or more independent samples
Mann–Whitney *U* test	Ordinal data	Two independent samples
Kruskal–Wallis test	Ordinal data	More than two independent samples
Wilcoxon signed rank	Ordinal data	Two non-independent samples
Friedman two-way analysis	Ordinal data	More than two non-independent samples
Kolmogorov–Smirnov test	Ordinal data	Similar to chi-square (but for ordinal data)

Measuring relationships: correlation and regression

Correlation
A statistical approach to examine the relationship between two variables. Uses an index to describe the strength of a relationship.

Marketers are frequently interested in the degree of association between two variables such as advertising and sales, temperature and ice cream sales, square footage of retail store and sales, average queue length and customer satisfaction scores. Bivariate techniques such as **correlation** analysis and regression analysis are used when only two variables are involved. If more than two variables are involved, then multivariate techniques are used. These are briefly described at the end of this chapter.

Bivariate analysis cannot be used to prove that one variable causes some change in another variable. It simply describes the degree of association between the two variables. Although a researcher may label each of the variables as being independent or dependent, this is not confirmed by either correlation or regression analysis. Independent variables are those variables that are believed to influence the dependent variable. As such, we can clearly assume that advertising is the independent variable and sales is the dependent variable. However, things may not always be so clear cut (e.g. in the case of credit-card usage and level of household debt, does the level of debt influence credit card usage or does credit-card usage influence household debt?).

Regression and correlation examine relationships in different ways. Regression analysis identifies the nature of the relationship using an equation, whereas correlation analysis uses an index to describe the strength of a relationship. To understand this fully, it is useful to look at a number of scatter diagrams (see Figure 9.3). These diagrams plot the variable that is considered to be dependent on the y axis and the independent variable on the x axis (for example, advertising would be on the x axis and sales would be on the y axis. Figure 9.3(a) suggests a positive linear relationship between x and y, whereas Figure 9.3(b) suggests a perfect negative linear relationship. Instead of a linear relationship, Figure 9.3(c) shows a nonlinear relationship, and more complex appropriate curve-fitting techniques are required to describe this relationship mathematically. Figure 9.3(d) shows no relationship between x and y. The correlation and regression techniques introduced in this chapter are only designed to capture the extent of linear association between variables and will not identify a curvilinear relationship.

Pearson's product moment correlation

The Pearson's product moment correlation approach is used with interval and ratio data. It produces the coefficient of correlation (R) which is a measure of the degree of association

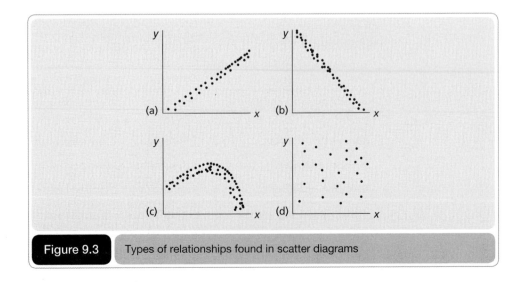

| **Figure 9.3** | Types of relationships found in scatter diagrams |

between x and y. The value of R can range from -1 (perfect negative correlation) to $+1$ (perfect positive correlation). The closer R is to either $+1$ or -1, the stronger the degree of association between x and y. If R is equal to zero, then there is no association between x and y.

The formula for calculating R is as follows:

$$R = \frac{n\sum xy - (\sum x)(\sum y)}{\sqrt{[n\sum x^2 - (\sum x)^2][n\sum y^2 - (\sum y)^2]}}$$

Pearson's product moment coefficient of correlation

To illustrate the computation and interpretation of Pearson's product moment coefficient of correlation, let us consider some data gathered by a manufacturer of photocopiers on worldwide sales. The following table contains data from a sample of 16 countries for the size of the salesforce and the revenues generated by sales during a six-month period.

Country	Number of sales personnel (x)	Sales (million euros) (y)	x^2	y^2	xy
1	45	5.85	2,025	34.22	263.25
2	32	4.06	1,024	16.48	129.92
3	16	2.09	256	4.37	33.44
4	8	1.05	64	1.10	8.40
5	33	4.31	1,089	18.58	142.23
6	18	2.33	324	5.43	41.94
7	10	1.27	100	1.61	12.70
8	3	0.38	9	0.14	1.14
9	22	2.93	484	8.58	64.46
10	23	2.79	529	7.78	64.17
11	26	3.37	676	11.36	87.62
12	24	3.12	576	9.73	74.88
13	41	5.33	1,681	28.41	218.53
14	37	5.00	1,369	25.00	185.00
15	19	2.79	361	7.78	53.01
16	11	1.30	121	1.69	14.30
Sum $\sum$	368	47.97	10,688	182.26	1,394.99

$$R = \frac{n\sum xy - (\sum x)(\sum y)}{\sqrt{[n\sum x^2 - (\sum x)^2][n\sum y^2 - (\sum y)^2]}}$$

$$R = \frac{16(1,394.99) - (368)(47.97)}{\sqrt{[16(10,688) - (368)^2][16(182.26) - (47.97)^2]}}$$

$$R = \frac{4,666.88}{4,678.20} = 1.0$$

This value of R indicates an almost perfect positive linear relationship between the number of sales personnel and the level of sales.

Spearman's rank-order correlation

Where the data is ordinal, Spearman's rank-order correlation is used. For example, if a researcher wants to examine the relationship between the rankings for advertising expenditure in an industry and the rankings for annual turnover, then the formula for Spearman's rank-order correlation coefficient should be used:

$$R_s = 1 - \left(\frac{6 \sum_{i=1}^{n} d_i^2}{n^3 - n} \right)$$

where d_i is the difference in ranks of the two variables and n is the number of items ranked.

Spearman's rank-order correlation

To illustrate the computation and interpretation of Spearman's rank-order coefficient of correlation, let us consider the following table showing the rankings for 14 companies in terms of advertising expenditure and annual turnover. Note that the rank of 1 indicates the highest expenditure and highest turnover.

Company	Advertising expenditure (x)	Annual turnover (y)	Difference in ranking (d)	(Difference in ranking)^2 (d^2)
A	1	2	1	1
B	8	6	−2	4
C	2	4	2	4
D	4	3	−1	1
E	3	1	−2	4
F	10	14	4	16
G	13	11	−2	4
H	5	5	0	0
I	14	13	−1	1
J	7	8	1	1
K	12	12	0	0
L	6	9	3	9
M	11	10	−1	1
N	9	7	−2	4
			Sum	50

$$R_s = 1 - \left(\frac{6 \sum_{i=1}^{n} d_i^2}{n^3 - n} \right)$$

where d_i is the difference in ranks of the two variables and n is the number of items ranked.

$R_s = 1 - (6(50)/(14^3 - 14))$

$R_s = 0.89$

Based on this coefficient, the two rankings are positively correlated. Higher rankings on one are associated with higher rankings on the other. The value of the correlation coefficient can be tested against the null hypothesis that states there is no relationship. This is done using a t distribution for a given sample size ($n = 14$) as follows:

$$t = R_s \sqrt{\frac{n-2}{1-R_s^2}} = 0.89 \times \sqrt{[(14-2)/(1-0.89)^2]} = 6.76$$

The tabulated value (see Table 3 in the Appendix) for t with $12(n-2)$ degrees of freedom is 2.18 (at $\alpha = 0.05$). As the calculated t value (6.76) is higher than the tabulated or critical value (2.18), the null hypothesis is rejected and so there is a positive relationship between a company's advertising expenditure and its annual turnover.

While the Pearson and Spearman rank-order correlation coefficients are effective in uncovering bivariate associations, there is one important caveat concerning their use. A low correlation coefficient does not necessarily mean there is no association; it only implies an absence of a linear association. A researcher should always explore the possible presence of a nonlinear association, especially when intuitively the researcher feels that the variables may be related. The easiest way of identifying a nonlinear association is to plot and examine a scatter diagram.

Simple regression analysis

Regression
A statistical approach to examine the relationship between two variables. Identifies the nature of the relationship using an equation.

Simple **regression** analysis is similar to the procedures used to calculate the Pearson correlation coefficient. However, whereas correlation analysis focuses on summarising the degree and the direction of association between variables as a single number, the purpose of regression analysis is to generate a mathematical equation linking those variables. In other words, regression analysis attempts to describe the gradient and direction of the line that goes through the plots on a scatter diagram. The equation that provides the description of the line can be used to forecast the value of the dependent variable for any value of the independent variable within the range examined by the regression analysis (for example, using past data to identify the likely sales impact of a change in advertising expenditure). When examining the association between two variables, the designation of one of the variables as the independent variable is more important to regression analysis than to correlation analysis. In regression analysis, it is only the dependent variable that is random; the independent variable is implicitly treated as a set of fixed numbers. In other words, the independent variable is seen as being set at a variety of fixed levels, at each of which the researcher observes the value of the dependent variable. This does not mean that regression analysis can prove that one variable definitely causes another. The specification of which variable is the dependent variable is done by the researcher using prior knowledge and theoretical considerations rather than by the regression technique. Similar to correlation analysis, regression analysis simply describes the relationship between the variables and does not explain it.

Least squares approach

The regression procedure that is widely used for deriving the best-fit equation of a line (see the line in Figure 9.4) for a given set of data involving a dependent and independent variable is the **least squares approach**. No straight line can perfectly represent every observation in a scatter diagram. As Figure 9.4 shows, there are discrepancies between the actual values and predicted values (values indicated by the line). The line does not go through every value. A number of lines could be drawn that would seem to fit the observations in the scatter diagram.

The least squares procedure identifies the line that best fits the actual data (better than any other line). The general equation for the line is $y = \hat{a} + \hat{b}x$ where $\hat{a}$ is the point at which the line intercepts the y axis and $\hat{b}$ is the estimated slope of the regression line, known as the regression coefficient.

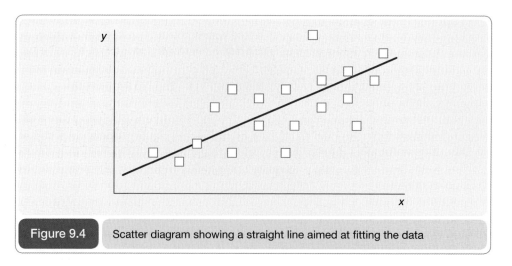

| Figure 9.4 | Scatter diagram showing a straight line aimed at fitting the data |

The values for $\hat{a}$ and $\hat{b}$ can be calculated using the following equations:

$$\hat{b} = \frac{\sum x_i y_i - n\bar{x}\bar{y}}{\sum x_i^2 - n(\bar{x})^2}$$

$$\hat{a} = \bar{y} - \hat{b}\bar{x}$$

where $\bar{x}$ is the mean value of x, $\bar{y}$ is the mean value of y and n is the sample size (number of units in the sample).

The following example uses the same data as was used for illustrating Pearson's product moment correlation to calculate B and $\hat{a}$.

Country	Number of sales personnel (x)	Sales (million euros) (y)	x^2	y^2	xy
1	45	5.85	2,025	34.22	263.25
2	32	4.06	1,024	16.48	129.92
3	16	2.09	256	4.37	33.44
4	8	1.05	64	1.10	8.40
5	33	4.31	1,089	18.58	142.23
6	18	2.33	324	5.43	41.94
7	10	1.27	100	1.61	12.70
8	3	0.38	9	0.14	1.14
9	22	2.93	484	8.58	64.46
10	23	2.79	529	7.78	64.17
11	26	3.37	676	11.36	87.62
12	24	3.12	576	9.73	74.88
13	41	5.33	1,681	28.41	218.53
14	37	5.00	1,369	25.00	185.00
15	19	2.79	361	7.78	53.01
16	11	1.30	121	1.69	14.30
Sum Σ	368	47.97	10,688	182.26	1,394.99
Mean	23	3.00			

$\hat{b} = \dfrac{1,394.99 - 16(23)(3)}{10,688 - 16(23)^2}$ $\hat{a} = < -b\xi$

$\hat{a} = 3 - 0.13 \times 23$

$\hat{b} = 0.13$ $\hat{a} = 0.01$

Thus the estimated regression function is:

$y = 0.01 + 0.13(x)$

According to the estimated regression function, for every additional 10 sales personnel, sales will increase by 1.31 million euros.

Strength of association R^2

In addition to the regression function, the researcher is frequently interested in the strength of the relationship between the variables. In other words, how widely do the actual values of y differ from the values predicted by the equation of the line?

The **coefficient of determination**, denoted by R^2 is the measure of the strength of the linear relationship between x and y. It specifically measures the percentage of the total variation in y that is 'explained' by the variation in x. If there is a perfect linear relationship between x and y (all the variation in y is explained by the variation in x and all values appear on the regression line) then R^2 equals 1. Finally, if there is no relationship between x and y, then none of the variation is explained by the variation in x and R^2 equals 0.

Country	Number of sales personnel (x)	Sales (million euros) (y)	$\hat{y}$	$y - \hat{y}$	$(y - \hat{y})^2$	$(y - \bar{y})^2$
1	45	5.85	5.86	−0.01	0.0001	8.133
2	32	4.06	4.17	−0.11	0.0121	1.128
3	16	2.09	2.09	0	0	0.825
4	8	1.05	1.05	0	0	3.795
5	33	4.31	4.30	0.01	0.0001	1.721
6	18	2.33	2.35	−0.02	0.0004	0.446
7	10	1.27	1.31	−0.04	0.0016	2.986
8	3	0.38	0.40	−0.02	0.0004	6.854
9	22	2.93	2.87	0.06	0.0036	0.005
10	23	2.79	3.00	−0.21	0.0441	0.043
11	26	3.37	3.39	−0.02	0.0004	0.138
12	24	3.12	3.13	−0.01	0.0001	0.015
13	41	5.33	5.34	−0.01	0.0001	5.438
14	37	5.00	4.82	0.18	0.0324	4.008
15	19	2.79	2.48	0.31	0.0961	0.043
16	11	1.30	1.44	−0.14	0.0196	2.884
Sum Σ	368	47.97	48.00	−0.03	0.2111	38.462
Mean	23	3.00				

Calculating the coefficient of determination using the data relating to the manufacturer of photocopiers:

$$R^2 = \frac{\text{Total variation} - \text{Unexplained variation}}{\text{Total variation}}$$

$$= 1 - \frac{\text{Unexplained variation}}{\text{Total variation}}$$

$$= 1 - \frac{\sum_{i=1}^{n}(y_i - \hat{y}_i)^2}{\sum_{i=1}^{n}(y_i - \bar{y})^2} = 1 - \frac{0.2111}{38.462} = 0.99$$

This is a very strong linear relationship between x and y, suggesting that almost all the variation in y is explained by the variation in x.

Multivariate data analysis

Multivariate data analysis
Statistical procedures that simultaneously analyse two or more variables on a sample of objects. The most common techniques are multiple regression analysis, multiple discriminant analysis, factor analysis, cluster analysis, perceptual mapping and conjoint analysis.

Multivariate data analysis is the term for statistical procedures that simultaneously analyse two or more variables on a sample of objects. For example, multivariate data analysis would enable the researcher to examine the relationships between advertising expenditure and number of salespeople, packaging costs and level of sales. Increased computer power has made it possible to examine complex relationships between multiple items with relative ease. The most common techniques provided by statistical software packages and used by marketing researchers are:

- multiple regression analysis;
- multiple discriminant analysis;
- factor analysis;
- cluster analysis;
- perceptual mapping;
- conjoint analysis.

Detailed explanation of the procedures involved in undertaking these techniques is beyond the scope of this book. However, the following subsections provide a brief description of the techniques and their application.

Multiple regression analysis

Multiple regression analysis
A statistical technique to examine the relationship between three or more variables and also to calculate the likely value of the dependent variable based on the values of two or more independent variables.

Multiple regression analysis enables a researcher both to understand the relationship between three or more variables and also to calculate the likely value of a dependent variable based on the values of two or more independent variables. In general, all of the variables require to be based on interval or ratio scales if they are to be suitable for multiple regression analysis (under exceptional circumstances, it may be possible to use nominal independent variables if they are recoded as binary variables). Multiple regression analysis is used for a variety of applications in marketing research including:

- estimating the impact of different marketing mix variables on sales or market share;
- estimating the relative importance of individual components of customer satisfaction on overall satisfaction;
- determining the impact of different customer characteristics on levels of purchasing.

Multiple discriminant analysis

Multiple discriminant analysis
A statistical technique used to classify individuals into one of two or more segments (or populations) on the basis of a set of measurements.

Multiple discriminant analysis is generally used to classify individuals into one of two or more segments (or populations) on the basis of a set of measurements. For example, the grouping may relate to brand usage, with respondents being either users or non-users of a brand. Multiple discriminant analysis enables a researcher to predict the likelihood of a person being a brand user based on two or more independent variables, such as size of weekly shop, income level, age, or purchasing levels of related products. This may allow the researcher to establish a model for classifying individuals into groups or segments on the basis of the values of their independent variables. The technique can also be used to identify which variables contribute to making the classification. Overall, the objective in discriminant analysis is to find a linear combination of the independent variables that maximises the difference between groupings and minimises the probability of misclassifying individuals or objects into their respective groups.

Factor analysis

Factor analysis is a procedure that studies the interrelationships among variables for the purpose of simplifying data. It can reduce a large set of variables to a smaller set of composite variables or factors by identifying the underlying dimensions of the data (e.g. measures of 'size' and 'value' in a study may be indicators of the same theoretical construct).

Reasons for performing factor analysis can be summarised as:

- It can provide insights from the groupings of variables that emerge. These insights might have practical or theoretical significance.
- It can reduce the number of questions, scales or attributes being analysed to a more manageable number.

In marketing research, factor analysis is most frequently used when analysing data coming from rating scales. Respondents may be asked to rate a service on a whole range of attributes; within this, satisfaction with the service employee may be measured through a range of attributes such as product knowledge, empathy with the customer, speed of service, clarity of communication, etc. A researcher may want to add some of these attributes together to develop a composite score or to compute an average score for the concept. Factor analysis will determine whether and how attributes can be combined into summary factors such as 'interpersonal skills' and 'technical ability'. Different weightings may require to be applied to the original attributes to determine the summary factors. A factor is thus a variable or construct that is not directly observable but that needs to be inferred from the input variables.

The most important outputs from factor analysis are the factor loadings and the variance-explained percentages. The factor loadings are used to determine the factors and describe the correlations between the factors and the variables. The variance-explained percentage help to determine the number of factors to include and how well they represent the original variables.

Factor analysis can generate several solutions for any data set. Each solution is called a factor rotation and is generated by a factor rotation scheme (e.g. Varimax rotation). Different rotations result in different factor loadings and different interpretations of the factors. Rotation simply means that the dimensions are rotated until suitable factors are identified. This highlights a weakness of factor analysis – it is a highly subjective process. The selection of the number of factors, their interpretation, and the rotation to select the factors (if one set of factors is disliked by a researcher, rotation may be continued indefinitely until a more suitable set is found) all involve the researcher's selective judgement. In order to increase the objectivity of the analysis and to determine whether the results of the analysis reflect something meaningful rather than being merely accidental, the following approach is frequently adopted: the sample is randomly divided into two or more groups and a factor analysis is run on each group. If the same factors emerge in each analysis, more confidence can be placed in the results.

Cluster analysis

Cluster analysis refers to statistical procedures used to classify objects or people into mutually exclusive and exhaustive groups on the basis of two or more classification variables. Frequently, marketing managers need to identify consumer segments so that marketing strategies can be developed and tailored to each segment. Such segments can be based on lifestyles, purchasing behaviour, socioeconomic characteristics, etc.

Although a number of different approaches and procedures are available for clustering, the underlying process involves determining the similarities among people or objects with regard to the variables being used for the clustering. At the most basic level this can be done plotting the characteristics of respondents on a scatter diagram and examining the patterns in the data. For example, Figure 9.5 shows the clusters relating to the purchases of toothpaste and variables relating to the importance placed on the reduction of tooth decay and the importance placed on price. The scatter diagram shows three clusters:

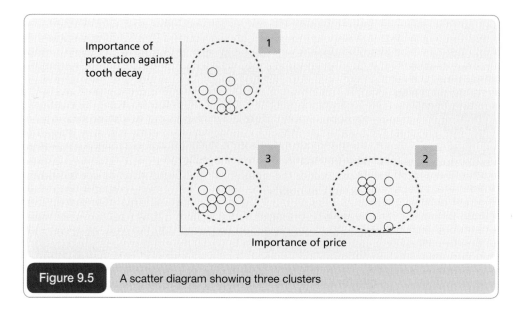

Figure 9.5 A scatter diagram showing three clusters

- **Cluster 1** includes those people who purchase toothpaste on the basis of protection against tooth decay and pay little attention to price.
- **Cluster 2** includes those people who purchase toothpaste on the basis of price and pay little attention to protection against tooth decay.
- **Cluster 3** includes those people who do not pay attention to either price or protection – they may be influenced by brand name, taste, appearance, type of dispenser, etc. (further scatter diagrams would be required to determine this).

Using scatter diagrams for cluster analysis is time consuming and can become an onerous task, particularly when considering a large number of variables or a large number of respondents. Scatter diagrams can sometimes be difficult to interpret if there are very large numbers of points plotted onto one two-dimensional diagram, never mind a diagram with three dimensions or more. However, there are computer programs available to undertake this task. The procedure they use involves algorithms that alter cluster boundaries until a point is reached where the distances between the points within the clusters is smaller than the distances between the points in one cluster and those in another. The computer will continue to assign and reassign data to clusters until it achieves the number of clusters that the researcher is seeking. The researcher will determine the optimum number by considering the practicalities of using the cluster information or by looking at the pattern of clusters and the distances between the clusters generated by the computer program at each iteration.

Perceptual mapping

Perceptual mapping
An analysis technique which involves the positioning of objects in perceptual space. Frequently used in determining the positioning of brands relative to their competitors.

Multidimensional scaling involves **perceptual mapping**, which is the positioning of objects in a perceptual space. This is particularly important in determining the positioning of brands relative to their competitors. For example, toothpaste manufacturers may want to assess the position of their branded products against those of the competition in terms of protection, price, taste, modernity, freshness of breath, and level of whiteness. Respondents will be asked to evaluate each brand on these attributes and the output from the data analysis is called a perceptual map. Such a map is usually two-dimensional; although three-dimensional maps are possible they are often more difficult to interpret. Where more than two dimensions are required, a series of two-dimensional maps is generally used.

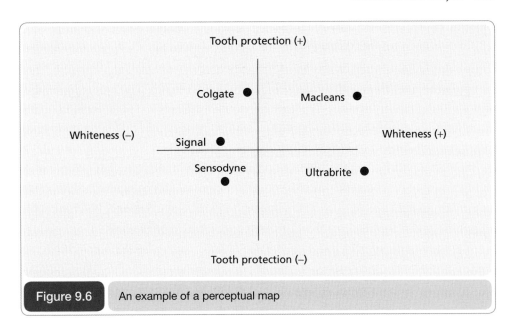

| Figure 9.6 | An example of a perceptual map |

Figure 9.6 shows an example of a perceptual map for toothpaste, it shows Macleans and Colgate as being perceived as better for tooth protection than the other brands, with Macleans and Ultrabrite being seen as performing better in terms of whiteness.

Conjoint analysis

Conjoint analysis
A statistical technique that provides a quantitative measure of the relative importance of one attribute over another. It is frequently used to determine what features a new product or service should have and also how products should be priced.

Conjoint analysis provides a quantitative measure of the relative importance of one attribute over another. It is frequently used by marketers to determine what features a new product or service should have and also how products should be priced. This is often used instead of the more expensive approach of full concept testing.

In assessing the importance placed on attributes by consumers, it is rare to find that only one attribute is important. People will buy their toothpaste on the basis of a combination of factors (e.g. price, protection against tooth decay, flavour, size of packet) rather than on the basis of one factor (e.g. flavour) only. In conjoint analysis, the respondent is asked to make trade-offs between the different attributes. Which attribute can be sacrificed? At what level of price does protection become less attractive? Sometimes the preferences may be in conflict; for example, high protection against tooth decay for a very low price. The aim is to find some form of compromise solution.

Trade-off data are collected in one of two ways: respondents are either asked to consider two attributes at a time or to assess a full profile of attributes at once.

The **full-profile approach** involves the respondents being given cards that describe a full product or service. This can best be described using a hypothetical banking product, which has only three attributes:

Interest rate	Means of delivery	Access to money
Low rate	Passbook	Immediate
High rate	Cash machine	Seven-day notice
	Internet	

For such a banking product, the design would consist of 12 combinations ($2 \times 3 \times 2$) as shown below:

Profile	Interest rate	Means of delivery	Access to money
1	Low	Passbook	Immediate
2	Low	Passbook	Seven-day notice
3	Low	Cash machine	Immediate
4	Low	Cash machine	Seven-day notice
5	Low	Internet	Immediate
6	Low	Internet	Seven-day notice
7	High	Passbook	Immediate
8	High	Passbook	Seven-day notice
9	High	Cash machine	Immediate
10	High	Cash machine	Seven-day notice
11	High	Internet	Immediate
12	High	Internet	Seven-day notice

Respondents can be asked either to rank-order the profiles in order of preference, or to assign a rating scale to each profile measuring overall preference or intentions to buy. The full-profile approach is similar to real life, in that consumers tend to consider all attributes at once when purchasing a product. However, as the number of attributes increases, the task of judging the individual profiles becomes very complex and respondents have difficulties in taking account of all the variations in the attributes.

An alternative approach is the pairwise (trade-off) approach where the attributes are presented in pairs. For example, in the bank product example, this would lead to three possible pairings:

1 Interest rate/Means of delivery;
2 Interest rate/Access to money;
3 Means of delivery/Access to money.

The pairings would be presented in grids similar to the following and respondents would be asked to put each combination in rank order of preference:

Means of delivery			
	Passbook	Cash machine	Internet
Low interest rate	6	5	3
High interest rate	4	2	1

Although the pairwise approach may lack the realism of the full-profile approach, it is generally easier for the respondent to make judgements between two attributes. Care must be taken to ensure that the number of attributes is not excessive, as the task may become repetitive and boring. If there is a very large number of attributes, a two-stage approach may be adopted where the respondent first classifies the attributes into various groups relating to importance. The pairings are only set up with the attributes that the respondent considers to be at least reasonably important.

The process can also be made less tedious by allowing respondents to input their decisions directly into a specialist computer package. The package can decide on the attributes to test on a real-time basis using the respondent's previous responses to select the next attributes to assess. Where a respondent has indicated that certain attributes or levels of attribute are totally unacceptable then these will not be presented again. The computer can also monitor the degree to which the model of preference that is emerging is actually explaining the choices made – when a good enough fit emerges, the interview can be ended.

Analysis of the data produces a set of utilities (a set of values/scores) for the various potential attributes of the product or service. These may look something like the following table, where the utilities are shown in brackets:

Set of utilities for respondent 1

Interest rate	Means of delivery	Access to money
Low rate (0)	Passbook (5)	Immediate (100)
High rate (100)	Cash machine (40)	Seven-day notice (70)
	Internet (30)	

By adding the various utilities, the total utility of a proposed product/service for each respondent can be calculated. This can enable the researcher to make estimates of the potential market share for each of the potential designs of products or services. However, a word of caution: when using conjoint analysis, the researcher should remember that it may not totally reflect reality, as consumers are unlikely to approach purchasing decisions in such a rational and deliberate manner. Customers may not be fully aware of all product features when buying a product or may be strongly influenced by branding or advertising.

Summary and an integrated approach

This chapter has attempted to introduce you to the key steps and most common approaches used by researchers when analysing quantitative data. The three main steps involve:

1 **Coding**: the transforming of responses into a form that is ready for analysis.
2 **Data entry**: entering of the data into a computer, either automatically or manually.
3 **Tabulation and statistical analysis**: the interpretation and communication of the meaning behind the data.

Quantitative data exists in one of four forms – nominal, ordinal, interval and ratio. The nature of each of these impacts on the types of tabulation and statistical analysis that are possible.

The main forms of statistical analysis can be categorised into:

- **Descriptive statistics**: measures of central tendency, measures of dispersion.
- **Statistical significance and hypothesis testing**: chi-square, Z test, t test.
- **Measuring relationships**: correlation and regression.
- **Multivariate data analysis**: multiple regression analysis, multiple discriminant analysis, factor analysis, cluster analysis, perceptual mapping.

All of these data analysis techniques introduced in this chapter are as relevant for quantitatively analysing customer data held within orgnisations as they are for analysing data from external secondary research or primary research sources.

The author is only too well aware that many students' eyes glaze over when confronted by formulas and statistics. Thankfully many of the analysis and questionnaire design software packages (such as Snap and those listed at the end of this chapter) remove the onerous tasks of applying formulas and calculating statistical outcomes. However, researchers do need to develop an awareness and understanding of the statistical techniques available and the meaning of their outputs. This chapter has attempted to provide this basic awareness and understanding. More detailed discussion of statistical techniques can be found in the books listed in the Additional reading section below, or on a website such as that run by Statsoft (electronic statistics website; **http://www.statsoft.com**).

Discussion questions

1 What does coding involve and how should a researcher go about post-coding responses to open-ended questions?

2 What is the difference between nominal and ordinal data?

3 What is the difference between interval and ratio data?

4 Describe the main measures of central tendency.

5 Explain the difference between mathematical differences and statistical differences.

6 Explain what is meant by the terms null hypothesis and alternative hypothesis.

7 For what purpose would you use the chi-square test. How is the chi-square test different from Z tests and t tests?

8 Explain the difference between correlation and regression.

9 Explain what is meant by multivariate data analysis.

10 Explain the difference between factor analysis and cluster analysis.

Additional reading

Devore, J.L. and Peck, R. (2011) *Statistics: The Exploration and Analysis of Data*, 7th edn. Duxbury Press, Belmont, CA.

Field, A. (2009) *Discovering Statistics Using SPSS*, 3rd edn. Sage Publications, UK.

Hair, J., Black, W.C., Babin, B.J. and Anderson, R. (2005) *Multivariate Data Analysis*, 7th edn, Pearson Education Harlow.

Johnson, R.A. (2004) *Statistics: Principles and Methods*, 5th edn. John Wiley, New York.

Koosis, D.J. (1997) *Statistics: a self-teaching guide*. John Wiley, New York.

Moore, D.S. (2006) *Statistics: Concepts and Controversies*, 6th edn. W.H. Freeman, New York.

Pallant, J. (2007) *SPSS Survival Manual: A Step by Step Guide to Data Analysis Using SPSS for Windows (Version 15)*. Open University Press, Milton Keynes, England.

Salkind, N.J. (2007) *Statistics for People Who (Think They) Hate Statistics*, 2nd edn. Sage, New York.

Wilcox, R.R. (1996) *Statistics for the Social Sciences*. Academic Press, London.

Quantitative analysis/questionnaire design software suppliers

Apian (SurveyPro): **www.apian.com**
CfMC (Mentor): **www.cfmc.com**
Creative Research Systems (The Survey System): **www.surveysystem.com**
FIRM (Confirmit): **www.confirmit.com**
Mercator (snap): **www.snapsurveys.com**
Merlinco (MERLIN): **www.merlinco.co.uk**
P-STAT: **www.pstat.com**
QPSMR: **www.qpsmr.ltd.uk**
SPSS: **www.spss.com**
VOXCO (StatXP): **www.voxco.com**

Reference

[1] Adapted from Phillips, A., Parfitt, J. and Prutton, I. (1989) Developing a rounder tea, *Market Research Society Conference Proceedings*, pp. 289–308. Published with the permission of the Market Research Society.

10 Presenting the research results

MTV and Microsoft were keen to fully understand global youth culture and appointed OTX, a global consumer research and consulting firm to undertake a worldwide study with 24,000 youngsters. Rather than presenting the results in a traditional PowerPoint presentation, the researchers put on an event in a London exhibition space for the clients. The event included giant headphones that blared out today's hottest music tracks, real-life teen diaries suspended from the ceiling and video voxpops – all of which served to help people who aren't young anymore understand those who are in their natural habitats.

Simon Ritter/Alamy

Some of the results were not surprising, while others offered unexpected comfort to the cynics. First of all, older people need to be careful before they start pontificating about the good old days when the neighbours all knew each others' names. Kids these days might get out less, but they probably have more friends than their parents at the same age.

Where concerned parents might see kids retreating from the 'real world' into technology, they are actually just connecting with the world in a way that, to them, is just as 'real' as anything else. To think that young people 'like' technology is wrong. In fact, most don't even notice it. Mobiles, computers and social networks are just ways for them to stay in touch with their friends.

Thanks to this new connectedness, they can discover music and culture that they wouldn't otherwise have come across. And teenagers with particular problems and concerns who can't find anyone to confide in on the playground, can easily find thousands on the Internet.

As interesting as the study itself is, the fact that the findings have been presented in a fun, funky exhibition open to the public, as well as targeting clients of MTV and OTX.

Maybe they tried a little too hard with the 'youth' styling, but it's certainly a much better way to grab clients' attention than even the most brilliantly crafted PowerPoint presentation.

Graham Saxton of OTX said: 'The point is to showcase a lot of insights about global youth culture that would be hard to present in more traditional ways. Researchers beat themselves up about adding value and getting findings in front of clients and yet most research is presented in the same old way, so we're trying to get away from that, and we'd love to do more of it. Clients are always looking for more engaging ways of research being communicated and this is one way of doing that – although it is an expensive way!'[1]

Learning outcomes

After reading this chapter you should:

- be aware of the need to understand your audience when doing a presentation or when writing a report;
- be aware of the key elements and format of the final report and oral presentation;
- understand some of the key guidelines for undertaking presentations;
- be aware of the main types of tables and graphs;
- be aware of some of the common dangers encountered in reporting and presenting.

Key words

audience's thinking sequence
bar chart
doughnut chart
line graph
oral presentation

pictogram
pie chart
research report
tables
word cloud

Introduction

The communication of the research results in the form of a research report or a verbal presentation is the culmination of the research project. This step is particularly important, as the clarity and relevance of the communication is critical to the client's final satisfaction with the marketing research project. A marketing manager may question the overall value and accuracy of the research if it is presented in a confusing and unconfident manner. The report provides a lasting impression of the quality of the research long after the project is finished. As such, it will play a big part in determining whether the researcher obtains further work from the client. This chapter provides guidelines for report writing in terms of structure, writing style, graphs and tables. It also discusses the preparation required for oral presentations. The pitfalls in both of these areas are also explored.

Understanding the audience

Audience's thinking sequence
The sequence of thoughts that people go through when they are being communicated with.

Researchers need to put themselves in the shoes of the clients and think through the specific information that the clients want to hear and also the likely manner in which they will want it communicated. One way of doing this is to consider the **audience's thinking sequence**, the sequence of thoughts that people go through when they are being communicated with. These can be illustrated as shown in Figure 10.1. Each of these thoughts has implications for the researcher:

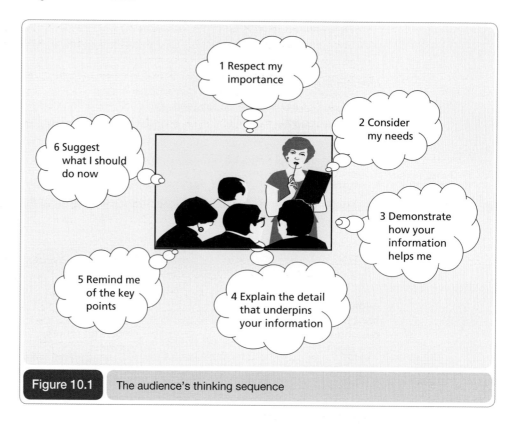

| Figure 10.1 | The audience's thinking sequence |

1 **Respect my importance**: no matter how big or small the research project, the audience are giving up their valuable time to read the researcher's report or attend the researcher's presentation. Members of the audience do not want to waste their time reading or listening to material that:

- is poorly presented (poor quality paper and poorly proofread);
- is unnecessarily long;
- is unclear and confusing;
- does not address the objectives set;
- is structured for the ease of the researcher rather than the needs of the audience.

Client quote

It is difficult to have confidence in a report if it is full of typographical and grammatical errors.

2 **Consider my needs:** the report or presentation should clearly provide evidence that the researcher is aware of the rationale for the research and is addressing the original research objectives. Relating the research findings to the marketing decisions that have to be made is critical. The material should take account of the reader's technical sophistication and their likely interest in different parts of the material.

3 **Demonstrate how your information helps me:** the audience wishes to see how the research addresses each of the research objectives and marketing decision areas. They are less concerned about different parts of the questionnaire but instead are more interested in what the findings mean to them and their organisation.

4 **Explain the detail that underpins your information:** the audience needs to be convinced that what is written or presented is accurate. They will therefore want to see the charts,

tables and actual respondent quotes that support the findings. Researchers should be anticipating the likely questions that the audience will have and should be attempting to pre-empt them in the report or presentation.

5 **Remind me of the key points:** no matter how long or short the presentation or report, there needs to be a summary of the key points. This concurs with the following maxim for communicating with an audience:

- **you should tell them what you are going to tell them** (explain the agenda of the report or presentation);
- **tell them** (i.e. the findings);
- **tell them what you have told them** (summarise and repeat the key points).

6 **Suggest what I should do now:** although the clients will be responsible for taking any marketing decisions resulting from the research findings, the researchers will normally be expected to provide recommendations about possible courses of action and issues to be addressed.

In addition to these immediate needs of the audience, it is important to realise that the report is a reference document. Long after the research has been completed, decision makers may return to the report as an input to further decisions or as a baseline or template for a follow-up research study. The report must therefore be self-explanatory and capable of being interpreted by a future audience who have had no involvement in the research project.

Understanding the current and future audiences for the research findings is critical to the successful preparation and planning of the report and presentation.

The marketing research report format

Research report
A final document produced at the end of a research study setting out the objectives, methodology, findings, conclusions, executive summary and recommendations of the research.

The exact format of a **research report** may vary from one research agency to another and also in response to specific client requirements. However, the majority of reports typically have the following components.

1 title page;
2 table of contents;
3 executive summary and recommendations;
4 introduction and problem definition;
5 research method and limitations;
6 research findings;
7 conclusions;
8 appendices.

The following subsections consider each of these in more detail.

Title page

The title page should include the title of the research study, information (name, address and telephone number) about the researcher or research agency, the name of the client, and the date of preparation. The title page should provide sufficient information to enable those who were not directly involved in the research to identify and contact those who were (either on the client or research side).

Table of contents

The table of contents should list the major headings and subheadings in the report with the appropriate page numbers. There may also be a list of tables and graphs.

Executive summary and recommendations

This section is very important as it may be the only section that is read by all of the senior decision makers in the client organisation. Certain managers may not have the time or inclination to read all of the report. This section should be no more than a few pages long and should normally be written after the other sections in the report have been completed. The summary should briefly describe the objectives of the study, the method adopted and the key research findings. The implications of the findings should also be explained, along with the researcher's suggested recommendations. Some clients may request researchers to exclude recommendations as the researcher may not be fully aware of the internal and external factors impacting on the decision area.

> **Researcher quote**
>
> Although the writing of the executive summary may be undertaken at the end, it should not be rushed, as it is the one area that will definitely be read by the most senior managers in the client company.

Introduction and problem definition

The introduction should set out the rationale and the detailed objectives for the study. In many ways, this will be similar to the background and objectives sections of the proposal. Some researchers simply copy these sections from the proposal and change the tense.

Research method and limitations

This section should set out details of the research approach adopted for the study. As such, it should cover the research method, questionnaire/discussion guide design, sampling approach and method of data analysis. Justification should be provided for the specific research approach adopted. Any limitations relating to a skewed sample, low response rate, timing of study, etc., should be highlighted as these may have a bearing on the study's findings and conclusions. In general, this section should not be any more than 4–5 pages long, with further technical details being placed in an appendix.

Research findings

This is the main part of the research report. The material should be divided into sections and structured in relation to either:

1 **the research objectives**, with each section describing the findings in relation to the information targets for each objective, or
2 **the customer segments being examined**, with each section describing the research findings in relation to different subsegments of the population. For example, one section may describe the results that relate to young couples, whereas another may focus on families and yet another may focus on the retired segment.

The findings should *not* be structured to reflect the different questions in the questionnaire. This may reflect the researcher's thinking process and analysis procedures, but it is unlikely to reflect those of the marketing decision maker. The structure should be logical and coherent, reflecting the original information needs and taking account of the audience's thinking process. The researcher should be trying to tell a story with a linked line of argument, which builds into a complete picture of the area under investigation. Key information should be supported with tables and graphs (guidelines for these are discussed later in this chapter).

For qualitative research, quoting the verbatim responses of the participants can bring the findings to life and increase the reader's interest and understanding.

Conclusions

The researcher should interpret the findings in the light of the research problems and identify the main implications for the client. The conclusions should be concise, highlighting the key findings and implications, and providing justification for these without going into excessively lengthy discussions.

Appendices

The questionnaire or discussion guide (and any showcards) should be included in the appendix, as should any tables or other material that is complex or specialised or not directly relevant to the research objectives. In other words, any material that may be of interest to the client but that may interrupt the flow and coherence of the document if it is included within the main body of the report should be placed in the appendices. If the researcher has used a large amount of secondary data, a reference list should appear in an appendix identifying the data sources, past studies, articles and books. When only a few citations are involved, these can simply be referenced in footnotes on the pages where they appear.

The oral presentation format

Oral presentation
A presentation of research findings delivered to a client in a face-to-face format by the researcher.

Making an effective **oral presentation** is sometimes seen as more difficult than writing a good report because of the direct interaction with the audience. It is certainly true that any lack of confidence during an oral presentation will result in the audience having doubts about the research results. This will be evident through more questions being posed and data being challenged. Therefore careful planning of an oral presentation is essential. Planning will revolve around the client's thinking sequence, which was highlighted earlier in this chapter.

The basic structure for a presentation should be as follows:

1 **Introduction**
   - thanking the audience for attending;
   - introducing the team doing the presentation (and any other members of the research team present);
   - explaining the format and structure of the presentation;
   - explaining the rationale for the study and the objectives of the project.
2 **Methodology**
   - a brief description of the methodology including the data-collection method, sample, time scales and any limitations.
3 **Key findings**
   - a brief presentation of the findings that are key to the objectives of the study, supported by graphs and tables;
   - the material should be aggregated into sections (possibly relating to individual objectives) as this will make it easier for the audience to assimilate.
4 **Conclusions and recommendations**
   - reiterating the key points to emerge from the research and their implications for decision making;
   - setting out recommendations;
   - inviting questions and comments from the audience.
5 **Questions**
   - handling questions posed.

A wide range of software packages, such as Microsoft's PowerPoint, are available to enable researchers to make high-quality, computer-controlled presentations or to make professional quality overheads. Whichever technology or package is used, the researcher should always ensure that it is compatible with the facilities and layout of the room where the presentation will be done.

> ### Researcher quote
>
> There is no point turning up with a lap-top computer and projector if there is no blank wall or window blinds.

Even with new technology, there are a number of basic presentation guidelines that the researcher needs to follow if quality communication is to be delivered:

- **Maintain eye contact**: the researcher should avoid reading detailed notes or staring at either the computer or presentation screen. Instead, regular eye contact should be maintained with the audience. This:
    - shows concern for the audience and their needs;
    - enables the researcher to note the reactions of the audience and possibly respond to these (speeding up or slowing down, providing further explanation);
    - maintains the interest of the audience (it is difficult to stay alert when you are constantly looking at the presenter's back or the top of their head);
    - builds trust or confidence in what the researcher is saying.

If the researcher is concerned about forgetting something, cue cards can be used. These are index type cards setting out brief notes that the presenter can hold in his or her hand.

- **Seek variety**: the researcher should avoid speaking in a monotone, using the same volume and pitch throughout. The audience will drift away and think about other things. For the same reason, variety should also be sought in the visuals used, mixing lists of bullet points with graphs and tables. Use pauses to break up the presentation and allow the audience time to digest the material.
- **Keep it simple**: over-complex visuals that are cluttered with elaborate diagrams or many words lead to confusion and boredom. Wording should be limited to the key words. The visuals are prompts for the researcher and the audience, and should not be seen as a proxy for the researcher's script. The typeface and graphics should be large enough to be viewed by everyone in the presentation room.
- **Check understanding**: throughout the presentation, researchers should regularly check with their audience that the material is clear and understood. If the researcher waits until the end to do this, he or she may find that the audience has not listened to the end of the presentation as they were so busy puzzling over the material on slide three. This becomes even more important when the presentation is being undertaken using video conferencing, if only to find out if all the members of the audience are still receiving a communication signal.
- **Provide handouts**: the provision of handouts saves the audience from taking notes, freeing the listener to pay attention to and participate more fully in the presentation. Many presentation software packages enable handouts to be produced at the same time as the visuals.

> ### Researcher quote
>
> I like to put the client's logo on the handouts and presentation charts – it makes it look more professional.

- **Act natural:** researchers concerned about their mannerisms or what their hands are doing are likely to look more awkward and less trustworthy than those who focus on what they are saying. Most people do not have mannerisms that are so distracting that they annoy an audience.
- **Finish on a high note:** the researcher should attempt to finish on a final summarising statement or key point rather than simply saying 'That's all I have to say, any questions?'. The emphasis should be on winding *up* the presentation and not winding it *down*. What is the lasting impression that the researcher wishes to leave with the audience?
- **Rehearse:** the researcher should rehearse the presentation and time it. Compare the time taken with the time available, allowing sufficient time for discussion and questions (possibly as much as an extra 25–30 per cent). Be prepared to be flexible: recheck the time available at the start of the presentation, and if an important decision maker is leaving early, ensure that the key points are communicated before he or she departs.
- **Clarify questions:** before answering questions, the researcher should pause to think carefully about what was asked. Frequently confusion in presentations results from researchers acting defensively and jumping in to answer questions that are slightly different from the ones that are being asked. A good technique is to write the question down. This indicates to the audience that the researcher is taking their points seriously. If the researcher is confused about what is being asked, they should seek clarification.

Integration | An international perspective

With the growth of multi-country research studies, many presentations are being made to clients located worldwide over video conferencing links. Video conferencing can create complications for the researcher and care should therefore be taken over:

- **Timing** – leave sufficient time for the presentation as they frequently do not start on time as a result of technical issues at the beginning of the call – either with the logging on process or with video-quality issues resulting from bad Internet connections or the existence of firewalls. If you have an hour scheduled for the presentation, it may be best to plan for 50 minutes.
- **Size of images and text** – the remote site might be using a layout that shows both the slides and person presenting, and this may shrink the presentation to a lower resolution. Large, clear images and text should therefore be used.
- **Complex animations** – be careful about using complex animations as they may be lost or distorted over a video link.
- **Check understanding regularly** – when the audience is remote from the presenter and clear eye contact is difficult, it is even more important to check that the audience understands and follows what is being said. This will be particularly important if the participants come from different countries and speak different languages.

Visual display of data

There is a saying that one picture is worth a thousand words. This is particularly true in the communication of research results. Tables and graphs can aid understanding by communicating the contents of written material in a very succinct and effective manner. They can also maintain the interest of the audience by providing breaks in the blocks of text or dialogue.

There are an infinite number of ways that tables and graphs can be produced and used. This section will set out the guidelines for the most popular: tables, pie charts, line graphs, bar charts, pictograms, word clouds and spider-type diagrams.

Table 1: Purpose of Customer Satisfaction Measurement Analysed by Industry Sector

	Retail	Hospitality sector	Financial services	Total
BASE	**64**	**48**	**48**	**160**
	%	%	%	%
To monitor customer attitudes and the organisation's performance in general	93	87	90	90
To identify particular problem areas in service delivery	86	64	76	76
To benchmark against data on competitors	36	45	30	37
To determine individual and team rewards/bonuses	36	23	50	36
To compare the performance of individual outlets	29	10	45	28
To feed into staff appraisals	14	20	23	19

Source: Strathclyde University (2011) Customer Satisfaction Report, p. 31

Figure 10.2   An example of a table

Tables

Tables
Visual displays that communicate written materials and statistics in a succinct and understandable manner.

There are a number of fundamental elements in **tables** that impact on their effectiveness at communication. Figure 10.2 shows an example table on the purpose of customer satisfaction measurement to illustrate some of these elements.

- **Title:** every table should be numbered and have a title. The number enables the table to be referred to in the text and the title should briefly describe the table's contents.
- **Base:** the base figures for the sample and subsamples should be shown. This is particularly important when percentages are being used in the table as a figure of 50 per cent may be less important when the base is 6 respondents in comparison to 6,000 respondents.
- **Ordering of data items:** wherever possible, data items in a table should be ordered with the largest items appearing at the top of the table. In the example in Figure 10.2, the elements are ordered in relation to the percentages appearing in the Total column. This enables the audience to quickly recognise the most important and frequent responses. The columns can also be ordered in this way with the segment that has the biggest subsample being in the first column. Although such a layout eases understanding, this should not be done at the expense of a more logical ordering, such as time period (Monday, Tuesday, etc.) or size category (0–14 litres, 15–29 litres, 30–44 litres, etc.).
- **Layout:** the table should incorporate plenty of space around each cell of data, and lines or boxes are also useful to distinguish between the different categories and figures. Any additional explanations or comments should appear in footnotes to the table (letters or symbols should be used for these footnotes to avoid additional confusion).
- **Source:** if the data comes from a published source, this should be cited at the bottom of the table.

Pie charts

Pie charts
Charts for presenting data which take the form of a circle divided into several slices whose areas are in proportion to the quantities being examined.

Pie charts are circles divided into several slices whose areas are in proportion to the quantities being examined. They are particularly useful for showing the decomposition of a total

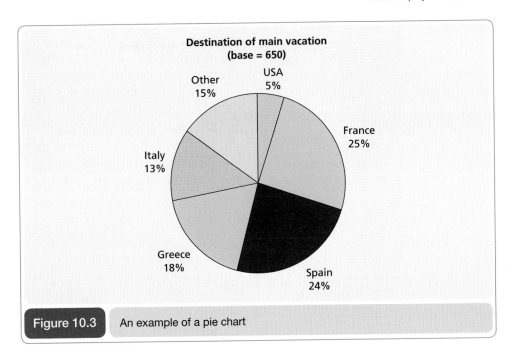

Destination of main vacation
(base = 650)

USA 5%
Other 15%
France 25%
Italy 13%
Greece 18%
Spain 24%

Figure 10.3   An example of a pie chart

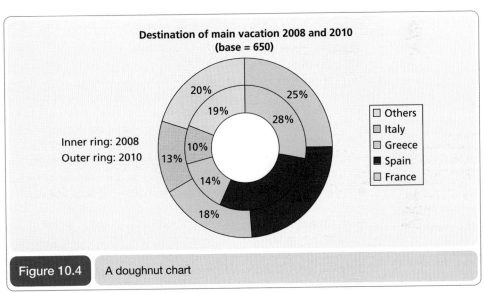

Destination of main vacation 2008 and 2010
(base = 650)

Inner ring: 2008
Outer ring: 2010

20%
19%
25%
28%
13%
10%
14%
18%

Others
Italy
Greece
Spain
France

Figure 10.4   A doughnut chart

quantity into its components (Figure 10.3). However, there should be no more than six or seven components, otherwise the chart becomes very cluttered and difficult to read. If there are many small categories (as was the case with the pie chart in Figure 10.3), these can be lumped into an 'Other' category to avoid overcrowding the chart. Using different colours or shading for the various slices improves the chart's effectiveness. As pie charts will normally show percentages, it is important that the base or sample size is shown. Also, the percentages for each segment should be included as some of the audience may have difficulty in determining the relative difference between segments.

A variety of pie charts is possible. For example, Figure 10.4 shows a derivative of the pie chart which takes the form of a 'doughnut'. The **doughnut chart** can be used to show different sets of data. For example, Figure 10.4 shows 2008 data in the inner doughnut and 2010 data in the outer doughnut. With many of the data processing packages that are now available, three-dimensional pie charts are also possible. These look impressive but can sometimes be difficult for the audience to interpret.

Doughnut chart
A form of pie chart which allows different sets of data (e.g. for different years) to be shown in the same chart.

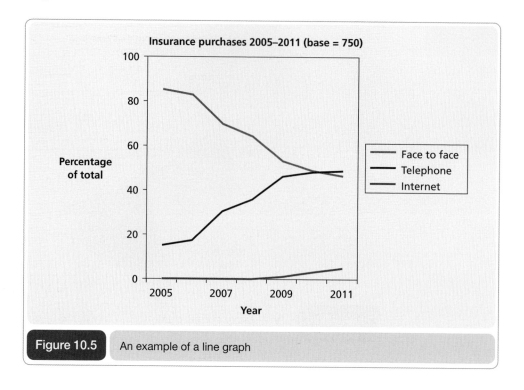

Figure 10.5 An example of a line graph

Line graphs

Line graph
A two-dimensional graph that is typically used to show movements in data over time.

A **line graph** is a two-dimensional graph that is typically used to show movements in data over time. Several series of data can be compared on the same chart using lines of different colours or format. A glance at Figure 10.5 shows the dramatic change in the way respondents purchased their insurance products over the period 2005–2011. In a similar way to pie charts, the base should be shown and the number of lines should be limited (with a maximum of around 4–5) otherwise the graph becomes cluttered and confusing.

Bar charts

Bar chart
A chart which uses a series of bars that may be positioned horizontally or vertically to represent the values of a variety of items.

A **bar chart** consists of a series of bars that may be positioned horizontally or vertically to represent the values of a variety of items. Figure 10.6 shows a bar chart representing the same data as shown using the pie chart in Figure 10.3. This raises the question as to when bar charts rather than pie charts should be used. The rule of thumb is that pie charts are better for illustrating relative data or percentages (e.g. market shares) where the number of items is less than six or seven components. Bar charts are more appropriate for illustrating actual or absolute numbers such as sales figures or where the number of items is more than seven. Stacked bar charts as shown in Figure 10.7 tend to be used instead of multiple pie charts when space within the report or presentation is limited.

Pictograms

Pictogram
A type of bar chart which uses pictures of the items being described rather than bars.

A **pictogram** is a special type of bar chart which uses pictures (such as bottles, cars, money) of the items rather than bars. An example of this is shown in Figure 10.8 relating to apples. Pictograms can be more interesting and appealing where the audience is unused to using statistics and graphs. This is one of the reasons why they are commonly used in newspapers and television programmes aimed at the general public.

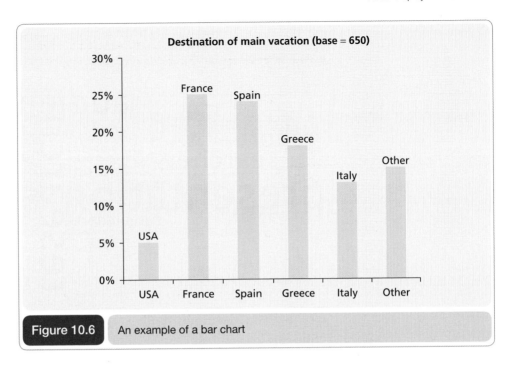

| **Figure 10.6** | An example of a bar chart |

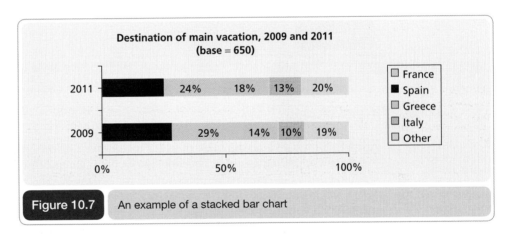

| **Figure 10.7** | An example of a stacked bar chart |

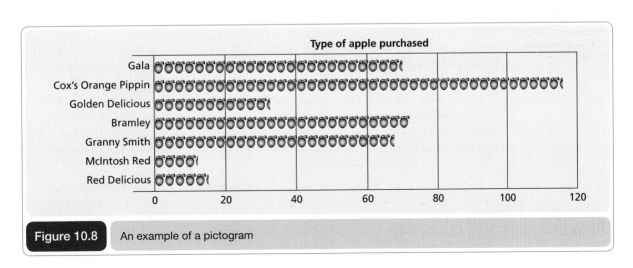

| **Figure 10.8** | An example of a pictogram |

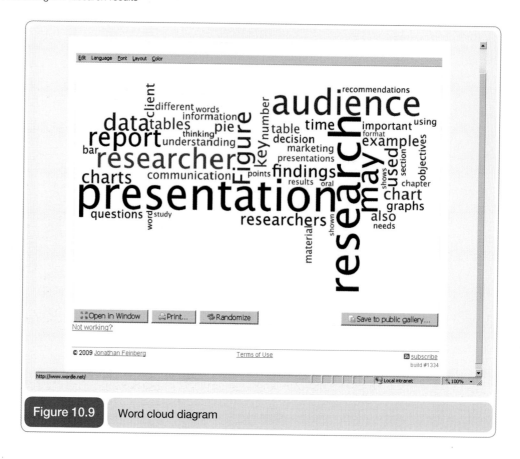

Figure 10.9	Word cloud diagram

Word clouds

Word cloud
A visual depiction of words used by respondents in qualitative research or the content appearing on social network sites or publications. The font size of the words is determined by the number of times a word has been used. The more that a topic or word is talked about, the bigger it is.

A **word cloud** is a visual depiction of words used by respondents in qualitative research or the content appearing on social network sites or publications. The font size of the words, is determined by the number of times a word has been used. The more a topic or word is talked about, the bigger it is. Some journalists use the tool to analyse the content of politician's speeches. Colour and layout can be manipulated to improve the presentation qualities on the cloud. Figure 10.9 below is constructed from an analysis of the words used in this chapter. There are a number of software programmes available which undertake the analysis and create the word clouds with Wordle (**www.wordle.net**) being probably the best known.

Spider-type diagrams

The spider-type diagrams (mind maps) described in Chapter 5 can also be used to present key findings and relationships in qualitative data. Using a diagram of this type (see Figure 10.10 below) can more clearly illustrate interconnections and examples of the actual words that respondents used. A variety of easy to use software exists to create such diagrams, an example is Mindgenius (**www.mindgenius.com**).

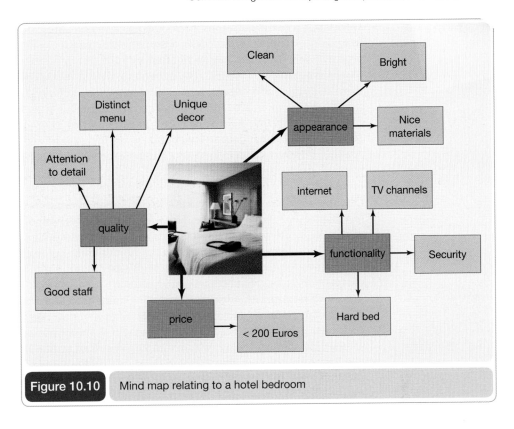

| Figure 10.10 | Mind map relating to a hotel bedroom |

Common dangers in the reporting and presentation of results

There are a number of areas where new researchers regularly fail to take account of the decision maker's thinking sequence. These are:

- **Assuming understanding:** some researchers will present tables and graphs in reports and presentations with very little commentary as to how the figures should be interpreted. The researchers may simply put up a visual of the data and repeat the numbers shown. It is dangerous to assume that the audience will interpret the data in the same manner as the researcher. It can be very tedious for the audience to read page after page of data without any explanation of what they mean. The audience will simply skip pages in the report or lose attention and start dreaming in the presentation.
- **Excessive length:** exceedingly long reports or lengthy presentations may give researchers the opportunity to demonstrate their extensive knowledge on a subject. However, they annoy decision makers as the key points get lost in the excessive detail and the results are devalued. Excessive length suggests a lack of clear thinking on the part of the researcher.

Client quote

Some researchers go on and on. They don't consider the fact that we have other meetings to attend and decisions to make. We therefore don't concentrate on what they are saying.

- **Unrealistic recommendations:** providing naïve recommendations which are beyond the financial capabilities of the client organisation or which do not take account of their organisational structures and overall strategy.
- **Spurious accuracy:** as computers may produce data to two or even three decimal places, some researchers also present them to this level. On many samples, particularly where the sample size is below 200–300 respondents, such accuracy is meaningless. For example, one recent marketing research report quoted figures of 47.08 per cent on a sample of 80 respondents. What does 0.08 per cent mean? It is around 1/15 of a respondent. Such spurious accuracy is totally misleading as it gives credibility to the data, which cannot be justified, particularly on a sample of 80. In the main, researchers should stick to whole numbers.
- **Obscure statistics:** some researchers may use obscure statistical techniques to cover up the fact that the data shows very little. This is becoming more common as a result of computer analysis being able to throw up all types of statistical measures (many of which involve very complex procedures) at the touch of a button. Although the researcher may believe that this will impress the client, it may result in a non-technical marketing manager rejecting the report, branding it as being too academic.
- **Too much gloss and no substance:** producing charts or an oral presentation which are very eye catching, colourful and entertaining but fail to communicate the information that the decision maker requires. For example, a PowerPoint presentation using animated features, sound, video clips and 3D effects may impress the client or may raise questions as to how much time was spent on the presentation rather than the data gathering and analysis. The client may miss the key points because he or she is too engrossed in examining the visuals. Alternatively, the visuals may not work as intended. For example, the projector, computer, lighting or the layout of the room may limit the effectiveness of any glossy presentation. With reports, these may be photocopied by the client, resulting in poor quality (or black and white) reproductions of complex graphics being seen by key decision makers.

Presentations on the Internet

The report or presentation can also be placed on the Internet or on a company's intranet, enabling decision makers to access the presentation, regardless of where they are in the world or when they need to access it. The presentation can take exactly the same format as it does when being done in a boardroom or meeting room. Reports can be provided as PDF files, which will provide the same graphical and layout format as the physical document, or can be turned into an interactive document where the reader can click on particular tables or sections to obtain further, more detailed information. Sound and even video clips from focus groups can be added. It should be noted, however, that the principles and guidelines outlined in this chapter are as relevant to communication via the Internet as they are to the more traditional methods of communication.

Summary and an integrated approach

Report-writing skills and presentation skills are very important to the successful communication of marketing research and marketing information researchers need to think from the reader's or audience's perspective and consider what it is that the clients want to hear, as well as the likely manner in which they will want it communicated. Understanding the audience's thinking sequence will assist with this. Research reports, presentations and Internet reports should be structured and prepared in a style which eases understanding, maintains interest and follows a logical sequence. Modern software has made the creation of impressive presentations available to almost everyone, but even with such technology, there are a number of basic presentation guidelines that the researcher needs to follow if a quality presentation that results in quality communication is to be delivered. These include maintaining eye contact, varying elements of the presentation, minimising complexity, checking understanding, providing handouts, acting naturally, finishing on a high note, rehearsing and clarifying questions.

A variety of tables and charts can be used to enhance the clarity and effectiveness of communication. This chapter has identified those that are most commonly used (tables, pie charts, line graphs, bar charts, pictograms, word clouds and spider-type diagrams) but there is an infinite number of possibilities. However, care must be taken to ensure that these ease understanding and do not cause confusion or mislead readers.

The chapter finished with a description of some of the most common flaws seen in the communication of marketing research results. Awareness of these should ensure that good research is not undermined by poor communication.

Discussion questions

1 In what ways should the content of a presentation differ from that of a report?

2 What are the key guidelines for producing tables?

3 By what criteria would you evaluate a research report? Develop an evaluation form for assessing these.

4 By what criteria would you evaluate an oral presentation? Develop an evaluation form for assessing these.

5 Why is the executive summary such a critical component of a research report?

6 Distinguish between findings, executive summaries, conclusions and recommendations.

7 In presentations, why is eye contact so critical?

8 Go through a quality Sunday newspaper and pick out any three graphical illustrations. Explain what types of charts they are and critically evaluate their strengths and weaknesses.

9 Describe the audience's thinking sequence and identify its implications for the researcher.

10 Think about all the good presentations that you have witnessed. What made them so good?

Additional reading

Abela, A. (2008) *Advanced Presentations by Design.* Wiley, USA.

Atkinson, C. (2007). *Beyond Bullet Points: Using Microsoft Powerpoint to Create Presentations that Inform, Motivate and Inspire.* Microsoft Press, USA.

Bradbury, A. (2010) *Creating Success: Successful Presentation Skills*, 4th Edn. Kogan Page, London.

Few, S. (2004) *Show Me the Numbers: Designing Tables and Graphs to Enlighten.* Analytics Press Oakland, USA.

Forsyth, P. (2010) *Creating Success: How to Write Reports and Proposals*, 2nd Edn. Kogan Page, London

Hague, P. and Roberts, C. (1994) *Presentation and Report Writing*. Kogan Page, London.

Websites

For word clouds: **www.wordle.net**
For spider-typediagrams: **www.mindgenius.com**

Reference

[1] Adapted from Bain, R. (2007) Disseminating research: MTV finds a more engaging – if expensive – alternative to PowerPoint debriefs: A public exhibition, *Research*, Nov 2007. p. 22.

Marketing research in action: case histories

These cases are included to provide examples of marketing research and how it is used. The cases help to illustrate some of the techniques and research approaches discussed elsewhere in the text. For each case, there are:

- links to the appropriate chapters in the text;
- potential topic areas for discussion;
- related websites.

Case 1
Lynx – launching a new brand

Case 2
Sony Ericsson – understanding the mobile phone market

Case 3
AIR MILES – researching advertising effectiveness

Case 4
The *Metro* – newspaper media research and understanding the reader

Case 5
Birmingham Airport – researching customer satisfaction

Case 6
Gü – establishing a community for research

Case 7
English Rugby – researching participation

Case 8
Malta and MTV – researching attitudes

Case 9
Allied Domecq – researching lifestyles

Case 10
Dove – researching beauty for a communications campaign

These case histories were originally published in *Research*, and have been reproduced here with the permission of the Market Research Society.

Case 1
Lynx – launching a new brand

Lynx Twist

Job Muscroft explains how consumers were drafted in to help Lynx launch its latest brand variant, Twist.

Unilever's Lynx (or Axe if you're outside the UK) is a global deodorant brand. The challenge it faces in product development and communications is to innovate constantly to keep its young consumers interested and engaged. The Lynx brand and insight team are always looking at ways of staying closer to their young consumers, in order to stay relevant.

A key strategy is to launch new variants of the product. Lynx has come up with some great products recently, including the hugely popular Dark Temptation, promoted by ads featuring a man made of chocolate. For the launch of the 2010 variant it was going to be important to build on this and reinforce Lynx's 'quality

Datacraft – QxQ Images/Alamy

fragrance' credentials once more. Face was commissioned to develop the new variant and its fragrance using co-creation, in an effort to generate engaging product concepts and communications based on strong, well-articulated consumer insights.

The brief

The brief was challenging in its simplicity for a deodorant brand: How can Lynx talk about freshness in a new and engaging way?

The approach

Face took Unilever all the way from insight to innovation and visualisation of ideas. While the emphasis of this brief was on concept innovation, it was very clearly rooted in insight all the way through. The approach was based on a mix of online and face-to-face techniques, gaining inspiration from the social web as well as co-creating with a group of talented, creative Lynx consumers.

The whole project unfolded over six weeks in the summer of 2008, leading to a fully realised and consumer-validated product concept that challenged the way Lynx talked about fragrance to guys.

An intrinsic part of the brief was the need to involve consumers directly in the creation of the new variant, and to ensure that they remained equal partners with brand, agency and fragrance house in its development. As Lynx is a global brand, those consumers needed to come from all over the world.

To do this, we adopted a three-stage methodology:

Stimulation: This phase consisted of an online social media monitoring and semiotic audit based on 'freshness', using a mix of content analysis, client data mining and desk research. This helped us to identify different aspects of 'freshness' which were used to stimulate and inspire the innovation process.

Creation: The stimulation phase was followed by a three-day co-creation workshop held in New York and involving 16 target audience consumers (both sexes, aged 16–24) from the UK, the USA and Latin America. Working alongside consumers were members of the Lynx global marketing team, the agency BBH New York and fragrance expert Ann Gottlieb.

The workshop was designed to be a planners' playground, crammed full of insight gained from working directly with consumers generating disruptive ideas and uncovering motivating language. By working together in groups with consumers, the Lynx team had a continuous stream of feedback that gave them a clear indication of which ideas were strong enough to be developed further.

The co-creation process was about much more than just getting consumers involved; with this kind of innovation it is crucial that key agencies are involved too. In this case BBH NY's planners and creatives had a chance to get engaged and inspired much earlier in the process than normal. This ultimately leads to a better communications brief, grounded in consumer insight.

While facilitators were on hand to intervene strategically at certain points, the workshop was designed first and foremost to encourage open thinking, collaboration and play. Co-creation exercises enabled consumers to show the Lynx team their fears, tactics and success stories in the mating game in an intimate environment. Insights were pooled in a group from crowd-sourcing sessions, enabling consumers and the Lynx team to identify fertile areas for idea generation.

The ideation process used on this project empowered the consumers to lead conversations and encouraged them to generate a huge number of ideas, then explore their potential in smaller groups. At this stage of the process the Lynx team were working as mentors in each of the consumer teams, bouncing ideas around and building on the stronger concepts together.

The breakthrough moment came from an unexpected source. The men got really excited by Ann Gottlieb's 'Fragrance 101' presentation which described the science behind fragrance. One of the co-creation groups quickly picked up on the fact that fragrances can transform over time particularly when they touch and react with skin. This insight into fragrance was quickly matched with the male need to keep women interested and led directly to the development of Lynx Twist, the fragrance that changes over time (from fresh to smooth). What is so interesting about the co-creative approach in this case was the fact that this simple idea, so well known in the Unilever deodorant business, was given flight because of the confidence and immediacy of working directly with consumers. Not only that: consumers and agencies were able to see immediately how to bring to life the idea of a fragrance that changes, through a name and a marketing concept.

Development: A final phase of online qualitative concept development was conducted in Argentina, the UK, the US and the Philippines, in a series of online focus groups with target audience consumers. This phase was crucial in order for the brand team to feel confident that leading with such an explicit fragrance message was going to be effective outside the workshop environment and that it could be linked to insights into the mating game.

While this phase is necessary to give a final burst of confidence and reassurance to the idea in a global context, what was unusual here is that we only took one concept into the follow-up development. This was because the Lynx/BBH team felt so confident with the ideas generated, as they had come directly from co-creating with consumers.

> 'If you look at what's happening online, the consumer has a voice as never before and brands need to listen more. Even if a brand doesn't want to engage with consumers on that level, it will be forced to.'
> David Cousino, Unilever

Lynx developed a concept that had buy-in from agencies, consumers and stakeholders in just six weeks, including validation. It enabled them to talk about fragrance in a new way, and enabled teams working on the concept to visualise very clearly where they were going with the idea very early on. This saved them time and money by allowing them to avoid the more traditional process of going backwards and forwards between agencies and consumers.

The findings

If there was one insight that drove the whole process of concept development it was that men were motivated by the idea of a fragrance that changed, and that this could be linked to broader ideas about changes in personal display, confidence and self-image.

The outcome

The concept generated through co-creation achieved extremely good scores in testing and sailed through to market. The result of the project is the launch of Lynx Twist, the first Lynx variant to lead with a strong fragrance message. David Cousino, Unilever's global consumer marketing insights director for the category, explains:

> 'This is totally unique as a new variant initiative. Twist is a fragrance that changes to keep her interested and keep you interesting. It was born from the insight stressed to us by these co-creators that girls get bored easily and the real challenge is to keep them hooked. A major benefit of the methodology is the purity and depth of the insight that you get. Insight is often back-filled from a proposition and so you can easily miss core opportunities to really engage with your target market in a deep-rooted way.'

Ann Gottlieb, the expert who was responsible for the fragrance brief, also explains why the approach was so different:

> 'I don't think that with all the Lynx variants I've worked on – which is probably now close to 25–30 of them – that I've ever been involved from the ground up, and with all of us starting with the project on equal footing we were all stakeholders in where the brand went. How right-on the guys were about a number of different things that I don't think would have occurred to us. They saw information that I don't think we would ever have gotten to.'

Lynx Twist was launched globally in January with a high-profile above-the-line and social media campaign including Lynx's first interactive film, starring model Keeley Hazell, Blake Harrison and Mike Fielding.

What next?

Co-creation is now an established innovation methodology at Unilever and has been used to develop a range of product concepts for Dove, Sure, Surf and Persil. We are now working with them on co-created brand planning in the food and beverage category. Cousino says: 'If you look at what's happening online, not just on the social networks, the consumer has a voice as never before and brands need to listen more. Even if a brand doesn't want to engage with consumers on that level, it will be forced to.'

Job Muscroft is managing director of co-creation agency Face.

This case history appeared in the April 2010 edition of *Research*, and is published with the permission of the Market Research Society.

Links in the text

Chapter 1 – The role of marketing research and customer information in decision making
Chapter 4 – Collecting observation data and monitoring online user-generated content
Chapter 5 – Collecting and analysing qualitative data

Potential areas for discussion

1 How does this approach compare with traditional marketing research?
2 Discuss the benefits of this type of engagement with customers.
3 What do you envisage as being involved in a semiotic audit based on 'freshness', using a mix of content analysis, client data mining and desk research?
4 What does this case tell us about the changing nature of the client – researcher relationship?

Related websites

Lynx: **www.unilever.co.uk/brands/personalcarebrands/lynx.aspx**
Face, The Co-Creation Planning Agency: **www.facegroup.co.uk**

Case 2
Sony Ericsson – understanding the mobile phone market

Seeking insight

When Sony Ericsson launched, it faced a wide range of challenges. Stephen Palmer examines the research behind its success.

In October 2001 the joint venture of Sony Ericsson Mobile Communications was formed; a new brand in a very competitive and fast-evolving industry. Tracking the development of that brand would be one of the key challenges of the new company. That meant understanding the legacy of the parent companies, as well as measuring how successfully Sony Ericsson was able to establish its own identity moving forward.

Hayden Richard Verry/Alamy

The senior management team recognised the need to engage with both employees and mobile phone owners in order to generate a clear understanding of current movements in the telecoms market, as well as of Sony Ericsson's brand image and its level of brand awareness.

In recent years, the mobile phone industry has been changing its focus: instead of selling handsets to first-time buyers, the majority of sales are now repeat buyers with more demanding requirements and higher expectations. In fact, the mobile phone replacement market now accounts for more than 50 per cent of purchases globally (around 250 million phones). Sony Ericsson needed market insight on how the renewal rate was evolving so that market-sizing forecasts could be as accurate as possible.

In addition, with technology advancing alongside user sophistication, Sony Ericsson needed to monitor customer perceptions of new mobile phone developments, such as imaging, gaming and connectivity. To be successful, the brand needed to differentiate itself from other competitors and own its territory.

Moreover, the company's international reach meant that it required consistent, credible and meaningful indexes on a global, regional and local level. The information would feed into the company's performance management systems and enable decisions to be made in a timely manner with confidence.

Research objectives

Working with TNS, the overall objectives of the study were to:

- generate company-wide performance indicators for brand health and identify the strengths and weaknesses of the Sony Ericsson brand in comparison to its competitors at global, regional and local market levels;
- provide full visibility on market development and buying/renewal trends to facilitate market forecasting;
- monitor and review advertising effectiveness and changes in brand share over time to inform future sales forecasting.

In such a fast-moving industry, it was essential to provide Sony Ericsson management with accurate and timely market and brand information to assess the development of the new brand and those of its competitors. Markets needed to be monitored continuously and findings made available quickly to enable strategic decisions to be made with confidence.

In order to understand the legacy of Sony Ericsson's parent companies, and to give full return on investment made in the past, results also had to be compared against an earlier tracking study. Furthermore, the study needed to incorporate easily and build on knowledge of Sony Ericsson proprietary target groups.

While consistency of results across countries was essential if insightful comparisons were to be made, this requirement needed to be balanced with that of best representing local markets. To ensure maximum buy-in at all levels across the company, and to provide individual markets with the most relevant data, TNS developed a flexible research programme able to incorporate local market adaptations in the interview process or methodology. To further facilitate the use of data across the company, information had to be easily and instantly accessible for further analysis when necessary – by all relevant employees within Sony Ericsson, regardless of physical location or time zone.

The project

Each month TNS interviews more than 3,500 consumers across 14 countries to represent the mobile phone industry globally and provide country-specific data in Sony Ericsson's key markets. The main study focuses on non-rejecters of mobile phones – that is, those who own a mobile, or who would consider acquiring one in the next 12 months. However, given the need for mobile phone market-sizing data, TNS also collect demographic information from mobile phone rejecters.

Telephone interviewing is the most cost-effective methodology in most countries. However, in markets where telephone penetration is too low to enable a representative sample to be reached, face-to-face interviewing is used. Random route-sampling specific to each country is used to obtain a representative sample of the total population for the purpose of market-sizing. In agreement with local Sony Ericsson offices, quotas are applied on the qualifying sample to represent the non-rejecter population aged between 16 and 65.

Quality and reliability of data is of course paramount and stringent checks and controls are applied at all stages. However, to maintain accuracy but minimise the time involved in data-checking, a bespoke online editing tool, Webeditor, has been developed. Using this, local agencies are able to submit data to a centrally maintained checking program that highlights any issues. Only once the data has successfully passed this check is it forwarded to the central team for processing.

To further reduce the lead-time from interviewing to reporting, TNS uses its analysis and reporting platform, WebMiriad. As Stephen Palmer, managing consultant, TNS Telecoms, who heads up the programme, explains: 'WebMiriad enables the development of template research reports that are tailored to local and regional markets. When new monthly data is input, all reports are automatically updated with the most recent results, rather than requiring new reports to be created for each wave of research.

'This system means that local and regional reports can be accessed within one week following the completion of fieldwork, allowing the project team to concentrate on the key objective of good consultancy – interpreting what the numbers actually mean for the client.'

While key personnel have access to data via WebMiriad, there is a wider need for reports to be made available in PowerPoint for access by a larger audience. Again, the accuracy and timing for these reports is critical and so an automated route was developed. Trend charts and cross tabulations are exported from WebMiriad and bespoke programs re-format and create reports. Analysis and summaries are added by the executive team, and nineteen reports are made available to more than 100 users globally by the second week in each month. To facilitate the dissemination of the reports, they are all posted on a web portal, TNSInfo.

Cecilia Guditz, senior manager, market research and intelligence at Sony Ericsson says, 'In order to make best use of the research across the company, it is critical that the data is comparable at an international level and that it is delivered promptly and in a format which is meaningful to all offices.'

Guditz explains that platforms such as WebMiriad and TNSInfo provide the client with considerable flexibility and control. '[These platforms] also allow us to specify levels of data access for different groups across the organisation. New data reports can also be run by members of the Sony Ericsson project team enabling trends data to be extracted simply and quickly without the risk of changing fixed data inputs.'

But delivery is not the end of the story. An added insight approach means that data analysis and interpretation is more than just a presentation of the figures notes Guditz. 'TNS clearly communicates what the research findings mean for our business . . . which we can use to shape strategy and policy moving forward.'

With the inclusion of reformatted back data from the Ericsson brand-tracking study, trends for both competitors and the parent companies can be viewed back to the beginning of 1999. They clearly show how the brand positioning has evolved and its impact on sales and performance.

For Guditz, too, it was vital for Sony Ericsson to have a research partner with a comparable international reach. 'TNS's global network of offices ensures that the research team are always on hand to create new reports and investigate emerging market trends. When required, bespoke research reports can be created and interpreted within 24 hours for client and board presentations using the very latest market data. Preparing such detailed, up-to-the-hour reports would not be possible without either such a committed TNS team or the use of advanced marketing information systems like WebMiriad.'

Evaluation and summary

Timed to coincide with the launch of the Sony Ericsson brand, the Consumer Market Tracker (CMT) project has allowed the company to follow the development of the new brand from its inception. The research findings have been well communicated and are now used by all parts of the organisation. This widespread acceptance and use of the findings in itself shows the strength of the programme, which TNS has now been running for three years.

Beyond that, however, the TNS research has also been used to inform major strategic decisions.

In 2002, for example, Sony Ericsson decided to take ownership of the imaging area. Today it is a market leader. Guided by the research, marketing communications activity for the promotion of the T610 handset focused specifically on imaging with excellent results. Strong sales of the phone helped to boost the brand's position within this new field, and Sony Ericsson also received an award for the Best Wireless Handset at the recent 3GSM World Congress.

The reason for the success of such a centralised project in a decentralised and regionalised organisation is certainly a consequence of the flexibility built into the CMT programme, which allows inclusion of local issues.

The final word goes to Riccardo Brenna, head of research and intelligence at Sony Ericsson. 'CMT has proven to be a very efficient and complete tool to evaluate our performance in different parts of the world. The research design is also flexible enough to make its roll-out quite easy and to answer to local knowledge needs. CMT is helping us to have a global view of our business and, at the same time, to look at the local specific issues. The objective for the future will be to make it even more actionable and focused on supporting our business development.'

Research into action

The impact that the research programme has had on Sony Ericsson's business from market unit level through to senior management is evident in the way that the results have been used.

- The results are used for annual target setting within the company
- The results are used in customer presentations, boards meetings and employee meetings to show the development of the brand. At a recent congress in Cannes, more than 50 presentations to key customers demonstrated the strength of the brand using results of the CMT study.
- The results of advertising campaigns around the world are measured through the study – as with, for example, the performance of both the print and TV campaigns for the T68i model.
- The continuous research findings play an important role in forecasting. The information gathered on the replacement market, in particular, is used as an early warning system to allow confidence in forecasting market volumes.
- Correspondence analysis and key-driver analysis have been used to understand more about the brand image and reasons for purchase of the main brands in the market.

Stephen Palmer is a director of TNS IT & Telecoms.

This case history appeared in the March 2005 edition of *Research*, and is published with the permission of the Market Research Society.

Links in the text

Chapter 6 – Collecting quantitative data
Chapter 10 – Presenting the research results

Potential areas for discussion

1 Discuss what is meant by a performance management system.
2 Why is telephone interviewing used?
3 Discuss the advantages and disadvantages of template reports.
4 Discuss the reporting procedures adopted by Sony Ericsson.
5 What does this case tell us about the changing nature of the client–researcher relationship?

Related websites

Sony Ericsson: **www.sonyericsson.com**
TNS: **www.tnsglobal.com**

Case 3
AIR MILES – researching advertising effectiveness

Loyal air force

A multimedia approach to research helped AIR MILES to develop its latest campaign; report by Sarah Hayward, Helen Mennis and Bethan Cork.

AIR MILES, founded in 1988, is the pioneer of customer loyalty schemes. Although hundreds of loyalty schemes have been introduced subsequently, including, more recently, online schemes, AIR MILES remains the UK's leading brand in this market with 6 million customers and 90 per cent awareness of the brand among its target audience – ABC1 adults aged between 25 and 54. The company has built up its business by forming part-

Mint Photography/Alamy

nerships through well-known companies through which customers collect AIR MILES.

The 'Who Joins Wins' campaign was developed by ad agency Bartle Bogle Hegarty. Anybody who joined the AIR MILES scheme during the campaign was entered into a prize draw, and was guaranteed a prize, ranging from a cinema ticket to one million AIR MILES. The marketing objective was to increase new registrations by 250,000 during the campaign.

The target audience for the campaign was ABC1 adults aged between 25 and 54. The campaign budget was in the region of £1m, so TV was not an option. Instead radio and press were used with additional point-of-sale material at petrol station forecourts and supermarkets. Radio advertising was used to arouse interest and generate excitement; press executions, which followed later, were designed to give more detail. Titles and stations were chosen to give greatest coverage of the target audience. Forty radio stations with an estimated coverage of 65 per cent of the target audience and 7.1 OTH (opportunities to hear); seven daily papers and six Sunday supplement magazines with an estimated coverage of 75 per cent of the target audience and 8.5 OTS (opportunities to see) were used.

Research was used to evaluate the advertising at all stages, from testing creative concepts through to analysis post-launch.

Forrest Associates undertook the qualitative research during campaign development. The objectives at this stage were twofold:

- to ascertain whether the key message was clear and understood;
- to gauge whether or not people felt a sense of 'you'd be mad not to take part'.

More specifically the following elements were tested:

- Did individual executions involve, communicate and motivate?
- Was the prize draw itself understood and did people feel it was relevant to them?
- Was the campaign promoting the AIR MILES brand fun, exciting and enjoyable?

Forrest ran eight focus groups: five groups of non-AIR MILES collectors (but non-rejecters of loyalty schemes) and three groups of current 'passive' AIR MILES collectors, who only currently collect with one AIR MILES partner. The primary purpose of the campaign was to increase the number of new AIR MILES collectors, but it also wanted to prompt 'passive' collectors to start collecting with another partner.

As a result of this work, AIR MILES gained an understanding of which executions had the greater appeal, and was able to structure the media buying to reflect this. BBH was also able to make changes to the radio ads.

Once the campaign had been finalised AIR MILES needed research to evaluate its effectiveness:

- Were people aware of it?
- What impact was it having on future behaviour?
- What was the effect of specific ad executions?

BMRB International was commissioned to undertake this stage of the advertising evaluation. There were a number of issues that we needed to address before designing the research.

A critical consideration for AIR MILES was sufficiently robust sample sizes to allow for analysis of key groups, in particular current and potential collectors. The former accounted for 11 per cent of the adult population and the latter, defined as people who either shopped at Sainsbury's, owned a NatWest credit card, owned a Vodafone or bought Shell petrol/diesel (key partners in the scheme), accounted for 34 per cent.

Within these groups it was important to provide enough people who recalled the advertising. Previous research conducted by AIR MILES had produced very low levels of recall with sample sizes too small to permit reliable sub-group analyses.

Finally, and true of almost every research project, the client had a restricted budget!

We decided the best solution was to conduct the research among a nationally representative sample of adults aged 18+ within the UK and not to restrict the sample to people who fell into the key groups only. This enabled us to compare the advertising effects among the target groups versus the rest of the population. We collected the information via a face-to-face omnibus survey enabling us to cost-effectively screen a large number of people to identify the 'niche' groups, with fieldwork costs shared by all the clients who had questions on the surveys used.

In order to maximise recall of the advertising we opted for multimedia technology for the interviewing. This is only marginally more expensive than traditional CAPI, with a small administration charge for the costs of preparing/editing ad clips, pressing them on to CD and despatching to the interviewers.

While the most obvious benefit of multimedia data collection is for TV advertising, here we felt there were advantages in integrating the radio ads into the computerised question-naire and playing them to respondents via soundcards:

- a number of different executions needed to be tested – we were able to guarantee effective rotation and hence eliminate any order bias;
- it avoided the expense of producing multiple tape copies and sending interviewers portable cassette players;
- it avoided the use of a free-phone number and the reliance on respondents agreeing to call it.

Three waves of research were conducted, before, during and after the campaign. A total of nine radio executions (six in Great Britain and three in Northern Ireland) and five press executions were tested at the second and third waves (mid- and post-campaign) of research. Each respondent was played three radio ads and shown three press ads towards the end of the interview. These were rotated (within media) so that each execution had an equal chance of being heard or seen first. In the words of Bethan Cork, research manager at AIR MILES: 'This is the most successful ad campaign research project we have ever undertaken. Armed with this research we will be able to develop clearly defined and targeted ad campaigns in the future.'

The key points that came out of the research that AIR MILES will take on board when developing future campaigns were that the role of the different media worked well to stretch the reach of the campaign; findings echoed what had been seen in earlier research, i.e. that a major barrier to collection is still a perception that AIR MILES can only be used for free air travel; and in terms of future intentions to collect AIR MILES, the greatest increase throughout the campaign was among 18-to-24-year-olds, a group which had never before been identified as potential collectors. If we had opted to research the target groups only and not recommended extending sample coverage to all adults this would not have been discovered.

The overall key learning from this research was that the messages used in future campaigns need to be kept as simple and clear as possible.

So was the advertising successful? Yes, in terms of meeting the marketing objective. The research showed that 14 per cent of adults not currently registered with the scheme would be likely to collect AIR MILES in the future. It was also successful by using two media that effectively complemented one another.

The main learning point, for AIR MILES and the ad agency, was the realisation that it is possible to cost effectively develop a robust and effective measurement of a multimedia campaign (be it a relatively modest one at £1m!), with careful thought and planning. One of the reasons it worked so well was the collaborative effect – all parties, the ad agency, the client and the research agency – worked closely together at every stage, from the development of the first creatives, to the final stage of the post-campaign tracking. And not only was the research effective, but 350,000 new customers registered to collect AIR MILES over the period of the campaign.

Sarah Hayward and Helen Mennis were Research Consultant and Director respectively at BMRB International. Bethan Cork was Research Manager at AIR MILES.

This case history appeared in the August 2000 edition of *Research*, and is published with the permission of the Market Research Society.

Links in the text

Chapter 5 – Collecting and analysing qualitative data
Chapter 8 – Sampling methods
Chapter 6 – Collecting quantitative data

Potential areas for discussion

1   Discuss the reasons for using eight group discussions.
2   What are your views on the sampling approach?
3   Why was an omnibus survey used?
4   Discuss the idea of using multimedia in the CAPI interviews.
5   Discuss other ways of measuring the effectiveness of media and multimedia campaigns.

Related websites

Air Miles: **www.airmiles.co.uk**
BMRB International: **http://kantarmedia-custom.com**

Case 4
The *Metro* – newspaper media research and understanding the readers

How did the *Metro* newspaper really get to know its readers?

Everyone knows that the young, urban professional is the holy grail for advertisers. Fortunately for *Metro*, they make up its core readership. The free weekly newspaper which is published by Associated Newspapers and distributed at key commuter points in eight UK cities sought a deeper understanding of its readers to complement existing industry sources such as the National Readership Survey (NRS) and Target Group Index (TGI). Its Urban Life project was won by BMRB Media, which has a track record of online and media research as well as building and managing panels

'The objectives and logistics of Urban Life are huge and have required great imagination and hard work to solve them,' said Doug Read, project director at *Metro*. 'It is exciting to extend the boundaries of media research and add massively to our consumer insight. BMRB have been a true partner in this project offering great expertise and project coordination.'

UpperCut Images/Alamy

As this young, mobile audience is hard to research via traditional data collection methods, *Metro* and BMRB chose a web-based methodology. An online approach fits with the readers' busy lifestyles and is readily available to the vast majority of them. It also has the advantage of allowing a fast turnaround of results, giving almost instantaneous polling.

Another effective response route for this group is to take advantage of its enthusiasm for mobiles and text messaging (SMS) by asking a small number of simple questions. Getting the permissions to conduct the research via e-mail and SMS required the building of a reader's panel.

Panel members were recruited through editorial content and adverts in the newspaper. Quota controls were put in place to achieve a demographic spread of members by gender, age and region. Click-to-web e-mails were sent out to notify, and then remind, members that a survey was ready for them to take. They simply had to link into the web survey and complete the questionnaires. The surveys could be left partway through and continued at a later stage and progress bars were employed to show the respondents when they were nearing the end of the questionnaires.

The panel was recruited on the basis that the members would take part in one survey and one mini-poll each month for six months. Each survey would cover a different topic such as shopping, travel, careers, finance and socialising, and also included questions on topical issues such as congestion charging, safety from crime and the war on terrorism. The results from each wave were combined with all the previous waves to create a single source database.

Attracting and retaining panellists

To recruit these young, urban professionals, BMRB had to present the panel as an exclusive and desirable proposition. An even greater challenge was maintaining the members' interest after recruitment and so classic panel maintenance principles were used.

Fostering a feeling of club membership increases commitment. For the *Metro* panel, a website for the members was created, providing feedback from previous surveys, details of the prize draws and news of the next surveys. *Metro* editor Kenny Campbell had direct input into the site.

Frequency and timing of contact is important in this situation as overburdening members will annoy them, but they may lose interest if contact is not frequent enough. Timing of when to send the survey link is therefore important and again, Campbell was involved in e-mails to panel members.

Use of incentives is also paramount. Substantial commitment should earn the members a substantial reward. Incentives should be of sufficient interest for all members, to avoid adding response bias, and be offered in a timely way to boost motivation when it starts to lag.

For this highly select audience, incentives need to be especially enticing. Genuinely exciting prizes were carefully selected and offered, such as £1,000 in Habitat or Red Letter Day vouchers. Appropriate use of language is key: members were addressed using language that reflected their age and level of education.

Given the nature of the project, it was important that everything from the questionnaires and website to the recruitment ads reflected the *Metro* brand to allow the research to benefit from the high brand affinity that many readers feel.

Throughout the life of the panel, the members were offered the chance to see results of the surveys via the members' website and editorial content in the newspaper itself. This helped to keep motivation high and give the members a real feeling that their opinion counted.

Questions, questions

Questionnaire design was key for getting the most out of the panel. Questions needed to be relevant, interesting and appealing to the members in order to keep their interest.

As the members all have busy lives and many were completing the survey at work, each main survey was kept to a maximum of 15 minutes. This is a standard consideration for any survey, but even more crucial where there is no interviewer present to encourage the respondent to complete the questionnaire.

In combining the results to all six 15-minute surveys, a database of considerable value was created without overburdening respondents. The key to the success of this approach was the response rate. Most of the members needed to complete all of the surveys, hence the importance of the panel maintenance infrastructure.

As well as the main surveys, we were able to use the panel to ask a few short questionnaires, or mini-polls, on topical issues, such as the firefighters' strike and celebrity kiss-and-tell stories. Results for the mini-polls were available on the day after the questionnaire was sent out.

Finally, we were also able to use SMS to ask a low number of very simple questions. SMS is ideal for asking time-specific questions such as 'Are you going out tonight?'

Providing insight

The results were used to show *Metro*'s core readership to be a confident, engaged and involved group of avid consumers with strong opinions on a wide range of issues. They tend to be pro-European, with a greater number in favour of adopting the euro than keeping the pound (43 vs 37 per cent), but interestingly the power to sway the results of a possible referendum will be down to the 20 per cent who are still undecided. They favour a softly-softly approach to cannabis and demand action to protect the environment.

These young urban professionals are highly ambitious in their desire to climb the career ladder, with 76 per cent saying that they want to get to the very top in their field – and are prepared to work long hours to achieve their goal. Two-thirds work more than 40 hours a week, with a third working more than 45 hours.

Given the above, it is unsurprising that holidays are very important – 38 per cent take three or more weekend breaks a year, as well as their main holiday.

Fashion shopping and retail therapy are popular pastimes among this group, with nearly half going to buy clothes and accessories at least once a month. One in ten are really hardcore shoppers who indulge in some retail therapy every week. In this and in most other respects, London readers were not hugely different from those outside of the capital.

There are, however, a couple of exceptions to this where London readers showed notable differences to their regional counterparts. Almost two-thirds of these Londoners have migrated to the capital from outside the South East region, whereas dwellers of other cities are much more likely to have come from around the same region. A possible reason for this is because Londoners rated career opportunities in their city much higher.

Londoners are also the most dissatisfied with their city's public transport. Three-fifths (59 per cent) of London panel members said that public transport was getting worse in London compared with an average of 47 per cent of other city dwellers for their cities.

These are just a couple of the insights *Metro* has gained into its readers. For *Metro*, an online panel created an attractive research proposition that described and reflected its audience. The results were relevant for use across its business – for editorial, advertising sales and marketing its brand.

From a research point of view, response rates were so successful for each main survey that the online panel approach proved to be an extremely effective way of achieving highly valuable insights into this hard-to-research group.

This case history was written by Jenny Sanders (an associate director in BMRB) and appeared in the April 2003 edition of *Research*, and is published with the permission of the Market Research Society.

Links in the text

Chapter 6 – Collecting quantitative data

Potential areas for discussion

1 Why does an organisation like the *Metro* newspaper require consumer insight?
2 Discuss the idea of using mobiles and text messaging for surveys.
3 What are your views on the manner in which the reader's panel was recruited?
4 Discuss the proposition that people who take part in panels may not be representative of *Metro* readers but may simply be representative of those people who want to take part in panels.
5 Discuss the value of incentives such as prize draws for panel members.

Related websites

BMRB Media: **http://kantarmedia-custom.com**
Metro: **www.metro.co.uk**
National Readership Survey: **www.nrs.co.uk**
Target Group Index: **www.kantarmedia-tgigb.com**

Case 5
Birmingham Airport – researching customer satisfaction

Airport blues

How do you measure the moods and emotions of all types of airport passenger? By a particular form of group discussion, says Tim Baker.

Birmingham International Airport (BIA) has enjoyed consistently high levels of customer satisfaction since measurement began. Passengers have always rated BIA more highly than its nearest serious competitors – Manchester, Heathrow and Gatwick – on all key measures: ease of access, staff attitudes, speed of processing and the provision of facilities.

BIA has become the airport of choice for many in the West Midlands and from further afield.

D. Hurst/Alamy

The measurement of customer satisfaction has been taken in the traditional UK airport way: specially trained and security-passed interviewers circulate in the airport, interviewing a representative sample of passengers, asking them to rate their satisfaction with each factor. All major airports in the UK operate exclusive fieldforces, providing a data collection facility for internal purposes that remains consistent and sensitive to the special circumstances of airports and their customers.

It became clear, however, that BIA risked becoming a victim of its own success. Increasing numbers of passengers were keen to use BIA as their preferred gateway, airlines had seen the benefits of offering services direct to the UK's second city, and the local authority which controlled the airport at the time was keen to benefit from the increased revenue opportunity such expansion offered. This was a compelling case, and plans for expansion were made.

The airport was to get an additional terminal building, the existing building was to be enlarged, and there were to be expanded car parking areas and increases in all the supporting infrastructure needed to facilitate a growth from around 6 million passengers a year to more than double this figure. Services inside the terminal buildings would also need to be developed – check-ins, security gates, catering, customer services, retail facilities, and so on. This would clearly signal a significant change in the character and atmosphere of Birmingham Airport.

Proud of its excellent customer satisfaction record, this projected expansion presented the authorities with two key service challenges:

- How to maintain the high ratings through the development process and as the new airport emerged? While it was inevitable that there would be disruption and inconvenience in the short term to customers (and staff), BIA needed to check for the roots of any dissatisfaction as the works progressed.
- How to ensure that satisfaction was being measured on the right criteria, using the right vocabulary? Through the changes, perhaps other 'new' issues would become more important to customers. This might also be the case once the developments were completed. It was clearly important that the ongoing quantitative measure remained flexible and could reflect the core issues. To this end, MRSL was commissioned by BIA to conduct a series of Insight On Site™ qualitative sessions with airport users.

Insight On Site™ is a unique qualitative research method developed by MRSL to allow group discussions to be conducted with respondent types that may be difficult to reach through conventional means. Originally designed for use at airports, the method is now used at exhibitions, visitor attractions and other places where people congregate to use the products or services under discussion.

Each session lasts between two and two-and-a-half hours, during which time between 16 and 30 respondents attend the discussion. Respondents are recruited at the time of the research by experienced interviewers. The method allows MRSL to gain the types of qualitative insight that are normally only available from group discussions, from people that would not normally be available or inclined to attend these discussions.

The sessions first commissioned provided a qualitative review of the departure process, from arriving at the airport through check-in, security, the use of the facilities, and so on. A corresponding view of arrivals was also obtained. Critically, we were able to provide a view to BIA management of the mix of moods and emotions felt by all types of passenger as they actually 'experience' the airport. A quite different view will be given (by, say, a commuting business passenger who cannot get a fresh breakfast) when the airport facilities are being discussed on site rather than being discussed at some later stage in a conventional group discussion. In addition to the regular quantitative analysis, management were thus given first-hand experiences from passengers of all types. This provided a more detailed understanding of response, and the reasons why ratings vary.

Passengers in airports are in a stressful situation. Typically, a passenger is not at rest until seated in the departure lounge. And many passengers will not visit an airport more than twice a year (indeed the bulk will visit only once or less often) and this effectively means that the passenger is rediscovering the experience each time. They may be sent to BIA by a travel company, or they may have chosen BIA as their preferred departure point. In either case, they will talk to friends, family and colleagues about the experience of BIA and this will affect the actions of many other potential visitors. The same can be said to be true of more frequent flyers: while they will accept mistakes that are corrected, they will be intolerant of continuous poor service, and will eventually vote with their feet. Importantly, they will also try to influence other flyers.

The Insight On Site™ sessions were conducted at regular intervals through the development process and continue to provide a regular dipstick monitor of customer moods. Specific areas where BIA has been able to respond quickly and effectively to customer needs include:

- Provision of information through the development process. Leaflets and other information about the development, the stages it would go through and the ways it would immediately inconvenience and ultimately benefit passengers had, of course, been made available to all visitors to the airport. We were able to quickly determine the most appropriate ways to communicate this information. In addition to leaflets that would need to be picked up by the customer, posters were put up showing various stages of the work and giving artists' impressions of the final phase. Other vantage points were also used to give customers information, so that BIA was perceived to be proactive, giving information rather than simply expecting customers to get the information for themselves.

- Determining the most appropriate retail mix in the departure lounge. Many customers had specific requirements of BIA which would help the airport maintain its distinct, personal and friendly character. Rather than simply emulate other airports, BIA has been able to build on particular customer responses and needs. This has been doubly important as duty free sales in the EC have ended and shops needed to offer a more tailored and attractive service.
- As a result of the group work, our quantitative surveys showed an increase in customer satisfaction for both retail and catering choice, with catering showing a 6 per cent increase in satisfaction and retail showing a 12 per cent increase.
- Identifying the key stress points for customers as they move through the airport. This identification gives a better understanding of the pressure points, why they exist and the specific needs of the customer as they go through them. This in turn helps to identify the need for specific staff training and leads to improved customer relations.
- A similar result has been obtained in security, one of the most stressful areas when passing through an airport. This area has shown a 6 per cent increase in satisfaction.
- A major cause of customer frustration at airports is not being able to find their way. This is a particularly complex issue. Both externally and internally, our work has helped BIA understand which signs work less well, where signs are needed so that they direct customers at the key points (that is, where does the customer pause and look for information and where do they simply carry on?), and the information that is needed on the signs.

These and other issues have been addressed for BIA so that the new airport is sensitive to customer needs and responsive to their issues. Our work has continued since the completion of the airport developments, providing board level feedback and insight into: all currently identified customer service issues; the vocabulary used by passengers; the changing needs of customers; and competitive performance.

In the old days we had to rely on conventional quantitative surveys and feedback from passengers. Now, qualitative feedback from on-site work provides first-hand information on both the negative and positive aspects of the airport, and we have been able to address these issues with the knowledge that we are satisfying our customers' needs.

Tim Baker was joint MD of MRSL.

This case history appeared in the December 2000 edition of *Research*, and is published with the permission of the Market Research Society.

Links in the text

Chapter 5 – Collecting and analysing qualitative data

Potential areas for discussion

1 Discuss your experiences of customer-satisfaction interviewers at airports.
2 What are your issues involved on carrying out research on-site and recruiting respondents in the departure lounge of an airport.
3 Discuss the advantages and disadvantages of rolling group discussions (where a large number of respondents enter and leave the group as it progresses and their flight departure time arrives). What other ways are there of gathering such data?
4 Discuss the concept of the branding of research approaches, such as Insight On Site™.

Related websites

Birmingham Airport: **www.birminghamairport.co.uk**

Case 6
Gü – establishing a community for research

Chloë Fowler reports on the creation of a customer community for Gü Chocolate Puds.

James Averdieck founded Gü Chocolate Puds in 2003 and this premium brand of posh chocolate puddings has been a huge success. So much so that in January the company was acquired for a tidy sum by Noble Foods.

Gü set out to revolutionise the chilled desserts category by creating luxurious but affordable puddings. Their growth strategy was based on innovation and distribution, and they intended their consumers to grow into the category alongside them.

However, Gü would be the first to admit that for the first few years they weren't always putting their consumers first. Or rather, if they were, it was out of a desire to create more recipes, product and pack formats rather than from starting with a consumer need. James had a great idea, Fred the chef whipped up a prototype, they tried it in the office and bingo – it launched.

For the most part they were spot on, but as the brand grew bigger and supermarket buyers

Keyfoto/Alamy

became more demanding, they realised that some launches were costing more than they were returning. They weren't entirely sure where the product–consumer alchemy was happening so they weren't always clear which bits to recreate.

Gü might also admit that their view of focus groups and market research was initially rather a dim one. We get that. The brand had been very successful without consumer input – investment in research seemed like an expensive, possibly lumbering process that might not deliver the reward they needed.

The brief

Gü gave us a pretty clear brief when we first met them two years ago: find a way to introduce consumer insight into each layer of the business (NPD, packaging, comms, category). Make it credible, commercial and engaging. Oh, and cheap!

The approach

Our relationship with Gü is continuous. They share the real business objectives behind their need for consumer insight with us – there's no messing about with tricksy subtext. Although we also conduct bespoke and standalone projects, our primary research approach has been to set up a community populated with their loyal fans so that Gü's conversations with their customers are just as frequent as their conversations with us.

We know brand communities aren't 'new news' (although our personal experience at managing them was rather scant when we started). We were open with Gü about this and the decision to create one was based on a joint desire to try something new – our cost structure reflected this.

We set the community up using free software from Ning. It's dead easy to learn and there's almost no technical jargon to prevent the amateur from having a go. We are in control of how it works and which features we include, and we feel that the look and feel of the site helps consumers feel at home and at ease and fits with Gü's brand values.

We specifically chose to let the population grow organically, with a small number of recruited fans recommending friends who invited more friends. This helped us maintain our promise of cost-effectiveness as we made it clear to the community that we were after their views based on the love of the brand, not the love of incentives. Of course we say thank you when we meet face-to-face, but it was important to us that we were speaking to people who really wanted to speak to us. As we suspected, the brand has such loyal and passionate fans that we've never had any trouble getting response to our questioning online or attendance at tasting and research sessions.

We think the high response rate is about more than just a love of chocolate. Consumers are captivated by cool brand stories and enjoy the fact that they can play some part in their growth. For the Friends of Gü there's genuine gratification that they have met and contributed to the story of one of their favourite brands.

We've used the community in several ways. We post questions on the forums and ask for responses – no surprises there. What does surprise us is how willing even the most fervent fans are to be honest about what disappoints and under-delivers. This is not a site for wanton fawning and if it was it wouldn't be as helpful in suggesting change. There are Gü team members involved in the forum from sales, marketing and NPD. They have all asked their own questions of their fans and arranged accompanied shopping trips independently of our hand-holding.

We have often asked for people to come along to sessions at Gü's offices. Sometimes these are straightforward tastings and at other times they provide us with opportunities to probe more strategic issues. Inviting people to Gü's HQ acts as an incentive in itself – fans can't wait to get to visit the chocolate factory.

As time has gone on, we have made it increasingly clear to Gü that communicating with their panel of fans does not and must not replace 'real' qual. We are talking to fans who start from a position of authority and whose knowledge of the brand has grown as their relationship with the community grows. However, for the purposes of what Gü needs to find out, this has suited them very well and when we need to recruit non-users or more ambivalent consumers, we recruit and research in the 'normal' way.

The findings

Over the past two years, particularly since the community was created, we've covered a lot of ground, both strategic and tactical. We've helped Gü understand which occasions beyond their core are most and least appropriate, we've tasted and refined numerous dessert concepts, we've reviewed pack messages and communication hierarchies, we've tested advertising ideas and explored the role of sub-brands and range architecture. All in all we've landed consumer insight at every point where it could possibly be relevant, which is pretty much everywhere. And that's most definitely something that wasn't there at Gü before.

The outcome

Gü's marketing and NPD teams seem much more confident in their decision-making now. They are able to provide evidence, internally and to buyers, that there's a real consumer need for what they've created. Sonia Kapadia, head of marketing and NPD, says: 'I come from the world of big brands, Pepsi and Walkers, where we didn't make any decision without talking to the consumer first. Before coming to Gü, we'd have a hunch and run with it. Now before we even get to that hunch we hear first from the consumer to understand what it is they want (or don't want) and then go for it. Marketing is all about giving consumers exactly what they want, and now we can do that with more confidence in our decisions.'

The insights we've gained have helped Gü build relationships with retailers too. Sales director Amelia MacLeod says: 'UK retailers, quite rightly, put the consumer at the heart of all their decision-making and for suppliers to be aligned with retailers' needs, we need to be doing the same thing. By gaining consumer insight from the word go, we're able to present compelling stories on how our range and NPD fit their strategy, confident in the knowledge that we'll be meeting the needs of our customers too.'

What next?

We are reviewing how to refresh and renew how we use the community and are dedicated to keeping the conversations with fans going. Our relationship with Gü is as strong as ever – our work is being taken directly into pitches for new business partnerships and we continue to be involved in new launches.

Razor has learnt a lot from the relationship too. In particular it's created a passion in our own business for working with entrepreneurial brands and start-up businesses. Directly as a result of our work with Gü we've created First Shave, a research approach designed for start-ups and entrepreneurs. We're taking what we've learnt and we're applying it to creating equally strong partnerships with some really funky brands.

Chloë Fowler is co-founder of Razor Research.

This case history appeared in the March 2010 edition of *Research*, and is published with the permission of the Market Research Society.

Links in the text

Chapter 4 – Collecting observation data and monitoring online user-generated content
Chapter 6 – Collecting quantitative data

Potential areas for discussion

1 Discuss the value of having an online community.
2 Discuss other ways of obtaining similar customer feedback
3 What approaches could you use to keep the community interested and refreshed?
4 Is the data you obtain from such a community likely to be biased? In what ways?
5 How would you get similar data from non-customers?

Related websites

Gü: **www.gupuds.com**
Ning: **www.ning.com**
Razor Research: **www.razorresearch.co.uk**

Case 7
English rugby – researching participation

Grassroots rugby is the winner with a new research initiative from the Rugby Football Union and its sponsors Zurich. Vivienne Wilson dons her mouthguard and tackles researchers and clients.

Mike Everett, managing director of MORI UK, is a rugby fan. He describes Jonny Wilkinson, the golden boy of English rugby as 'better than Beckham. He can really kick a ball', and waxes lyrical about the enlightening joys of the game. One suspects that when MORI won the contract for a major piece of research from the Rugby Football Union, Everett was over the moon. 'Having a passion is helpful,' he says. 'As long as you realise that you've got to be fair, and that you need to keep an eye on every angle.'

clive thompson rugby/Alamy

Researching sport is difficult as it can be many faceted. There is a world of difference from a football kickaround in the park to the multi-million pound wheeling and dealing of Old Trafford or, in the case of rugby, from the crowds of Twickenham belting out 'Swing Low, Sweet Chariot' to scrumming down in a field on a rainy Saturday afternoon. However, soon the RFU hopes these two ends of the rugby spectrum will collide. The RFU has its eye on the Rugby World Cup, held this month. England is a serious contender for the title and the RFU wants to build on the excitement and the team's (hopeful) success in the competition to boost involvement in the game at grassroots level. 'There won't be another opportunity to generate such enthusiasm for the game for a long time', says Peter Hasler, head of sports research at MORI (incidentally is the fastest growing department in the agency).

Time out

The RFU and its Premiership sponsor Zurich realised that this was an ideal point to rethink the strategy for encouraging involvement in rugby. The notion of using market research to achieve this came from a conversation between James Hill, corporate marketing director from Zurich and Terry Burwell, community rugby and operations director at the RFU.

'We asked ourselves at Zurich: "What do responsible sponsors do?"' says Hill, '"What would really make a difference in the sport?" We know that there are difficulties with participation. But how much is that to do with leisure time, and how much is that to do with the game itself?' The man at the RFU charged with the difficult task of getting people out onto the rugby pitch (and keeping them there) is Terry Burwell. 'If you're going to make any strategic decision about the direction of the sport and how you want it to grow, you need to know the size of your market and the current trends and issues that affect it,' he explains. 'We needed to get some robust data to form our plans.'

Therefore, a piece of research was planned, paid for and commissioned by Zurich (the final bill for the project will come in at around £100,000). The front runners from the start were MORI and the Henley Centre, both of whom had been involved either with Zurich or the RFU. In the final analysis the work went to MORI. 'We wanted an organisation with a profile name because it can add to the weight of the research,' says Hill.

One, two, three . . . Go!

The research project was split into three stages and had a very simple aim: to establish current participation trends and the factors affecting them with a view to raise the profile of community rugby and increase participation levels.

The first stage was the desk research of trend and context analysis. 'To put rugby into context you can't look at it in isolation,' says Hasler. 'We looked at other sports and talked to a range of people about use of the Internet and working time and other issues.' MORI also looked at information they already held. 'We've got quite a lot of data in-house, we did a young people's sports survey for Sport England and a sports tracking survey that looks at participation,' he explains.

The background contextualisation was followed by qual and quant stages. 'We interviewed people right across the board. We interviewed teenage rugby players, heads of governing bodies, teachers and referees,' says Everett.

Perhaps unsurprisingly there was no shortage of researchers who wanted to get involved with this kind of work. 'People are always keen to work on these kinds of surveys,' says Hasler, who confesses to being more of an all-round sports fan than a rugby enthusiast. However, as Everett points out, 'Being a sports fan can help as people who like sport have a certain outlook on life and if you don't understand it, you just don't understand it! And it's important that interviewers know what they are talking about because it's easy to go down the wrong route in sport.'

Rugby – making an impact

The survey was conducted by MORI UK between January and April 2003.

It is the most comprehensive survey ever undertaken into the state of rugby union in England, with 1,476 participants.

The following participated: administrators, ex-amateur players, rugby development officers, club officials, journalists, local authority sports practitioners, amateur players, referees, teachers, spectators, TV viewers and RFU Rugby student liaison officers.

One of the most important concepts to come out of the survey is the idea of the 'Rugby Journey,' i.e. people experience rugby in different contexts at different times in their lives. If participation is to increase, the RFU must now help foster strong links between stages in that journey. For example, between secondary schools and local clubs.

Game plan

While there is no doubt that this was a major piece of fieldwork, the main challenge was dealing with the enormous amount of data in slightly different formats, and coming up with a reporting and analytical framework.

'The process of research is often as useful to the client as the end product,' says Everett. In this case it was scenario planning that really helped the communication of results and the development of the process. 'I like scenario planning,' continues Everett. 'When you write about the future it feels very real. Then you go back and look at what happened and how it came about. We came up with three scenarios of the game playing out till 2006.'

However, the scenarios that MORI came up with for the RFU and Zurich will not appear in the final findings report which will be released to the media. Terry Burwell, explains: 'There were negative parts of the report that were critical about what we've done or not done and we will be open about them. However, if we published the worst case scenario, that we call "the withered rose", people would focus in on that. The scenarios are in our consciousness and in our planning but not something that is right for general release.'

Tackle problems

The results have also been used internally to bolster the position of the development team. 'The RFU is an incredibly political organisation,' says Everett, 'and Terry is really impressive, he loves the game and has a clear vision about how the game has to develop from the grass-roots. We wanted to use the research project to help him win some people over within the organisation.'

Managing internal clients and expectations is a difficulty known to many in-house researchers. In this case there was also difficulty of persuading colleagues that research is worth the money. 'It's a bit of a catch-22,' says Burwell. 'Many of us feel that £100,000 could be spent practically in the field.' However, if rugby has to compete with other pastimes to win participants, it needs to see itself as a brand, however unappealing that may sound. In many ways this is the real commercialisation of sport, as bodies such as the RFU use the tools of successful brand building, such as MR, to keep ahead of the game. Burwell is keen to keep his feet on the ground though. 'With research, you have to ask: "do you let it lead you in one direction or do you lead with it?" I think we have probably got the right mix here.'

The ultimate results of this research will be easy to measure. Are there more people playing rugby in 2006? Has the lure of a cold wet Saturday afternoon beaten the lure of the TV, internet and a whole host of other distractions? What comes now is vital. The report will undoubtedly help the RFU make the sport more popular but whether it gets people out on the pitch is another question. If England win the World Cup and more people watch rugby, but fewer people are playing the game, is that a success? 'It is and it isn't,' sums up Everett. 'That's very difficult for them.' And here is the crunch – research is just the first step. The RFU and Zurich can now make the distinction of what is within rugby's control and what isn't. For example, they claim that there is not enough sport played in secondary schools. The RFU can now lobby with other sports bodies, using the information gained through research to strengthen their case.

As Mike Everett talks about the project with ill-concealed passion, it's obvious that he is one rugby fan who hopes that this research will help keep rugby alive and where it really matters. At the heart of sport in the UK.

This case history appeared in the October 2003 edition of *Research*, and is published with the permission of the Market Research Society.

Links in the text

Chapter 2 – The marketing research process
Chapter 10 – Presenting the research results

Potential areas for discussion

1 Could the research objectives have been achieved in any other way?
2 How would you determine the number of interviews to do with the different interest groups?
3 What is meant by the comment: 'With research, you have to ask, do you let it lead you in one direction or do you lead with it.'
4 Should such a study also include respondents who have no interest or experience playing rugby?

Related websites

MORI: **www.ipsos-mori.com**
Zurich Insurance: **www.zurich.com**

Case 8
Malta and MTV – researching attitudes

Sun, sea, sand and surveys

Sam Elphinstone explains how research helped Malta's tourist authority assess its efforts to use music to attract younger visitors.

The challenge

With idyllic beaches, a laid-back atmosphere and fascinating history, it's easy to see why the island of Malta is a well-established holiday destination. But while it has always been popular among families and older travellers, the younger demographic has been less visible. The Malta Tourist Authority (MTA) wanted to unmask the island's younger side, and attract more 16-to-34-year-olds to the island.

Liz Boyd/Alamy

Identifying music as a means to drive visits, MTA collaborated with MTV, one of the world's most powerful youth entertainment brands, to develop Malta Music Week, the perfect platform to showcase the lively side of Maltese life. The five-day festival would include club nights, beach parties and street concerts, culminating in an MTV event.

MTA embarked on a partnership with Viacom Brand Solutions International (VBSI), the sales and sponsorship division of MTV Networks International. The collaboration would align Malta Music Week with a globally recognised brand, finishing the festival on a high and making it an international event. In July 2007, the Isle of MTV Malta Special was launched, catapulting Malta into the spotlight and enabling MTV's youth audience to see a new side of the island, through events on the ground and a one-hour TV special.

Knowing that evaluation and measurement of the event would be crucial, VBSI turned to 2CV to investigate the impact that the Isle of MTV event had on consumer attitudes towards the holiday destination during 2008 and 2009.

'Being able to demonstrate the effectiveness of event activity has become more important as our clients are increasingly trying to assess their return on investment.'
Lisa Cowie, insight manager, VBSI

The brief

Our brief from VBSI was to measure how the Isle of MTV event affected young peoples' perceptions of Malta as a tourist destination, whether the exposure on MTV encouraged a greater number of young tourists to book a holiday to the island, and if the brand partnership was successful in shaping Malta as an ideal holiday destination. Our experiential division, 2CV:EXP, would record the shifting perceptions in attitudes to Malta from those attending and measure the value of the partnership between the MTA and MTV.

The approach

Using our new experiential model we were able to generate sufficient data to compare different activities.

The research was carried out during the 2008 and 2009 festivals, allowing us to provide insight into the impact of the event in shifting younger tourists' perceptions of Malta and establish what elements of the event drove positive behaviour.

In 2008, the evaluation involved interviewing 200 people at the event and 2,400 people in previous online interviews. In 2009, the evaluation was developed into a three-step process involving data collection at the event, post-event and among a control sample.

The research in 2009 captured the immediate feelings and perceptions of the consumer at the point of experience by conducting 300 face-to-face interviews at the event. This gave us the chance to monitor and consider responses within context when looking at overall findings. Interviewers from a local agency were used to target the non-Maltese members of the crowd; a target profile of 16-to-34-year-olds was required, with a good balance of males and females. Each interviewer spent five minutes with each respondent conducting a quantitative questionnaire.

Data were captured on PDAs, which helped capture respondent curiosity and allowed a quick turnaround. The study replicated the one carried out in 2008, so findings were fully compatible and could be compared.

Four weeks later, 100 consumers who had been interviewed at the event were recontacted to carry out a further interview online. This allowed 2CV to understand the attendees' experiences and the resulting beliefs and actions. Information gathered could then be mapped, comparing intended behaviour against the outcome.

The third stage was to survey a control cell to provide baseline measures and isolate how successful the activity and brand partnership had been in driving shifts in perceptions. This was done by asking 100 matched-sample people who hadn't attended the event a similar battery of questions to those asked at (and after) the event.

The findings

The results of the research demonstrated the positive effect of the MTV and MTA partnership, with the Isle of MTV event attracting younger tourists to the island. Results showed that the island was also able to demonstrate other reasons why it's a great place for young holidaymakers, aside from the festival – the weather, the people and the beauty of the island. Eighty-eight per cent of respondents agreed that 'Malta is the perfect holiday destination for people like me', a 59 per cent increase on the control group. Research also highlighted the impact of word-of-mouth in promoting the event, with 7 out of 10 respondents questioned four weeks later having talked about Malta on Facebook. This demonstrated the lasting effect of the activity, while giving Malta wider exposure across different channels.

The event delivered a better experience of Malta than expected, and aligned the island with a previously unseen side, one which appealed far more to the younger tourist looking for a lively destination. With 82 per cent of respondents claiming there was more to Malta than they had thought, it was clear that visitors were engaging with more than just the music.

The outcome

Our framework measures and evaluates experiential activity during and after a campaign, so we were able to provide MTV with feedback on what people thought of the event and the outcomes it delivered. This gave them the insight needed to prove that the Isle of MTV event can forge deeper, longer-lasting relationships with consumers.

Although there was some impact from the global recession, there was a year-on-year shift in attitudes and perceptions, which we will continue to develop and monitor in the future.

Lisa Cowie, insight manager at VBSI, said: 'Being able to demonstrate effectiveness of event activity has become more important as our clients are increasingly trying to assess their return on investment.'

What next?

MTV presented the results to the MTA as part of its wider research studies, demonstrating the effectiveness of the brand partnership in changing the perceptions of Malta in the minds of the younger demographic.

With Isle of MTV now in its fourth year, 2CV returned earlier this year to build on previous research. Using the same methodology as in 2009, we expanded the approach to include interviews with Maltese residents to allow a comparison of how the event affects locals and visitors and how effective the brand partnership has been in driving a change in perception.

Sam Elphinstone is Research Director at 2CV.

This case history appeared in the September 2010 edition of *Research*, and is published with the permission of the Market Research Society.

Links in the text

Chapter 6 – Collecting quantitative data
Chapter 7 – Designing questionnaires
Chapter 8 – Sampling methods

Potential areas for discussion

1 Discuss why a three-step process for data collection was used in 2009.
2 Discuss how you would sample when carrying out the research at the event.
3 Discuss the value of re-contacting people who had already been interviewed.
4 Thinking about the nature of a concert, when and where (during the event) should the research company undertake the interviews?

Related websites

Isle of MTV: **www.isleofmtv.com**
Malta Tourist Board: **www.visitmalta.com**
2CV Research: **www.2cv.co.uk**
TNS: **www.tns-global.com**

Case 9
Allied Domecq – researching lifestyles

Getting to know you

Adult emergent drinkers are a vital market for the alcoholic drinks industry. Shirley Acreman and Bill Pegram explain how Allied Domecq commissioned an innovative study to understand this group, and how the findings made an impression on the drinks company's business managers.

Markets are becoming ever more competitive, with new brands competing for a share of consumers' hearts and minds. Building a relationship with consumers is a challenge facing all organisations, but particularly so in the case of 'emergent drinkers' – those of legal drinking age up to 25. These consumers are highly experimental, and our only safe assumption is that their consumption habits will probably not follow on from those of preceding generations.

PhotoSpin, Inc./Alamy

In 1997, Allied Domecq Spirits & Wines (ADSW) recognised the danger of being distanced from this crucial group, particularly across geographical markets. We were not looking to understand a current user group per se, but rather to gain insight into the factors influencing brand adoption as these young drinkers mature.

Working with Pegram Walters International (PWI), a unique programme of research was created. The objectives went far beyond an exploration of their current usage and attitudes towards spirits, and encompassed an exploration of their personal values, their feelings about their lives, their universe, their hopes and dreams. The project required a willingness to think beyond current market conditions and business objectives.

The broad objectives of the research – covering an elusive respondent set – clearly required an approach that would be both informal and unconventional. It needed to venture beyond 'traditional' MR in order to maximise the quality of data. Moreover, because of the innovative nature of the project, it required a high level of openness, communication and trust between client and agency, to ensure that the information was both usable and relevant. In research terms, there were two clear challenges:

- gathering information from this difficult-to-access consumer group;
- integrating the information back into the organisation.

Gaining access to the adult emergent drinker

We believed that, to gain real insight into the emergent drinker community we would have to take into consideration two realities: nobody can understand a community better than the community itself; and information alone cannot provide valuable insight, which can only be developed from the blending of community understanding with external analysis.

Access to the community was provided via the development of the 'information gatherers' (IGs) concept. IGs would be representatives of the adult emergent drinker target group. They would participate in the research in order to interpret the dynamics of their own community for us.

To accomplish this, we recruited adult emergent spirits drinkers, who were required to understand the objectives of our research project and to be able to communicate concepts. In this way, they would not only provide feedback on their own needs and actions but, more important, would also be able to gather and interpret information from their peer group. IGs would become, effectively, both respondents and researchers, with the ability to provide us with rich, value-added insight.

We believe that one of the key successes of this programme was our policy of maintaining honesty at all stages of the programme. By being completely open about what we were setting out to do with the participants, by sharing our hopes and expectations with them, we empowered the IGs to have a stake in our project. As a result, they felt as committed to gaining valuable insight as we did. However, the recruitment of IGs also required both ADSW and the research agency to step away from established comfort zones and let go of control – two key ingredients to any programme of innovation.

Overall there were three stages to the research design in each market. In the first instance we conducted one-hour depth interviews. There were three clear objectives for this stage of research: to understand personal viewpoints on marketing and lifestyle issues; to clarify and/ or narrow down topics for subsequent exploration at the workshop stage; to recruit appropriate 'information gatherers' (IGs). Depth interviews were conducted to understand what was happening in respondents' lives. We invited them to undertake 'homework' such as essays on their lives, and to bring along items of personal importance to stimulate discussion. From this stage we began to formulate hypotheses on issues such as how they saw themselves and their future, relationships, self-discovery, and opting in or opting out of the system. In each market, from 20 depth interviews, 10 respondents were retained as IGs to accompany us through the rest of the programme. We believed that it was important to conduct the bulk of the research in the environments in which alcohol was consumed. We rented out leading edge bars where we invited 50 adult emergent drinkers to participate in workshops.

From the time the participants entered the venue, the role of ADSW and the research agency became purely observational, with the IGs leading the discussion throughout. We designed a task guideline, empowered the IGs with an understanding of our needs, and left them to it. As an additional record, the workshops were video-recorded. Because of the way in which they had been recruited, the IGs felt a real responsibility to get the right information. The participants felt comfortable within their peer group and, in the more natural bar environment, fed back real, relevant and honest information. Moreover, both respondents and IGs respected the process, allowing them to 'buy into' the research. On the night following the workshops, we reconvened focus groups with the IGs to discuss what actually happened, and their interpretation of what it actually meant. In this way, we were able to collect concentrated data: what we observed, what the consumers said, how it was reported back to us, and an initial understanding of what it all might actually mean.

Communicating the findings within ADSW

To infuse the exercise with knowledge, learning and a sense of adventure, we invited ADSW business teams to spend a day of discovery with us. We began the day by holding breakout sessions that included ADSW marketing and sales personnel, and their key agencies. The purpose was to gauge current assumptions about adult emergent drinkers, and where necessary to dispel some myths. Then we 'met' the generation. We felt that the best way to do this was to create fictional characters for the adult emergent drinker generation. These would enable ADSW marketing managers to visualise the consumers when developing NPD or communication strategies. The personalities we created were brought to life using actors from the generation. In France, for example, the clients were able to meet Matthias, Stephanie, Seb, Justine and Stan.

These five characters symbolised the richness and the diversity of the generation. They were not meant to represent a segmentation of the market – rather, they were intended to reflect a collage of adult emergent drinkers in order to help business managers enter into a relationship with this consumer group.

Each of the characters engaged with the audience via dialogue, discussing for example their lifestyle, behaviours, in/outs, values, concerns and expectations for the future, as well as their current attitudes towards alcohol. In addition, the audience was presented with workshop 'souvenirs', notebooks with pictures and 'bios' of the character types where they could take notes during the presentation. We then reconvened the work groups to summarise learning. The effect was immediate: with the bar as a cue, business managers were able to step into a new world and easily meet and interact with their consumers. Moreover, their 'consumers' were eager to explain what was and wasn't important to them. This multi-media/multi-layered presentation of findings allowed information to be assimilated both visually, audibly, and kinaesthetically.

In order to ensure that the information remained topical, useful and easily accessible, we felt it was important to create a vehicle for ongoing communication and dialogue with the audience. To achieve this, we created a high impact 'magazine' to bring the research to life after the presentation. We refer to this as a 'magazine' and not a research report, to reflect the lifestyle of the consumer group in question: it contained images, layouts and fonts typically associated with the generation. This magazine, together with the videos containing live footage of the actors and the workshop, was distributed throughout ADSW.

Ongoing innovation

We believe that this was an important exercise in terms of combining creativity of process and reportage with real business needs. We often state the need to 'get into consumers' minds', and we use creative/projective techniques to really understand what consumers are thinking. However, where, as researchers, we fall short is that we too frequently forget to devote the same amount of time to understanding and to the context of our clients' businesses.

Such was the success of the research format that the research agency developed CommunityInsight – an information-gathering process that aims to access primary target groups. CommunityInsight is based on the same two very simple premises:

- nobody can understand a community better than the community itself;
- information alone cannot provide valuable insight, which can only be developed from the blending of community understanding with external analysis.

We now have successfully replicated this model in other markets and continually look for new opportunities to innovate.

Shirley Acreman was insight director, Allied Domecq Spirits & Wines, UK. Bill Pegram was managing director, Pegram Walters International.

This case history appeared in the November 1999 edition of *Research*, and is published with the permission of the Market Research Society.

Links in the text

Chapter 1 – The role of marketing research and customer information in decision making
Chapter 5 – Collecting and analysing qualitative data
Chapter 10 – Presenting the research results

Potential areas for discussion

1 Discuss the characteristics of emergent drinkers.
2 Discuss the need for an informal and unconventional research approach with this market.
3 'Nobody can understand a community better than the community itself.' Does this place a question mark over all marketing research?
4 Discuss the advantages and disadvantages of using 'information gatherers'.
5 Are respondents honest when they talk to their peer group?
6 Discuss the ethical and moral issues regarding the provision of alcohol at group discussions.
7 Discuss the methods used to feedback information to the clients (days of discovery and magazines).
8 Discuss the proposition that valuable insight can only be developed from the blending of community understanding with external analysis.

Related websites

Allied Domecq: **www.allieddomecq.com**
Pegram Walters International (now part of Synovate): **www.synovate.com**

Case 10
Dove – researching beauty for a communications campaign

The beauty myth

Dove's Campaign for Real Beauty made the headlines on its launch last year. Teams from StrategyOne and Dove reveal the story behind it.

In the spring of 2004, Dove launched its Campaign for Real Beauty in the United Kingdom with a print ad campaign like no other before it. The campaign was in collaboration with celebrity photographer Rankin and featured a group of very real women celebrating their very real body types, including fuller figures not typically portrayed in advertising. These six ordinary women were recruited off the street and chosen for their confidence and spark – baring all in their underwear without having been airbrushed or re-touched in any way.

Blend Images/Alamy

Chord to action

The campaign spurred instant discussions everywhere and really seemed to strike a chord. As the *Evening Standard* commented: 'Hoorah! After many, many years of being assured by the fashion and beauty industries that women adore and aspire to the ultra-glamorous, perfect images of models on billboards and in glossy magazines, we have proof that, well, we bloody well don't.'

The global advertising campaign, launched in October 2004, added further grist to the mill by questioning whether 'model' attributes, such as youth, slimness and symmetrical features, are required for beauty – or are completely irrelevant to it. Each ad presented an image of a woman whose appearance differs from the stereotypical physical ideal, and asks the reader/viewer to judge the woman's looks by ticking a box.

The big picture

But the Campaign for Real Beauty is more than just an advertising campaign. It consists of many different strands including:

- the creation of a forum for women to participate in a dialogue and debate about the definition and standards of beauty in society;
- fundraising initiatives (sponsored by the Dove Self-Esteem Fund) to help young girls with low body-related self-esteem;
- self-esteem workshops with young girls in schools to help them foster a healthy relationship with and confidence in their bodies and their looks;
- the establishment of the Program for Aesthetics and Well-Being at Harvard University, through a grant from Dove, which will continue to examine the way we think and talk about beauty in popular culture and the effect that this has on women's wellbeing;
- the creation of a global touring photography exhibit (Beyond Compare, Women Photographers on Beauty), showcasing diverse images of female beauty from 67 female photographers, and demonstrating that beauty is about much more than stereotypes.

Beauty and the beach

The initial idea for this approach to beauty came from Dove's awareness that its brand was primarily associated with its eponymous soap bars. It wanted to develop a new 'beauty brand' platform to support product extensions into a range of shower gels, moisturisers, shampoos, and so on. The company wanted to avoid using mainstream images of beauty that it felt were unrealistic and unattainable, but did not know what an alternative platform would be.

So, Dove commissioned StrategyOne, the specialist research and strategic consulting arm of Daniel J Edelman, to conduct a global research programme to provide the company with authoritative, legitimate data on which to build its new beauty philosophy. It wanted to explore what beauty means to women today and why that is. Further, Dove wanted the study to assess whether it was possible to talk and think about female beauty in ways that were more authentic, satisfying and empowering.

Body of evidence

StrategyOne adopted a rigorous approach to the project. Materials in 22 languages from 118 countries were reviewed to examine existing research and writing on beauty, appearance and self-worth. The review was conducted by the specialist secondary research and media analysis group of StrategyOne and tapped multiple databases provided through the National Library of Medicine and PubMed, as well as the Reuters and Dow Jones newswires and the Factiva News database. This helped to determine the current body of knowledge on the topic, and to identify gaps that would enable Dove to add positively to the debate.

Obtaining expert guidance and support from leading thinkers and academics then fed into the design and interpretation of the primary research and the development of a white paper. These experts included Dr Nancy Etcoff, a professor at Harvard University and author of *Survival of the Prettiest* and Dr Susie Orbach, visiting professor at the London School of Economics and author of *Fat is a Feminist Issue*.

Primary, quantitative research was then commissioned from Mori among women aged between 18 and 64 in ten countries around the world: the US, Canada, Great Britain, Italy, France, Portugal, Netherlands, Brazil, Argentina and Japan. A total of 300 women were interviewed in each country, except for the United States, where 500 were interviewed. No references to the brand or its parent, Unilever, were made during the survey, so that participants were unaware of Dove's sponsorship of the investigation.

Breaking ground

The global literature review confirmed that no one had undertaken a comprehensive study of this nature – so there was definitely scope for Dove to take this idea further and take ownership of this important issue.

And the results of the quantitative research gave Dove the information it needed to communicate with women in a new, but highly relevant and meaningful way.

The study also showed that women globally hold remarkably similar views on beauty – with the exception of the Japanese on some measures. It demonstrated that authentic beauty is a concept lodged in women's hearts and minds and seldom articulated in popular culture or affirmed in the mass media. As such, it remained unrealised and unclaimed. 'The study shows that women are less satisfied with their beauty than with almost every other dimension of life except their financial success,' notes Etcoff. 'There is enormous room for improvement.'

Importance of attributes in Making a Woman Beautiful	
	% of total respondents
Happiness	89
Kindness	86
Confidence	83
Dignity	81
Humour	78
Intelligence	75
Wisdom	72
Appearance of skin	67
Overall physical appearance	64
Facial appearance	62
Sense of style	61
Body weight/shape	56
Hair styling	54
Youthfulness	51
Professional success	49
Sexiness	46
Financial success	43
Spirituality/religious faith	42
Make-up/cosmetics	36

Pretty vacant

The study also confirmed that this idea of beauty appears to have been replaced by a narrower definition that is largely located in limited ideals of physical appearance. It appeared that the word 'beauty' has – in many ways – become functionally defined as 'physical attractiveness'.

This definition of beauty has been powerfully communicated through the mass media and has been assimilated through popular culture. It is this ideal that many women measure themselves against and aspire to attain. However, because this ideal is extremely difficult to achieve, women find it difficult to think of themselves as beautiful, with four in ten strongly agreeing that they do not feel comfortable describing themselves as beautiful. 'The study does not suggest that women are self-loathing or in despair or mere victims,' explains Etcoff. 'Far from it. But they do not feel the power and pride of beauty either.'

Beautiful minds

Nonetheless, the study found that two-thirds of women strongly agreed that physical attractiveness is about how one looks, whereas beauty includes much more of who a person is. Women rated happiness, confidence, dignity and humour as powerful components of beauty, along with the traditional attributes of physical appearance, body weight and shape, and even a sense of style.

The respondents also saw beauty in many different forms:

- 77 per cent strongly agreed that beauty can be achieved through attitude, spirit and other attributes that have nothing to do with physical appearance;
- 89 per cent strongly agreed that a woman can be beautiful at any age; and
- 85 per cent stated that every woman has something about her that is beautiful.

'At the heart of this study is a result which is highly significant,' claims Orbach. 'Women regard being beautiful as the result of qualities and circumstance: being loved; being engaged in activities that one wants to do; having a close relationship; being happy; being kind; having confidence; and exuding dignity and humour. Women who are like this look beautiful. They are beautiful.'

Not only did women agree that happiness is the primary element in making a woman beautiful, but 86 per cent strongly agreed that they themselves feel most beautiful when they are happy and fulfilled in their lives. Furthermore, 82 per cent agreed that: 'If I had a daughter, I would want her to feel beautiful, even if she is not physically attractive.'

In addition, although women laid some of the blame for the perpetuation of inauthentic beauty on popular culture and the mass media, they also believed that that mass media can help reconfigure popular culture so that true beauty becomes the new standard.

Pillar talk

The study delivered on four pillars of success. It provided credible and ownable insight in the needs of women, publicly validating the way women feel about and perceive beauty – and shining a light on the way they believe beauty could – and should – be democratised.

It provided content for outreach: utilising scientific and media-centric lines of questioning, the study ensured authority as well as media receptivity. It validated the Campaign for Real Beauty strategy, ensuring that it would resonate with women globally and become a catalyst for change. And finally, it created thought leadership equity, allowing the company's innovative thinking and unique approach to secure its leadership position in the beauty category and beyond.

The results of the survey clearly demonstrated the potential for Dove to become the voice for 'real beauty' and a vehicle for dialogue, engagement and action. And, as we have seen in the advertising, Dove really has taken on board the findings of the survey by using everyday women as models, representing a range of different body weights, shapes, ages and ethnic backgrounds.

As Silvia Lagnado, global brand director at Dove, says, 'At Dove, we have the simple mission, to make women feel beautiful every day.'

The authors of this case are: Jennifer Scott, President of StrategyOne; Janette Henderson, Director of StrategyOne London; Tomas Emmers, Global Dove CMI Director – skin and masterbrand; and Erin Iles, Dove Masterbrand Marketing Manager, Canada.

This case history appeared in the July 2005 edition of *Research*, and is published with the permission of the Market Research Society.

Links in the text

Chapter 1 – The role of marketing research and customer information in decision making
Chapter 5 – Collecting and analysing qualitative data
Chapter 10 – Presenting the research results

Potential areas for discussion

1 Discuss the appropriateness of the sample size of 300 women in nine countries and 500 in the United States.
2 The research consisted of secondary research, expert opinion and a major multinational quantitative survey. Discuss the implications of there being no qualitative research with women.
3 StrategyOne is the research and strategic consulting arm of Daniel J Edelman, a public relations company. Discuss the proposition that many companies undertake research studies for publicity and Public Relations purposes rather than to aid decision making.
4 Discuss the value of gathering expert opinion.

Related websites

Dove: **www.mydove.com**
StrategyOne: **www.strategyone.com**
MORI: **www.ipsos-mori.com**

Current issues in marketing research

These issues are included to provide examples of the key debates and challenges in the marketing research industry today. The issues are real and help to illustrate the changing nature of the marketing research industry. For each issue, there are:

- links to the appropriate chapters in the text;
- potential topic areas for discussion;
- related websites.

Issue 1
Marketing research versus customer insight

Issue 2
Merging marketing research with customer databases

Issue 3
Observation and surveillance cameras

Issue 4
Declining response rates

Issue 5
Challenges of business-to-business research

Issue 6
Difficulties in achieving representative samples

Issue 7
Research and social media

Issue 8
Multi-mode interviewing

Issue 9
Using technology for data collection

Issue 10
Clients going direct to respondents

Issue 11
International research

Issue 12
The respondents' view of research

These articles on issues were originally published in *Research/Research Decisions* and have been reproduced here with the permission of the Market Research Society.

Issue 1
Marketing research versus customer insight

In sight of change

Is the renaming of clientside market research departments just a cosmetic exercise or does it point to a fundamental shift in the role and status of MR? Ken Gofton investigates.

As new members introduced themselves at April's meeting of the Association of Users of Research Agencies, one thing stood out above all else: the wide range of job titles now in use on the clientside of the industry.

Today, inhouse professionals are as likely to be called consumer insight managers, customer insight managers or planners, as they are research managers – so much so, that AURA plans to investigate the extent to which the inhouse research function is being restructured and repositioned.

[apply pictures]/Alamy

The move is one more sign of what is arguably a fundamental change under way in client companies. A number of recent 'Clientside' features in *Research* – General Mills, GuinnessUDV, Van den Bergh – have highlighted the increased importance now given to the 'consumer insight' function within MR buyers.

Andrew Grant, European and Marketing Insights Manager for Ford, puts this more dramatically when he suggests it is a case of change or die for inhouse research departments. 'The clientside researcher must innovate or die. The encroachment of data suppliers and insight consultants could squeeze the clientside research function altogether.'

However, management styles and corporate structures are very prone to fashion swings, so is the move to 'consumer insight' just a relabelling exercise? Professor Tim Ambler of London Business School believes the change undoubtedly includes a certain amount of rebadging. 'I'm not against that,' he adds. 'It can be helpful, and market research people do need to market themselves better internally. But that's second prize. First prize is rethinking how consumer insight fits into the company as a whole.'

Andrew Marsden, Category Marketing Director, Britvic Soft Drinks, says: 'We changed our consumer research team to consumer insight four years ago. Having extended that thinking to the trade research side, we now have a category insight department. It is far more than a change of name.

'I grew up with market research managers who spent their lives writing action standard documents, and whose business was buying data. They have to become strategic contributors. Insight to me is exactly what it says – it gives strategic direction to the knowledge the business requires.' Raoul Pinnell, head of global brands at Shell, agrees that the industry is seeing a basic shift. 'Market research managers used to be the deliverers, the people who ensured that the processes were proper and thorough. They are now being asked to contribute to the analysis. It means they are not just managing the process, but managing the information, which in modern life is where the power lies. It is a genuine contribution to boardroom thinking, where they want to know what conclusions you draw.'

The rapid adoption of the consumer insight idea means that there is both some uncertainty about its origins, and some variation in the terms used. But AURA chairman Leslie Sopp is convinced it is not mere fashion. He sees it as a reaction to a genuine business need.

'To a large extent it reflects pressure on businesses to deliver and develop – in other words, it's driven by shareholders and customers,' he says. 'If there's a further element, it's the growth of IT, which makes the task more difficult because there are so many streams of information coming into the organisation.'

There's broad agreement that the concept embraces the bringing together of the many sources of information available to a company, of which market research is just one strand.

Consultant Peter Mouncey, formerly responsible for customer relationship strategy development at the AA, says: 'In the 1970s the only real source of consumer data was market research in its various forms. Today, it's only one of many, alongside customer and lifestyle databases, scanner data, loyalty schemes and geodemographics.

'The dilemma is to know how to pull all these sources together, understanding the strengths and weaknesses of each. It requires a much wider application of the researchers' skills, and the need to be able to have influence – an internal consultancy role if undertaken properly.'

The insight teams at some companies have programmes in place to help their marketing colleagues develop skills in identifying consumer insights for themselves. The key requirements in the consumer insight approach are an ability to assimilate information from a much wider range of sources, to adopt a much more proactive role, and be able to contribute to strategy development.

And the reason for it all, according to Mouncey, is that 'the source of competitiveness in today's world is the brand, customer service and the breadth and depth of the relationship with the customer. All of which presupposes a well-developed understanding of consumer needs, attitudes and behaviour'. Or as Ambler puts it: 'Consumer insight is what marketing is all about.'

When the Royal Bank of Scotland acquired NatWest, it was decided to retain the two brands and separate marketing teams. However, the research functions were merged a year ago to form a Customer and Market Insight Department.

Everyone now works across both brands, explains the department's head, Maryan Broadbent. Segment managers are responsible for developing understanding of areas such as small business, or customer categories such as young adults. A much flatter structure has been adopted, with an increase in the number of research managers, now rebranded 'planners', and fewer support staff.

There's an emphasis, too, on adding more value. Routine work like designing questionnaires is now farmed out to the company's agencies, while the team undertakes much more analysis of competitor activity.

'We are trying to convey that we don't just sit here and wait for our internal clients to ask us to do a survey. We are not a post box. We should be proactively looking at the organisation's information needs,' adds Broadbent.

A slightly different slant on the changed role comes from Andrew Grant of Ford. 'Insi[...] he says, 'allows us to viscerally understand our consumers rather than know they are 35–49 and male. Producing products, services and advertising targeting a specific consumer yields better loyalty and affinity.

'We're looking more for the "aha" than for the two decimal places of statistical significance, or the 20 reasons why two data sets are not directly comparable.'

The changes within client companies, even where they result in new challenges for suppliers, are welcomed by some on the supplyside. Andrew Vincent, Managing Director of Business & Market Research, says it's a positive development because it reflects a wish on the part of clients to get more out of their market research and to understand its role in the context of other sources of knowledge.

For example, it has become more common for clients to ask what the research actually means, even to demand, 'What would you do if it was your decision?'. This is more of a consulting role, says Vincent, 'and some agencies are not comfortable with that'.

Clive Nancarrow of Bristol Business School questions whether all the researchers involved in 'consumer insight', internal and external, have a sufficiently deep appreciation of marketing issues. 'There are major human resource issues to be thought through for consumer insight to be a reality – a culture change rather than just a name change.'

This article appeared in the May 2001 edition of *Research*, and is published with the permission of the Market Research Society.

Links in the text

Chapter 1 – The role of marketing research and customer information in decision making

Potential areas for discussion

1 Is the renaming of clientside marketing research departments just a cosmetic exercise?
2 What does it mean when it says researchers have to become strategic contributors?
3 Does IT make the information-gathering task more difficult?
4 What new skills does a marketing researcher require?
5 What are the advantages and disadvantages of a marketing research department being proactive.
6 Is customer insight a culture change rather than just a name change?

Related websites

AURA: **www.aura.org.uk**
Royal Bank of Scotland: **www.rbs.co.uk**

Issue 2
Merging marketing research with customer databases

Raiding the databank

Clients are increasingly merging their market research and database marketing functions in a bid to get more out of their data. Noëlle McElhatton investigates a major dilemma for the MR industry.

When the Royal Bank of Scotland wanted to revise its customer contact strategy last year, the UK's seventh largest bank interviewed a representative sample of customers about their contact preferences. Would customers support or oppose being phoned with an offer of a customer service review – in other words, a meeting to discuss their finances? Two-thirds said 'yes, please'.

Nothing unusual about this exercise, you might think. Not unusual, but just how useful?

Dmitriy Shironosov/Alamy

Crucial to the finance industry, and any service industry for that matter, is the concept of customer value management, or the ability to segment and target a company's most profitable customers.

Which is why, for the above project, the Royal Bank of Scotland then added information from its internal database on product holding and gender, together with derived data like contribution, a profitability measure the bank uses. By overlaying one data set on top of the other, it discovered that the customers making the bank the most money – 93.56 per cent of contribution – overwhelmingly supported the idea of being offered a review.

Welcome to the world of merging MR and databases, a practice fast becoming the norm for client companies with large transactional databases and relationship marketing strategies. Banks, retailers and utilities, among others, now believe that overlaying internal MR surveys onto databases is vital to improving response rates from direct marketing through the greater consumer understanding that MR can provide. While databases have volume, so the argument goes, they lack the depth of the MR study. By putting MR data on to databases and finding individual matches, clients get to know their customers better at an aggregate level.

With current or threatened competition in many markets – finance and utilities especially – clients need to extract the most value out of their databases, prompting them to take MR-overlaying extremely seriously.

'It has to happen – it's a natural progression of database development,' says Tom Kerr, Head of Analysis and Research at Bank of Scotland (no relation to Royal Bank of Scotland). 'We're moving into an age of "customer first", and all organisations have a responsibility to utilise information they have access to without further bothering the customer for non-essential information to provide the service he or she demands.'

Moves to overlap database marketing and market research are stepping up a gear, as companies like Boots, Royal Bank of Scotland and Sun Life of Canada restructure to integrate the disciplines more closely, from shifting the furniture so that teams sit together to full integration of database and research databases. Many are conducting the overlay themselves and redefining the role of MR in the process. Meanwhile, the ethical arguments rage on.

Five years ago, Carola Southorn was Group Marketing Services Manager at travel and financial services company Saga and foresaw this trend. She spearheaded the development of guidelines for researchers handling databases, a milestone at the time. Now, she says, 'the Market Research Society ethos on the two being very separate has been overtaken by events'.

The merger process involves matching up customer databases to internal MR. Names and address are then stripped off and models are developed to predict into what segment a customer or prospect falls. In particular, clients are looking for groups for whom their share is small, but the opportunity is big.

Berry Consulting is one of the few agencies selling the practice to clients. Julian Berry, MD, explains the lure of MR for database managers: 'What client databases lack is anything beyond their own customers' transactions. But if you can attribute somebody to a particular segment and you know how that segment is behaving in the market, then you've got quite a different marketplace. The only way you can do this is by modelling MR data onto databases.'

Clients say the urge to merge is being driven from the top. Marketing directors are concerned with the quality and relevance of market data, not its source. At Royal Bank of Scotland both the Head of Marketing Information and Research, Maryan Broadbent, and her database counterpart, Tim Crick report to the bank's Director of Retail Marketing, Ian Henderson. 'It's no good me telling Ian what customers think, and Tim telling him how they behave,' Broadbent explains. 'We need to understand how attitudes and behaviour are related. Ian asks us not to give him independent views – to go away and give him a consolidated picture.' One notable example of structural integration is found at Whitbread, the leisure and restaurant group, where the database team reports to Martin Callingham, the Group Head of MR. Callingham agrees this set-up is not the norm: it's the result of his own initiative two years ago to bring Whitbread's many brand databases in-house.

Because MR was the most numerate and computer-literate department in the company, it was the natural site for the databasers. However, it's organised in such a way that the database unit could easily be demerged from MR, in that external database suppliers report directly to John Belchamber, Database Marketing Manager, and the function is separately funded.

The lesson from Callingham's experience is that senior management support is essential to cut through any politics surrounding the integration. He needed the support of his main board to overcome resistance from the group's various marketing directors. Likewise Kerr believes support by Bank of Scotland at the highest levels was vital to gaining approval for the merger of the bank's customer database and external MR database.

Without senior buy-in, ethical nervousness and good, old-fashioned turf wars can stymie cooperation. Jane Goldsmith is Client Director at First T, a joint venture between database marketing consultancy Dunn Humby and BMRB, to sell applications of MR products to databases.

She says: 'Where MR and database marketing are two very separate functions it's difficult to get representatives from both departments to buy in, or even attend meetings together. There are instances where you go in to speak to one side and they won't pass the information on to their colleagues.'

The last two years have seen the evolution of customer insight groups charged with getting a customer view which combines knowledge from databases and MR. Goldsmith cites the UK's largest grocer, Tesco, as a clued-in proponent of the joint discipline. 'Tesco's customer research unit is made up of people with database expertise and a full understanding of their behavioural and transactional data. All the information in that group is shared.'

In May, Bank of Scotland brought database marketing into its strategic analysis unit alongside MR. 'It's so much more closely knit,' says Kerr, who has moved from being a researcher into involvement in all aspects of database development.

Goldsmith believes that given the tensions likely to exist between database and MR teams, some sort of guidelines should be drawn up as to how to work together. At Royal Bank of Scotland, cross-disciplinary teams meet to tackle specific issues like customer retention, where all participants agree and sign off terms of reference before they start.

Clients like John Buckle, MR Manager at Alliance & Leicester, and Kerr say they are baffled by the turf wars that occur in some companies. 'We do have more to gain from working with each other,' Buckle says.

'Database marketing is very broad brush. If response rates of 2–3 per cent are deemed to be highly successful, it still suggests that there's 97 per cent who are still being hit inappropriately with the wrong product or at the wrong time. That's where the extra insight of MR will be called upon to refine the process.'

Buckle believes a purist stance by MR would be a strategic mistake. 'MR has a problem in that it's not seen as the commercial side of marketing, whereas database marketing has the ear of senior marketeers because it appears more actionable.' MR can't afford to be a brake on the marriage process, or otherwise databasers will go elsewhere for their data, lifestyle companies being the obvious alternative source.

Years ago, while he was at NOP, Kerr found it strange that the power of research should not be used within database marketing. Now as a client he says it is something that research cannot afford not to do. After he joined Bank of Scotland four years ago, he implemented the concept of integrating external and internal data into a standalone marketing 'workbench'.

'You can't underestimate its power,' he says. 'If research doesn't exist within that, then its value will further diminish and could effectively become obsolete.'

This article appeared in the September 1999 edition of *Research*, and is published with the permission of the Market Research Society.

Links in the text

Chapter 1 – The role of marketing research and customer information
Chapter 3 – Secondary data and customer databases

Potential areas for discussion

1 What are the advantages and disadvantages of merging information from marketing research surveys with databases?
2 Discuss the proposition that 'organisations have a responsibility to utilise information they have access to without further bothering the customer for non-essential information to provide the service he or she demands'.
3 Discuss the proposition that the marketing research department manages the company databases.
4 In Whitbread, why would the Marketing Directors be resistant to integration?
5 Why are there likely to be tensions between database and marketing research teams?
6 How does integration fit within the MRS or ESOMAR codes of conduct?

Related websites

Royal Bank of Scotland: **www.rbs.co.uk**
Boots: **www.boots-plc.com**
Sun Life of Canada: **www.sunlife.com**
Saga: **www.saga.co.uk**
Whitbread: **www.whitbread.co.uk**
Bank of Scotland: **www.bankofscotland.co.uk**
Dunn Humby: **www.dunnhumby.co.uk**
Tesco: **www.tesco.com**
Alliance & Leicester: **www.alliance-leicester.co.uk**
GfK NOP: **www.gfknop.co.uk**

Issue 3
Observation and surveillance cameras

Watching you, watching me

A fair proportion of your life is being recorded by surveillance equipment. Robert Bain reports on research's attempt to get behind the camera.

Ever had the feeling you're being watched? Being observed and recorded by security cameras isn't unusual anymore. But increasingly, the same video surveillance technology that has become so central to security in public places, is being used to research people's behaviour.

The Halverson Group is one of the firms doing just that. In the US CCTV took a leap forward in the post-9/11 security drive, and Halverson's Video-Driven Behavioral Analytics (VDBA)

Image Source/Alamy

technique was propelled by the advances in video technology and coding. The crucial change was that the new system was digital – allowing much quicker and more sophisticated analysis.

'There's quite a body of research showing that if you improve satisfaction and commitment of employees, the customer experience is much stronger,' says founder Ron Halverson. 'But when it comes to actual improvement in engagement and customer experience, companies are having a hard time. At the real moment of truth when employees are interacting with customers, there's not that really detailed insight.'

This is where video really comes into its own, especially as research shows shoppers tend to operate on 'autopilot', making it hard for them to understand or describe their own buying decisions. Digital technology then streamlines the analysis process by automatically detecting movement and tracking individual shoppers. This can be tied in with till records to see what people ended up buying, and even with recordings from headsets worn by employees.

Being seen

It's all part of a world where data about our lives is constantly and routinely collected, sometimes for 'necessary' purposes like security, sometimes for research, and often almost incidentally.

So how do people feel about being watched? The answer seems to be that they don't give it much thought.

Partly due to suspicion of measures that could threaten freedom of speech, the US has little in the way of data privacy law or standards for video surveillance in research. So, while identifying individuals is prohibited, and signs must tell shoppers they are being filmed, researchers like Halverson can tap into these systems as they like.

Over in the UK people are both more accustomed to CCTV surveillance, and more awake to its potential dangers. Not only are there far more cameras – one for every 14 people – there is also a livelier public discourse on the subject, and more rigorous legislation controlling its use.

Shooting restrictions

The heavy use of CCTV in the UK has prompted warnings of an erosion of civil liberties, and the Information Commissioner, who oversees issues of privacy and information access, has spoken of the risk of 'sleepwalking into a surveillance society'. The commissioner may have a point, but just as important as what he said is the fact that an independent figure has been appointed to say it at all.

Data protection law covers all but the most basic CCTV systems in the UK, and the Market Research Society's own rules state that, if video surveillance is used for research, signs should be displayed to make people aware that they are being filmed, by whom, and for what purpose.

Whether or not the rules make a difference is another question. A 2004 survey of CCTV in 1,400 locations in Europe by a team from Berlin's Technical University found that less than half of systems had appropriate signage, contact details were often missing, and enquiries about who operated systems went unanswered in 43 per cent of cases.

John Griffiths used a UK supermarket chain's CCTV systems while working for Grey Integrated in the 1990s. He has no qualms about researchers using security footage for commercial purposes. 'It's harmless – this kind of stuff is captured on a regular basis. Surely it's simply a form of observation, and do you have to get the permission of people you're observing? I don't think so. It's an established research technique.'

Shoppers in their sights

In any case, it seems people are so used to being watched that researchers have nothing to gain from not being upfront. UK agencies ID Magasin and Nunwood both use video surveillance for shopper research, and display signs with a contact number for anyone with questions – but the phone rarely rings. 'They just accept that it's part of everyday life,' says ID Magasin's research director Claire Arnold.

Siamack Salari has been doing video ethnography with Everyday Lives for eight years, accompanying people about their usual activities with a camera. In his experience, concerns about attitudes to being filmed exist predominantly in clients' heads. 'People say "Nobody in this country's going to be willing to let you film them, they're very private." But they're all the same. We've done Dubai, Japan, China, Malaysia, North America, Western Europe – all no problem. We're all exposed to so much material and media content now, it's very everyday.' Salari also attaches importance to the relationship between the person filming and the person being filmed. 'We tell our researchers that if the household knows as much about you as you know about them, then you've done a good job.'

Families on film

Online researcher BrainJuicer took things a step further by setting up surveillance cameras inside a family home (although not without the family's cooperation). The Family Cam experiment used wireless technology to film the family of four for six months. Users could watch live online, remotely controlling the cameras and zooming in on areas of interest, as well as being able to access edited highlights later. News of a more targeted follow-up project in partnership with Unilever suggests the experiment had more than just novelty value, and CEO John Kearon is now talking of plans for Bar Cam and Car Cam.

Even in this setting, where the people on camera were in on it, BrainJuicer had to seek legal advice before embarking on the project, to make sure all the correct hoops were jumped through. The family had to sign disclaimers, and a big friendly sign was erected to make sure any visitors to the home also knew they were being filmed.

But Kearon said he was surprised at how positively people responded to the idea of cameras in their homes. 'We just asked our panel in the UK if anyone would be willing, and from about 30,000 people we had about 250 families say yes. So it seems people are intrigued by it.' Concerns about privacy were straightforward to deal with, said Kearon, as long as they were handled 'with respect'.

Video-based research is on the rise as it becomes cheaper and easier, and demand for deeper consumer insight grows. ID Magasin's Arnold says: 'It's understanding how people are actually behaving. When we do questionnaire research, people pre-empt what they want you to hear. So it's really to get under the skin of how people are behaving and not how they say they're behaving.'

Nunwood began using video surveillance for shopper studies recently, in response to increasing client demand. 'In many markets it's becoming a complex business to sell what your product or proposition is,' said retail consultant Ian Addie. 'There's that much more competition chasing you, that you need to work harder than you ever did to provide something that's truly appealing to the customer. CEOs and board directors are far more in tune with trying to understand what customers are thinking and feeling.' It's also an ideal medium for making sure insights are properly disseminated and capture high-level attention.

But this is still an expensive way to do research. One of the main selling points of Halverson's VDBA technique is that it harnesses the investment that companies have already made in security systems. 'Our view is that it's being underutilised from a marketing and operational research standpoint,' Halverson says.

Kearon believes costs could be driven down through a Web 2.0 approach – making surveillance systems more openly accessible and sharing the laborious analysis work. With many users examining the footage and adding their own searchable tags to items of interest, things could be made easier for everyone. 'We won't know until we get the scale . . . but the idea is that by making it open to academics or ad agencies, the more people using it, the more useful it becomes.'

This article appeared in the October 2007 edition of *Research*, and is published with the permission of the Market Research Society.

Links in the text

Chapter 2 – The marketing research process
Chapter 4 – Collecting observation data and monitoring online use-generated content

Potential areas for discussion

1 Discuss the ethics of using CCTV cameras for marketing research.
2 Discuss the conflict of getting informed consent and being able to observe real behaviour.
3 Discuss the types of material for marketing research purposes that could effectively be collected through CCTV cameras.
4 Discuss the advantages and disadvantages of such an approach.
5 Explore the analysis issues associated with observation research.

Related websites

The Halverson Group: **www.halversongroup.com**
ID Magasin: **www.tnsmagasin.com**
Nunwood: **www.nunwood.com**
Brain Juicer: **www.brainjuicer.com**

Issue 4
Declining response rates

The perfect response

How can the research business keep its respondents engaged? Robert Bain considers whether a more social and interactive approach to the research process is called for.

In their 2009 book *The Disloyal Company*, Chuck Chakrapani and David Scholz argue that transactions between businesses and their customers tend to be based on 'market norms', and that the only way to build loyalty is to start basing them on social norms too. In other words, treat people like people – recognising and reciprocating honesty, trust and loyalty. This means raising the stakes, because if a company adopts social norms, then fails to live up to them, it makes things even worse.

D. Hurst/Alamy

Here's an idea: the same thing applies to research and respondents (although 'engagement' is probably a better word than 'loyalty' unless you're recruiting people for some sort of ongoing project). If anything, social norms are even more important when dealing with respondents than when dealing with customers.

Unfortunately the research industry hasn't done a great job of taking on board the concerns of respondents. The term 'bad respondent' exemplifies the tendency to shirk responsibility when methods aren't working. As Andrew Cooper of Verve puts it, if someone's not answering surveys properly, 'That's not a people problem, it's a communications problem'.

So what does it mean to adopt 'social norms' in your relations with respondents, rather than just doing what you can get away with?

Telling people that their views are important hasn't stopped response rates from tumbling. Let's face it, MR is about asking people to help your business make more money, so don't be surprised if their desire to play along wears thin when you present them with matrix after matrix of obscure brands and attributes to compare.

The most important thing, surely, is to make certain that people have a good experience in return for their input. At the simplest level this means producing surveys that are well-designed, clearly written and most of all not too long. If you put a bad survey in front of someone they will justifiably feel slighted and very likely become a bad respondent.

Too often the respondent experience is the responsibility of nobody in particular. How many agencies employ someone to look at questionnaires from the respondent's point of view? Is the same attention paid to these communications as to marketing materials, for example? It's not that people don't understand the issues, it's just that there's a lack of discipline and leadership. The client decides they want to add a couple of questions, the agency sighs and backs down, the questionnaire ends up being written by committee and takes 40 minutes to fill in.

If you're using a random sample you'll most likely never see the respondent again so you can afford to worry less about this, but if you're using a panel you can expect to feel the effects directly.

Going beyond survey quality, treating people in accordance with social norms means allowing them to communicate on their terms, not yours. This month we carry results of a survey by eDigitalResearch which paints an optimistic picture, suggesting that people do like doing research as long as it's on their own terms – which increasingly means they expect some sort of social or interactive element.

Fiona Blades of Mesh Planning and Rachel Brown of Oxfam gave a paper at last year's Esomar Congress on how respondents are 'co-creating the research process'. Not only can they offer feedback on what it's like to take part in research, they can also be surprisingly insightful about how techniques and methodology could be improved. 'The marketing literacy of participants is changing and researchers should listen,' Blades and Brown wrote.

Blades says respondents are becoming 'professionalised' and that this is a good thing. 'They know what works and what doesn't, and they are quite professional in that sense. I've learned quite a lot from them,' she said.

It often takes a respondent's perspective to point out where a survey is poorly written, she said. 'If there's a question and they can't quite answer it within a structured online question-naire, once they've had the experience of having to put in a half truth, they feel disillusioned because they don't feel you're that interested in what they really think. That would only have come about through asking people what they thought about the survey.'

Taking a 'social' approach to respondent relations isn't necessarily easy. It means experimenting, investing and innovating. It can also mean challenging research guidelines. eDigitalResearch's survey suggests that the desire for anonymity among respondents is actually not as strong as the desire for social interaction. Research industry codes insist on protecting anonymity in order to win trust and prevent sugging, but often what respondents really want is the freedom to interact with others.

Web 2.0 technology is, of course, a major element in the changing relationships between respondents and research – although it's tricky to tell whether social media has created, accelerated or simply revealed these trends.

Client incentives are another point of contention – in the UK the Market Research Society banned them in order to adhere to data protection rules separating marketing and research. The fact that in many cases (online communities in particular) respondents welcome some sort of engagement with the client brand is a secondary concern.

Perhaps treating people right also means calling them something different. The word 'respondent' gives the impression that we do the talking and they simply respond. It's pain-fully Web 1.0. What about participant? Or partner? Or customer? Or collaborator?

Last month Communispace's Diane Hessan said that in the future, 'engagement will trump sample size'. The agencies that ignore the social norms will chug along without much engagement, having an increasingly difficult time getting people to take part in research. Others will earn respondent engagement and reap the rewards.

This stuff shouldn't really be too difficult. It is, after all, a researcher's job to understand how people behave and why, but in the rush to become experts on why people buy yoghurt or download ringtones we can forget to be experts in how and why people take part in research in the first place.

Some in the industry are more scared than others about the future of survey research. Jay Leve of Survey USA believes that telephone research (i.e. his business) is in its dying days. 'Ringing someone's phone without warning and asking if they have 20 minutes to spend with you flies in the face of everything that's going on in the world today,' he told *Research* last year. Nor does he see much of a future for online research in its current form, describing web-based surveys that recruit via pop-ups and email invitations as 'dead ends'. Research, Leve believes, must be conducted on terms that are favourable to the respondent first and foremost.

Pete Comley of Virtual Surveys believes that we're approaching the point of 'peak panel', when respondents' tolerance of online panel invites hits its peak and the only way is down. The recession and the trend for short, sharp surveys may have bought us a little time, but we'll start feeling the effects in a few years, Comley says. He hopes that salvation lies in online communities and other techniques such as co-creation that encourage a triangular relationship between respondent, client and agency. These areas are growing rapidly in comparison with traditional methods, so will this more equitable type of respondent relationship spread to other types of research?

One of the biggest obstacles to changing your approach is the belief that the shortcomings of established techniques are unavoidable, or that they don't have shortcomings. They're not – we've only put up with them because we've been so anxious to avoid other problems. But with respondent participation becoming scarcer that equation has changed.

The thing to remember is that all research methodologies are a trade-off. And if Diane Hessan is right about engagement trumping sample size, the best trade-off may not be the one you thought it was.

This article appeared in the March 2010 edition of *Research*, and is published with the permission of the Market Research Society.

Links in the text

Chapter 5 – Collecting and analysing qualitative data
Chapter 6 – Collecting quantitative data
Chapter 7 – Designing questionnaires
Chapter 8 – Sampling methods

Potential areas for discussion

1 Discuss the reasons for the decline in response rates.
2 Why do falling response rates make random probability sampling more difficult?
3 Discuss the provision of respondent incentives.
4 How can satisfaction with marketing research be measured?
5 What training should interviewers receive?
6 How do you make interviews interesting?
7 What are the characteristics of a good interviewer?
8 What are the key things that should be done to raise response rates?

Related websites

eDigitalResearch: **www.edigitalresearch.com**
ESOMAR: **www.esomar.org**
MRS: **www.mrs.org.uk**

Issue 5
Challenges of business-to-business research

Mind your own business

Business-to-business research presents challenges not only to the client but also to the researcher. Peter Shreeve discusses the ins and outs of poking your clipboard into other people's business.

It is a marketer's dream to understand customers on a one-to-one basis and to provide tailored communication, and products and services. Most consumer business research provides data at the aggregate level, offering guidance on segment-based strategies, while permission marketing techniques allow marketers to push marketing messages and move closer to the one-to-one goal.

In some types of research, such as customer satisfaction, gaining permission from customers to

Christian Lagerek/Alamy

allow their details and views to be passed to the client moves organisations towards the one-to-one relationship goal. In business-to-business research this is characterised through key account research where attributed account profile information is reported. With this in mind, let's look at the steps required to provide data that businesses can act upon and take into their organisations to drive customer commitment.

Samples vs client base

Using a representative sample of a business-to-business market can present a serious challenge to researchers. Business listings are all well and good, but difficulties inevitably arise. There is little or no homogeneity in the business world; people with a number of different job titles may perform the same function; and what counts as a decision maker, anyway? Time must be taken to make sure the source sample reflects the needs of the research.

On the other hand, agencies might be tasked with researching the client's own business customers or channel partners. The challenge arises when companies rely on a relatively small number of customers for the bulk of their revenue. You are then potentially researching the whole client base rather than a small sample representative of a much larger set.

This provides researchers with a chance to produce information that can impact on the bottom line. If you're asking questions of the actual customers, then responding to the answers they give must directly impact on your business. This kind of research takes on a different role within the business to standard sample-based surveys.

Engaging the client

There are arguments against doing this type of research. Clients may say that they have a key account management system or that key account managers provide them with feedback.

It's possible to see the research as a threat rather than a complementary tool. A key account manager, by definition, will provide a subjective viewpoint of their clients and might only identify issues they think are important.

Researchers do not offer the Holy Grail but a means to help clients understand their customers through an objective appraisal of the relationship. The researcher has a different end goal and can pull together the views of all key accounts. Research is critical to get a good understanding across a customer base. It doesn't replace a key account management structure, but key account managers cannot carry it out.

Not all companies have a research function, and this can sometimes lead to a lack of recognition about the benefits of research. And of course, those people that benefit most from this kind of research are rarely the research buyers themselves.

Finding budget for a survey of this nature is about engaging all of the stakeholders. The project has to obtain the wholehearted buy-in and support from the customer-facing teams to have the desired effect.

It is well recognised that business decision-making processes are different from those of consumers. But as researchers we can still provide the client with meaningful and actionable information based on these processes. In an organisation there will always be an understanding of how or why purchasing decisions are made; the information we provide is complementary.

Engaging the customers

Engaging the customers in the research to elicit the highest possible response rate is the next stage. We are reliant upon accurate customer databases. While this task should be relatively easy because we are dealing with a smaller number of establishments, we find that most organisations still do not have up-to-date listings of the key contacts.

Much of the information is stored informally with sales mangers and key account managers in electronic and paper-based systems. This in itself can be revealing. One such example uncovered data that was three years out of date, stopping the project in its tracks before it had even started and informing the organisation it needed to change. Where projects span many countries the potential inconsistency escalates.

Depending on the nature of the project, cooperation could be required from both decision-makers and users. Either way, pre-notification, where practical and possible, can greatly improve response rates. Cooperation rates are usually above 50 per cent and can reach 75 per cent–80 per cent in some cases.

There is always some refusal to be interviewed on the grounds of company policy or time pressures. But it may also be an indication of their feelings towards their supplier – are they just another supplier of products and services or a strategic partner? Given this, and the fact that the pool from which to draw samples is smaller, our clients tend to want to understand more about the reasons for refusal than those in general consumer research.

One of the key differences between this type of research and sample survey research is that data can be used to drive both strategic and tactical individual account changes. Within the pre-notification process and the questionnaire we tell respondents that the company wishes to identify them as individuals for the development of individual account plans. Communicating the client's intentions at the start helps us increase the likelihood of obtaining respondent attributable data.

Doing the research

If a business is new to carrying out this kind of research into their own customer base, a qualitative stage amongst a selection of key accounts should be used. This will drive the focus, content and terminology used in the quantitative stage of the research.

As with most research, the choice of data-collection method is dependent on a number of issues. Even if your client has a strong relationship with their clients, a postal-based methodology does not always elicit a high enough response rate, particularly for this type of research. And this can often fail to communicate the importance of a survey. There are similar problems with web-based surveys, aside the obvious problems of access to the web. Budget availability is a primary consideration. Face-to-face interviewing of key accounts through a semi-structured interview should glean the most detailed information, but the unclustered nature of respondents and subsequent costs usually prevent us from suggesting this as an approach for this type of quantitative research. More often than not our research tasks involve multicountry studies. This tends to indicate the centrally controlled CATI-style research. The benefits of CATI in this instance are the ability to:

- double-check that the respondent is the correct person, and keep a tighter control on sample, quota control and routing, thus ensuring and improving the quality and accuracy of the data collected;
- speed up the turnaround from implementation to completion;
- expedite changes to questionnaires in response to client or agency suggestions;
- make appointments and carry out interviews at the convenience of the respondent;
- allow the interviewer to probe during the one-to-one interaction, if necessary.

The primary focus of this type of research is the measurement of current performance and the identification of areas for improvement or for new service offerings. We can put this in the context of competitor organisations' performance (actual or perceived). We can measure all the key factors that impact on the relationship with each key account rather than just satisfaction per se.

Once we've done all this, and having engaged the key stakeholders in the research at the beginning of the process, we need to report the data in a way that maintains their interest while the research is being carried out and beyond the reporting.

Feedback

The transparency of the research allows instant client feedback on customers' attitudes towards them based on several criteria. If a customer has anything they wish to discuss with the client that is urgent it is identified.

While this information can be collected and passed to the client (if permission is granted) the key thing is that the client is set up to respond. The research normally involves questions identifying whether the customer is at risk. Other techniques include the need to report when scores on key questions drop below an agreed level.

The debrief needs to provide the stakeholders with a number of different things: an overview; the key differences between customer types; the key issues; the strengths and weaknesses identified on elements that form the dynamics of the relationship; and performance-improvement planners.

The session should be like a workshop. Let the clients ponder on the implications. How are they going to make some of these changes? Do the results surprise them? Do they confirm what they knew already but are surprised at the impact on the relationship?

The results at this stage are shown in aggregate form. Electronic reporting can engage users of the information whether they were in attendance at the debrief meeting or not. Through the use of dynamic reports users can examine data by different cuts at their leisure, to let them explore the points made in the presentation in more detail, usually through a few sheets rather than pages and pages of slides. The data then become even more actionable through the use of profiles on an account-by-account basis in an attributable rather than an anonymous way. This enables key account teams to produce targeted performance improvement: exactly what is it that customer X wants and how does this compare to the average response?

While the use of individual account profiles based on the survey data clearly has its benefits for account management, if these are combined with internal data the power of the data is so much greater. Companies who properly account-manage will have information relating to the account's importance to the organisation, defined in terms of revenue or profitability.

At the strategic level, research can be used to understand the triggers for likely defection, or simply where competitors are rated more highly.

Once this is combined with the importance of a specific customer, the organisation gets to understand how much of its business is at risk and which accounts it needs to target to ensure they stay committed. The next stage is crucial. After the survey, clients should communicate with each key account in a creative and positive manner what action will be taken as a result, both within that account and throughout the organisation. In most cases, it does not need to do this through advertising as with the broader markets – it can tell them directly.

This style of research then lends itself to periodically repeated studies to measure how customers view the performance of the organisation – have they recognised the changes made? However, this is a bit 'chicken and egg', as they need to see change to be convinced of the benefits of taking part again.

Key to the success of this type of business-to-business research is communication. Internal and external customer expectations need to be managed carefully. It also points to including research needs as part of CRM-based strategies. We are still a long way from research featuring at the core of CRM, but we have to start somewhere. At least with key account research the task, in theory, should be easier.

Peter Shreeve was client service director at Maritz Research.

This article appeared in the May 2002 edition of *Research*, and is published with the permission of the Market Research Society.

Links in the text

Chapter 3 – Secondary data and customer databases
Chapter 6 – Collecting quantitative data
Chapter 8 – Sampling methods
Chapter 10 – Presenting the research results

Potential areas for discussion

1 What are the ethical issues relating to the reporting of attributed account profile information?
2 Discuss the concept of decision makers.
3 Discuss the need for marketing research in a key account management system.
4 Discuss the value of pre-notification in a survey.
5 Identify the strengths and weaknesses of CATI for business-to-business research.
6 Discuss the likelihood of respondents being honest in their feedback.
7 Explain the relationship between CRM and marketing research.

Related websites

The Customer Management Community: **www.mycustomer.com**
Maritz Research: **www.maritzresearch.com**

Issue 6
Difficulties in achieving representative samples

The data dilemma

Do tumbling response rates and shrinking turnaround times make a mockery of representative samples? Mike Savage of *Research* hears why MR must make a stand.

Research: In today's climate of falling response rates and clients wanting data turned round ever more quickly, are we deluding ourselves when we still try to seek representative samples?

Corrine Moy (Director of Statistics, NOP): Sure, clients want data turned around ever more quickly but there is absolutely no question that they are still seeking, and expect, representative samples. Our job is to make judgements on how best to deliver representative samples given the conditions of any project we undertake.

DBURKE/Alamy

Ken Baker (Statistical Consultant): Without representative samples we don't have an industry – we are no different from the data collecting methods adopted by database marketing companies. We shouldn't be deluding ourselves – we should be attempting to represent the population, and moreover, we have tools to represent the population better than we had 20 years ago.

Research: **To what extent do you think response rates and commercial pressures from clients undermine the quest for true representativeness?**

Baker: It's difficult to do a strict probability sample with time pressures because you need call-backs. That puts the onus on getting a high-class quota sample. With the new tools at our disposal, such as geodemographic systems, we should be able to get something like representation without taking the time a probability sample would. There's no earthly reason why these things are incompatible, given that you design your survey well enough.

Moy: In terms of designing samples to produce representativeness, I would argue we are better than we have been in the past. We have more resources, our knowledge has increased from all the development work that has gone on. The demographic information we have about the population at large makes it easier to produce balanced samples which improve the quality of what we are trying to do.

Baker: The problem is you never know whether you've got systematic bias in your sample with non-probability means. Where is the non-response coming from? Up to a point we can set quotas to counter that, but declining response rates are a worry because they may be creating hidden systematic bias. We can put so much more structure on our actual survey designs but if there is any systematic bias, declining response rates will increase the error.

I am worried about declining response rates. At least the tools that we've got have increased in quality. Sampling techniques have improved quite a lot over the last 20 years. Whether everybody is taking advantage of these improvements, I don't know.

Research: **What are the other issues that prevent the industry from attaining representative samples?**

Baker: If you're not in a probability situation you've got different probabilities of likelihood of being available for interview; you've then got the problem of over-researched people not wanting to give you an interview, and so on. Aside from that, the only real issue is: are research companies prepared to pay the price for good-quality, non-probability sampling? If they are, they should be able to redress the balance up to a point.

Moy: There's always a cost pressure. If a client wants to carry out a survey for half the cost of a perfect survey then you've got to make some decisions. In a sense it doesn't cost a lot more to produce a decent sample than a poor one. There are inevitably cost pressures but the real issues are response rates and time available.

Research: **If the benefits are much greater, shouldn't agencies be able to persuade clients to pay a bit more?**

Moy: Sometimes what happens is that clients go to competitive tender for a job and you will see a price differential which is the result of different methodologies. It may well be the cheaper bid will win out but the methodology may not be quite so sound. Now, maybe the client has taken an informed decision about trading off accuracy or purity for cost, or maybe they just don't know. Some clients don't have the knowledge to make the judgement but I have to say I think the majority of them do – that's a relatively infrequent occurrence.

Research: **How big an issue is awareness of statistical methods among research buyers? There are more pressures and broader responsibilities for clientside departments, who pay less attention to the details and rely more on trust.**

Baker: Why should the onus be on the research buyer? They should be able to buy on trust. It's up to the research provider to make sure their systems are well founded for the problem in hand.

Moy: We have some highly skilled, highly informed clients who know exactly what they are doing. They may not necessarily be good statisticians but know about the issues that produce good research. Equally we have clients who are less well informed, often primarily because research isn't even their main function. There, if you've got a relationship of trust they can lean on the agency for advice. It's slightly more difficult when they go out for competitive bid because they are having to make decisions based on the knowledge they have.

Research: **There's also an issue with the scope of the data user – it's not just the research department anymore. How far is it possible to educate all the data users?**

Moy: This is where finding a balance between rigour and practicality becomes important. We can't afford to sit in our ivory towers and pontificate about how a perfect survey should be conducted. The bottom line is, if it's not available to the client when they need it, it's not going to be of any use to them. Ultimately they're either not going to buy it, or, even if they buy it, they won't be able to use it, and that will compromise their choice when they think of doing research the next time. Research buyers come from disparate backgrounds. Our task is to find the balance between giving the information they need to make informed decisions, and not overwhelming them or trying to turn them into researchers. That's a business skill and in our industry the most successful people are those who blend business and research skills.

Research: **There is a worry that research buyers are not fully aware of the strengths and weaknesses of data on which they base commercial decisions. Data can appear authoritative on a computer screen.**

Baker: It does seem to give it a degree of credibility. Sampling is just one issue behind the data you see. A more fundamental issue is the questioning technique. I can't prove this but if I were to say 'where's the main source of error in market research?', it wouldn't be sampling error at all – it would be simply the wrong question at the wrong time in the wrong place, over-fatigued respondents answering by rote and therefore not saying what they mean at all – they just want to get rid of you – and so on. That leads to a much more fundamental issue. How can we keep our respondents interested in the subject and how can we avoid making the fundamental mistakes of questionnaire design? That is where the major problems lie, rather than in sampling error.

Research: **What would you say are the main alternatives to representative sampling?**

Baker: There is a bad alternative to probability sampling – a poorly designed quota sample. Maybe it is cheaper but I doubt whether it's that much cheaper to justify doing it. Some of the alternatives for minority products are things like snowball sampling, where you try and find maybe a shop where they sell this minority product and you stand outside until you've found somebody, and try and interview them and see if they know anybody else. These sorts of techniques are rather like using databases – you've got no idea what the probability is. You don't even know what the universe looks like. These techniques are only useful when there's virtually no alternative. As long as we try, whenever practical, to represent the population as well as possible, that's what we should be doing.

Research: **Even though the Internet is not representative of the population, it is an attractive medium for data collection. The lure of that may push the industry away from statistical representativeness.**

Moy: For some people I'm sure it will, but hopefully whichever agency is doing research for those people will be able to inform them of the trade-off they are making. There is no doubt that the Internet is sexy at the moment. If you're looking for views from business people or early adopters the Internet is a good vehicle. However, as coverage is not yet universal, it will not produce good representation of the general population. If you're looking for a rounded view of that general population, then it may well be in a year's time we are looking at the digital TV route and the interactivity there, effectively carrying out what we perceive as Internet surveys over TV sets. That may turn out to be a much quicker way of getting a representative sample, rather than over the Internet.

Baker: You can also set up a panel of Internet people where you actually give them a PC and access to the net and show them how to use it and so on. Things like that might be the way forward with net research.

Moy: We can learn a lot from our colleagues in the States because they're ahead of us in this game, given that Internet penetration is much higher there. There's a lot of experience there that can inform how we do things. There's also quite a lot of work being done here that looks at bias that comes from using Internet samples and how to deal with that. If the Internet is the only way that gives you data in the time frame that you need, then we have to accept that and find ways to accommodate our objectives within an Internet sample. The only thing I would add to that is you could do an overnight telephone survey and that may well be a better solution in some cases. It really does depend on the situation.

Research: **The other issue with the Internet is that it moves the research agency away from the client. It can be automated, removing the opportunity to educate the client or warn them about the data they are using. Is this a danger?**

Baker: I think this is a major danger. The more we communicate with our clients about the limitations of what it is we are doing, the better.

Moy: We carry out a lot of large surveys where we harness the processes to set up very sophisticated web delivery systems. This clearly tends to be for bigger clients but there they will have a very deliberate, well thought-out policy of dissemination within their organisation. There's actually quite a lot of thought that goes into those kind of processes when we set up web delivery of data. That's one side of the argument. I suppose the other end of it is there is so much data available on the web for people to get their hands on. We can't be expected to police the whole world.

Baker: I think as an industry we should be setting the standards for what it can and can't do via industry bodies such as the Market Research Development Fund, which in the 80s looked at hot methodological issues such as telephone research and data fusion. We should be doing the same things on Internet research, but it seems to me that there are far too many busy people to volunteer their time than there were 10 to 15 years ago. That is an industry problem. But this is what we ought to be doing – have an industry body saying: what are the problems with this? What are the recommendations? What's good about it? What can it do, what can't it do? I'd like to see the industry looking into things like this.

Research: **Do you think this is feasible? We live in a time-poor age.**

Baker: We certainly do, but there are some outstanding brains floating around who may be willing to do this – people who have theoretically retired but maintain a big connection with the industry. Perhaps we should be recruiting those people to look into the technical problems rather than expecting very, very busy people to give more of their time. Perhaps we should slightly change tack about the way we go about it, but the thing is, it needs to be done.

Moy: There is less collaborative work going on. Having said that it doesn't mean there's no collaborative work going on. As I said earlier, a lot of work has been published from the States. Because the Internet is such a big issue, there is a commercial imperative which wasn't there with the advent of telephone research. There are a lot of technological issues now with Internet research which didn't really exist with telephone research. The combination of the pressure of work on people's time and, to an extent, more commercial pressure to keep developments under wraps, means there is less collaboration in research into research. But there's still quite a lot of stuff going on. It's the responsibilities of researchers to keep themselves up to date with that kind of work.

Research: **What form will representativeness take in the future?**

Baker: The industry is changing but representative sampling has got to keep up with it. The moment we start to decline in standards in terms of representation then what's our product? What are we selling?

Simply, we have to find more and more ingenious ways to represent the population as well as we can. It is so important to keep in touch with our roots. At the moment we seem to have a whole series of developments like net research going on without any concerted industry investigation. I am not talking about a witch hunt or anything like that, I'm just saying, now we've been in this for some time, can we establish the rules?

All the time the Internet universe is changing anyway. What the rules are today may not be the rules in five years' time. But the need for representation will always be there.

Moy: What we've managed to do as an industry is convince ourselves and our clients, despite the arguments to the contrary of some academics, that it is possible to produce representative samples, and therefore reliable data, based on quota sampling. I don't think that's going to change. It may well be harder to achieve those samples and there may be larger issues around non-response bias if response rates continue to fall, but it's the responsibility of the industry to arrest that trend. There will undoubtedly be more panel research going on. That will service a particular need. The emphasis is still on achieving that holy grail – the representative sample. The challenge for us is: what different mechanisms do we need in our changing environment to achieve what has been the constant aim from 60 or 70 years ago when market research was in its infancy? I don't think the ultimate aim has changed and I don't think for the majority of research it will ever change.

This article appeared in the September 2000 edition of *Research*, and is published with the permission of the Market Research Society.

Links in the text

Chapter 6 – Collecting quantitative data
Chapter 8 – Sampling methods

Potential areas for discussion

1 What is a truly representative sample?
2 To what extent is a quota sample representative?
3 Why are there increased time pressures on surveys?
4 Should clients have an awareness of statistical methods or is there a need for more clarity in the way that researchers report statistics?
5 Discuss the issue of over-fatigued respondents.
6 In what ways can we keep respondents interested in research?
7 Discuss the value of the Internet for survey research.
8 Discuss the issues relating to sampling and Internet-based research.

Related websites

GfK NOP: **www.gfknop.co.uk/**

Issue 7
Research and social media

Could social networks, such as MySpace and Facebook, provide an invaluable source of respondents for the insight industry? Tim Phillips talks to some of those who have begun to tackle the challenges posed by this burgeoning phenomenon.

Social networking or, in the techie argot, 'Web 2.0' is potentially a medium for reaching hard-to-find demographic groups, and a fantastically rich opportunity to discover hard-to-find insight. Social networking certainly attracts a big audience. The size of the online population – and the preponderance of young, active users who are happy to communicate for fun – would seem to be the answer to every researcher's prayers. Having struggled to recruit panels of this type of consumer for years, a few sites have managed to recruit millions of them in a matter of months. The more important question for MR professionals is: will they be happy to participate in research? And if they are, what sort of insight will this research create?

At the most basic level, research agencies can write applications which can try to marry their skills with the opportunities of social networks. Mario Menti, the Solutions Architect at GMI, has been involved in translating research to a particular type of social network: he is writing code for virtual researchers in Second Life. 'Second Life is more than social networking.

lifestylepics/Alamy

It's a virtual lifestyle. I've helped create software that can survey users, and create virtual interviewers who can engage with people inside Second Life. We've only run a couple of trials so far, but there's a lot of interest.'

A friendly face

The professionals who are actively recruiting subjects among social network users warn that this isn't another panel recruitment task. 'You need to be much more engaging and user-friendly,' says Job Muscroft, the managing director at the Face Group, which has created a project called Headbox to use social networks to investigate the opinions of 16–25-year-olds. Eventually aiming to have access to 30,000 active users, Headbox uses techniques like online focus groups conducted using instant messaging to find out what they think about certain topics. Muscroft believes that the traditional focus group technique of recruiting subjects for a one-off session won't work. 'We can host groups from people anywhere in the UK, create an ongoing dialogue. With traditional groups, it's almost impossible to get the guys back in the room again when you have finished the first session. We're interested in involving them in the whole creative process, not just in researching one thing. So we can come back to them and say, "What do you think of this?" I think excitement is generated by what we're working with, what they are doing. We don't see them as respondents; they will only engage through ownership of what they are doing. We are harnessing their creativity and insight.'

Among the early clients for this approach are Unilever and Carphone Warehouse, but Muscroft claims that many other brands are hungry to tap into this approach. For market researchers, he says, this creates the need to speak to participants in ways they can understand, and treat them as equals. 'Traditional researchers in their 40s or 50s might struggle. The biggest difference is language. You need to understand and use the language that they use online, but it's a very rich environment. You can learn far more about what gets them excited.'

Excitement is all

Like Muscroft, Mark Earls, an expert on social networks who runs Herd Consulting and is the author of *Herd: How to Change Mass Behaviour by Harnessing Our True Nature*, also thinks the key to using social networks is using the 'E' word: excitment. 'One of the fictions we've sustained is that there's a wall between us and them, like a viewing facility. It's clearly showing people in their social context, which we don't do very often, because our industry has a bias towards abstracting people. People are social animals, and that's what matters. It allows us not just to ask them questions, that's not the point. The point is to see what really gets them excited.' Excitement is different to interest, buzz or hype, he says. 'There's a world of difference even in the traditional focus group setting between a product that people like, or that fits the brief, and one that generates spontaneous excitement. Even using questions and answers is very controlling: the working assumption is that we are in control of the process, and we aren't.'

Energy and insight

For Fiona Blades, the managing partner at MESH Planning, a great advantage of social networks for clients is that they can harness this spontaneous energy and use it for simple, immediate insight that's driven by the participants. 'I look at things from a planning perspective, where you get insight from wherever you can find it. If you can only run a couple of groups, you milk them dry rather than buying research by the yard.'

The participants that take part in MESH research are encouraged to simply text when they experience something relevant to the project, and give an opinion. They have their own forum, dubbed 'The Boardroom' for discussion. 'We ask our participants to effectively become field-workers for us. The boardroom is its own little social network A poll isn't going to work. You have to understand the context in which they gave the answer. Give them something to do, empower them to change things.'

Traditional statistical modelling techniques aren't appropriate in this environment, says Max Kalehoff, the vice president of marketing at Nielsen BuzzMetrics. 'We need to put aside our white gloves and the idea that we work in some kind of laboratory. It's a participative dynamic. They have value precisely because they are involved with us,' he says. 'Do you wash the individuality out of people you are studying to make some statistical projection? No. This enables you to tap into individuals that it would be almost impossible to tap into otherwise. If the goal is to project what you find to an overall population, then no, social networks are probably not good. The opportunity here is to research some specific niches. It might not satisfy some statistical measure of survey quality, but this is a whole new discipline that's arising, closer to anthropology.'

The involvement is a relationship, and that means more than a simple thank you. It also implies that clients will have to take the step of letting research continually influence the design and marketing of a product. 'It's a process of continuous learning, interacting with real people, and that's a powerful idea. But continuous learning is based on a relationship, and that relationship doesn't end just because you've finished your survey,' he warns. 'Brand marketers have to make a decision today, to find new, unconventional customers.'

Unless marketing, development and research all speak with one voice, and unless the participants see the results of their input and are rewarded for it in a meaningful way, the process will inevitably lose momentum. Grant McCracken, the author of *Culture and Consumption* and *The Long Interview*, thinks brands must show participants that their contribution has made a difference. 'I certainly don't want anyone "just dropping in" uninvited on groups I belong to on Facebook. Incentives could take several forms and the one I like the best would be a contribution to some cause or other. There then has to be some way for the group to show how much "social capital" it has created.'

It's a radically different model for market research, but at MESH, Blades says that their client feedback is surprisingly open to these new ideas, and especially the insight that more impressionistic research can give. 'Some of the most traditional clients are very aware. They are asking for evidence from our research groups to show their managers that things are changing. They don't just accept numbers from us, they can accept pictures, quotes, anything.'

Nike is one of the brands that has gone one step further, and created its own social network. Nike+ is a range of products which logs your running activity on your iPod and allows you to upload your results to a community on the Internet. It gives Nike insight into how its products are being used, and what customers think of its products.

'At some point you have to take a leap, you have to be courageous,' says Nick Law, the executive creative director of interactive agency R/GA, which won a Cyber Lion at Cannes in 2007 for the Nike+ campaign. He says that to create a valid network, marketing departments have to reassess their core business: offer something useful, and don't just tell customers to buy things. 'The whole point of the digital environment is that it is much more than what traditional agencies do, which is all about outbound messaging,' he says, 'It's a fundamentally democratic medium.'

This article appeared in the August 2007 edition of *Research*, and is published with the permission of the Market Research Society.

Links in the text

Chapter 4 – Collecting observation data and monitoring online user-generated content

Potential areas for discussion

1 Why is social media an appropriate tool for reaching hard to find demographic groups?
2 Discuss the value to the client of research using social media.
3 Discuss the value to the respondent of research using social media.
4 Discuss the concept of relationship between reviewer and respondent.
5 Discuss the proposition that researchers need to tread lightly to avoid being seen as the corporate gate crasher.
6 What sampling issues arise with such an approach?
7 Discuss the proposition that Facebook is just a passing fad.
8 Discuss the view that this approach is only appropriate for new product development.

Related websites

Facebook: **www.facebook.com**
Face Group: **www.facegroup.co.uk**
Nielsen BuzzMetrics: **www.nielsen-online.com**

Issue 8
Multi-mode interviewing

Different strokes

Mixed-mode research, where one research survey might embrace several different fieldwork methods side by side, is a relatively recent development. It may be achieved by conducting some interviews in, say, CATI and others on the web. Or it may take this a stage further, and allow respondents to switch modes part way through: a variation I refer to as *multi-mode interviewing*.

Research agencies have been reluctant to add mixed-mode research to their toolkits. There

John Tomaselli/Alamy

are mutterings of irreconcilable modal differences, and the subject is quietly ignored. So last year, I decided to investigate the area in some detail, not just from the technological perspective, but from a methodological standpoint as well.

Those who dare to mix modes find it does improve response rates, sometimes quite dramatically if respondents get to choose the mode for themselves. John Allison and Chris O'Konis, researchers at the US financial firm Fidelity, writing in *Quirks* magazine (July 2002), found that a staggering 88 per cent of their customers contacted by CATI agreed to participate in the web survey. While this certainly included a number of covert soft refusals, some 54 per cent of them did complete the web survey, and a small proportion also completed the survey on the telephone.

But completion rate is not the only issue. More insidious is the effect of low response on coverage. A mixed-mode approach will inevitably expose the inbuilt tendencies of some modes to favour certain types of respondent.

CATI, especially on consumer surveys, has been observed to favour female participants, older respondents, the less well educated and those outside of urban areas. Web surveys tend to favour males, the young, the better educated and so on. Mixing modes allows you to turn these in-built biases to your advantage.

It is an aspect of mixed mode research that has gained the interest of social researchers, who have been pioneers in this field. Quota sampling and weighting (methods treated with suspicion if not disdain in social research), can do nothing to ensure proper representation of more marginalised, socially excluded groups. Only face-to-face contact will. Yet, as Hester Rippen reported in a case study in last year's *Research IT Review*, for a study aiming for 90,000 completes, in-person interviews across the board would be far too costly and time consuming. However, by using face-to-face selectively, the research agencies involved scored a balanced response and achieved the target of 60 per cent participation.

Mixed-mode research deserves more attention than it is getting from agencies at present. But my research also revealed that it deserves better attention to detail from the software manufacturers. Simply bolting a web module onto a CATI system does not make a true multi-modal research system: there are several layers of challenges to overcome.

Coverage and calibration – the major research hurdles

At a research level, the challenge is twofold. The first is sampling. Different modes display different characteristics in terms of coverage, especially when defined in terms of non-response. As already noted, some groups are harder to reach by one more than another. The second, which is often quoted as the justification for not doing mixed-mode research, is the variability in response or 'modal effect' experienced between different modes. Notionally, for example, the respondent gives a different response because she is responding on the web as opposed to the phone or paper.

Research has shown that there are some systematic differences in the kinds of responses obtained by each mode. However modal variation is a question of degree, and is covertly present in every unimodal survey. A virtue of mixed mode research is its ability to make this explicit and allow you to take it into account when it might matter.

How mode can influence answers given

- Computer-assisted methods provide more complete responses, and web surveys tend to be more complete than CATI.
- Verbatim responses tend to be longer on the Internet than on the telephone. However, some of this difference may still be a social rather than a psychological difference, as web respondents tend to be more articulate.
- Where stimulus material is presented on screen, respondents tend to give longer and more detailed responses.
- Answers to scale questions vary by mode. CATI respondents tend to favour the extreme points whereas web respondents tend to use the entire range of the scale.
- On socially sensitive subjects, respondents will admit to more on the web than they will via CATI or CAPI interview, or on paper.

Reducing complexity is the greatest technical challenge

The central challenge of true mixed-mode research is to minimise the operational complexity of combining both administered and self-completion interviewing across a range of devices and methods, and end up with data in the same place and in the same format, ready for analysis. Get this wrong, and you can find fieldwork costs can treble.

I contacted ten of the major software manufacturers to ask them what capabilities they had built into their solutions.

SPSS, with its Dimensions range, uses the concept of the multi-modal player that will self-adjust your survey instrument to the mode. While web and paper are implemented, CATI is still represented by two legacy products that do not support this.

Nebu, Askia, Pulse Train's new Bellview Fusion range, MI Pro and Sphinx had strong templating capabilities that also let surveys self-adjust between modes.

Nebu, Askia and Pulse Train handled modal switching particularly well, which is supremely important in multi-mode studies. Askia has an inbuilt preferred contact mode in its sample definition. Nebu provided two complementary mode-switch methods: 'dynamic' where interviewers or respondents can switch at any time, and 'static' which is script induced. Both then handle the messy business of despatching e-mails, or setting up CATI appointments.

Bellview Fusion offers similar flexibility by being able to 'abandon' an interview at any point, switch it back to the previous mode and even integrate it with its dialler, so an interviewer could be on the phone to a struggling web respondent in a matter of seconds.

All six mentioned so far proved the much-needed consolidated results database. Askia and MI Pro have good solutions for bringing offline interviews (CAPI, or in MI Pro's case, paper) back into the mix.

The ingenuity dries up in these first-generation, multi-mode products when it comes to tackling the research issues of calibration, coverage and controlling the modal influence. Opinion One takes modal bias very seriously, and controls the whole online experience to make it identical in all its three modes (kiosk, CAPI and web). It also contains a question type that allows controlled, closed-list recording of spontaneous mentions in web and kiosk interviews, by using an approximate on a concealed list, so you can follow on prompted questions using the same closed list. No one has tackled the sampling issues and there was little evidence of any understanding of the more research-centric issues. Mixed-mode surveys remain a challenge because, as yet, no one package yet contains all of the features necessary to do it properly. Technology providers are understandably reluctant to put more effort into developing features that few agency customers are using.

Mixed-mode research offers one of the most serious ways to tackle falling response rates. The issues of modal variation are not insurmountable, and neither are the technical challenges. The research methodologist Don Dillman (at the University of Washington Social and Economic Research Center) no longer sees mixed mode as an option in the future. At a recent Gallup symposium, he made this challenge: 'Survey organisations, whether they are in universities, in private-sector organisations or in government organisations, are going to have to change dramatically in some ways in order to do effective surveys as we bring these new technologies online and still use our other technologies where they work.'

Key features of the ideal multi-mode research

- One common survey authoring for all modes;
- different templates applied automatically to different modes to ensure each looks right;
- mode-specific text alternatives, in addition to support for foreign language translations;
- a single database for all survey data, updated in real-time;
- the ability to determine the mode of initial contact from the sample;
- easy, instant switching of any interview from one mode to another;
- automated concealment of any interviewer-recorded data when switching a self-completion mode;
- support for reminders and rule-based switching back to the original mode if the contact goes cold;
- management tools that let you view progress across all modes and identify separate modes;
- real-time quota controls that operate across all modes;
- support for mode-specific questions or question types;
- ability to tag and analyse questions by the mode of answering.

This article is written by Tim Macer and appeared in the March 2004 edition of *Research in Business*, pp. 19–20 , and is published with the permission of the Market Research Society.

Links in the text

Chapter 6 – Collecting quantitative data
Chapter 7 – Designing questionnaires
Chapter 8 – Sampling methods

Potential areas for discussion

1 Why have research agencies been reluctant to undertake mixed-mode research?
2 Which types of interview mode are likely to suit which types of people?
3 Discuss the sampling issues involved in mixed mode studies.
4 Discuss the proposition that people's responses will vary depending on the mode of the interview.
5 Should respondents be able to switch mode at any point of an interview?
6 Discuss the issue of declining response rates.

Related websites

University of Washington Social and Economic Research Centre: **www.sesrc.wsu.edu**
Askia Software: **www.askia.com**
MI Pro: **www.mipro.no**
Nebu Software: **www.nebu.com**
Pulse Train Software: **www.confirmit.com**

Issue 9
Using technology for data collection

How has technology made fieldwork more reliable and more efficient?

For even the most capable field-work provider, the client from hell is the one that meddles and tinkers – and is still e-mailing over changes as the fieldwork goes live. For the buyer, the nightmare is not knowing that a hugely expensive survey is going badly wrong, until the results beg more questions than they answer and it is too late to repair the damage. Today, technology can help everyone avoid these expensive mistakes by making what was historically a closed process into an open one,

Simon Belcher/Alamy

and allowing both parties to anticipate and correct errors. In the worst case, they now make it possible to take decisive corrective action, perhaps only sacrificing an hour of online or telephone interviewing, or a day of CAPI interviewing, not the whole job.

Most of today's software used to support fieldwork done on the Internet can permit client access to monitor work before and during fieldwork. Mistakes or problems undetected by one pair of eyes can often be picked up by another, especially those with more subject-specific expertise, as the client will often have. Increasingly, these features are now spreading to CATI and CAPI systems too, allowing remote monitoring from anywhere you can open a web browser. The older technologies, notably Quancept or Surveycraft or the old Bellview CATI, did not offer such a way in, but their modern equivalents, like mr Interview, Bellview Fusion, Nebu, Voxco and others too, provide web access to their back-office functions. This means the fieldwork company can set up specific logins which let each client see their own work in progress.

Usually, the level of access can be tailored to fit in with your comfort zone, or that of your supplier. For example, a client may be able to view reports but not adjust quotas, whereas fieldwork managers, even when out of the office, will have the ability to modify quotas or make other changes. Having early sight of preliminary results is one of the major benefits of web-enabled interviewing software. Yet the fear of the meddlesome client is, more often than not, causing fieldwork providers to close off these options, or at least not to advertise them to their clients. Some fear that the client may spot an error before they do – something which can be considered to be an advantage, rather than a disadvantage. Others express the fear that giving clients access to partial results can result in false conclusions being drawn too early. But are these good enough reasons to keep the client in the dark? In a complex business such as information gathering, not everything will always go to plan. As anyone involved in customer satisfaction research will testify, problems, even trite errors, are unlikely to damage relationships in the long term provided that the recovery is swift and effective. Client access to fieldwork systems not only means that there is more than one interested party watching what is going on: it can also mean better early detection and a more fully informed decision about how best to react. In the past, reacting quickly has been particularly difficult to achieve with face-to face fieldwork, due to the inertia imposed by printing and distributing questionnaires and quota rosters to a distributed fieldwork force. The first generation of CAPI often conspired to increase this inertia, making it hard to recall or correct interviews once fieldwork had started, and impossible for interviewers to get round the problem. Now, companies are starting to experiment with wireless communications, so that quotas can be checked in real time, and completed results beamed back to the central database as soon as each interview is completed. These can also speed up the distribution process and allow for some controlled changes to be made to interview scripts even after the survey has gone into the field. For example, codeframes can be extended on the fly, in the way they can in CATI, to save interviewer and respondent time in handling semi-open questions such as product lists. There is hope that online CAPI should eventually reduce fieldwork cost, by eliminating wasted interviews and reducing physical distribution costs. Data-communication costs, at less than the price of a second-class postage stamp per interview, now make this extremely viable.

In urban areas, network coverage tends to be good enough now to be workable. But the cost of the hardware today, even though it has come down dramatically, means there is usually a mountain of capital investment that the fieldwork company has to climb before any savings can be realised. For the foreseeable future, speed and improved quality rather than cost are likely to be the greatest benefit. Others are looking to using mixed-mode interviewing to achieve cost reduction. Leave on one side the arguments about whether mixed-mode results are to be trusted, apart from observing that some of the most effective mixed-mode research is currently being done by national statistics offices and by social researchers, where response rates below 85 per cent are likely to result in the fieldwork being abandoned! The trick is to shift as many interviews online as is possible and only use the more expensive methods where respondents are unable or unwilling to self-complete on the web. But to actually save any money, your fieldwork agency must be using one of the new-generation, web-enabled systems, such as those we mentioned earlier. If not, any potential savings will be consumed in extra programming time, as a different script is written for different unconnected interviewing systems for CATI, CAPI and web.

The modern tools also make it easy for interviews to switch from mode to mode. For example, after an initial contact on the phone, the respondent is offered the option to complete online. A very truthful inducement can be offered that it will be quicker and more convenient if they have access to the Internet. If the respondent agrees, then their e-mail address is captured, and the system instantly generates an e-mail containing the link to the survey. In reverse, several of the new systems also provide a 'call me' button, from the web survey, which results in an interviewer placing an outbound call to the respondent, and transfers the web interview to CATI mode. There are plenty of other areas where an enlightened use of technology can result in huge administrative time savings.

This article appeared in the June 2005 edition of *Research Decisions*, pp. 19–22, and is published with the permission of the Market Research Society.

Links in the text

Chapter 2 – Collecting quantitative data
Chapter 10 – Presenting the research results

Potential areas for discussion

1 Discuss the advantages and disadvantages of permitting client access to monitor fieldwork (from a client's perspective and then from a researcher's perspective).
2 Why would you change quotas once a survey has started?
3 Discuss the issue of mixed-mode interviewing.
4 What issues arise from changing interview scripts once they are in the field?
5 Discuss the changing roles and relationships of the clients and the agencies.

Related websites

University of Washington Social and Economic Research Centre: **www.sesrc.wsu.edu**
Nebu Software: **www.nebu.com**
Voxco Software: **www.voxco.com**

Issue 10
Clients going direct to respondents

Direct approach

An increasing number of clients are cutting out the research 'middle man' and talking directly to their customers. Mike Savage looks at the growth of 'direct-to-consumer' programmes, and the implications for MR suppliers.

When Microsoft UK set up special forums for its staff to meet their customers, it did so as a direct result of research – the software giant's customers were complaining that they had had enough of it. 'They didn't want to be surveyed by people over the web,' reveals Microsoft UK's Customer Loyalty Manager, Valerie Bennett. 'They wanted to come and talk to Microsoft face-to-face.' Now they can, on 'Theme Days' organised by Bennett to talk over issues of common concern with Microsoft personnel.

Iain Masterton/Alamy

Market research is no longer seen as the de facto solution to business problems; and Microsoft is not the only company that views the days when MR alone could interpret customer behaviour as over. With its roots in retail, where managers were encouraged to mingle with customers on the shop floor, the practice of going direct to the consumer has now spread in various guises to companies as diverse as Ford, Birds Eye Walls, Barclays and BSkyB.

Often these programmes are run by the research department, which has had to adapt to a new role. No longer the sole intermediary between a company and its customers, in-house researchers are taking a step back to coordinate customer contact and tie the results of these meetings in with existing research programmes.

'We are primarily facilitators of consumer insight with responsibility for identifying those which can be most powerfully harnessed to drive our brands,' explains Bill Parton, market research controller for Kraft Foods. 'Ultimately, however, it is our brand and customer marketers who must translate insights into strategy and execution. To do this it is not enough to intellectually understand the insight; they need to feel it. The only way they can do this is through direct experience.'

Kraft Foods first introduced direct-to-consumer techniques in November 1998, with the initial aim of helping to build broader understanding of its consumers' lives. It has since become part of the company's culture. Parton says that the biggest challenge for researchers and marketers alike is to go beyond behaviour, to understand what really motivates consumers. To do this Kraft is trying to help its people develop some of the skills employed by research. 'It's not about the future of research,' Parton states. 'It's about the future of marketing. They are the guys who have to come up with the ideas.'

Meeting people who place their choice of instant coffee near the bottom of life's priorities can provide a much-needed change of view for marketers who steep themselves in a category day after day. 'It's a good reality check,' comments Gavin Emsden, Beverages Research Manager at Nestlé. 'Even going to groups and sitting behind the glass is not the same as sitting down with the consumer and talking with them.'

'It is tremendously powerful in getting your store to think about the customer,' enthuses Asda's Head of Market Research, Darryl Burchell, who is teaching staff how to get the most out of focus groups and accompanied shops. 'If you work in a store day in, day out, you see the store from an operational perspective, rather than a customer's perspective. What better way to see the customer's perspective than to accompany them on a shopping trip?'

Direct-to-consumer programmes also spread the experience of customer insight to a far wider audience than is reached by traditional market research, Burchell points out. The majority of MR may still be done by Burchell and his team, but they alone do not have the resources to research each of Asda's 227 stores.

While direct-to-consumer programmes could be described as a 'quick and dirty' way of getting research done, few clientside researchers regard these as threatening the work of MR suppliers. Kraft Foods conducts many direct-to-consumer studies at early stages of development long before it becomes economically sensible to commission MR. Bill Parton believes this early work-out for fledgling ideas leads to better briefs for research projects.

The aims of Van den Bergh Foods' direct-to-consumer programme, 'Consumer Connexion', are very different to the learning it gets from market research data, points out Group Insight Manager Stephen Donaldson.

'This programme is subjective by its design and nature. This is not an objective piece of market research.' The three-year-old programme hasn't affected Van den Bergh's appetite for basic MR data, Donaldson stresses. 'Market research still plays the role of the voice of the consumer in our business decision making. This [Consumer Connexion] is making you more aware of your customers and giving you a better understanding of them, so you make better decisions.'

Donaldson believes companies that encourage direct customer contact will thrive and is hoping that Van den Bergh's parent, Unilever, will use his experiences as a model throughout the entire group. However, direct-to-consumer programmes are not easy to introduce. Time-consuming get-togethers that have no immediate benefit are not easy to initiate in companies working to a goal-driven culture. The programmes also have to be carefully managed, to make sure managers lacking in research experience don't jump to the wrong conclusions, and to maintain the freshness that gives the programmes their value.

Despite the hurdles, direct-to-consumer is growing. It is one way of maximising learning from a tightly controlled budget. Management buy-in is easier to come by if the board has adopted a philosophy of customer focus. Direct-to-consumer offers an edge over the competition in a market where customers are increasingly perceived to be calling the shots.

'This kind of approach will only become more common,' observes Karen Wise, joint MD for Martin Hamblin's consumer and business division. 'Our clients are looking for additional insights and involvement with their end users and we appreciate that this practice can do this. However, there's a strong argument that without the professional skills that an agency has, a lot is lost.' Wise suggests convening three-way workshops where the client, its customers and the research agency all work together. 'Through encouraging our clients to meet their customers face to face, we will involve them more in the research process and be able to engage them further in the findings – crucial for the success of any project.'

Even if companies are not operating schemes on the scale of Asda or Van den Bergh Foods, contact with consumers has become a common component of company induction and training programmes. The market research industry is also seeing a growth in the use of methodologies which bridge traditional MR and direct-to-consumer techniques, such as extended focus groups where traditionally passive viewers emerge from behind the mirror after a group to address issues they are interested in directly to the participants.

However, the growth of direct-to-consumer techniques also sounds a note of warning that research buyers are no longer satisfied with traditional research. Although some clients say direct-to-consumer programmes have not dented research budgets, agencies should also take note of companies like Microsoft UK, where the take-up of direct-to-consumer techniques forms part of a more fundamental shift in attitudes to research. The growth of new ways of interrogating the consumer will not eat into research budgets only as long as MR can keep proving its worth.

Companies move closer to their consumers

Asda – Customer Listening Programme

How long has it been running?
Since 1992.

Who manages it?
Coordinated/facilitated by the market research department.

Who takes part?
All managers within the business, both at Asda House and instore.

How often is it run?
Frequency varies by department, but typically at least once a month.

What methods are used?
The programme includes focus groups, moderated by Asda personnel, with a mixture of professionally recruited respondents and customers who had complaints or suggestions, and accompanied shops. Customer suggestion cards reviewed weekly.

Van den Bergh Foods (now part of Unilever Bestfoods) – Consumer Connexion

How long has it been running?
Since 1997.

Who manages it?
The consumer insight department (formerly called market research) with an external agency, QRS.

Who takes part in it?
All departments – marketing, R&D, sales, etc.

How often is it run?
Ad hoc, depending on individual needs.

What methods are used?
Methods include but not limited to: in-home visit; store visit; cooking sessions; friendship pairs; mini-groups; and others.

Nestlé – Unnamed informal, ad hoc use

How long has it been running?
There has been marketing/sales contact with consumers going back many years. This has become more regular over the last two years.

Who manages it?
Market Intelligence – whoever is responsible for the product area the approach is being used on.

Who takes part in it?
Market Intelligence, marketing and, as appropriate, staff from the category, technical and sensory departments.

How often is it run?
No fixed time scale.

What methods are used?
Generally group discussions or depths – usually accompanied shops or in-home interviews, but use other methods as well, such as accompanied visits to coffee shops.

This article appeared in the October 2000 edition of *Research*, and is published with the permission of the Market Research Society.

Links in the text

Chapter 1 – The role of marketing research and customer information in decision making
Chapter 2 – The marketing research process

Potential areas for discussion

1 What are the benefits of going directly to customers?
2 Discuss the proposition that 'it is not enough to intellectually understand the insight; they (marketing personnel) need to feel it'.
3 What implications do 'direct-to-consumer' programmes have for marketing research agencies?
4 Why do you need both customer contact and marketing research?
5 What are the key weaknesses of the customer contact approach?
6 Discuss the value of extended group discussions.

Related websites

Microsoft UK: **www.microsoft.com/uk**
Ford: **www.ford.com**
Van den Bergh: **www.unilever.com**
Bird's Eye Walls: **www.birdseyefoods.com**
Barclays: **www.barclays.co.uk**
BskyB: **www.sky.com**
Kraft Foods: **www.kraft.com**
Asda: **www.asda.co.uk**

Issue 11
International research

Think global, act local

In a global market, say Kate Anderson and Holly Edmunds, the key to success is a combination of local knowledge and good management controls.

Remember the days when an international project would cover the UK, France, Germany and, at a push, that strange country called 'Benelux'? Well, those days are no more. International now means global, with single projects often spanning mature and developing markets across Europe, North America, Asia-Pacific (APAC) and, increasingly, Latin America and the Middle East. Successful coordination of projects on such a scale requires local knowledge, research skills and meticulous attention to quality control.

[apply pictures]/Alamy

Do the right thing

But first and foremost it requires a strong grasp on ethics. Several associations and organisations publish guidelines, but those most applicable to the global research field are embedded in the International Code of Marketing and Social Research Practice developed jointly by the International Chamber of Commerce (ICC) and the European Society for Opinion & Marketing Research (ESOMAR). It provides guidelines for ethical practices between clients and vendors, and vendors and respondents.

As well as ensuring that you treat local partners appropriately, it is critical to stay focused on the welfare of your own staff. Following a couple of scares years ago in which one researcher bore witness first-hand to a military coup and another's hotel was placed under siege, RS Consulting implemented a very strict travel policy that removes ambiguity from the decision of whether travel should be undertaken, and does not leave potentially tricky decisions to the individual researchers.

We now adhere to the Foreign Office's recommendations on travel hot-spots; and will veto travel requested by a client if it considers the risk too great. But staff are also at liberty to refuse to travel on grounds of personal safety, even if the Foreign Office deems the market in question safe and the company veto has not been applied.

This does not mean that a travel hot-spot becomes a research no-go zone. Rather, pragmatic solutions must be found that enable direct access to local research teams without risking the wellbeing of staff.

You can, for example, hold briefings and debriefs in the nearest safe market. When the Foreign Office embargoed travel to Indonesia, RS Consulting researchers met their Indonesian research partners in Singapore.

Similarly, you could choose a supplier from a neighbouring market to cover the hot-spot in question. We conduct an annual market-sizing study covering 20 markets worldwide; the study is highly complex, and briefing the field teams and monitoring the initial interviews face-to-face are critical quality controls. Rather than exclude Colombia on the grounds that neither the agency nor its client wishes to send staff there, we have commissioned an Argentinian provider to deliver the Colombian fieldwork, thereby giving its staff direct access to the fieldwork team without placing them in any peril.

A simple plan

When considering the methodological approach for a global project, the challenge is to achieve the maximum consistency across markets while also catering for cultural and regional differences. One size so rarely fits all, and market differences can impact on every aspect of the job. The answer is to keep it simple. Sometimes you just have to defer to the lowest common denominator and design the project around the constraints imposed by the least advanced market. For example, while a web-based adaptive conjoint approach may be feasible in a developed market, elsewhere reality is likely to dictate the need for a paper-based, full-profile exercise.

Local partners are a key source of information and should be consulted at the design stage rather than once the research approach is a fait accompli. And, when asking for advice, make sure you ask the right question: 'What approach would you recommend?' is always better than 'Is approach X doable?'

Close cooperation with experienced local providers is, in fact, crucial. For example, standard focus groups are do-able in Japan, but inadvisable. Group dynamics are often hampered by observance of social hierarchy which seriously compromises the quantity and the quality of the information yield. Local partners conduct hundreds of focus groups each year and may not advise against them, but results tend to be inferior to those from groups in other markets – especially for B2B audiences. Close discussions with local partners have revealed mini-groups, friendship groups and depth interviews as good alternatives.

Similarly, web surveys can be implemented in France, but – unless you are using a panel provider with suitable measures in place to counter low strike rates and to incentivise participation effectively – the attrition rate between invites and completes is likely to cause you many a sleepless night. Indeed you may exhaust your sample source before filling your quotas.

Soap of the day

But there are some things that local research partners are just not going to volunteer. An obvious example would be if they are pretending to be something they are not. This is particularly true of start-ups in developing markets. Imagine the consternation when one RS Consulting project manager visited a prospective research partner in India only to discover that the company was a soap factory that had decided to diversify. Needless to say, its suitability as a provider of fieldwork on high-tech product adoption beggared belief.

Obviously the time for such surprises is when evaluating partners, not once the project you have commissioned from them starts to go mysteriously and horribly wrong! Wherever possible, seek references from reputable clients, discussing these directly and in person if at all possible. But you should also visit your potential partner's operations, and meet with key members of the management team.

Boomtown rats

There is little you can do to influence the dynamics of local employment markets. For example, the Chinese market is booming and good agency staff rapidly move on to bigger and better things. This makes it difficult to ensure that adequately trained staff are allocated to your project, let alone to develop working relationships with key staff such as project managers, moderators and interpreters.

The solution is to focus efforts on vetting the local staff allocated to your projects and to training and briefing local project team members to deliver the standard of work you expect.

Mr 10 per cent

In dealings with US fieldwork vendors, you will no doubt have noted their tendency to quote a price +/– 10 per cent. Strangely enough, in over 38 years of combined experience of dealing with US vendors the two authors can count on the fingers of one hand the number of times they experienced a 10 per cent reduction in costs due to the project's being easier to complete than expected!

Worse still, some vendors, having quoted a fixed price (+/– 10 per cent of course) think nothing of adjusting their cost per interview on a daily basis in accordance with the strike rate.

Again, sadly, it would appear that the only way for prices to go is up. All you can do is pick your vendors carefully, lay down strict rules for prices adjustments and work on the assumption that the +10 per cent charge will apply.

Clear as mud

Instead of worrying whether your local partner has a clear grasp of requirements, you can ask the local team to play back to you, in their own words, the tasks they have been charged with. This method will unearth misunderstandings you couldn't have hoped to anticipate and is particularly critical in Asian markets where a reluctance to appear rude by saying no makes the question 'Is everything clear?' pointless.

Rules of the road

1 **Always maintain respect for the local culture and customs.** Awareness of public holidays and of social taboos and laws (particularly on personal data privacy and payment of incentives) can be key.
2 **Never assume that knowledge of one market can act as a proxy for understanding neighbouring markets.** You are particularly likely to come unstuck if you apply this practice to costings. If you thought Sweden was expensive, just wait until you cost an identical project in Norway!
3 **Be forthcoming with local partners.** For research to succeed on a global scale, you must provide them with information to the best of your ability and also accept their inputs. They are your best source of local information, and you need to have a relationship based on mutual trust.
4 **Ensure that you have direct access to the local researchers, not just the expat research director.** Make it clear that you want to meet the researchers warts-and-all and that this won't scare you off. This should help ensure that you receive up-to-date status reports on your project as well as timely notification of issues arising.
5 **Back-checking of translations is vital.** The omission or misinterpretation of a single word – or the erroneous cut-and-paste of a paragraph – can drastically alter your questionnaire.
6 **You can't run these projects on a nine-to-five basis.** Accept the need for early morning calls to Asia and late night calls to the US to keep abreast of the project. No news is not good news: never assume that all is ticking along nicely. Work on the basis that there will be problems, and understand that your core function as manager of international research is to seek out and rectify them.

Kate Anderson is a director of RS Consulting Ltd, UK; Holly Edmunds is managing partner of RS Consulting LLC, US

This article appeared in the July 2005 edition of *Research*, and is published with the permission of the Market Research Society.

Links in the text

Chapter 2 – The marketing research process

Potential areas for discussion

1 Choose two countries and discuss the cultural and regional differences that may impact on marketing research.
2 How will the growth in online surveys impact on international research projects?
3 Discuss how you would evaluate potential partners.
4 Which countries would you consider to be the most difficult to undertake research in? Why?

Related websites

For up-to-the-minute information on travel hot-spots and immunisation requirements, consult the Foreign Office's site: **www.fco.gov.uk**

For useful information on languages spoken, time zones and public holidays, use **www.wrc.lingnet.org/areastd.html**, and for worldwide country statistics, visit **www.worldbank.org/data/countrydata/countrydata.html**

Issue 12
The respondents' view of research

Derek Eccleston, research director of eDigitalResearch, takes a look at how survey respondents really feel about taking part in research, and how we can make sure they keep doing it.

The way consumers interact with one another and the world in general is changing rapidly. The explosion in social media networks and online forums has provided more channels through which consumers can interact and engage with brands. Consequently, CEOs and senior executives are looking at new and faster ways to tap into the consumer consciousness. Some tried and tested survey methods are no longer satisfying these needs and there is now more competition than ever in the market research industry.

But why do some research methods work well where others fail? To answer this we decided to ask the respondents themselves to gauge what motivates them and what would keep them engaged.

Respondents want to influence products and services

'I enjoy doing surveys and I have been very pleased to see the outcome . . . (seeing a newspaper ad or a DVD cover for example where I saw various suggestions of styling before a choice was made and the designs went "public").'

Craig Holmes/Alamy

'I enjoy doing them and feel I might make a difference. I recently did an online one about different websites. One site was very bad and I made this quite clear. I noticed that this company has now got a new website and feel my input helped to change this.'

'I got a real buzz from seeing an advert the other day that I had commented on when it was in development.'

The first thing that becomes clear is that people take part in surveys because they want to influence products and services. Eighty-two per cent agreed or strongly agreed that they are motivated to take part in market research because they want to influence what future products or services look like. Almost nobody disagreed with this – a result that some may find surprising.

The second biggest motive was people wanting their voices to be heard while, interestingly, 74 per cent of people take part because they enjoy the experience of participating. Less than half overall said they only take part for the incentive or reward.

Market research draws in those who want to be listened to and make a difference, but people are creatures of comfort and will only participate if it is quick, easy and convenient to do so. People will not go out of their way to give their opinion. If we do not respect respondents' time, do not acknowledge their contribution and do not communicate with them on a relevant and interesting subject, we risk discouraging participation. The importance of acknowledgement is confirmed by the 58 per cent who stated that incentives or rewards do make them much more likely to take part in a survey.

Respondents expect to be in control of when and how they communicate

'I like that I am able to complete them in my own time, in my own home and not have my time taken up by an interviewer calling at my house or telephoning me.'

'(I) can do it at my leisure and not be pressured.'

'It enables me to understand the questions properly and take time to consider my answer.'

'I can take it when it is convenient to me and spend as much time as I like doing it.'

'I am in control! I can do it when I feel like it.'

People like to have control over the survey process and complete surveys in their own time and on their own terms. Respondents were more ready to spend longer doing online surveys – around half said that the appropriate length for an online survey was between five and ten minutes, while for phone surveys the same proportion said the right length was five minutes or less. Twenty-nine per cent said ten to fifteen minutes was OK for online, more than double the number who thought that was an appropriate length for a phone survey. Anything over fifteen minutes was considered too long for either sort of survey by more than 80 per cent of respondents.

Perhaps surprisingly, given what we hear about response rates and survey fatigue, over a fifth of respondents in our survey said they would take part in more market research in the future than they do now. Most said the same and hardly anyone said less. There's certainly room for that result to be better but, all in all, our industry does appear to be delivering a positive respondent experience.

Respondents are social

'It is great to meet a diverse number of people and to hear everyone's opinions and to be able to bounce ideas around.'

'I like the experience of the group discussion with people from all over the country. It is interesting to chat together and a lot of opinions can be expressed quickly.'

'(I like having) the opportunity to discuss a topic with a group of people rather than just putting my own opinion across.'

Respondents like to be in control of when and how they communicate, but other aspects that market researchers need to consider are the fact that people are social and expressive, and want to share views with others without restriction.

Respondents want to enjoy the experience

> 'I enjoy the interaction between the participants. It is interesting to share views. Sometimes other people's views make me see things in a new light.'

The general feeling among respondents was the genuine desire to meet or share their views through group discussions. As evidenced earlier in our survey, people like to express their views, and responses to this question highlight the fact that people find it a more enjoyable experience if they can express themselves publicly, without the veil of anonymity that survey research guidelines generally require.

Respondents don't want restrictions on how they express themselves

> '(I like it because) we are given more options/ability to answer questions: i.e. not just multiple-choice answers.'

Respondents also found it more enjoyable to be given open questions, as opposed to multiple-choice, as this gave them more opportunity to express their views. It's a finding that points to a bright future for online qualitative and Web 2.0 techniques that allow interaction.

Having addressed motivations and enjoyment, we can understand why some research approaches are working better than others – respondents vote with their fingers. One thing is clear: building respondent-focused research is about more than just mode, it is about method.

We have witnessed this ourselves in the different response rates that we have got through sending out online surveys to clients. It is much more beneficial to actively manage the client panel, as this places the respondents at the heart of a multi-layered engagement plan which sees response rates in the range of 30–50 per cent. Where the panel is not actively managed, response rates drop to just 10 per cent.

It is clear that we can achieve higher response rates if we build programmes that encourage a sense of influence, where the process is enjoyable, fun and social, and where the surveys are flexible and convenient.

A great example of this is the success of online communities such as the one we run for New Look, where the traditional question and answer dynamic is disrupted by customers offering insights without being asked. This is achieved by making the content engaging and making consumers feel like they are making a difference to the products and services.

The future

There is a clear and sizeable opportunity for emerging online methodologies, and also for traditional focus groups, with their perceived higher incentive levels.

When we asked which type of survey invitations respondents would accept in the future, almost 50 per cent said online focus groups or mini communities – more than said they would participate over the telephone. This is despite low familiarity with these online methods, with only 16 per cent of the sample having already taken part in online focus groups or communities for research before. There is a similar picture for web chats, with 28 per cent saying they would accept an invitation to take part whereas only 4 per cent have already participated in a web chat. While 38 per cent said they would attend a traditional focus group, 98 per cent said they would complete an online survey.

We need to keep in mind, of course, that an online survey itself has limited scope for judging attitudes to online surveys in comparison with the alternatives. But even within the online sphere, the enthusiasm for new and different approaches, particularly those involving interaction and a social element, is encouraging.

Consumers enjoy a richer and more flexible set of communication options today and this is shaping the expectations, preferences and behaviour we witness in market research. While certain motivations will endure, we expect to see an ongoing evolution of the respondent experience, shaped in part by technologies such as Twitter and Facebook or whatever the next one might be.

Survey methodology

An online survey was sent to two panels: eGlobalPanel, which is a general consumer panel owned by eDigitalResearch, which is incentivised through a prize draw but is also a recruitment pool for qualitative sessions, and a well-known access panel where respondents receive a direct monetary payment equivalent per survey.

Fieldwork was conducted between 15 and 25 January 2010. We collected a total of 1,501 completes, measured as those who reached the end of the survey. These were split fairly evenly between eGlobalPanel (721 completes, which was a 49 per cent response rate) and the third-party panel (780 completes, 14 per cent response rate).

The modal time taken to complete the survey was 6m to 6m 30s. We acknowledge an inherent weakness in the idea of asking for feedback on a range of different research types through a single mode, but we see the findings as informative despite that obvious limitation.

This article appeared in the March 2010 edition of *Research*, and is published with the permission of the Market Research Society.

Links in the text

Chapter 6 – Collecting quantitative data
Chapter 7 – Designing questionnaires

Potential areas for discussion

1 Discuss the extent to which these findings reflect your ideas of surveys.
2 What are your expectations as to how these views are going to change in the future?
3 Discuss the role of incentives in obtaining respondent cooperation.
4 Discuss the future of marketing research.

Related websites

eDigitalResearch: **www.edigitalresearch.com**

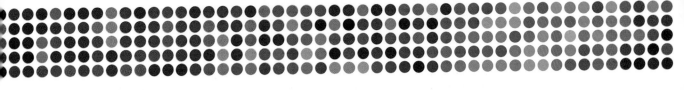

Appendix 1

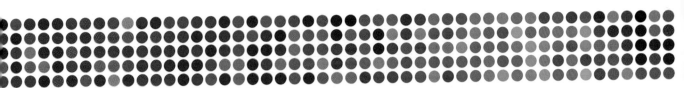

Table 1 Standard normal distribution: Z values

Values in this table give the area under the curve between the mean and Z standard deviations above the mean. For example, for $Z = 1.75$, the area under the curve between the mean and Z is 0.4599.

Z	0.00	0.01	0.02	0.03	0.04	0.05	0.06	0.07	0.08	0.09
0.0	0.0000	0.0040	0.0080	0.0120	0.0160	0.0199	0.0239	0.0279	0.0319	0.0359
0.1	0.0398	0.0438	0.0478	0.0517	0.0557	0.0596	0.0636	0.0675	0.0714	0.0753
0.2	0.0793	0.0832	0.0871	0.0910	0.0948	0.0987	0.1026	0.1064	0.1103	0.1141
0.3	0.1179	0.1217	0.1255	0.1293	0.1331	0.1368	0.1406	0.1443	0.1480	0.1517
0.4	0.1554	0.1591	0.1628	0.1664	0.1700	0.1736	0.1772	0.1808	0.1844	0.1879
0.5	0.1915	0.1950	0.1985	0.2019	0.2054	0.2088	0.2123	0.2157	0.2190	0.2224
0.6	0.2257	0.2291	0.2324	0.2357	0.2389	0.2422	0.2454	0.2486	0.2518	0.2549
0.7	0.2580	0.2612	0.2642	0.2673	0.2704	0.2734	0.2764	0.2794	0.2823	0.2852
0.8	0.2881	0.2910	0.2939	0.2967	0.2995	0.3023	0.3051	0.3078	0.3106	0.3133
0.9	0.3159	0.3186	0.3212	0.3238	0.3264	0.3289	0.3315	0.3340	0.3365	0.3389
1.0	0.3413	0.3438	0.3461	0.3485	0.3508	0.3531	0.3554	0.3577	0.3599	0.3621
1.1	0.3643	0.3665	0.3686	0.3708	0.3729	0.3749	0.3770	0.3790	0.3810	0.3830
1.2	0.3849	0.3869	0.3888	0.3907	0.3925	0.3944	0.3962	0.3980	0.3997	0.4015
1.3	0.4032	0.4049	0.4066	0.4082	0.4099	0.4115	0.4131	0.4147	0.4162	0.4177
1.4	0.4192	0.4207	0.4222	0.4236	0.4251	0.4265	0.4279	0.4292	0.4306	0.4319
1.5	0.4332	0.4345	0.4357	0.4370	0.4382	0.4394	0.4406	0.4418	0.4429	0.4441
1.6	0.4552	0.4463	0.4474	0.4484	0.4495	0.4505	0.4515	0.4525	0.4535	0.4545
1.7	0.4554	0.4564	0.4573	0.4582	0.4591	0.4599	0.4608	0.4616	0.4625	0.4633
1.8	0.4641	0.4649	0.4656	0.4664	0.4671	0.4678	0.4686	0.4693	0.4699	0.4706
1.9	0.4713	0.4719	0.4726	0.4732	0.4738	0.4744	0.4750	0.4756	0.4761	0.4767
2.0	0.4772	0.4778	0.4783	0.4788	0.4793	0.4798	0.4803	0.4808	0.4812	0.4817
2.1	0.4821	0.4826	0.4830	0.4834	0.4838	0.4842	0.4846	0.4850	0.4854	0.4857
2.2	0.4861	0.4864	0.4868	0.4871	0.4875	0.4878	0.4881	0.4884	0.4887	0.4890
2.3	0.4893	0.4896	0.4898	0.4901	0.4904	0.4906	0.4909	0.4911	0.4913	0.4916
2.4	0.4918	0.4920	0.4922	0.4925	0.4927	0.4929	0.4931	0.4932	0.4934	0.4936
2.5	0.4938	0.4940	0.4941	0.4943	0.4945	0.4946	0.4948	0.4949	0.4951	0.4952
2.6	0.4953	0.4955	0.4956	0.4957	0.4959	0.4960	0.4961	0.4962	0.4963	0.4964
2.7	0.4965	0.4966	0.4967	0.4968	0.4969	0.4970	0.4971	0.4972	0.4973	0.4974
2.8	0.4974	0.4975	0.4976	0.4977	0.4977	0.4978	0.4979	0.4979	0.4980	0.4981
2.9	0.4981	0.4982	0.4982	0.4983	0.4984	0.4984	0.4985	0.4985	0.4986	0.4986
3.0	0.4986	0.4987	0.4987	0.4988	0.4988	0.4989	0.4989	0.4989	0.4990	0.4990

Table 2 Chi-square distribution

Entries in the table give chi-square values, where α is the area or probability in the upper tail of the chi-square distribution. For example, with 10 degrees of freedom and a 0.05 area in the upper tail, chi-square = 18.307.

Degrees of freedom	Area in upper tail									
	0.995	0.99	0.975	0.95	0.90	0.10	0.05	0.025	0.01	0.005
1			0.001	0.004	0.016	2.706	3.841	5.024	6.635	7.879
2	0.010	0.020	0.051	0.103	0.211	4.605	5.991	7.378	9.210	10.597
3	0.072	0.115	0.216	0.352	0.584	6.251	7.815	9.348	11.345	12.838
4	0.207	0.297	0.484	0.711	1.064	7.779	9.488	11.143	13.277	14.860
5	0.412	0.554	0.831	1.145	1.610	9.236	11.071	12.833	15.086	16.750
6	0.676	0.872	1.237	1.635	2.204	10.645	12.592	14.449	16.812	18.548
7	0.989	1.239	1.690	2.167	2.833	12.017	14.067	16.013	18.475	20.278
8	1.344	1.646	2.180	2.733	3.490	13.362	15.507	17.535	20.090	21.955
9	1.735	2.088	2.700	3.325	4.168	14.684	16.919	19.023	21.666	23.589
10	2.156	2.558	3.247	3.940	4.865	15.987	18.307	20.483	23.209	25.188
11	2.603	3.053	3.816	4.575	5.578	17.275	19.675	21.920	24.725	26.757
12	3.074	3.571	4.404	5.226	6.304	18.549	21.026	23.337	26.217	28.299
13	3.565	4.107	5.009	5.892	7.042	19.812	22.362	24.736	27.688	29.819
14	4.075	4.660	5.629	6.571	7.790	21.064	23.685	26.119	29.141	31.319
15	4.601	5.229	6.262	7.261	8.547	22.307	24.996	27.488	30.578	32.801
16	5.142	5.812	6.908	7.962	9.312	23.542	26.296	28.845	32.000	34.267
17	5.697	6.408	7.564	8.672	10.085	24.769	27.587	30.191	33.409	35.718
18	6.265	7.015	8.231	9.390	10.865	25.989	28.869	31.526	34.805	37.156
19	6.844	7.633	8.907	10.117	11.651	27.204	30.144	32.852	36.191	38.582
20	7.434	8.260	9.591	10.851	12.433	28.412	31.410	34.170	37.566	39.997
21	8.034	8.897	10.283	11.591	13.240	29.615	32.671	35.479	38.932	41.401
22	8.643	9.542	10.982	12.338	14.042	30.813	33.924	36.781	40.289	42.796
23	9.260	10.196	11.689	13.091	14.848	32.007	35.172	38.076	41.638	44.181
24	9.886	10.856	12.401	13.848	15.659	33.196	36.415	39.364	42.980	45.559
25	10.520	11.524	13.120	14.611	16.473	34.382	37.652	40.646	44.314	46.928
26	11.160	12.198	13.844	15.379	17.292	35.563	38.885	41.923	45.642	48.290
27	11.808	12.879	14.573	16.151	18.114	36.741	40.113	43.194	46.963	49.645
28	12.461	13.565	15.308	16.928	18.939	37.916	41.337	44.461	48.278	50.993
29	13.121	14.257	16.047	17.708	19.768	39.087	42.557	45.722	49.588	52.336
30	13.787	14.954	16.791	18.493	20.599	40.256	43.773	46.979	50.892	53.672
40	20.707	22.164	24.433	26.509	29.051	51.805	55.758	59.342	63.691	66.766
50	27.991	29.707	32.357	34.764	37.689	63.167	67.505	71.420	76.154	79.490
60	35.535	37.485	40.482	43.188	46.459	74.397	79.082	83.298	88.379	91.952
70	43.275	45.442	48.758	51.739	55.329	85.527	90.531	95.023	100.425	104.215
80	51.172	53.540	57.153	60.392	64.279	96.578	101.879	106.629	112.329	116.321
90	59.196	61.754	65.647	69.126	73.291	107.565	113.145	118.136	124.116	128.299
100	67.328	70.065	74.222	77.930	82.358	118.498	124.342	129.561	135.807	140.169

Table 3 *t* distribution

Entries in the table give *t* values for an area of probability in the upper tail of the *t* distribution. For example, with 10 degrees of freedom and a 0.025 area in the upper tail, $t_{.025} = 2.228$.

Degrees of freedom	Area in upper tail				
	0.10	0.05	0.025	0.01	0.005
1	3.078	6.314	12.706	31.821	63.657
2	1.886	2.920	4.303	6.965	9.925
3	1.638	2.353	3.182	4.541	5.841
4	1.533	2.132	2.776	3.747	4.604
5	1.476	2.015	2.571	3.365	4.032
6	1.440	1.943	2.447	3.143	3.707
7	1.415	1.895	2.365	2.998	3.499
8	1.397	1.860	2.306	2.896	3.355
9	1.383	1.833	2.262	2.821	3.250
10	1.372	1.812	2.228	2.764	3.169
11	1.363	1.796	2.201	2.718	3.106
12	1.356	1.782	2.179	2.681	3.055
13	1.350	1.771	2.160	2.650	3.012
14	1.345	1.761	2.145	2.624	2.977
15	1.341	1.753	2.131	2.602	2.947
16	1.337	1.746	2.120	2.583	2.921
17	1.333	1.740	2.110	2.567	2.898
18	1.330	1.734	2.101	2.552	2.878
19	1.328	1.729	2.093	2.539	2.861
20	1.325	1.725	2.086	2.528	2.845
21	1.323	1.721	2.080	2.518	2.831
22	1.321	1.717	2.074	2.508	2.819
23	1.319	1.714	2.069	2.500	2.807
24	1.318	1.711	2.064	2.492	2.797
25	1.316	1.708	2.060	2.485	2.787
26	1.315	1.706	2.056	2.479	2.779
27	1.314	1.703	2.052	2.473	2.771
28	1.313	1.701	2.048	2.467	2.763
29	1.311	1.699	2.045	2.462	2.756
30	1.310	1.697	2.042	2.457	2.750
40	1.303	1.684	2.021	2.423	2.704
60	1.296	1.671	2.000	2.390	2.660
120	1.289	1.658	1.980	2.358	2.617
infinity	1.282	1.645	1.960	2.326	2.576

Appendix 2

Snap Getting Started Guide

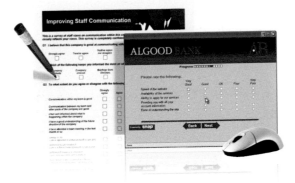

Should you require any technical support for the Snap survey software or any assistance with software licences, training and SurveyShop research services please contact us at one of our offices.

Details can be found at **www.snapsurveys.com** or under **About Snap 10** in the **Help** menu of the software.

snap

Contents

Snap

A Snap survey in seven easy steps

Snap is powerful, adaptable and flexible... As a software tool, it is powerful for designing, publishing and analysing surveys. It is adaptable in that it can design surveys for the web, email, paper, scanning, phone, PDAs, kiosks and tablet PCs. It is flexible in that any survey can be set up as "multi mode", using any combinations together in the same survey, such as web and paper, or kiosk, PDA and scan.

Finally, when all your replies have been received, there's no need to export your data to a spreadsheet or a stats program, Snap has it all. From tables to charts; from filters to weights, from descriptive to multivariate stats, it's all there in one software program.

This guide teaches you how to create and publish a web survey in seven easy steps. Snap provides you with both a structure for setting up your questions, together with a template that will generate a good looking questionnaire without you having to worry about fonts, buttons and the layout.

A Snap survey in seven easy steps

At the end of the seven steps you will have a questionnaire that looks like this...

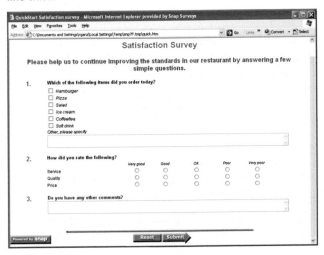

The next stage is to enhance the questionnaire by adding some graphics, together with routing so that only "relevant" questions are asked. We'll also access a question or two from one of the libraries supplied with the software.

Once that's complete, we'll show you how to generate an alternative "mode" to enable respondents to be able to complete the questionnaire if they don't have access to the web. In our example, we'll create a paper version.

Finally, we'll look at the analysis of a survey. We'll provide you with several hundred completed questionnaires and show you how to generate professional tables as well as a selection of charts.

So let's get started.....

Step 1: Start a new survey

When you first start Snap you are presented with the **Survey Overview Window** showing a list of the surveys stored in your current working directory in Documents and Settings.

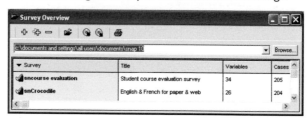

1. Click 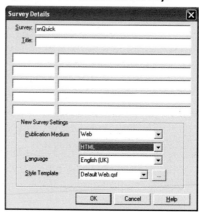 at the top of the **Survey Overview Window. A Survey Details** dialog box appears.

2. In the **Survey** field, type in a unique identifier, e.g. *Quick*.

3. Press [**Tab**] and enter a description in the field marked **Title**. Notice that as you tab to the **Title** field, Snap automatically prefixes the survey with the letters *sn*.Type in a title of **QuickStart Satisfaction Survey**.

4. Set the **Publication Medium** to **Web** and **HTML**. By default, **Language** is defined by your system and the **Style Template** is

A Snap survey in seven easy steps

set to Default Web.qsf. The style template determines the layout of your web questionnaire, together with the fonts and the buttons used in your questionnaire. Leave these as they are.

5. Click **[OK]** to create the questionnaire

The **Survey Details** dialog box is replaced by the **Questionnaire Window**, which opens in Design Mode and contains no questions, just a framework.

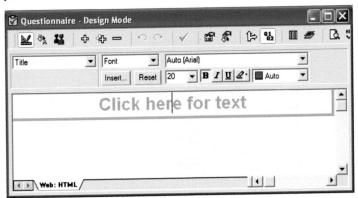

You are now ready to start creating your questionnaire… But first…

Snap has over a dozen different types of questions and fields. These range from multi-choice questions to open questions, from free text to numeric answers, from titles and subtitles to notes and instructions. As with Microsoft Word, each of these has a style and this makes it easier for you to enter the question text and the answer labels and Snap will format the questionnaire for you.

In addition, Snap includes complete templates that have been created for our users, and are designed with particular tasks in mind. The Default Web template has been designed for web surveys and includes all the buttons, the colours, the background, the fonts, the drop down lists and the layout for a web survey.

It is important to point out that none of the templates are fixed – you merely use them as guides. If you want to alter a specific question

7

Step 2: Adding headings

layout, you can. Snap will keep all your changes with that particular survey.

Step 2: Adding headings

You can add headings and sub-headings anywhere in your survey. The Default Web template has been set up so that the styles **Title** and **Sub Title** are assumed to start the questionnaire.

The **Questionnaire Window** should be open. If not, then click on the ⬚ button on the main toolbar. You will see a blank questionnaire showing a highlighted area for the **Title** of the survey.

The toolbar at the top of the window already shows a **Style Name** of **Title**.

The default setting for the **Title** is blue text in Arial font on a cream background.

1. In the area marked "**Click here for text**", type "Satisfaction Survey".

    You can change the look of the text by selecting it and choosing a different font and size from the drop-down menus in the toolbar.

2. Press [**Enter**] when you have set up your title. An area for a **Sub Title** appears.

A Snap survey in seven easy steps

3. Type "Please help us to continue improving the standards in our restaurant by answering a few simple questions." in this area. The default setting for **Sub Title** is centred Arial text.

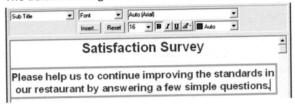

4. Press [**Enter**] when you have set up your sub-title.

That's how to put headings in your survey. You can select Title, Sub-title or Instruction styles at any time to put in any text you like.

Now let's move on and set up a few questions……..

Step 3: Add your first question

After you enter the subtitle and press [**Enter**], Snap creates Q1. By default, this is created as a multi-choice question. The question style is shown as **Multi Choice** on the toolbar.

The first question to add to the survey is about items purchased in the restaurant. The respondent will be presented with a list of options, and they can select as many as they wish. This is a **Multi Choice** question.

9

Step 3: Add your first question

1. An area is marked "Click here for text". Type "Which of the following items did you order today?"

2. Press the [**Tab**] key on your keyboard. The cursor moves into an area to the right of the first box. Type "Hamburger" and press [**Tab**] to move to the next line. Snap creates a selection box for that option.

3. Continue with the text for the other items and press [**Tab**] after each one:

"Pizza" [**Tab**]   "Salad" [**Tab**]

"Ice cream" [**Tab**]   "Coffee/tea" [**Tab**]

4. For the last code, "Soft drink", type it in but press [**Enter**] at the end instead of [**Tab**]. This tells Snap that you have finished this question and want to start a new one.

10

A Snap survey in seven easy steps

Step 4: Add a space for respondents to write their own answer

It's likely that your list of items will not be exhaustive, so it is wise to add a space to allow the respondent to enter anything that is not on the list. This is done using an **Other** question (which collects free format text or numbers).

When you press [**Enter**] after completing the first part of question 1, Snap creates Q2 by default. You can change this to create the structure to set up a section at the end for those answers not listed.

1. Select Q2 if it is not selected.

2. Use the ▼ button to the right of the words **Multi Choice** to display the other style names. Select **Other**. This allows you to enter free format text and moves the text of the question up to just below the previous question so it looks like part of it. The question name (Q1a) is hidden.

    1. **Which of the following items did you order today?**
        ☐ Hamburger
        ☐ Pizza
        ☐ Salad
        ☐ Ice-cream
        ☐ Coffee/tea
        ☐ Soft drink

        Click here for text

3. Click the box marked "Click here for text" and type "Other, please specify." The box that's been created should be sufficient to store whatever's written as the default setting is 100 characters. You'll see later how we can alter the size of the box to hold more data.

That's all you need to create this type of question, so press [**Enter**] and Snap will move on to create the next question...

11

Step 5: Adding your second question

The next task is to create a **Grid** question. This is simply a series of **Single Response** questions organised in the form of a grid. Their construction and operation during later stages of data entry and analysis are basically the same as other **Multi Choice** questions. It is their appearance on the questionnaire that sets them apart.

1. If you haven't already done so, press [**Enter**] to complete question 1. Snap creates the structure to set up question 2. Click the ▾ button to the right of the words **Multi Choice** to display the other style names and select **Grid First**. This allows you to set up the headings for the first of a series of grid questions.

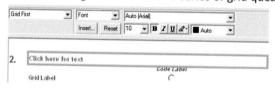

2. Type "How did you rate the following?" and press the [**Tab**] key on your keyboard.

   The cursor moves to the list of codes across the top of the first grid question.

3. Type "Very good" and press [**Tab**]. Type "Good" and press [**Tab**]. Type "OK" and press [**Tab**]. Type "Poor" and press [**Tab**]. Type "Very poor" and since this is the last code to be set up, press [↓] instead of [**Tab**].

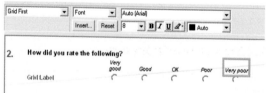

4. The cursor will move to the text of the first **Grid label**. Type "Service" and press [**Tab**]. Type "Quality" and press [**Tab**].

A Snap survey in seven easy steps

5. For the last question, type "Price" but instead of pressing [**Tab**], press [**Enter**] to complete the grid and move to a new question.

Snap recognises that these are single-response questions in an HTML survey so sets the choices as radio buttons.

Step 6: Ask for their comments

The last question is totally free format to allow the respondent to record any feedback comments whatsoever. Snap has automatically started to create Q3 and all you need to do is to change it from a **Multi Choice** question to an **Open Ended**.

1. Use the ▼ button to the right of the words Multi Choice to display the other style names and select Open Ended. This will allow you to enter free format text as a reply. Type "Do you have any other comments?"

    3. ┌─────────────────────────────────────┐
        │Click here for text   │
        └─────────────────────────────────────┘

2. The default capacity for this box is 100 characters and it appears as a single line. If you think more space is needed, select the question and hold down the [**Ctrl**] key and press the [**+**] key to make the line longer. (Press [**Ctrl**] and [**-**] to make the line shorter. You can also alter the option on the toolbar formatting option from **Font** to **Boxes** and change the number displayed in the **Size** field to the right.)

3. You have successfully created a short questionnaire. Click ✓ to save your work.

Step 7: Publishing the questionnaire

Once you have designed your questionnaire, the next step is to publish and check it.

Either select **File | Publish** or press [**Ctrl**] and [**Shift**] and [**W**]

13

Step 7: Publishing the questionnaire

The Publish Questionnaire dialog box opens. This allows you to specify exactly how your survey will be published.

Setting the output file name and location

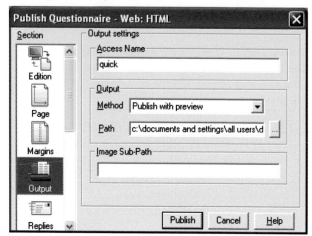

1. Select **Output** in the left-hand column.

2. Type a name that identifies your survey in the **Access Name** field.

3. Select **Publish with Preview** as the **Output Method**. This displays your survey as it would appear in a web browser immediately after it has been published.

4. If you wish, press the [...] button to browse for a new path where your survey will be stored.

14

A Snap survey in seven easy steps

Setting the way you will receive responses

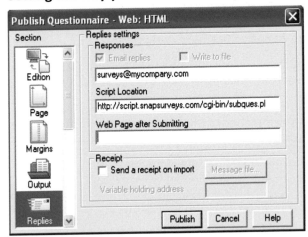

1. Select **Replies** in the left-hand column of the **Publish Questionnaire** dialog.

2. Enter the email address that responses will be sent to in the **Responses** field. (This would normally be your own or a colleague's email address.)

    The responses to your web survey will be sent to a special script (or computer program) on our server that will convert them into emails that are sent back to this address.

    This allows you to import email responses from your current Inbox when you run Snap.

3. Press **[Publish]** to publish the survey and create a folder containing all the necessary files.

15

Adding something extra to your survey

In seven easy steps, you've learnt how to create your first survey and publish it. That may be enough for many of you and you may want to move straight on to analysing your survey results.

For those of you that want to take your survey one step further, we'll show you how to:

- Add extra questions from one of the SurveyPak question libraries.

- Add some graphics.

- Alter some of the questions and move them to new locations.

- Add some routing so that some questions are only asked when certain conditions are met.

16

Adding something extra to your survey

The result will look something like this…

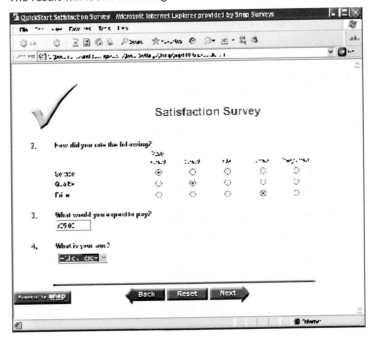

The first step is to create a copy of your questionnaire, so that you can always go back to the original version.

1. Make a copy of your survey

1. Make a copy of your survey

When you first start Snap, you are presented with the **Survey Overview** window as shown below. If you still have a survey shown on the screen...

1. Click the 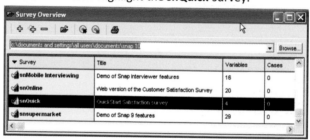 button on the main toolbar to return to the **Survey Overview** window. Highlight the *snQuick* survey.

▼ Survey	Title	Variables	Cases
snMobile Interviewing	Demo of Snap Interviewer features	16	0
snOnline	Web version of the Customer Satisfaction Survey	20	0
snQuick	QuickStart Satisfaction survey	4	0
snsupermarket	Demo of Snap 9 features	29	0

2. To copy or clone an existing survey, highlight the survey you want to copy, (in this case **SnQuick**), and then click 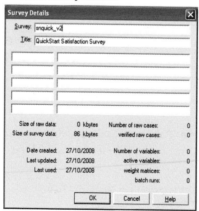 at the top of the **Survey Overview Window.** A new dialog box will appear entitled **Survey Details**.

18

2. Accessing questions from the SurveyPak question library

SurveyPaks contain frequently used questions that can be copied directly to a Snap survey, avoiding the need to specify the question from scratch. You can then edit the question within the survey. You access the **SurveyPaks** from the **Reference Window.**

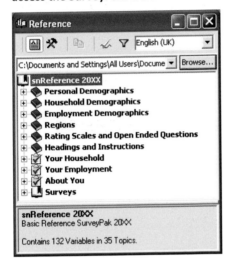

1.　Open the **Reference Window** by clicking on the 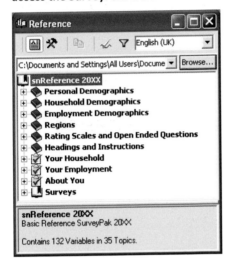 button of the main program toolbar. Close all other windows except for the **Questionnaire Window**.

2.　Select **Window | Tile** so that the two windows are arranged side by side on the screen.

3.　Double-click on the **SurveyPak** named **snReference20XX** to open it if it has not opened automatically. (The exact name of the SurveyPak may vary according to your release of Snap.)

4.　Double-click **Personal Demographics** and then **Age**.

2. Accessing questions from the SurveyPak question library

5. Select the question **Age of respondent**. The question is displayed in the bottom part of the window in the style it will appear in your current output (Web:HTML)

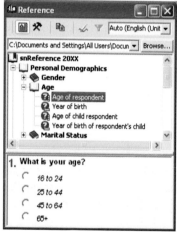

6. Now it's time to drag the question from the **SurveyPak** into the questionnaire. With the mouse hovering over the Age question, click on the left button, and as you move it, the mouse will change to 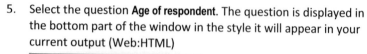. Keep the left button pressed and move the mouse from the **Reference** window on the left to the Questionnaire window on the right. As you move the mouse over the questionnaire it changes again:

   ~ insert the new question **before** this question.

   ~ **replace** this question with the new one.

   ~ insert the new question **after** this question.

   When you release the mouse button, the new question is dropped in the position indicated and will adopt the same look and feel as all the existing questions in your survey.

20

Adding something extra to your survey

Wherever you place the Age question, it is now part of your questionnaire. You can make changes to the text or add, edit or delete codes in the list. Snap will allocate a number to your new question wherever you've placed it.

7. To move your Age question, click anywhere on the question so that a green border appears around the question, and then use the [**Ctrl**] and [↓] or [**Ctrl**] and [↑] to move the question to its final location. Snap will automatically renumber the question as you move it. Move the Age question until it appears as **Q3**.

8. To alter the Age question from a **Multi Choice** with boxes to a **Drop down** list, highlight the **Age** question so a green box appears for editing.

    Then click ▼ next to **Multi Choice** on the toolbar to display the list of styles and select **Drop down**. If this is not visible, select **More Styles...** to see the second series of alternatives on the list.

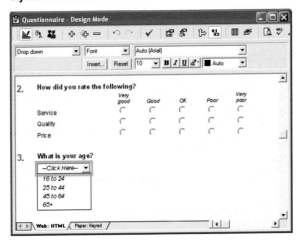

9. You've no more need for the SurveyPak libraries in this exercise so you can now close the **Reference** window.

21

3. Adding a logo to the title

3. Adding a logo to the title

1. Select the title of the questionnaire. (When selected it has a green border around it.)

2. Select **Background** in the Toolbar topic dropdown list and click the **[Picture]** button.

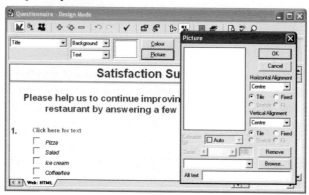

3. Click the **[Browse...]** button. The folder \Images\ opens by default. Change to the sub-folder \Images\Icons

4. Select the file *tick_icon.gif* and click **[Open]**. The **Picture** dialog opens displaying your choice. Pull down the **Horizontal Alignment** drop-down list and select **Left** in to insert the picture at the left-hand end of the title text. Set the radio buttons to **Fixed** to put one copy of the picture in a fixed position.

22

Adding something extra to your survey

If you wish, use the **Colourize Gif** box to change the image to a colour of your choice.

1. Click **[OK]** to return to the Questionnaire window. The logo will be inserted into the title.

2. Click ✓ to save the changes to the questionnaire.

4. Inserting breaks between questions

When you are creating a survey for display on the Web, it is important that people do not miss out questions because they are not immediately visible. When you are creating a web survey, it is sensible to put a break at the end of each screen. This makes a series of buttons appear at the bottom of each screen, aiding navigation through the survey.

Assume that Q1 adequately fills the first screen and you want Q2 to appear on the next screen.

1. Click on **Q2** in either the question text or question number. This will then be highlighted with a green border.

2. Press **[Ctrl]+[S]** to insert a page break above the question. (You can also select **Break** from the Toolbar topic list and check the **Page Break** box.)

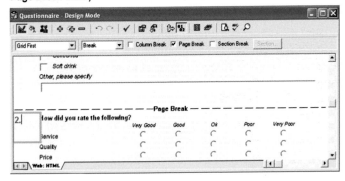

23

5. Only asking questions of specific respondents

3.   Click ☑ to save the changes to the questionnaire.

5. Only asking questions of specific respondents

Rarely in a survey do you ask every respondent every question. It is quite typical to only ask questions based on replies to other questions in the survey. To show this in operation, create an extra question of **What would you expect to pay?** and only ask this question of those people who rated the restaurant in terms of **Price** in Q2 as **Poor**. Anybody who replied either **Good** or **OK** will not be asked the question.

1.   Put your cursor on the line Price, and press **[Enter]** to create a question beneath it. Snap generates a new question with the same type (in this case, a **Multi Choice**). For a question to record a number (such as price) it needs to be **Open Ended**.

2.   On the Toolbar options, alter the style from **Multi Choice** to **Open Ended**.

3.   Type "What would you expect to pay?" in the selected text box.

By default, open-ended questions have a response type of literal. This means that anything can be entered in the box. To ensure that respondents enter a number (either as words or digits) you must convert the response type to a quantity. You can then perform calculations on the result.

1.   Right -click on the question you have just added and select **Variable properties** from the drop-down menu (or press **[Alt]+[Enter]**). The Variable Properties dialog appears.

24

Adding something extra to your survey

2. Select **Quantity** from the **Response** drop-down list.

3. Scroll down the list of variable properties using the bar on the right-hand side

    The Source Pattern reads (Default Quantity). This is how Snap can understand numbers written as words or figures. Since you know that the respondent is entering currency information, you can set the parameters to be slightly more specific.

4. Change the **Source Pattern** field from **(Default Quantity)** to **Currency**. Snap will now recognise not only a number, it will also accept a currency character such as $ or £.

25

5. Only asking questions of specific respondents

5. Click **[OK]**. The box for the response shrinks as Snap assumes a shorter response for a quantity.

6. Now you can create the routing to decide who gets asked this question.

Creating a routing rule

1. With the cursor on **Q3**, right-click the mouse and select **Routing Rules** from the context menu. Alternatively, click the 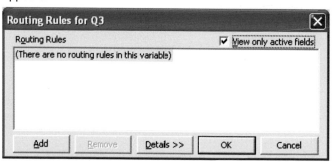 button on the Questionnaire Design toolbar. The Routing Rules dialog appears.

Routing Rules for Q3	⊠
Routing Rules	☑ View only active fields
(There are no routing rules in this variable)	

    Add   Remove   Details >>   OK   Cancel

2. Click 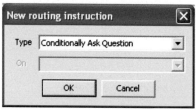 to create a new routing rule.

New routing instruction ⊠

Type Conditionally Ask Question ▼

On

OK   Cancel

3. Select **Conditionally Ask Question** from the **Type** box and click **[OK]**. This means that the question will only be asked (and be visible) if the conditions you set are met.

Adding something extra to your survey

4. The Rule Details dialog appears. The cursor is located in the **If** box.

5. Type "**Q2c=(4,5)**". Q2c is the third line of question two. **4** means that the respondent has selected the fourth answer "Poor" and **5** means the fifth answer "Very Poor". Putting **(4,5)** means they have answered either "Poor" or "Very Poor".

6. Click **[OK]**. A small arrow appears to the left of the question. You can double-click it to see the Rule details dialog.

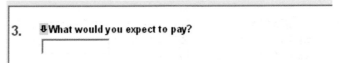

7. Press **[Ctrl]+[S]** to insert a page break above this question.

5. Only asking questions of specific respondents

Checking your survey with routing

When you publish and preview your survey, you will need to check that all the routes through your survey work the way you expect them too. Enter replies and see that the new Q3 only appears when either Poor or Very Poor are selected in the Price question for Q2.

Creating a paper version of your survey

Even when you are distributing your survey via the Internet, you may need to have a paper version of the same survey. This can be sent to people who do not have Internet access. It is also easier for people to comment on a paper version of the survey, if you have any concern about the questions.

✓ Satisfaction Survey

Please help us to continue improving the standards in our restaurant by answering a few simple questions

Q1 Which of the following items did you order today?

Hamburger .... ☐
Pizza .... ☐
Salad .... ☐
Ice cream .... ☐
Coffee/tea .... ☐
Soft drink .... ☐
Other, please specify

Q2 How did you rate the following?

	Very good	Good	OK	Poor	Very poor
Service	☐	☐	☐	☐	☐
Quality	☐	☐	☐	☐	☐
Price	☐	☐	☐	☐	☐

Q3 What is your age?

Under 18 .... ☐
18 to 28 .... ☐
28 to 38 .... ☐
38 to 48 .... ☐
48 to 58 .... ☐
58 to 68 .... ☐
68 to 78 .... ☐
78 or more .... ☐

Q4 Do you have any other comments?

29

5. Only asking questions of specific respondents

1. Open your survey and click the Editions and Style Templates button 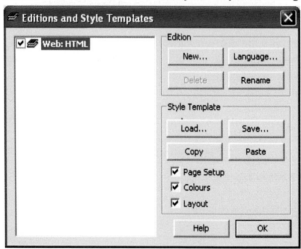. The **Editions and Style Templates** dialog opens.

2. Click **[New...]**, then select **Paper** as the publication medium.

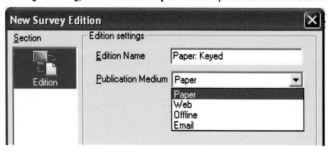

3. Click **[OK]**.

4. Click **[Load...]** to display the **Open** dialog box.

Creating a paper version of your survey

5. Select **Default.qsf** from the Styles folder to access the template for a paper survey and click **[Open]**.

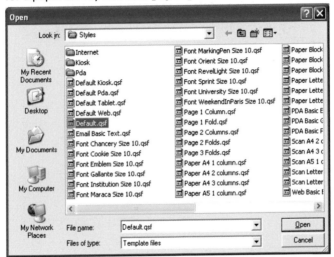

6. Click **[OK]** on the **Editions and Style Templates** dialog.

Snap creates a new tab entitled **Paper:Keyed** to display the paper version of the same questionnaire.

Removing page breaks from the paper edition

Although Snap has created a single database to store the structures of your questionnaire, you can make changes to editions of the same questionnaire – certain questions can be hidden, others can be phrased slightly differently, or even appear in a different la**nguage**. All these capabilities cannot be covered in this brief introduction, but you can remove the page breaks set up for the web survey in the paper one, so that the questionnaire will fill the printed page.

1. Click anywhere in the question (**Q2**) below the page break.

2. Press **[Ctrl]+[S]** to remove the page break. Remove any other page breaks in the same way.

31

Publishing and printing your paper questionnaire

To publish and print your paper questionnaire,

- Press **[Ctrl]+[Shift]+[W]** or select **File|Publish**

  or

- Click the Print Preview button .

The Printing Options dialog appears. It has a Publish button if you have selected **File|Publish**, and a Print button if you have gone through the Print preview.

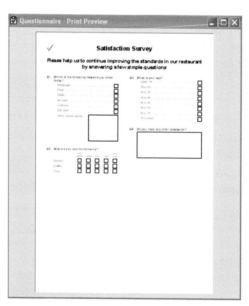

To print a single proof copy, click **[Print]** or **[Publish]**, as appropriate. Once you have proofed and checked your questionnaire, you can print multiple copies by clicking the **[Number of Copies...]** button.

snap

Collecting replies to your survey

Many of you will be more interested in seeing how a questionnaire is designed, published and analysed, rather than the mechanics of getting replies back in Snap. This section is designed for those of you who want to see what goes on behind the scenes.

Once you've created your questionnaire and **Published** it, you're ready to bring the replies from respondents back into Snap for analysis. Since you've created both a web and a paper version of the questionnaire, you can see how you get replies from both sources into Snap.

Importing responses from your HTML questionnaire into Snap

When you published the snQuick survey, you specified an email address to collect the replies to your survey.

The replies will be sent to you in the form of email messages, one message per respondent. You must import these messages into your survey in order to record respondents' replies. The instructions below assume that you are using an email client such as Outlook Express on your local PC.

Importing responses from your HTML questionnaire into Snap

1. You will see that the message has arrived in the **Inbox** of your email package. Each completed questionnaire will arrive as a separate email entitled **Snap Survey Submission.** In the Subject box, it will specify the name of the survey – **Internet Submission of** followed by the name of the survey, likely to be **Quick**.

```
***START SURVEY DATA***
:USERID:=99999S/999
V4=1;2
:FORMAT:=HTML
submit.x=17
V9=Apple Pie
:SURVEY:=Quick v2
:CHARSET:=windows-1252
:EMAIL:=surveys@mycompany.com
:PUBVER:=1
V5=3
:FORMID:=1
V12=1
V16=2
***END SURVEY DATA***
```

There's no need to open any of them. If you do want to view the contents of the email, you'll need to reset the email back to being **Unread** before importing it into Snap. The image shown here is a sample of the data that is contained within the email received in the **Inbox**.

Collecting replies to your survey

2. In Snap, click the  button on the main toolbar to open the **Data Entry** window and choose **File | Import**.

3. Set the **Format** to be **MAIL format**, and click **[OK]**.

    Snap will scan your mailbox for unread messages and turn messages containing replies for the current survey into new data cases.

    The **Data Import** dialog box contains an option to **Recheck mail box every ... seconds**. Once you have selected this option and specified the recheck period, leave Snap running in the background. It will download unread messages automatically at the designated time. The imported data is immediately ready for analysis in the form of tables, charts and statistics.

    The email message must be left unread and must be located in the main **Inbox** of your email package. Snap cannot scan sub-directories for messages, nor will it check messages that are marked as read.

    Any messages that are not recognised will be left as unread mail. These can be viewed with the mail system as normal.

35

Enter the replies from the paper questionnaire

Enter the replies from the paper questionnaire

1. From the **Survey Overview** window, open the *Quick* survey, i.e. the survey that you created at the beginning of this tutorial.

2. Click the ▨ button on the main toolbar to open the **Data Entry** window.

3. Click the ▨ button on the **Data Entry Window** toolbar to switch to **Questionnaire Mode**. The window title should be **Data Entry - Questionnaire Mode (Test Case)**.

4. Click the ✚ button to tell Snap that you wish to enter data for a new **Case**. The text just below the button should change from **Test Case** to **New case 1 of 1**.

5. Click on the **Code Boxes** for **Pizza**, **Salad** and **Soft drink**. A tick will appear in each box. If you accidentally clicked on one of the other boxes then simply click that box again to remove the tick.

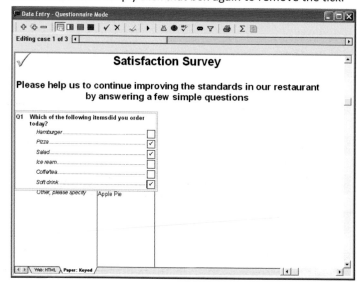

36

Collecting replies to your survey

6. Press [**Enter**] to move to the next question. In this case the next question is question 1a, asking for other foods bought. Press [**Enter**] again to leave this box blank and move to the next question. A message box appears to check that it was meant to be omitted. If you would prefer to complete it, click [**No**] and add **Apple Pie**, else click [**Yes**].

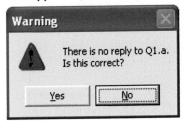

7. In the grid question, you can either use the mouse to select your responses or use the keyboard. To use the keyboard press [**1**] to select the first code when the question is selected. Press [**Enter**] to move to the next part of question 2 and enter another response (**1**, **2**, **3**, **4** or **5**).

8. Press [**Enter**] to move to the next question. Note that the routing functions here too. If you selected **Poor** for Q2c, you will be taken to Q3 **What would you expect to pay**. If not, you will be taken to the Open ended Q4.

9. Enter appropriate responses (a comment such as **The food was cold**) and press [**Enter**] after each question.

10. When you completed the questionnaire you are given the options:

11. Select [**Continue**] to save the data and move on to Case 2.

12. When you have finished the last case, select [**End**] and all the data will be saved.

37

Enter the replies from the paper questionnaire

By default, you must press [**Enter**] after each completed reply in
Snap. This is a safety setting for new users. Experienced users can
change the setting so that the [**Enter**] key is not required; Snap
moves from one field to the next as soon as a valid reply is keyed in.

To do this, open the **Tailor | Data Entry** dialog box and select
Continuously instead of **Individually. Click [Keep]** to use this
setting from now on.

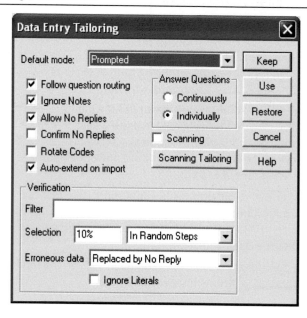

Analysing your survey results

To help you start analysing a survey, we've provided you with a sample survey called **SnCrocodile**. It already has over 200 completed replies.

A topline analysis of your survey

A unique feature of Snap is its ability to display the results of a survey in the form of a questionnaire. This is a clear and easy way of viewing a top-level summary of the survey and can easily be printed. More detailed analyses will then follow in the form of tables and charts.

1. Click the ⬚ button on the main toolbar to open the **Survey Overview** Window. Select the *snCrocodile* survey and either double-click on the mouse or click ⬚ .

2. The **Survey Details** dialog box will appear. Click **[OK]** to open the survey and display the **Questionnaire - Design Mode** window. If it does not, click the ⬚ button on the main toolbar.

39

Creating a table from one or more questions

3. Click the ![icon] button in the **Questionnaire** window to switch to
   Questionnaire - Data View Mode.

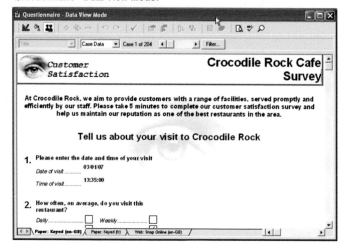

4. Click the ![arrow] button next to **Case Data**, and select **Counts**. The
   number of respondents giving each answer will be shown. For
   example, 18 of the 204 visitors ate at the restaurant every day.

5. Select the **Percentage** radio button. The questionnaire will now be
   presented with the percentage value shown for each of the
   questions. You'll now see that the 18 daily visitors represent 9%
   of our total. Use the vertical scroll bar to view more of the
   questionnaire.

Creating a table from one or more questions

Frequency tables are the quickest and easiest method of tabulating
single questions. You can produce them in Snap just by specifying the
name of the question or questions.

You can use Snap to calculate percentages in tables, filter results to
look at subsets of data and apply scores to results.

Analysing your survey results

1. Click 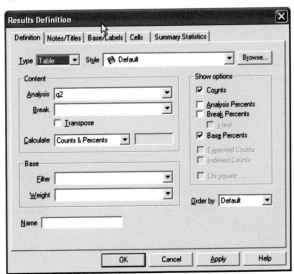 to create a table. The **Results Definition** dialog box appears.

2. In the **Analysis** field, type **"Q2"**. Note that:

    The **Style** field has automatically accessed a style for the table, and will select the style last accessed by the user, in this case *Default.tsf*.

    The drop-down list for the **Calculate** field should show **Counts & Percents**.

3. In the **Show options** section, select **Base Percents**. **Counts (**how many cases fall into each category) should already be selected; if not, select it now. **Base Percents** shows all answers as a percentage of the base, i.e. total number of respondents.

    Click the **Notes/Titles** tab. You can enter headings for your table here. By default, the **Title** field contains the text {ANALYSIS}.This makes the text for Q2, **Frequency of visit,** automatically appear as the title.

41

Cross-tabulating a group of questions
_____

4. Press **[OK]** to build the frequency table.

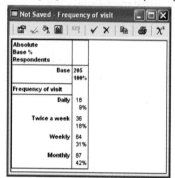

5. Click ✓ to save the table. The name of the saved table, "AN8: Frequency of visit", will appear in the table's **Title Bar**.

   Do not close the window containing this table, as it will be used in the instructions on the next page.

Cross-tabulating a group of questions

You can also cross-tabulate one question against other questions. For example, you could analyse the frequency of visits and break the results down by age. This example drags the question response to be analysed directly into the table from the Variables window (instead of using the 🖼 button to show the definition).

1. Click the  button to open the **Variables Window**.

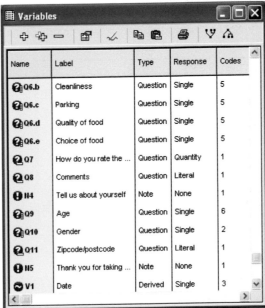

You should now have two open windows: one containing a list of variables in the survey and another showing the table produced in the previous section.

If the table is not open:

~ Click the ▦ button to open the **Results Window**.

~ Double-click the table, or select it and click the 🏠 button.

2. Arrange the two windows with the **Variables Window** on the left and the table of Q2 on the right.

3. Check the list of variables to make sure that Q9 is showing.

43

Producing a 3-D bar chart

4. Click and hold on Q9. As soon as you move the mouse, the cursor changes to ![cursor icon]. Drag Q9 into the box above the base figure. The cursor changes to show you are adding a column. Release the mouse to build the new table.

Absolute Base % Respondents	Total	Age Under 18	18-24	25-34	35-44	45-54	55+
Base	204	59	43	38	36	20	8
		29%	21%	19%	18%	10%	4%
Frequency of visit							
Daily	18	9	5	4	-	-	-
	9%	4%	2%	2%	-	-	-
Twice a week	35	11	8	8	7	-	1
	17%	5%	4%	4%	3%	-	0%
Weekly	64	16	8	16	16	4	4
	31%	8%	4%	8%	8%	2%	2%
Monthly	87	23	22	10	13	16	3
	43%	11%	11%	5%	6%	8%	1%

The window title automatically updates to show the new analysis definition.

To alter the table further, click ![icon] to display the **Results Definition** dialog box. Snap supports **Counts** and any combination of the three percentages. Check the required values in **Show options**, and press **[OK]**.

Producing a 3-D bar chart

To convert the cross-tabulation into a bar-chart:

1. Click ![icon] to display the **Results Definition** dialog.

Analysing your survey results

2. Change the **Type** to **Chart**.

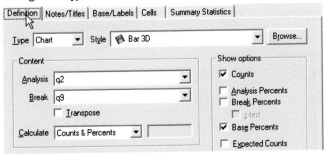

3. Choose **Bar 3D** as a style from the drop-down list and click **[OK]**. A 3-dimensional bar chart will be displayed.

<u>Frequency of visit by Age</u>

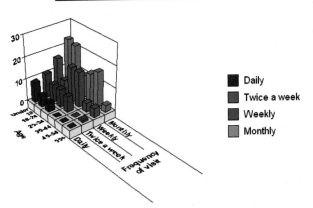

To rotate the chart, hold down the **[Ctrl]** key and press the left mouse button. The cursor changes to ⚓ . You can then drag the chart round with the mouse and look at it from different angles. Release the mouse and the chart will remain as you've set it.

45

Producing a 3-D bar chart

Moving the legends on the chart

4.   With the mouse anywhere over the chart, right-click on the mouse and select **Chart Designer** from the context menu. **The Chart Designer** dialog appears.

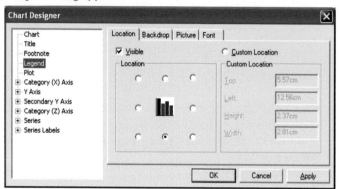

5.   Select **Legend**.

6.   Click the **Location** tab and check **Visible**.

7.   Click the radio button at the position where you want the Legend to appear.

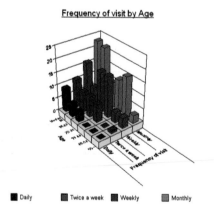

46

Analysing your survey results

8.   Click **[OK]** to apply the changes.

Changing from a bar chart to another type of chart

You can easily change the type of chart. There are three ways of changing the format of your charts.

- Select a different template from the **Results Definition** box

- Use the **Chart Designer** to make small adjustments

- Use the **Chart Wizard** option to quickly alter the layout.

1.   Open the window containing the bar chart from the previous section if it is not already open.

2.   Right-click to display the context menu and then select the **Chart Wizard** option.

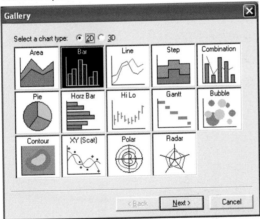

3.   Select a chart type from the **Gallery** dialog box. For simplicity, produce a 2-D version of the 3-D chart. Select the **2-D** radio button at the top of the dialog box and make sure that **Bar** is selected.

47

Changing from a bar chart to another type of chart

4.   Click **[Next>]**. The Style dialog appears.

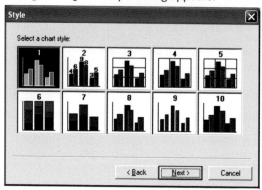

5.   Select the first option displayed and click **[Next>]** to display the layout options.

6.   Click **[Next>]** to display the **Axes** options.

7.   Click **[Finish]** to build the chart and return to the **Results** window in Snap.

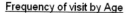

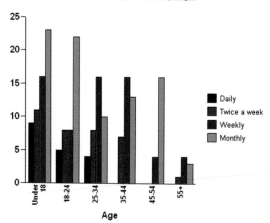

48

Analysing your survey results

Saving and retrieving tables and charts

All tables and charts definitions can be saved with the survey. The next time you access a survey the tables and charts are automatically updated to reflect any new respondents that have been added to the survey.

To save a table or chart you have created, click [✔] in its window toolbar.

If you do not wish to save the table or chart click [✕].

To view your saved tables and charts, click [▦] or select **View | Results**.

The **Results Window** displays the list of saved tables and charts. Select the one you wish to look at and double-click on it to open it.

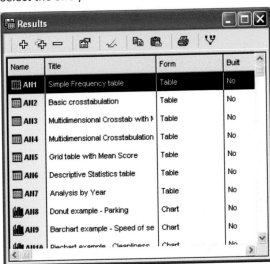

snap

Your notes

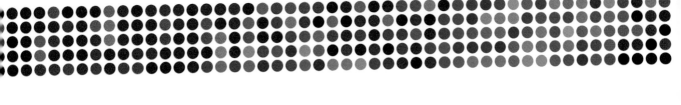

Glossary

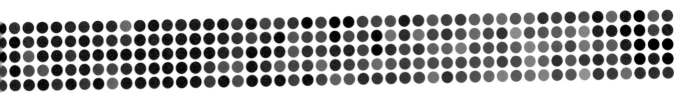

Access panels A database of individuals who have agreed to be available for surveys of varying types and topics. Rising rates of refusals and non response, make it more difficult to recruit for a single survey, therefore sampling from a pool of potentially willing marketing research respondents can be seen as an appropriate way of saving time and money.

Accompanied shopping A specialised type of individual depth interview, which involves respondents being interviewed while they shop in a retail store and combines observation with detailed questioning.

Alternative hypothesis The hypothesis where some difference or effect is expected (i.e. a difference that cannot occur simply by chance).

Ambiguous question A badly constructed question which results in respondents and researchers reading different meanings into what is being asked, resulting in inappropriate or unexpected answers.

Animatics A type of stimulus material where key frames for a television advertisement are drawn or computer generated with an accompanying sound track.

Annotation method An approach taken to analyse qualitative data using codes or comments on the transcripts to categorise the points being made by respondents.

ANOVA Analysis of variance. A test for the differences among the means of two or more variables.

Area sampling A type of cluster sampling in which the clusters are created on the basis of the geographic location of the population of interest.

Audience's thinking sequence The sequence of thoughts that people go through when they are being communicated with.

Audits An examination and verification of the movement and sale of a product. There are three main types: wholesale audits, which measure product sales from wholesalers to retailers and caterers, retail audits, which measure sales to the final consumer, and home audits, which measure purchases by the final consumer.

Bar chart A chart which uses a series of bars that may be positioned horizontally or vertically to represent the values of a variety of items.

Beauty parades The procedure of asking a number of agencies to present their proposals verbally to the client company. The procedure is used to assist clients in selecting the research agency that will undertake a research project.

Blog An abbreviated title for the term web log, meaning a frequent, chronological publication of personal thoughts and ideas. Twitter is a form of microblogging service that allows an individual to publish their blog type opinions and ideas in short Tweets (text-based messages of up to 140 characters).

Brand mapping A projective technique which involves presenting a set of competing brand names to respondents and getting them to group them into categories based on certain dimensions such as innovativeness, value for money, service quality and product range.

Brand personalities A projective technique which involves respondents imagining a brand as a person and describing their looks, their clothes, their lifestyles, employment, etc.

CAPI Computer-assisted personal interviewing. Where lap-top computers or pen-pad computers are used rather than paper-based questionnaires for face-to-face interviewing.

Cartoon completion A projective technique which involves a cartoon that the respondent has to complete. For example, the cartoon may show two characters with balloons for dialogue. One of the balloons sets out what one of the characters is thinking or saying, while the other is left empty for the respondent to complete.

CATI Computer-assisted telephone interviewing. CATI involves telephone interviewers typing respondent's answers directly into a computer-based questionnaire rather than writing them on a paper-based questionnaire.

CATS Completely automated telephone interviews which use interactive voice technology and require no human interviewer. Respondents answer the closed-ended questions with their touch-tone telephone.

Causal research Research that examines whether one variable causes or determines the value of another variable.

Census Research which involves collecting data from every member of the population of interest.

Chat rooms An Internet-based facility that can be used for online focus groups where individuals are recruited who are willing to discuss a subject online usually using text.

Chi-square A statistical test which tests the 'goodness of fit' between the observed distribution and the expected distribution of a variable.

Closed question A question that requires the respondent to make a selection from a predefined list of responses. There are two main types of closed questions: dichotomous questions with only two potential responses and multiple-response questions with more than two.

Cluster analysis A statistical technique used to classify objects or people into mutually exclusive and exhaustive groups on the basis of two or more classification variables.

Cluster sampling A probability sampling approach in which clusters of population units are selected at random and then all (one-stage cluster sampling) or some (two-stage cluster sampling) of the units in the chosen clusters are studied.

Coding The procedures involved in translating responses into a form that is ready for analysis. Normally involves the assigning of numerical codes to responses.

Coefficient alpha *See* Cronbach alpha.

Coefficient of determination Measure of the strength of linear relationship between a dependent variable and independent variables.

Concept boards A type of stimulus material which uses a set of boards to illustrate different product, advertising or pack designs.

Conclusive research Research aimed at evaluating alternative courses of action or measuring and monitoring the organisation's performance.

Confidence level The probability that the true population value will be within a particular range (result +/– sampling error).

Conjoint analysis A statistical technique that provides a quantitative measure of the relative importance of one attribute over another. It is frequently used to determine what features a new product or service should have and also how products should be priced.

Constant sum scales A scaling approach which requires the respondent to divide a given number of points, usually 100, among a number of attributes based on their importance to the individual.

Construct validity An analysis of the underlying theories and past research that supports the inclusion of the various items in the scale. It is most commonly considered in two forms: convergent validity and discriminant validity.

Content analysis The analysis of any form of communication, whether it is advertisements, newspaper articles, television programmes or taped conversations. Frequently used for the analysis of qualitative research data.

Content analysis software Software used for qualitative research which basically counts the number of times that pre-specified words or phrases appear in text.

Content validity A subjective yet systematic assessment as to how well a rating scale measures a topic of interest. For example, a group of subject experts may be asked to comment on the extent to which all of the key dimensions of a topic have been included.

Continuous research *See* Longitudinal research.

Contrived observation A research approach which involves observing participants in a controlled setting.

Convenience sampling A non-probability sampling procedure in which a researcher's convenience forms the basis for selecting the potential respondents (i.e. the researcher approaches the most accessible members of the population of interest).

Convergent validity A measure of the extent to which the results from a rating scale correlate with those from other scales or measures of the same topic/construct.

Cookies Text files placed on a user's computer by web retailers in order to identify the user when he or she next visits the website.

Correlation A statistical approach to examine the relationship between two variables. Uses an index to describe the strength of a relationship.

Critical path method (CPM) A managerial tool used for scheduling a research project. It is a network approach that involves dividing the research project into its various components and estimating the time required to complete each component activity.

Cronbach alpha A statistical test used to measure the split-half reliability of a summated rating scale. Also known as coefficient alpha.

Cross-sectional research Research studies that are undertaken once only involving data collection at a single point in time providing a 'snapshot' of the specific situation. The *opposite* of longitudinal research.

Cross-tabulations Tables that set out the responses to one question relative to the responses to one or more other questions.

Customer database A manual or computerised source of data relevant to marketing decision making about an organisation's customers.

Cut-and-paste method of analysis A method for analysing qualitative research data where material is cut and pasted from the original transcript into separate sections or tables relating to each topic. Cutting and pasting can either be done physically using scissors or using a word processing computer package.

Data analysis errors Non-sampling errors that occur when data is transferred from questionnaires to computers by incorrect keying of information.

Data analysis services Organisations, sometimes known as 'tab shops', that specialise in providing services such as the coding of completed questionnaires, inputting the data from questionnaires into a computer and the provision of sophisticated data analysis using advanced statistical techniques.

Data cleaning Computerised checks made on data to identify inconsistencies and to check for any unexplained missing responses.

Data conversion The reworking of secondary data into a format that allows estimates to be made to meet the researcher's needs.

Data display Summarising and presenting of information in order that relationships or connections can be identified and conclusions can be drawn.

Data elements The individual pieces of information held in a database (e.g. a person's name, gender or date of birth). These elements mean little independently but when combined they provide information on a customer or group of customers.

Data entry The transfer of data from a questionnaire into a computer either directly in computer-assisted interviewing, or by an operator copy-typing the responses from questionnaires, or the optical scanning of printed questionnaires.

Data errors Non-sampling errors that occur during data collection or analysis that impact on the accuracy of inferences made about the population of interest. The main types of data error are respondent errors (where respondents give distorted or erroneous answers), interviewer errors and data analysis errors.

Data fusion Data fusion involves the fusing together of different types of information to present a more complete picture of an individual or a group of individuals.

Data mining An activity where highly powerful computers are used to dig through volumes of data to discover patterns about an organisation's customers and products.

Data protection legislation Legislation created to protect against the misuse of personal data (i.e. data about an individual person).

Data validation The verification of the appropriateness of the explanations and interpretations drawn from qualitative data analysis.

Database A collection of related information that can be accessed and manipulated quickly using computers.

Deduplication The process through which data belonging to different transactions or service events are united for a particular customer. Software will be used to either automatically eliminate duplicates or identify potential duplicates that require a manual inspection and a decision to be taken.

Degrees of freedom (d.f.) The number of observations (i.e. sample size) minus one.

Depth interview *See* Individual depth interview.

Descriptive research Research studies that describe what is happening in a market without potentially explaining why it is happening.

Descriptive statistics Statistics that help to summarise the characteristics of large sets of data using only a few numbers. The most commonly used descriptive statistics are measures of central tendency (mean, mode and median) and measures of dispersion (range, interquartile range and standard deviation).

Dichotomous questions Questions with only two potential responses (e.g. Yes or No).

Directories A listing of individuals or organisations involved in a particular activity. May be available in printed format, CD-ROMs or on the Internet.

Discriminant validity A measure of the extent to which the results from a rating scale do not correlate with other scales from which one would expect it to differ.

Discussion guide *See* Topic list.

Disproportionate stratified random sampling A form of stratified random sampling (*See* Stratified random sampling) where the units or potential respondents from each population set are selected according to the relative variability of the units within each subset.

Double-barrelled question A badly constructed question where two topics are raised within one question.

Doughnut chart A form of pie chart which allows different sets of data (e.g. for different years) to be shown in the same chart.

Editing The process of ensuring that questionnaires were filled out correctly and completely.

E-mail survey A self-completion survey that is delivered to pre-selected respondents by e-mail. The questionnaire can take the form of text within the e-mail or can be sent as an attachment (either as a word-processor document or as a piece of software which runs the questionnaire).

End-piling A situation where almost all responses appear in a few categories at one end of a measurement scale.

Ethnography A form of participant observation that involves the study of human behaviour in its natural setting. For example, a researcher may accompany consumers (sometimes with a video camera) as they engage in a wide range of activities such as going on a shopping trip with friends. It involves the researcher exploring the interactions between group members, their reaction to various events and experiences, how they consider different courses of action and take decisions.

Executive interviews Quantitative research interviews with business people, usually undertaken at their place of work, covering subjects related to industrial or business products and services.

Experimental research Research which measures causality and involves the researcher changing one variable (e.g. price, packaging, shelf display, etc.), while observing the effects of those changes on another variable (e.g. sales) and controlling the extraneous variables.

Exploratory research Research that is intended to develop initial ideas or insights and to provide direction for any further research needed.

External data Secondary data that are sourced from outside the organisation requiring the research to be conducted.

Eye tracking The use of equipment in the observation and recording of a person's unconscious eye movements when they are looking at a magazine, a shop display or a website.

Face-to-face survey Research which involves meeting respondents face-to-face and interviewing them using a paper-based questionnaire, a laptop computer or an electronic notepad.

Factor analysis A statistical technique that studies the interrelationships among variables for the purpose of simplifying data. It can reduce a large set of variables to a smaller set of composite variables or factors by identifying the underlying dimensions of the data.

Field agencies Agencies whose primary activity is the field interviewing process focusing on the collection of data through personal interviewers, telephone interviewers or postal surveys.

Focus groups *See* Group discussions.

Frequency distributions *See* Holecounts.

Full-service agencies Marketing research agencies that offer the full range of marketing research services and techniques. They will be able to offer the entire range of qualitative and quantitative research approaches as well as be capable of undertaking every stage of the research from research design through to analysis and report writing.

Funnel sequence A sequence of questioning that moves from the generalities of a topic to the specifics. Funnel sequencing is particularly critical where answers to earlier specific questions could bias the answers to later questions. It is also important where the researcher wishes to ensure that respondents are only asked questions that are specifically relevant to them.

GANTT chart A managerial tool used for scheduling a research project. It is a form of flowchart that provides a schematic representation incorporating the activity, time, and personnel requirements for a given research project.

Geodemographic profiling A profiling method which uses postal addresses to categorise different neighbourhoods in relation to buying power and behaviour.

Grounded theory A set of analysis techniques that were developed in the 1960s by two medical sociologists, Glaser and Strauss (1967). It is more commonly used by academic researchers rather than marketing research practitioners in areas where little is known about a subject or where a new approach to understanding behaviour is required. It is a systematic method of generating theory and understanding through qualitative data collection and analysis.

Group depth interviews *See* Group discussions.

Group discussions Also known as focus groups or group depth interviews. These are depth interviews undertaken with a group of respondents. In addition to the increased number of respondents, they differ from individual depth interviews in that they involve interaction between the participants.

Group dynamics The interaction between group members in group discussions.

Group moderator The interviewer responsible for the management and encouragement of participants in a group discussion.

Hall tests Research undertaken in a central hall or venue commonly used to test respondents' initial reactions to a product or package or concept. Respondents are recruited into the hall by interviewers stationed on main pedestrian thoroughfares nearby.

Hidden observation A research approach involving observation where the participant does not know that they are being observed.

Holecounts The number of respondents who gave each possible answer to each question in a questionnaire. Sometimes known as frequency distributions.

Hypothesis An assumption or proposition that a researcher puts forward about some characteristic of the population being investigated.

Hypothesis testing Testing aimed at determining whether the difference between proportions is greater than would be expected by chance or as a result of sampling error.

Implicit assumption A badly constructed question where the researcher and the respondent are using different frames of reference as a result of assumptions that both parties make about the question being asked.

Independent samples Samples in which the measurement of the variable of interest in one sample has no effect on the measurement of the variable in the other sample.

Individual depth interview An interview that is conducted face-to-face, in which the subject matter of the interview is explored in detail using an unstructured and flexible approach.

Information explosion The major growth in information available in a wide range of formats from a wide range of sources. This growth has principally resulted from improvements in the capabilities and speeds of computers.

In-home/doorstep interviewing Face-to-face interviews undertaken within the home of the respondent or on the doorstep of their home.

Internal data Secondary data sourced from within the organisation that is requiring the research to be conducted.

Internet monitoring The measurement undertaken by web-based retailers and suppliers to monitor the number of times different pages on their sites are accessed, what search engines bring people to the site, what service provider browsers are used as well as tracking the specific time at which the site is accessed. Using cookies, the retailers may also be able to identify when users revisit the site.

Internet panel A panel of people recruited through the Internet for marketing research purposes. Based on the profile of each individual participant, the panel operator sends out personalised e-mail alerts identifying surveys that they would like the participant to complete. For each completed survey, the participant's will either be credited with a cash sum or will be entered into a prize draw.

Interquartile range A measure of dispersion that calculates the difference between the 75th and 25th percentile in a set of data.

Interval data Similar to ordinal data with the added dimension that the intervals between the values on a scale are equal. That means that when using a scale of 1 to 5, the difference between 1 and 2 is the same as the difference between 4 and 5. However, the ratios between different values on the scale are not valid (e.g. 4 does not represent twice the value of 2).

Interviewer bias Bias and errors in research findings brought about by the actions of an interviewer. This may be influenced by who the interviewer interviews, how the interview is undertaken and the manner in which responses are recorded.

Interviewer errors *See* Interviewer bias.

Interviewer guide *See* Topic list.

Interviewer Quality Control Scheme (IQCS) A quality-control scheme for interviewers in the UK. The scheme is aimed at improving selection, training and supervision of interviewers and is jointly run by the Market Research Society, the Association of Market

Survey Organisations, the Association of British Market Research Companies, the Association of Users of Research Agencies, and a number of leading research companies.

Judgement sampling A non-probability sampling procedure where a researcher consciously selects a sample that he or she considers to be most appropriate for the research study.

Kiosk-based survey A survey often undertaken at an exhibition or trade show using touch-screen computers to collect information from respondents. Such computers can be programmed to deliver complex surveys supported by full colour visuals as well as sound and video clips. They can be much cheaper to administer in comparison with the traditional exit survey undertaken by human interviewers.

Leading question A badly constructed question that tends to steer respondents toward a particular answer. Sometimes known as a loaded question.

Least squares approach A regression procedure that is widely used for deriving the best-fit equation of a line for a given set of data involving a dependent and independent variable.

Lifestyle databases Databases that consist of data derived from questionnaire responses to 'lifestyle surveys'. Such surveys make it clear to respondents that the data is being collected for the creation of a database rather than for marketing research purposes.

Lifetime value The present value of the estimated future transactions and net income attributed to an individual customer relationship.

Likert scales A scaling approach which requires the respondent to state their level of agreement with a series of statements about a product, organisation or concept. The scale using the descriptors Strongly agree; Agree; Neither agree nor disagree; Disagree; Strongly disagree is based on a format originally developed by Renis Likert in 1932.

Line graph A two-dimensional graph that is typically used to show movements in data over time.

List brokers Organisations that sell off-the-shelf data files listing names, characteristics and contact details of consumers or organisations.

Loaded question *See* Leading question.

Longitudinal research A study involving data collection at several periods in time enabling trends over time to be examined. This may involve asking the same questions on a number of occasions of either the same respondents or of respondents with similar

characteristics. Sometimes known as 'continuous' research.

Mall intercept interviews *See* Street interviews.

Marketing concept The proposition that the whole of the organisation should be driven by a goal of serving and satisfying customers in a manner which enables the organisation's financial and strategic objectives to be achieved.

Marketing decision support system (MDSS) An interactive computerised information source designed to assist in marketing decision making.

Marketing research The collection, analysis and communication of information undertaken to assist decision making in marketing.

Marketing research process The sequence of activities and events involved in undertaking a marketing research project.

Mean The arithmetic average which is calculated by summing all of the values in a set of data and dividing by the number of cases.

Measures of central tendency Measures that indicate a typical value for a set of data by computing the mean, mode or median.

Measures of dispersion Measures that indicate how 'spread out' a set of data is. The most common are the range, the interquartile range and the standard deviation.

Mechanised observation A research approach involving observation of behaviour using automated counting devices, scanners or other equipment.

Median When all of the values in a data set are put in ascending order, the median is the value of the middle case in a series.

Metric data A name for interval and ratio data.

Mixed-mode studies Research studies that use a variety of collection methods in a single survey (e.g. using the same questionnaire online and face to face) in order to improve response rates.

Mode The value in a set of data that occurs most frequently.

Multiple-choice questions Questions that provide respondents with a choice of predetermined responses to a question. The respondents are asked to either give one alternative that correctly expresses their viewpoint or indicate all responses that apply.

Multiple discriminant analysis A statistical technique used to classify individuals into one of two or more segments (or populations) on the basis of a set of measurements.

Multiple regression analysis A statistical technique to examine the relationship between three or more variables and also to calculate the likely value of the dependent variable based on the values of two or more independent variables.

Multi-stage sampling A sampling approach where a number of successive sampling stages are undertaken before the final sample is obtained.

Multivariate data analysis Statistical procedures that simultaneously analyse two or more variables on a sample of objects. The most common techniques are multiple regression analysis, multiple discriminant analysis, factor analysis, cluster analysis, perceptual mapping and conjoint analysis.

Mystery shopping A form of participant observation which uses researchers to act as customers or potential customers to monitor the processes and procedures used in the delivery of a service.

Netnography Sometimes known as online ethnography and webnography, netnography is the ethnographic study of communities on the World Wide Web. It generally involves a researcher fully participating as a member of the online community.

Newsgroups Internet-based sites that take the form of bulletin boards/discussion lists on specific topics. They involve people posting views, questions and information on the site.

Nominal data Numbers assigned to objects or phenomena as labels or identification numbers that name or classify but have no true numeric meaning.

Non-metric data A name for nominal and ordinal data.

Non-probability sampling A set of sampling methods where a subjective procedure of selection is used resulting in the probability of selection for each member of the population of interest being unknown.

Non-response errors Errors in a study that arise when some of the potential respondents do not respond. This may occur due to respondents refusing or being unavailable to take part in the research.

Non-sampling error Errors that occur in a study that do not relate to sampling error. They tend to be classified into three broad types: sampling frame error, non-response error and data error.

Normal distribution A continuous distribution that is bell-shaped and symmetrical about the mean. This means that in a study, 68.27 per cent of the observations fall within plus or minus one standard deviation of the mean, approximately 95.45 per cent fall within plus or minus two standard deviations, and approximately 99.73 per cent fall within plus or minus three standard deviations.

Null hypothesis The hypothesis that is tested and is the statement of the status quo where no difference or effect is expected.

Observation A data gathering approach where information is collected on the behaviour of people, objects and organisations without any questions being asked of the participants.

Omnibus surveys A data collection approach that is undertaken at regular intervals for a changing group of clients who share the costs involved in the survey's set-up, sampling and interviewing.

One-way mirrors Used in qualitative marketing research to enable clients and researchers to view respondent behaviour during a discussion. Behind the mirror is a viewing room, which consists of chairs for the observers and may contain video cameras to record the proceedings.

Online communities A community of individuals who interact online focusing on a particular interest or simply to communicate.

Online group discussion These are group discussions or private chat rooms where a group is recruited who are willing to discuss a subject online usually using text (webcam and microphone are sometimes used). Participants are recruited by phone, e-mail or through an online special interest group. They react to questions or topics posed by the moderator and type in their perceptions or comments taking account of other participants' inputs.

Online survey A self-completion questionnaire which is delivered via the Internet. It may appear on the computer screen as a standard questionnaire where the respondent scrolls down the page completing each question. Alternatively, it can take the form of an interactive questionnaire with questions appearing on the screen one at a time.

Open-ended questions Questions that allow respondents to reply in their own words. There are no pre-set choices of answers and the respondent can decide whether to provide a brief one-word answer or something very detailed and long. Sometimes known as 'unstructured' questions.

Oral presentation A presentation of research findings delivered to a client in a face-to-face format by the researcher.

Ordinal data Numbers that have the labelling characteristics of nominal data, but also have the ability to communicate the rank order of the data. The numbers do not indicate absolute quantities, nor do they imply that the intervals between the numbers are equal.

Paired interview An in-depth interview involving two respondents such as married couples, business partners, teenage friends or a mother and child.

Panel research A research approach where comparative data is collected from the same respondents on more than one occasion. Panels can consist of individuals, households or organisations, and can provide information on changes in behaviour, awareness and attitudes over time.

Participant observation A research approach where the researcher interacts with the subject or subjects being observed. The best-known type of participant observation is mystery shopping.

Participant validation A validation technique that involves taking the findings from qualitative research back to the participants/respondents that were involved in the study and seeking their feedback. If the feedback verifies the explanations and conclusions, then the researcher can be more confident about the validity of the findings.

Pearson's product moment correlation A correlation approach that is used with interval and ratio data.

Perceptual mapping An analysis technique which involves the positioning of objects in perceptual space. Frequently used in determining the positioning of brands relative to their competitors.

Photo sorts A projective technique which uses a set of photographs depicting different types of people. Respondents are then asked to connect the individuals in the photographs with the brands they think they would use.

Pictogram A type of bar chart which uses pictures of the items being described rather than bars.

Pie chart A chart for presenting data which takes the form of a circle divided into several slices whose areas are in proportion to the quantities being examined.

Pilot testing The pre-testing of a questionnaire prior to undertaking a full survey. Such testing involves administering the questionnaire to a limited number of potential respondents in order to identify and correct flaws in the questionnaire design.

Placement tests The testing of reactions to products in the home and where they are to be used. Respondents are given a new product to test in their own home or in their office. Information about their experiences with and attitudes towards the products are then collected by either a questionnaire or by a self-completion diary.

Population of interest The total group of people that the researcher wishes to examine, study or obtain information from. The population of interest will normally reflect the target market or potential target market for the product or service being researched. Sometimes known as the target population or universe.

Postal surveys Self-administered surveys that are mailed to pre-selected respondents along with a return envelope, a covering letter and possibly an incentive.

Primary data Data collected by a programme of observation, qualitative or quantitative research either separately or in combination to meet the specific objectives of a marketing research project.

Probability sampling A set of sampling methods where an objective procedure of selection is used, resulting in every member of the population of interest having a known probability of being selected.

Product/service review sites Online sites that allow individuals to feedback their views on products and services. These sites may be independent or operated by manufacturers, retailers and other forms of intermediaries.

Professional codes of conduct Self-regulatory codes covering acceptable practices in marketing research developed by the professional bodies responsible for the research industry (e.g. the Market Research Society or ESOMAR).

Profilers Organisations that gather demographic and lifestyle information about consumers and combine it with postal address information. They take this base information and use it to segment an organisation's database of existing customers into different lifestyle and income groups. They may also be used to identify additional prospective customers whose characteristics match those of an organisation's existing customers.

Programme evaluation and review technique (PERT) A managerial tool used for scheduling a research project. It involves a probability-based scheduling approach that recognises and measures the uncertainty of project completion times.

Projective questioning Sometimes known as third-party techniques, this is a projective technique that asks the respondent to consider what other people would think about a situation.

Projective techniques Techniques used in group discussions and individual depth interviews to facilitate a deeper exploration of a respondent's attitudes towards a concept, product or situation.

Proportionate stratified random sampling A form of stratified random sampling (*See* Stratified random sampling) where the units or potential respondents from each population subset are selected in proportion to the total number of each subset's units in the population.

Purchase intent scales A scaling approach which is used to measure a respondent's intention to purchase a product or potential product.

Qualitative research An unstructured research approach with a small number of carefully selected individuals used to produce non-quantifiable insights into behaviour, motivations and attitudes.

Quantitative research A structured research approach involving a sample of the population to produce quantifiable insights into behaviour, motivations and attitudes.

Questionnaire design process A stepped approach to the design of questionnaires.

Quota sampling A non-probability sampling procedure which involves the selection of cells or subsets within the population of interest, the establishment of a numerical quota in each cell and the researcher carrying out sufficient interviews in each cell to satisfy the quota.

Range A measure of dispersion that calculates the difference between the largest and smallest values in a set of data.

Ratio data Actual 'real' numbers that have a meaningful absolute or zero. All arithmetic operations are possible with such data.

Regression A statistical approach to examine the relationship between two variables. Identifies the nature of the relationship using an equation.

Related samples Samples where the measurement of interest in one sample may influence the measurement of the variable of interest in another sample.

Reliability of scales Refers to the extent to which a rating scale produces consistent or stable results. Stability is most commonly measured using test-retest reliability and consistency is measured using split-half reliability.

Research brief A written document which sets out an organisation's requirements from a marketing research project. This provides the specification against which the researchers will design the research project.

Research proposal The submission prepared by the research agency for a potential client specifying the research to be undertaken. On the basis of the research proposal, the client will select an agency to undertake the research. The proposal becomes the contract between the agency and the client company.

Research report A final document produced at the end of a research study setting out the objectives, methodology, findings, conclusions, executive summary and recommendations of the research.

Respondent errors Non-sampling errors that are caused by respondents inadvertently or intentionally giving distorted or erroneous responses. Respondents may give erroneous answers because they fail to understand a question and do not want to admit their incomprehension.

Role playing A projective technique which involves a respondent being asked to act out the character of a brand.

Sample A subset of the population of interest.

Sampling The selection of a sample of respondents that is representative of a population of interest.

Sampling error The difference between the sample value and the true value of a phenomenon for the population being surveyed. Can be expressed in mathematical terms: usually the survey result plus or minus a certain percentage.

Sampling frame A list of the population of interest from which the researcher selects the individuals for inclusion in the research.

Sampling frame error A bias that occurs as a result of the population implied by the sampling frame being different from the population of interest.

Scaling questions Questions that ask respondents to assign numerical measures to subjective concepts such as attitudes, opinions and feelings.

Scanner-based research Collecting sales information using electronic scanners reading barcodes at the checkouts of retailers and wholesalers. The information collected feeds into audits.

Screening questionnaire A questionnaire used for identifying suitable respondents for a particular research activity, such as a group discussion.

Search engines Internet-based tools for finding web addresses which contain collections of links to sites throughout the world and an indexing system to help you find the relevant sites. Examples include AltaVista, Yahoo! and Lycos.

Secondary data Information that has been previously gathered for some purpose other than the current research project. It may be data available within the organisation (internal data) or information available from published and electronic sources originating outside the organisation (external data).

Self-administered surveys Surveys where the respondent completes the questionnaire with no help from an interviewer. The questionnaire can be delivered to the respondent via the mail (postal surveys), by hand, by fax or online (e-mail, web surveys).

Semantic differential scales A scaling approach which requires the respondent to rate a brand or concept using a set of bipolar adjectives or phrases (e.g. helpful and unhelpful; friendly and unfriendly). Each pair of adjectives is separated by a seven-category scale with neither numerical nor verbal labels.

Sentence completion A projective technique which involves providing respondents with an incomplete sentence or group of sentences and asking them to complete them.

Shelf impact testing equipment *See* Stand-out equipment.

Simple random sampling A probability sampling method where every possible member of the population has an equal chance of being selected for the survey. Respondents are chosen using random numbers.

Simulated test markets A research approach used to predict the potential results of a product launch and to experiment with changes to different elements of a product's marketing mix. Rather than testing in retail stores, simulated test markets rely on simulated or laboratory-type testing and mathematical modelling.

Snowball sampling A non-probability sampling procedure where additional respondents are identified and selected on the basis of referrals of initial respondents. It tends to be used where the population of interest is small or difficult to identify.

Social networks Online social networks allow individuals to communicate with one another, construct a public or semi-public profile of themselves as well as share a variety of content.

Spearman's rank-order correlation A correlation approach for ordinal data.

Specialist service agencies Marketing research agencies that do not offer the full range of services (*See* Full service agencies) but tend to specialise in certain types of research. For example, a specialist agency may only do research in a specific market sector, such as the automotive sector or children's products, or in a geographic region of the world. Alternatively, the agency may be a specialist in terms of the research techniques it undertakes, focusing on telephone research or qualitative research.

Spider-type diagrams Diagrams used to organise data in the analysis of qualitative research data.

Split-half reliability Measures the internal consistency of a summated rating scale and refers to the consistency with which each item represents the overall construct

of interest. The method involves randomly dividing the various scale items into two halves. High correlations between the two halves suggests internal consistency of what is being measured

Standard deviation A measure of dispersion that calculates the average distance that the values in a data set are away from the mean. The standard deviation of different sets of data can be compared to see if one set of data is more dispersed than another.

Stand-out equipment Sometimes known as 'shelf impact testing equipment', this is used to determine the visual impact of new packaging when placed on shelves next to competitors' products.

Stapel scales A scaling approach which is a variation of the semantic differential scaling approach. It uses a single descriptor and ten response categories with no verbal labels.

Statistical significance If the difference between two statistical measures is large enough to be unlikely to have occurred due to chance or sampling error, then the difference is considered to be statistically significant.

Stimulus materials Materials used in group discussions and individual depth interviews to communicate the marketer or advertiser's latest creative thinking for a product, packaging or advertising to the respondents.

Storyboards A type of stimulus material where key frames for a television advertisement are drawn consecutively, like a comic strip.

Stratified random sampling A probability sampling procedure in which the chosen sample is forced to contain potential respondents from each of the key segments of the population.

Street interviews Interviews where respondents are approached and recruited while they are shopping or walking in town centres. In North America, these are known as 'mall intercept interviews'.

Structured observation A research approach where observers use a record sheet or form to count phenomena or to record their observations.

Systematic sampling A probability sampling approach similar to simple random sampling but which uses a skip interval (i.e. every *n*th person) rather than random numbers to select the respondents.

***t* test** A hypothesis test about a single mean if the sample is too small to use the *Z* test.

Table A visual display that communicates written materials and statistics in a succinct and understandable manner.

Tabular method of analysis A method for analysing qualitative research data using a large sheet of paper divided into boxes.

Target population *See* Population of interest.

Telephone interviewing Quantitative research where the interviewing is undertaken over the telephone.

Television viewing measurement The procedures used in the measurement of the number of viewers watching a particular television programme. In the UK, around 5,100 households have electronic meters attached to their television sets to register when the set is turned on and to what channel it is tuned.

Test-retest reliability Measures the stability of rating scale items over time. Respondents are asked to complete scales at two different times under as near identical conditions as possible. The degree of similarity between the two measurements is determined by computing a correlation coefficient

Text analysis software Software used for data analysis in qualitative research. Such software helps segment the data and identify any patterns that exist.

Third-party techniques *See* Projective questioning.

Topic list Sometimes known as an 'interviewer guide'. It outlines the broad agenda of issues to be explored in an individual depth interview or group discussion. It may also indicate the points at which stimulus material or projective techniques should be introduced.

Transcript A detailed 'word for word' record of the depth interview or group discussion setting out the questions, probes and participant answers

Triangulation Using a combination of different sources of data where the weaknesses in some sources are counterbalanced with the strengths of others. The term 'triangulation' is borrowed from the disciplines of navigation and surveying, where a minimum of three reference points are taken to check an object's location.

Twitter A microblogging service. *See* Blog

Type I error Rejection of the null hypothesis when it is actually true.

Type II error Failing to reject the null hypothesis when it is actually false.

Universe *See* Population of interest.

Unstructured questions *See* Open-ended questions.

User-generated content Online material such as comments, profiles photographs that is produced by end users.

Validity Whether the differences in the subject to be measured were actually measured by the research scale.

Video conferencing The bringing together of a group of individuals using a video link and telecommunications. Can potentially be used for group discussions, particularly where the respondents are located in various parts of the world.

Viewing rooms Specialist facilities/locations for group discussions. They are set out in the form of a boardroom or living-room setting with video cameras or a large one-way mirror built into one wall. Some are owned by research agencies, but the majority are independent and available to anyone willing to pay the hourly room-hire rates.

Web 2.0 Web applications that facilitate interactive information sharing, interoperability and collaboration on the Internet.

Web analytics The collection, analysis and reporting of internet data for the purposes of understanding and optimising web usage.

Web survey *See* Online survey.

Weighting The process of adjusting the value of survey responses to account for over- or under-representation of different categories of respondent. Weighting is used where the sample design is disproportional or where the achieved sample does not accurately reflect the population under investigation.

Word-association tests A projective technique that involves asking respondents what brands or products they associate with specific words. In addition to the direct outputs regarding brand imagery, it is also a very useful technique for building rapport within a group discussion and getting everybody contributing and involved.

Word cloud A visual depiction of words used by respondents in qualitative research or the content appearing on social network sites or publications. The font size of the words, is determined by the number of times a word has been used. The more that a topic or word is talked about, the bigger it is.

Z test A hypothesis test about a single mean where the sample size is larger than 30.

Index

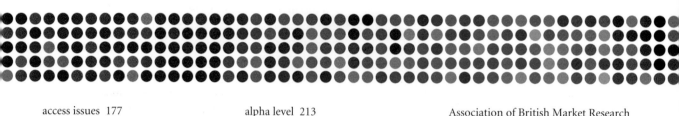

fy nodiadau **ad⏻lygu**

CBAC TGAU

FFISEG

Jeremy Pollard

HODDER
EDUCATION
AN HACHETTE UK COMPANY

CBAC TGAU Ffiseg

Addasiad Cymraeg o *WJEC GCSE Physics* a gyhoeddwyd yn 2017 gan Hodder Education

Ariennir yn Rhannol gan
Lywodraeth Cymru
Part Funded by
Welsh Government

Cyhoeddwyd dan nawdd Cynllun Adnoddau Addysgu a Dysgu CBAC

Mae cyn-gwestiynau papurau arholiad CBAC wedi'u hatgynhyrchu gyda chaniatâd CBAC.

t. 26 (brig) © Washington Imaging/Alamy Stock Photo, (gwaelod) © ACORN 1/Alamy Stock Photo; t. 34 © sciencephotos/Alamy Stock Photo; t. 35 (chwith) © Berenice Abbott/Science Photo Library; (de) © Andrew Lambert Photography/Science Photo Library; t. 46 © Morrison1977 - iStock via Thinkstock/Getty Images

Er y gwnaed pob ymdrech i sicrhau bod cyfeiriadau gwefannau yn gywir adeg mynd i'r wasg, nid yw Hodder Education yn gyfrifol am gynnwys unrhyw wefan y cyfeirir ati yn y llyfr hwn. Weithiau mae'n bosibl dod o hyd i dudalen we a adleolwyd trwy deipio cyfeiriad tudalen gartref gwefan yn ffenestr LlAU (*URL*) eich porwr.

Polisi Hachette UK yw defnyddio papurau sy'n gynhyrchion naturiol, adnewyddadwy ac ailgylchadwy o goed a dyfwyd mewn coedwigoedd cynaliadwy. Disgwylir i'r prosesau torri coed a gweithgynhyrchu gydymffurfio â rheoliadau amgylcheddol y wlad y mae'r cynnyrch yn tarddu ohoni.

Archebion
Bookpoint Ltd, 130 Park Drive, Milton Park, Abingdon, Oxon OX14 4SE
ffôn: (44) 01235 827720
ffacs: (44) 01235 400401
e-bost: education@bookpoint.co.uk
Mae'r llinellau ar agor rhwng 9.00 a 17.00 o ddydd Llun i ddydd Sadwrn, gyda gwasanaeth ateb negeseuon 24 awr. Gallwch hefyd archebu trwy ein gwefan: www.hoddereducation.co.uk.

ISBN 978 1 510 44308 2

© Jeremy Pollard, 2017 (yr argraffiad Saesneg)

Cyhoeddwyd gyntaf yn 2017 gan

Hodder Education,
an Hachette UK Company,
Carmelite House,
50 Victoria Embankment
London EC4Y 0DZ

© CBAC 2018 (yr argraffiad hwn ar gyfer CBAC)

Llun y clawr © J.R. Bale / Alamy Stock Photo

Teiposodwyd yn Bembo Std Regular 11/13 gan Integra Software Services Pvt. Ltd., Pondicherry, India

Argraffwyd yn Sbaen

Mae cofnod catalog y teitl hwn ar gael gan y Llyfrgell Brydeinig.